Lara Letizia Milione

Enhancing the Credibility of Resolution

An Analysis of the Impact of Recovery and Resolution Planning and Loss-Absorbing Capital Requirements on the Credibility of Bail-In

Nomos

The Deutsche Nationalbibliothek lists this publication in the Deutsche Nationalbibliografie; detailed bibliographic data are available on the Internet at http://dnb.d-nb.de

a.t.: Diss., Univ. Frankfurt am Main, 2022

ISBN 978-3-8487-7489-0 (Print)
978-3-7489-3280-2 (ePDF)

British Library Cataloguing-in-Publication Data
A catalogue record for this book is available from the British Library.

ISBN 978-3-8487-7489-0 (Print)
978-3-7489-3280-2 (ePDF)

Library of Congress Cataloging-in-Publication Data
Milione, Lara Letizia
Enhancing the Credibility of Resolution
An Analysis of the Impact of Recovery and Resolution Planning and Loss-Absorbing Capital Requirements on the Credibility of Bail-In
Lara Letizia Milione
302 pp.
Includes bibliographic references.

ISBN 978-3-8487-7489-0 (Print)
978-3-7489-3280-2 (ePDF)

Onlineversion
Nomos eLibrary

1st Edition 2022

Meinen Eltern

Vorwort

Die vorliegende Arbeit wurde im Sommersemester 2021 dem Fachbereich Rechtswissenschaft der Goethe-Universität Frankfurt am Main als Dissertation vorgelegt. Der Stand der Literatur wurde bis dahin berücksichtigt. Mein herzlicher Dank gilt meinem Doktorvater Herrn Professor Dr. Tobias Tröger, LL.M. (Harvard), dessen herausragende Lehre und unnachahmliche Art Stein des Anstoßes für diese Dissertation waren. Insbesondere die Jahre, die ich als Wissenschaftliche Mitarbeiterin an seinem Lehrstuhl verbringen durfte, haben mich geprägt und werden mir immer in bester Erinnerung bleiben. Herrn Professor Dr. Peter von Wilmowsky, LL.M. (Berkeley) danke ich für die zügige Erstellung des Zweitgutachtens und den angenehmen Prüfungsbeisitz. Der Friedrich-Ebert-Stiftung danke ich für die finanzielle und ideelle Förderung meines Promotionsvorhabens.

Ein großer Dank gilt ebenso meinen ehemaligen Kolleginnen und Kollegen des Lehrstuhls sowie des Forschungsinstituts SAFE, deren Kameradschaft und Diskussionsbereitschaft einen großen Beitrag zu dieser Arbeit geleistet haben und die mich auch über die Promotionszeit hinaus weiter begleiten. Insbesondere möchte ich hier Frau Rechtsanwältin Dr. Theresa Kreft und Herrn Richter Dr. Andreas Roth nennen, für deren Freundschaft allein sich die Promotionszeit bereits gelohnt hat. Auch möchte ich meinem Lebensgefährten Herrn Rechtsanwalt Martin Elias Kalbhenn für den seelischen und technischen Beistand danken, für die Hilfe bei der Endredaktion dieser Arbeit und einfach dafür, ein großartiger Partner zu sein. Auch meinen Schwiegereltern, Frau Ulrike Kalbhenn und Herrn Friedhelm Kalbhenn, sei an dieser Stelle für ihren Beistand und ihre Warmherzigkeit gedankt. Mein größter Dank gebührt jedoch meiner Familie und dabei insbesondere meinen Eltern, Frau Monika Milione und Herrn Calogero Milione, die mir gezeigt haben, dass Intelligenz und die wichtigen Dinge im Leben keines akademischen Abschlusses bedürfen. Durch ihre selbstverständliche Förderung und liebevolle Unterstützung haben sie mir das Studium und die Entstehung dieser Arbeit erst ermöglicht. Dafür und für so vieles mehr bin ich ihnen unendlich dankbar. Ihnen ist diese Arbeit gewidmet.

Frankfurt am Main, Oktober 2022
Lara Letizia Milione

Content Overview

Inhaltsverzeichnis 11

List of Abbreviations 17

PART 1 – INTRODUCTION 21

Introductory Remarks 21

Scope and Objective of the Thesis 32

Course of the Thesis 33

PART 2 – CREDIBILITY OF RESOLUTION PROCEDURES AND CURRENT LACKS 35

The Importance of Credible Resolution Procedures 35

Result of Part 2 124

PART 3 – RECOVERY AND RESOLUTION PLANNING – IMPACTS ON CREDIBILITY 125

The Impact of Recovery and Resolution Planning on the Credibility of Bail-In 125

Result of Part 3 177

PART 4 – LOSS-ABSORBING CAPITAL REQUIREMENTS – IMPACTS ON CREDIBILITY 178

The Impact of Loss-Absorbing Capital Requirements on the Credibility of Bail-In 178

Result of Part 4 232

PART 5 – ATTEMPTS TO FIND SOLUTIONS TO THE IDENTIFIED IMPEDIMENTS 234

Possible Solutions to the Identified Impediments of Recovery and Resolution Planning 234

Possible Solutions to the Identified Impediments of Loss-Absorbing Capital Requirements 255
Result to Part 5 274

PART 6 – SUMMARY OF THESES 275

References 279

Content

List of Abbreviations 17

PART 1 – INTRODUCTION 21

Introductory Remarks 21

Scope and Objective of the Thesis 32

Course of the Thesis 33

PART 2 – CREDIBILITY OF RESOLUTION PROCEDURES AND CURRENT LACKS 35

The Importance of Credible Resolution Procedures 35

Why the Credibility of Resolution is So Important 36

The Current Lack of Credibility in the Resolution Framework 39

Complexity in Bank Structures 48

Asset Size 52

Legal and Organizational Structures 53

Number of Legal Entities and Distribution of Banking Groups and Activities Across Jurisdictions 54

Governance Arrangements 55

Discrepancies in Institutions' Technical Infrastructure 55

Institutional Structure: Business Models 57

Results 58

No Adequate Modification Measures Ex Ante 58

Results of Ex Ante Evaluation 59

Ex Post: Lack of Sufficient Funding for Resolution 59

A Junction Before Resolution: Precautionary Recapitalization 62

The Current Framework of Precautionary Recapitalization 63

Application of Precautionary Recapitalization in Italy – Unveiling the Problems 65

Precautionary Recapitalization – Quo Vadis? 70

The Available Funding Sources and the BRRD's Burden-Sharing Cascade 73
The Good: Private Funding 75
National Insolvency Proceedings 75
Internal Private Funding Instruments – Bail-In 79
Reducing the Pool of Bail-inable Instruments through Articles 44(2) and 44(3) BRRD 80
Exemption of Senior Debt Holders 84
Bail-inable Instruments in the Cross-Border Context 86
Conclusion 87
External Private Funding Instruments 88
The Ugly: Sector Funding 89
Pre-Funded Funds – DGS and EDIS as Sector-Funded Financing 89
The Bad: Public Funding 95
European Stability Mechanism – Direct Recapitalization Instrument 96
Results of *Ex Post* Evaluation 105
Excursus: Limits to the No-Bailout Policy – The Role of Public Financing 106
Quod Erat Demonstrandum: Emergency Liquidity Assistance 109
Emergency Liquidity Assistance for Solvent Institutions – An Overview 111
The Current Problem 117
Results 119
When is Resolution Credible? 120
Credibility Ex Ante: Recovery and Resolution Planning 120
Credibility *Ex Post:* Loss-Absorbing Capital Requirements 123
Result of Part 2 124

PART 3 – RECOVERY AND RESOLUTION PLANNING – IMPACTS ON CREDIBILITY 125

The Impact of Recovery and Resolution Planning on the Credibility of Bail-In 125

The Potential of RRP to Enhance Credibility Ex Ante Resolution Decision 125

Remedy for the Lack of Predictability 125

Remedy for Complexity 126

Remedy for Missing Modification Measures 128

Identification of Possible Impediments to the Potential of Recovery and Resolution Planning 130

Impediments Concerning Recovery and Resolution Planning 130

Potential Divergences Between Authorities – Cross-Border Coordination 131

Protection of Own Markets, Market Players and Depositors 138

Planning as an Inconvenient Standard Exercise – Adding More Complexity 139

Drawing-up of Plans Takes Place in Times of Stability – Optimism Bias 143

Costliness of Recovery and Resolution Plans 144

Predictability of the Actual Crisis Scenario at Some Future Date 146

Impermanence of Banks' Structures and the Topicality of Recovery and Resolution Plans 148

Opaque Data Production and Collection Process – Templates 149

Recovery Planning Process – Building Blocks 151

Resolution Planning Process – Building Blocks 151

Evidence from Institutions Undertaking Planning 153

Templates 154

Planning Capacity for Systemic Crises 157

Gateway to Political Influence – Enforceability of Plans 160

Impediments Concerning Resolution Plans 161

Principal-Agent Conflict 164

Issues with Resolution Plans Relying on Institution-Provided Information 165

Unintentionally Incorrect Information 167

Faulty Processing or Valuation of Information 169

Intentionally Incorrect Information 169
Outlook: Determination of MREL Quote 171
Conclusion 172
The Problems with Modification Measures 172

Result of Part 3 177

PART 4 – LOSS-ABSORBING CAPITAL REQUIREMENTS – IMPACTS ON CREDIBILITY 178

The Impact of Loss-Absorbing Capital Requirements on the Credibility of Bail-In 178
Convergence of MREL and TLAC – the European Proposal 179
Minimum Requirements for Own Funds and Eligible Liabilities 181
Total Loss-Absorbing Capacity 183
Integrated Approach – Commission Proposal 185
The Potential of LACRs to Enhance Credibility Ex Post Resolution Decision 186
Identification of Possible Impediments to the Potential of Loss-Absorbing Capital Requirements 189
Implementation, Monitoring, and Maintenance Costs 189
Implementation of Integrated LACRs is Complex and Difficult to Understand 191
Eligibility of Instruments – Qualitative Requirements 192
Pricing of LAC Instruments 195
Debt Subordination – New Article 108 BRRD 198
Potential Investors and Holders of MREL-Eligible Instruments 203
Possible Investors 204
Retail Investors – Households – SMEs 204
Banks and Other Financial Institutions 207
Deduction of Cross-Holdings 208
Risk Transportation from the Banks to the Market – Who Remains? 209
Imposition of Losses on Specific Classes of Creditors Could Give Rise to Adverse Systemic Effects 210
Problem of Certain Banks in Complying with Loss-Absorbing Requirements 211
Scope and Level of Application 212
MREL Guidance – New Article 45e BRRD 215

Calculation Process 217
Denomination – Underlying Uncertainty 219
The Impact of Recovery and Resolution Planning – First Level of Uncertainty 221
Discretion in Setting the Recapitalization Amount – Second Level of Uncertainty 225
Unclear Adjustment Mechanisms – Third Level of Uncertainty 227
The TLAC as an International Standard Being Transposed into National Law 228
Current Shortfall and Transposition 230
Result of Part 4 232

PART 5 – ATTEMPTS TO FIND SOLUTIONS TO THE IDENTIFIED IMPEDIMENTS 234

Possible Solutions to the Identified Impediments of Recovery and Resolution Planning 234
Is Improvement of Recovery and Resolution Planning Necessary at All? 234
Proposals in Detail: Measures to Improve Recovery and Resolution Planning 236
Strengthening and Clarifying the Framework for Cross-Border Cooperation of Supervisory and Resolution Authorities 237
Enhancing Data Management 241
Special Training to Enhance Internal Data Provision 242
Full-Time RRP Employees 243
Development of a Standardized Template for a Single Distributor that Shares Relevant Data with Recipient – Information Intermediary 244
Updating of Institutions' IT Infrastructure 246
Automated Data Submission 247
RegTech as an Antidote to Major Data Management Problems 248
Make Plans Enforceable – Penalize Non-Compliance – Prevent Political Influence 249
Structural Reform of the Banking Sector 250
Open Issues 254

Possible Solutions to the Identified Impediments of Loss-Absorbing Capital Requirements 255
Proposals in Detail: Measures to Improve Loss-Absorbing Capital Requirements 255
Adoption and Maturation of the Reforms 256
Defining Dependable Eligibility Criteria 257
Enhancing the Pricing of MREL Instruments 258
Solution to the Subordination Problem 259
Solving the Investor Problem – Adequacy of Holders of Loss-Absorbing Debt 260
Disclosure Requirements and Provision of Mandatory Information to Potential Investors 261
Find Resilient and Adequate Holders for Loss-Absorbing Instruments – Buy-Side Monitoring 263
Setting-up Specific Bail-in Bonds 264
What to do with Legacy Holdings – Resolution Planning? 264
Flexibility Needs of Different Business Models 267
O/DSIBs – Scope and Level of Application 269
MREL Guidance 270
Solutions to Calculation Problems 271
Making the Calculation Process More Predictable 271
Making the Calculation Process More Accurate 272
International Transposition of TLAC 273
Shortfall and Transposition 273
Result to Part 5 274

PART 6 – SUMMARY OF THESES 275

References 279

List of Abbreviations

AG	Aktiengesellschaft
Art./Arts.	Article/Articles
AT1	Additional Tier 1
BaFin	Bundesanstalt für Finanzdienstleistungsaufsicht
BCBS	Basel Committee on Banking Supervision
BoC	Bank of Cyprus
BPE	Banco Popular Español
BRRD	Bank Recovery and Resolution Directive (Directive 2014/59/EU)
CBR	Combined Buffer Requirement
CET 1	Common Equity Tier 1
CMG	Crisis Management Group
CoCos	Contingent Convertible Bonds
Consob	Commissione Nazionale per le Società e la Borsa
CRD	Capital Requirements Directive (Directive 2013/36/EU)
CRR	Capital Requirements Regulation (Regulation (EU) No 575/2013)
DGS	Deposit Guarantee Scheme
DGSD	Deposit Guarantee Scheme Directive (Directive 2014/49/EU)
DPM	Data Point Model
DRI	Direct Recapitalization Instrument
EBA	European Banking Authority
ECB	European Central Bank
EDIS	European Deposit Insurance Scheme
ed/s.	editor/s
EEA	European Economic Area
EFSF	European Financial Stability Facility
EFSM	European Financial Stability Mechanism
e.g.	exempli gratia
ELA	Emergency Liquidity Assistance
EPFS	Extraordinary Public Financial Support
ESM	European Stability Mechanism

et al.	et alia
et seq.	et sequentes/and the following
EU	European Union
FDIC	Federal Deposit Insurance Corporation
FINREP	Financial Reporting
FSB	Financial Stability Board
GDP	Gross Domestic Product
GFST	Government Financial Stabilization Tools
GSIB	Global Systemically Important Bank
ibid.	ibidem
i.e.	id est
IFRS 9	International Financial Reporting Standard 9
IMF	International Monetary Fund
IRT	Internal Resolution Team
IT	Information Technology
ITS	Implementing Technical Standards
LAA	Loss Absorption Amount
LAC	Loss-Absorbing Capital
LACR	Loss Absorption Capital Requirements
LDR	Liability Data Report
LoLR	Lender of Last Resort
LRE	Leverage Ratio Exposure
MCC	Market Confidence Charge
MDA	Maximum Distributable Amount
MiFID II	Markets in Financial Instruments Directive (Directive 2014/65/EU)
MPE	Multiple Point of Entry
MPS	Monte dei Paschi di Siena
MREL	Minimum Requirements for Own Funds and Eligible Liabilities
NCWO	No Creditor Worse Off
NPL	Non-Performing Loans
NRA	National Resolution Authority
OSIB	Other Systemically Important Bank
para.	paragraph
P2G	Pillar 2 Guidance
RAP	Resolvability Assessment Process

RCA	Recapitalization Amount
RRP	Recovery and Resolution Planning
RTS	Regulatory Technical Standards
RTS on MREL	Regulatory Technical Standards on MREL (Regulation (EU) 2016/1450)7
RWA	Risk-Weighted Assets
SA	Standardized Approach
SAG	Sanierungs- und Abwicklungsgesetz
SIB	Systemically Important Bank
SIFI	Systemically Important Financial Institution
SME	Small and Medium Enterprises
SPE	Single Point of Entry
SRB	Single Resolution Board
SREP	Supervisory Review and Evaluation Process
SRF	Single Resolution Fund
SRM	Single Resolution Mechanism
SRMR	Single Resolution Mechanism Regulation (Regulation (EU) No 806/2014)
SSM	Single Supervisory Mechanism
SSMR	Single Supervisory Mechanism Regulation (Regulation (EU) No 1024/2013)
T2	Tier 2
TBTF	too big to fail
TFEU	Treaty on the Functioning of the European Union
TLAC	Total Loss-Absorbing Capacity
UK	United Kingdom
US	United States of America
XBRL	eXtensible Business Reporting Language

PART 1 – INTRODUCTION

Introductory Remarks

After financial markets were shaken up by the global financial crisis in 2007[1] and the eurozone crisis in 2009,[2] a rethinking of the stability of banks in times of distress was precipitated, encompassing legislators, policy makers, politicians, financial actors, and society equally. What followed was one of the most extensive legislative undertakings of modern times, changing the legal and financial world substantially. Although, in this period, a tremendous number[3] of legal acts have been passed in the

1 See, among many, J. Crotty, 'Structural causes of the global financial crisis: a critical assessment of the 'new financial architecture'', *Cambridge Journal of Economics* 33 (2009), 563–80; J. Carmassi, D. Gros and S. Micossi, 'The Global Financial Crisis: Causes and Cures', *Journal of Common Market Studies* 47 (2009), 977–96; E. Helleiner, 'Understanding the 2007–2008 Global Financial Crisis: Lessons for Scholars of International Political Economy', *Annual Review of Political Science* 14 (2011), 67–87; O. Merrouche and E. Nier, *What Caused the Global Financial Crisis? - Evidence on the Drivers of Financial Imbalances 1999-2007*, IMF Working Paper (2010).

2 C. Hadjiemmanuil, 'Bank Resolution Financing in the Banking Union' in J.-H. Binder and D. Singh (eds.), *Bank Resolution: The European Regime* (Oxford: Oxford University Press, 2016), pp. 177–210, pp. 179, 181 *et seq.*

3 The substantial reform of the financial and regulatory framework largely revolves around the work of global initiatives (such as the Basel Committee on Banking Supervision (BCBS)) that set global standards. In this regard, the most relevant European pieces of legislation include *Regulation (EU) No 575/2013 of the European Parliament and of the Council of 26 June 2013 on prudential requirements for credit institutions and investment firms and amending Regulation (EU) No 648/2012 OJ L 176, 27.6.2013, p. 1–337* (Capital Requirements Regulation, henceforth: CRR), *European Directive 2013/36/EU of the European Parliament and of the Council of 26 June 2013 on access to the activity of credit institutions and the prudential supervision of credit institutions and investment firms, amending Directive 2002/87/EC and repealing Directives 2006/48/EC and 2006/49/EC, OJ L 176, 27.6.2013, p. 338–436* (Capital Requirements Directive, henceforth CRD), *Directive 2014/59/EU of the European Parliament and the Council of 15 May 2014 establishing a framework for the recovery and resolution of credit institutions and investment firms and amending Council Directive 82/891/EEC, and Directive 2011/24/EC, 2004/25/EC, 2005/56/EC, 2007/36/EC, 2011/35/EU, 2012/30/EU and 2013/36/EU, and Regulations (EU) No 1093/2010 and (EU) No 648/2012, of the European Parliament and of the Council OJ L 173, 12.6.2014, p. 190–348* (Bank Recovery and Resolution Directive, henceforth: BRRD) and

eurozone alone, all such regulation across the financial world enshrined the following principle: states – and thus ultimately taxpayers – shall no longer be financially responsible for institutions[4] that get into trouble but were previously considered too big, too complex, or too intertwined to fail[5] (collectively referred to as 'TBTF') and therefore needed to be kept alive through bailouts.[6] It became apparent that the only alternative to bailout at that time, namely the existing national regimes for normal insolvency proceedings, were unfit and would produce undesired results if applied. Thus, a certain resentment against their application spread. As a consequence, in many cases, these regimes were not regarded as a genuine alternative to bailout[7] and were not applied, leaving the public

---

Regulation (EU) No 806/2014 of the European Parliament and of the Council of 15 July 2014 establishing uniform rules and a uniform procedure for the resolution of credit institutions and certain investment firms in the framework of a Single Resolution Mechanism and a Single Resolution Fund OJ L 225, 30.7.2014, p. 1–90 (Single Resolution Mechanism Regulation, henceforth: SRMR). For a systematic overview on banking legislation, see K. Langenbucher, T. H. Tröger, L. Milione, A. Roth, D. Kolassa, S. Honnefelder, A. K. Krischel, S. d. Lemos Peixoto, C. Lindemann, R. Maier, I. van Es and R. Silvestri, *EU Mapping 2017: systematic overview on economic and financial legislation: Study for the ECON Committee* (Luxembourg: Publications Office of the European Union, 2017), pp. 13 *et seq.*

4 'Institution' in the context of this thesis is defined as it is in the BRRD, as a credit institution (as defined in point (1) of Art. 4(1) of Regulation (EU) No 575/2013, not including the entities referred to in Art. 2(5) of Directive 2013/36/EU) and investment firms (as defined in point (2) of Art. 4(1) of Regulation (EU) No 575/2013 that is subject to the initial capital requirement laid down in Art. 28(2) of Directive 2013/36/EU). All other technical terms used herein have the same meaning as given to them by the BRRD, if not defined otherwise.

5 S. Gleeson and R. Guynn, *Bank Resolution and Crisis Management: Law and Practice*, First edition (Oxford: Oxford University Press, 2016), pp. 7–8; for the US approach to tackling too-big-to-fail, see Scott K. E., Jackson T. H. and Taylor J. B. (eds.), *Making failure feasible: How bankruptcy reform can end "too big to fail"*, Hoover Institution Press publication (Stanford, California: Hoover Institution Press, Stanford University, 2015), no. 662.

6 M. Pagano, 'Lessons from the European financial crisis' in E. Faia, A. Hackethal, M. Haliassos and K. Langenbucher (eds.), *Financial Regulation: A Transatlantic Perspective* (Cambridge, United Kingdom, New York: Cambridge University Press, 2015), pp. 23–48, pp. 25 *et seq.*; J. P. Krahnen and L. Moretti, 'Bail-In Clauses' in E. Faia, A. Hackethal, M. Haliassos and K. Langenbucher (eds.), *Financial Regulation: A Transatlantic Perspective* (Cambridge, United Kingdom, New York: Cambridge University Press, 2015); Binder J.-H. and Singh D. (eds.), *Bank Resolution: The European Regime* (Oxford: Oxford University Press, 2016) p. vi.

7 See recital (1) BRRD. For a deeper analysis showing why normal insolvency regimes do perfectly apply to commercial companies but not to banks, see Gleeson

to bear the massive expenses of bank rescues[8] and eventually destabilizing entire economies. This situation and the resulting reactions of taxpayers, stoked by negative media coverage across the world, would finally lead to a change. In Europe, this was the birth of what we today refer to as the European Banking Union.[9]

But why were people so reluctant to apply the existing national insolvency regimes that it became necessary to find a superior alternative? First, national insolvency proceedings actually terminated institutions, thereby destroying value,[10] and depleted the availability of the socially and economically important functions the respective banks used to provide. Second,

---

and Guynn, *Bank Resolution and Crisis Management*, pp. 3–5, J. Armour, 'Making Bank Resolution Credible' in N. Moloney, E. Ferran and J. Payne (eds.), *Oxford Handbook of Financial Regulation* (Oxford: Oxford University Press, 2015), pp. 453–86, pp. 456 *et seq.*

8 For a detailed analysis of costs associated with bank rescues within the financial crisis, see European Commission, *The effects of temporary State aid rules adopted in the context of the financial and economic crisis, SEC(2011) 1126 final*, Commission Staff Working Paper (2011) retrievable at http://ec.europa.eu/competition/publications/reports/working_paper_en.pdf accessed 1 October 2022.

9 For insight into the development of the Banking Union, see European Commission, *Communication from the Commission to the European Parliament and the Council - A Roadmap towards a Banking Union COM(2012) 510 final*; European Commission, *Banking Union - restoring financial stability in the Eurozone*, Press Release/Memo (2014) retrievable at http://europa.eu/rapid/press-release_MEMO-15-6164_en.htm?locale=en accessed 1 October 2022; European Commission, *Communication to the European Parliament, the Council, the European Central Bank, the European Economic and Social Committee and the committee of the Regions on completing the Banking Union COM(2017) 592 final*; European Commission, *Completing the Banking Union by 2018*, Fact Sheet retrievable at http://europa.eu/rapid/press-release_MEMO-17-3722_en.pdf accessed 1 October 2022. For secondary literature on the Banking Union see Binder J.-H. and Gortsos C. V. (eds.), *The European Banking Union: A compendium* (München, Oxford, Baden-Baden: C.H. Beck; Hart; Nomos, 2016); D. Schoenmaker, 'The Banking Union: An Overview and Open Issues' in T. Beck and B. Casu (eds), *The Palgrave Handbook of European Banking* (London: Palgrave Macmillan UK, 2016), pp. 451–74.

10 The destroyed value arising from a bank's liquidation goes beyond the nominal value of the claims and the rights of claimholders to future cash flows. For example, insolvency proceedings would impede the liquidity-providing function of deposits while hedges would be destroyed by the loss-participation of risk-shifting derivatives. See T. H. Tröger, 'Optimal Bail-In Tools - Observations From A European Perspective' in D. Arner, D. Busch, E. Avgouleas and S. Schwarcz (eds.), *Systemic Risk in the Financial Sector: Ten Years After the Great Crash* (Centre for International Governance Innovation, 2019); J. H. Sommer, 'Why Bail-In? And How!', *Economic Policy Review* 20 (2014), 207-228, pp. 214, 216.

liquidation is a lengthy process, and is unsuitable in a situation where a quick reaction is needed. Third, and most importantly, the national insolvency proceedings provided no mechanisms to cope with the complex idiosyncrasies and systemic effects[11] of big[12] banks' failures in the 21th century.[13]

Therefore, the problem was not only that a bank as an institution itself faced insolvency and ceased to exist[14] but rather that some banks were so interconnected, so complex, or simply so big that insolvency would spill over, contaminating all kinds of creditors, other banks, and other states, thereby posing a threat to the economy and the financial system[15] in one country or even several countries. This presented governments and regulators with an unenviable dilemma. The affected parties expected governments to save the struggling banks (and governments themselves were not exactly unwilling to do so, since they believed the systemic

11 These effects can occur because: the failing bank is a counterparty for a wide range of market participants; or because, due to liquidity shortness, it is forced to fire-sell assets, which leads to negative price movements, damaging other institutions. or because the defaulting of such institutions can spread (irrational) panic in the market through rumor, leading other institutions to possibly fail as well. See T. H. Tröger, 'Too complex to work: A critical assessment of the bail-in tool under the European bank recovery and resolution regime', *SAFE Working Paper* No. 179 (2017), p. 5 retrievable at SSRN https://ssrn.com/abstract=3023184 accessed 1 October 2022; M. K. Brunnermeier, 'Deciphering the liquidity and credit crunch 2007 - 2008', *The Journal of Economic Perspectives: a Journal of the American Economic Association* 23 (2009), 77–100.

12 As will be shown in the course of this thesis, it is not only the failure of big banks that can have systemic effects. The failure of medium-sized banks or even small banks can have negative consequences on the market, if they provide certain critical functions or are systemic in a domestic context.

13 For an extensive analysis of macro- and micro-economic effects of bank insolvencies, see M. M. Göhner, *Bail-in oder Bail-out?: Bankeninsolvenzen aus wirtschaftspolitischer Perspektive*, Wirtschaftspolitische Forschungsarbeiten der Universität zu Köln (Baden-Baden: Tectum Verlag, 2018), Band 63, pp. 22–27.

14 Although this motif might also have persuaded some states to save their banks through bailout, saving a bank as an institution because it was considered a 'national champion' or a 'prestige object' was not the main reason for the refrainment from normal insolvency proceedings.

15 Contagious effects can occur through various means, one being the direct connection of banks' balance sheets, since one liability of an institution is the asset of another institution, firm, or state. But contagious interconnection can also be traced down to correlation in investment strategies or depositors' wrong inferences causing bank runs, which have a compounding effect on each other, further intensifying the contagion. See Armour, 'Making Bank Resolution Credible', pp. 457 *et seq.*

and economic consequences of regular insolvency to be worse, so they too would benefit from a rescue), which in turn aggravated the situation in sovereign debt markets.[16] Due to this doom-loop,[17] tumbling banks posed a direct financial and economic risk to their home country and its taxpayers. If a given bank was considered important for the real economy and the financial system, and insolvency would have meant a threat[18] to the stability of this system, the government of the relevant state would try to save it through monetary means by socializing the costs of the rescue, better known as bailing it out.[19] Not only did this bailout come at a sub-

---

16 M. Yiatrou, *Bank Resolution Credibility and Economic Implications*, ADEMU Working Paper Series (2016), p. 2 retrievable at http://cadmus.eui.eu/bitstream/handle/1814/50205/ADEMU_2016_038.pdf?sequence=1&isAllowed=y accessed 1 October 2022; Armour, 'Making Bank Resolution Credible', p. 453.

17 V. de Bruyckere, M. Gerhardt, G. Schepens and R. Vander Vennet, 'Bank/sovereign risk spillovers in the European debt crisis', *Journal of Banking & Finance* 37 (2013), 4793–809, E. Farhi and J. Tirole, 'Deadly Embrace: Sovereign and Financial Balance Sheets Doom Loops', *The Review of Economic Studies* 85 (2018), 1781–823, Faia E., Hackethal A., Haliassos M. and Langenbucher K. (eds.), *Financial Regulation: A Transatlantic Perspective* (Cambridge, United Kingdom, New York: Cambridge University Press, 2015), p. 24.

18 Normal insolvency proceedings take time to identify and realize the available assets, to find the accounts of debts owing, and then to pay the creditors in accordance with the creditor hierarchy, which means creditors must bear the liquidity risk associated with the delay in insolvency proceedings. This procedure can aggravate potential contagious effects. See Armour, 'Making Bank Resolution Credible', pp. 455, 459.

19 Krahnen and Moretti, 'Bail-In Clauses', p 125. There is a rather long history of bank bailouts in Europe. Between 2008 and 2014, in 11 Member States, the fiscal impact of bailout exceeded 3 % of the 2014 GDP with Ireland reaching an outstanding 31.1 %, followed by Greece, Cyprus, and Slovenia. See: European Central Bank, *Economic Bulletin Issue 6/2015* retrievable at https://www.ecb.europa.eu/pub/pdf/ecbu/eb201506.en.pdf?b58dfa168a33d6dc69a2d397d0982e45 accessed 1 October 2022; and S. Micossi, G. Bruzzone and M. Cassella, 'Fine-tuning the use of bail-in to promote a stronger EU financial system', *CEPS Special Report* No. 136 (2016), p. 1 retrievable at https://www.ceps.eu/system/files/CEPS%20SR%20No%20136%20Bail-in%20StateAid%20and%20Public%20Interest.pdf accessed 1 October 2022. In Germany, there were numerous bailouts, including in recent times the SachsenLB, IKB Deutsche Industriebank in 2007, Hypo Real Estate in 2008, Commerzbank, BayernLB, LBBW, and WestLB. These banks were considered rather big and interconnected so the German government granted them public financial injections. On the other hand, 23 banks between 2008 and 2012 were sent into insolvency, such as Partin, Weserbank or Gontard & MetallBank in Germany – this was unsurprising as these were small banks with little importance in terms of the financial system's health. See C. Dohmen,

stantial fiscal cost[20] and consequently at an enormous cost to taxpayers, it also created incentives for banks to speculate on supporting state responses and to rely on fiscal help in the event they ever got into trouble again, which again caused moral hazard,[21] excessive risk-taking and opportunistic behavior among banks and their stakeholders. As a result, especially big, complex, or intertwined banks were tempted to rely on the financial safety net provided by states that would cushion them in case of financial distress, because they knew they were considered too big or too important to fail. Consequently, customers and investors anticipated such a subsidy, failed to evaluate the risk adequately,[22] and did not monitor the institu-

---

Finanzwirtschaft: Wie alles zusammenhängt, Zeitbilder, 1. Aufl. (Bonn: Bundeszentrale für Politische Bildung, 2014), pp. 162, 164.

20 In the period of 2008 to 2014, total gross fiscal support of euro area governments to the financial system amounted to approximately 8 % of the region's GDP, C. Hadjiemmanuil, 'Limits on State-Funded Bailouts in the EU Bank Resolution Regime' in G. B. Navetti, G. Calzolari and A. F. Pozzolo (eds.), *European Economy: Banks, Regulation, and the Real Sector* (Rome: Europeye, 2016), pp. 91–117, p. 92. Although slightly diverging numbers exist, the EU Member States and central banks approved a total of 5045 billion euros between 2008 and 2016 for recapitalizations, impaired asset measures, guarantees, and other liquidity measures. Of this amount, 1946.9 billion euros was actually used, see European Commission, *State Aid Scoreboard 2017: Aid in the context of the financial and economic crisis* Figure 1 – Total amounts of state aid to banks approved and used in the EU over the period 2008–2016 (in billion EUR) retrievable at http://ec.europa.eu/competition/state_aid/scoreboard/state_aid_scoreboard_%202017.pdf accessed 1 October 2022; K.-P. Wojcik, 'Bail-in in the Banking Union', *Common Market Law Review* 53 (2016), 91–138, pp. 91 *et seq.* Approximately 80 % of the total support consisted of loans and guarantees to strengthen the liquidity position of the banks, see W. P. de Groen, *Cash outflows in crisis scenarios: Do liquidity requirements and reporting obligations give the Single Resolution Fund sufficient time to react?*, In-Depth Analysis for the Economics and Monetary Affairs Committee of the European Parliament (2018) retrievable at http://www.europarl.europa.eu/RegData/etudes/IDAN/2018/614507/IPOL_IDA(2018)614507_EN.pdf accessed 1 October 2022.

21 E. Avgouleas and C. Goodhart, *A Critical Evaluation of Bail-ins as Bank Recapitalisation Mechanisms*, Centre for Economic Policy Research Discussion Paper (2014), available at SSRN https://ssrn.com/abstract=2478647 accessed 1 October 2022; Wojcik, 'Bail-in in the Banking Union', pp. 100 *et seq.*; J. Zhou, V. Rutledge, W. Bossu, M. Dobler and N. Jassaud, *From bail-out to bail-in: Mandatory debt restructuring of systemic financial institutions*, IMF staff discussion note (Washington, DC: Internat. Monetary Fund, 2012), 2012/3..

22 Evidence was found that a positive relationship between bailout expectations and risk-taking exists. See L. Dam and M. Koetter, 'Bank Bailouts and Moral Hazard: Evidence from Germany', *Review of Financial Studies* 25 (2012), 2343–80.

tions, resulting in banks' risk-taking being underpriced[23] and increasing the probability and severity of future crises.[24] Furthermore, these implicit subsidies caused rating agencies to give the respective institutions better ratings, which in turn lowered risk premiums and as a consequence the banks' refinancing costs, which thereupon increased the banks' profits.[25] Consequently, many investors shifted their money from smaller to bigger banks, since they also knew that the government would not let the bank go into insolvency. They thought "why not charter an unsinkable ship?" This phenomenon fostered the assumption that the financial strength of a Member State[26] would determine the riskiness of its banks, as a financially strong economy[27] can more easily rescue a troubled bank. This assumption disrupted cross-border lending and incentivized ring-fencing of national liquidity and entities, even within the same banking group. Eventually, on a macroeconomic level, the bailout of mismanaged institutions that proved (and in the future will most likely continue to prove) incapable of surviving[28] runs counter to economic considerations in the majority of cases. Bailing-out such troubled banks prevents market consolidation

23 G. H. Stern and R. J. Feldman, *Too Big to Fail: The Hazards of Bank Bailouts* (Washington, DC: Brookings Institution Press, 2009), ch. 3.; Micossi, Bruzzone and Cassella, 'Fine-tuning the use of bail-in to promote a stronger EU financial system', p. 2.

24 Hett/Schmidt found that market participants rationally adjust their bailout expectations in reaction to government interventions. For an overview of, and data on, the impact of bailout expectations on market discipline see F. Hett and A. Schmidt, *Bank Rescues and Bailout Expectations: The Erosion of Market Discipline During the Financial Crisis*, Safe Working Paper Series (2016) retrievable at SSRN https://ssrn.com/abstract=2365686 accessed 1 October 2022.

25 The Bank of England estimated that this overreaching in favor of systemic banks has an approximate value of one trillion US dollars annually. See Dohmen, *Finanzwirtschaft*, p. 162.

26 Evidence for this may be found in Schäfer et. al, who found that banks in European crisis countries are much more strongly affected by bail-in rumors than banks from other countries. They stated that this is because fiscal capacity is one important determinant of bail-in expectations. See A. Schäfer, I. Schnabel and B. Di Weder Mauro, 'Bail-in expectations for European banks: Actions speak louder than words', *CEPR Discussion Paper* DP11061 (2016) retrievable at SSRN https://ssrn.com/abstract=2723322 accessed 1 October 2022.

27 Zhou, Rutledge, Bossu, Dobler and Jassaud, *From bail-out to bail-in*, 2012/3, p. 20.

28 For the problem of 'zombie banks' or 'the walking dead dilemma' see, amongst others C. Gandrud and M. Hallerberg, *How not to create zombie banks: lessons for Italy from Japan*, Bruegel Policy Contributions retrievable at http://bruegel.org/wp-content/uploads/2017/03/PC-06-2017-030317.pdf accessed 1 October 2022. For recent developments see Y. Onaran, 'Zombie Banks', Bloomberg, 11 July 2017

and deprives other better-managed banks of market opportunities. These effects can decrease social welfare and the financial stability in the medium term.[29]

To help overcome this plight and in order to save taxpayers' money from bailouts, the European legislator equipped the Banking Union with the following three remedial features: a Single Supervisory Mechanism (SSM)[30]; a Single Resolution Mechanism (SRM)[31] (the SSM and SRM were both based on a Single Rulebook)[32]; and a European Deposit Insurance Scheme (EDIS)[33]. These were designed to complement existing national deposit guarantee schemes. Although the setting up of the EDIS as a third component has attracted some major resistance – especially from Germany[34] – and its proposals are still ongoing and have not yet been adopted

---

retrievable at https://www.bloomberg.com/quicktake/zombie-banks accessed 1 October 2022.

29 Göhner, *Bail-in oder Bail-out?*, Band 63, pp. 30–40; J. P. Krahnen, *Banking Failures: Consolidation is Better than Rescue: Bailing out ailing banks distorts competition*, SAFE Policy Blog (2017) retrievable at https://safe-frankfurt.de/policy-blog/details/banking-failures-consolidation-is-better-than-rescue.html accessed 1 October 2022.

30 *Regulation (EU) No 1022/2013 of the European Parliament and of the Council of 22 October 2013 amending Regulation (EU) No 1093/2010 establishing a European Supervisory Authority (European Banking Authority) as regards the conferral of specific tasks on the European Central Bank pursuant to Council Regulation (EU) No 1024/2013 OJ L 287, 29.10.2013, p. 5–14* (2013) (henceforth: SSMR).

31 *Regulation (EU) No 806/2014 of the European Parliament and of the Council of 15 July 2014 establishing uniform rules and a uniform procedure for the resolution of credit institutions and certain investment firms in the framework of a Single Resolution Mechanism and a Single Resolution Fund OJ L 225, 30.7.2014, p. 1–90* (henceforth: SRMR).

32 Key elements of the Single Rulebook are the CRD IV, which transposes Basel III capital requirements; the *Directive 2014/49/EU of the European Parliament and of the Council of 16 April 2014 on deposit guarantee schemes, OJ L 173, 12.6.2014, p. 149–178* (Deposit Guarantee Scheme Directive, henceforth DGSD); and the BRRD.

33 EDIS would complement the existing national deposit-guarantee schemes, along with EU legislation that already insures the protection of all deposits up to 100 000 euros. Through a single fund, EDIS would ensure equal and more financially-equipped protection of all Banking Union depositors in case of failure. See European Commission, *Completing the Banking Union by 2018*, p. 2.

34 See only recently the rejection of the proposal in the German parliament: Deutscher Bundestag, *Antrag zu dem Vorschlag für eine Verordnung des Europäischen Parlaments und des Rates zur Änderung der Verordnung (EU) Nr. 806/2014 im Hinblick auf die Schaffung eines europäischen Einlagenversicherungssystems KOM(2015) 586 endg; Ratsdok. 14649/15 - Drucksache 19/2525* (2018). Not only was Germany

by the European Parliament and the Council,[35] the introduction of the SSM and SRM has been relatively smooth. For now, both the SSM and the SRM are fully operational in all participating Member States forming the Banking Union.[36]

With these problems in mind, the European legislator created the centerpiece of the Banking Union, a framework for the recovery and resolution of credit institutions and investment firms,[37] namely the Bank Recovery and Resolution Directive (BRRD).[38] The aim of the BRRD was to redress the technical and economic challenges of bank failures by infusing the European Banking Union project with several fundamental and innovative notions. One of the most important ideas behind the BRRD was that banks, once failed, need to be resolved in the most cost-effective and orderly way, setting aside costly public bailouts and providing an alternative to the unsuitable and slow-mode national insolvency regimes.

There is a widespread consensus that by setting up the BRRD, Europe – at least theoretically – came up with a competent way to deal with failing banks and to provide alternatives to both undesirable bailouts and

---

reluctant in relation to setting up the EDIS, but already in the process of setting up the European Stability Mechanism (ESM), the successor of the EFSM and the EFSF, Germany tried to fend off and resist the centralization of resolution funding. It was afraid that this would amount to an *ex post de facto* mutualization of the costs from past national supervisory failures. See Hadjiemmanuil, 'Bank Resolution Financing in the Banking Union', p. 195.

35 European Commission, *Completing the Banking Union by 2018*. However, the development of the EDIS was recently discussed by the European Commission; see European Commission, *Communication to the European Parliament, the Council, the European Central Bank, the European Economic and Social Committee and the committee of the Regions on completing the Banking Union COM(2017) 592 final*, pp. 9–13.

36 On the completion of the Banking Union, see European Commission, *Communication to the European Parliament, the Council, the European Central Bank, the European Economic and Social Committee and the committee of the Regions on completing the Banking Union COM(2017) 592 final.*

37 In the following, credit institutions and investment firms together are referred to as 'institutions' in the context of Art. 2(23) of the BRRD.

38 *Directive 2014/59/EU of the European Parliament and the Council of 15 May 2014 establishing a framework for the recovery and resolution of credit institutions and investment firms and amending Council Directive 82/891/EEC, and Directive 2011/24/EC, 2004/25/EC, 2005/56/EC, 2007/36/EC, 2011/35/EU, 2012/30/EU and 2013/36/EU, and Regulations (EU) No 1093/2010 and (EU) No 648/2012, of the European Parliament and of the Council OJ L 173, 12.6.2014, p. 190–348* . The BRRD was a product of the recommendations made by the Basel Committee's Cross-border Bank Resolution Group and the Financial Stability Board.

unsuitable insolvency proceedings. From now on, banks that are failing or likely to fail,[39] but are considered too big or too important to undergo normal insolvency proceedings, shall be put into resolution.[40] In this regard, the introduction of the bail-in tool represented the most notable and innovative resolution tool.[41]. Conceptualized as the reverse scenario of bailout – since not the government but the creditors themselves are put in charge of absorbing losses and recapitalizing the institution through write-down and conversion of debt or other liabilities according to a pre-defined hierarchy[42] – the new tool renders the industry more risk-conscious and responsible[43] while at the same time avoiding having to use public funds to finance bailouts and the negative consequences attached thereto.

But obviously the mere fact that the European legislator changed the law and set up a framework that – at first glance – looks conclusive does not mean that all pre-existing challenges and distortions will be eliminated right away. The main parts of the new legislative framework are experimental in nature since they have no meaningful precedents that could be used as guidance. This leaves a high level of uncertainty about central legal and economic aspects,[44] especially with respect to the growing dimension of EU and non-EU cross-border banking coordination. In addition, as the BRRD only emerged in May 2014, the banking industry as well as financial market participants will need time to adjust to the new rules and to rid themselves of the old habits and mindsets that were prevalent pre-Banking Union and pre-BRRD. Lastly, as dealing with failing banks is a highly political issue, political considerations and the interference of

---

39 Art. 32(4) BRRD sets out the circumstances under which an institution can be deemed failing or likely to fail.

40 Resolution, according to Art. 2(1)(1) BRRD, is defined as "the application of a resolution tool or a tool referred to in Art. 37(9) in order to achieve one or more of the resolution objectives referred to in Art. 31(2)." For a detailed introduction of the institutional setting of the resolution procedure within the Banking Union, see D. Busch, 'Governance of the Single Resolution Mechanism' in D. Busch and G. Ferrarini (eds.), *European Banking Union* (Oxford: Oxford Univ Press, 2015), part III, ch. 9; Jahn U., Schmitt C. and Geier B. M. (eds.), *Bankensanierung und -abwicklung: Handbuch*, 1. Auflage (München: C.H. Beck, 2016), pp. 236 *et seq.*

41 Art. 43 BRRD.

42 Art. 48 BRRD.

43 Tröger, 'Too complex to work', p. 3; on the influence on banks' risk-taking incentives U. Vollmer and H. Wiese, 'Minimum capital requirements, bank supervision and special resolution schemes. Consequences for bank risk-taking', *Journal of Financial Stability* 9 (2013), 487–97, p. 489.

44 Binder and Singh (eds.), *Bank Resolution*, p. vii.

a strong banking industry lobby might frustrate legal endeavors, making it hard to advocate for unpopular but reasonable approaches. Against this backdrop, the bail-in instrument had a truly difficult start. Despite being legally innovative and having a strong cross-border reference, it was faced with suborn preservation of old habits and a lack of political will.[45]

Therefore, in order to continuously pursue the defined objectives and to counteract initial difficulties, the legislator took further action in various areas. In 2015/2016 two new instruments have been introduced in order to promote the successful implementation of bail-in. One of them is the prophylactic recovery and resolution planning[46] obligation (henceforth RRP), which would ideally help banks, supervisors, and resolution authorities through preventive planning and thorough preparation for any necessary action in the event of financial distress. Meanwhile, the second is the introduction of additional loss-absorbing capital requirements (henceforth LACR) for institutions, which go beyond the regular capital requirements identified in Basel III and which can be used to absorb losses in case of resolution, to recapitalize banks afterwards, and to help them regain market confidence. Both of these closely linked[47] instruments are intended to facilitate bail-in: the first through giving structure and feasibility *ex ante*, and the second through giving substance and reliability *ex post*. As of now, RRP as well as LACR are in the course of being implemented: both instruments, despited not being entirely finalized, have attempted their first baby steps already.

---

45 Although initially strongly supported by politicians in response to public agitation, the bail-in tool was to a certain extent unpopular right from the beginning, as will be elaborated in detail as this thesis proceeds, see *infra* under Part 2, A.II.2.a. – *A Junction Before Resolution: Precautionary Recapitalization*. However, this reluctance is much more attributable to external factors and the poor design of the instrument rather than to the underlying principle of the concept "bail-in" that was, and still is, predominantly supported.

46 Arts. 4–14 BRRD and 8–11 SRMR.

47 The amount of loss-absorbing capital requirements, especially the MREL, is determined throughout the process of recovery and resolution planning and is set by the resolution authority. *Vice versa*, the resolution plan will only work smoothly, if the required loss-absorbing capital backs the envisaged resolution strategy.

Scope and Objective of the Thesis

One of the most important undertakings of the Banking Union project – along with the aim of stopping banks from failing *ab initio*[48] through supervision and making them more resilient – is to discourage the use of public money to bail-out banks in case of failure by setting up a viable resolution framework. The creation of the bail-in tool was a major innovation and leap forward in turning away from publicly-funded bailouts. It tackled the root of the problem by providing an antidote to the distorted behavior of market participants and the consequences of longstanding bailout policy, and simultaneously encouraged a viable alternative concept for the future. However, recent resolution episodes in the EU draw a different, more pessimistic picture. Broad discretion within the resolution framework and the continuing propensity to use public funds ultimately means the bail-in tool has so far failed to defeat old habits and the negative repercussions of years of public bailouts. Bail-in, in its current state, seems to be a flaky and unpredictable concept that falls short of achieving its ambitious policy goal. Additionally, resolution in general seems to apply arbitrarily and it can be presumed that this is caused to a great extent by problems pertaining to the bail-in tool. This raises concerns with respect to future bank failures and the success of the EU's resolution endeavors. Therefore, the issue with public bailouts (and all forms that such unwanted public intervention can take) is not yet resolved, and it is this very predicament that serves as the subject matter of the present thesis.

Deriving from one of the guiding principles of resolution, namely the credibility of resolution,[49] the following analysis aims to provide insight into whether two newly-created instruments – recovery and resolution planning on the one hand, and LACR on the other hand – are able to

48 Thole states that there is a shift from *ex post* regulation to *ex ante* regulation; see C. Thole, 'Bank Crisis Management and Resolution: Core features of the Bank Recovery and Resolution Directive', *SSRN Electronic Journal* 2014, p. 3 retrievable at SSRN https://ssrn.com/abstract=2469807 accessed 1 October 2022.

49 Unless otherwise indicated, the term 'credibility of resolution' in the context of this thesis always refers to the credibility of private or institutionally-funded resolution without public participation, meaning only through resolution tools with an emphasis on the bail-in tool and funded according to the BRRD burden-sharing cascade, ergo without any other funding sources. For an attempt to define the term credibility, see *supra* under Part 2, A.I. – *Why the Credibility of Resolution is so Important.*

improve the current situation of the bail-in tool.[50] As only well-functioning and sound undertakings would be able to achieve this ambitious objective, both instruments undergo extensive examination. Within such examination, a comprehensive disclosure of inherent impediments will provide valuable information to policy makers and legislators, and will form the basis for attempts to find possible solutions to the identified impediments and to indicate a direction for further legislative approaches. The overarching ambition of the thesis, therefore, is to help make both recovery and resolution planning, as well as LACR instruments, sustainable remedies for the current lacks in the resolution regime that will restore, or at least contribute to restoring, the credibility of resolution in general and bail-in in particular.

Course of the Thesis

As a first step, and in the process creating a meta-level, the case for credibility as the thematic anchor of the topic is clarified together with an explanation of why there is such a strong need for (reinstated) credibility in resolution (Part 2, A.I. – *Why the Credibility of Resolution is so Important*). Then, the current state of the credibility of resolution and bail-in is examined. With the help of examples of recent cases of bank failure in the EU, the section concludes that two major lacks continue to hamper the ideal functioning of the new bail-in regime and undermine its credibility. First, there is over-complexity, a lack of predictability, and an absence of modification measures *ex ante* resolution decision (Part 2, A.II.1. – *Ex Ante: Lack of Predictability, Complexity and Missing Modification Measures*). Second, a lack of adequate private funding *ex post* resolution also exists (Part 2, A.II.2. – *Ex Post: Lack of Sufficient Adequate Funding for Resolution*). These two findings are tested against the recent use of Emergency Liquidity Assistance (Part 2, A.II.4. – *Quod Erat Demonstrandum: Emergency Liquidity Assistance*). As the credibility of resolution action was identified as the prerequisite for a functioning bank-resolution framework,

50 Although often used as a set of tools during resolution, the other BRRD resolution tools are mainly left out of this discourse, in which no statement is provided as to whether the examined instruments (RRP or LACR) might also facilitate the functioning of these tools. When speaking of 'resolution' in general, reference is made to resolution procedures where bail-in would be a reasonable resolution tool.

eradicating the current lacks should be prioritized in legislative endeavors. It will be shown that two directions of impact must be heeded to make bail-in-related resolution procedures more credible: the *ex ante* as well as the *ex post* stage of resolution must be enhanced (Part 2, A.III. – *When is Resolution Credible?*).

With the contribution of *ex ante* predictability, the instrument of recovery and resolution planning will be made fruitful. The contribution of *ex post* bindingness, sufficiency, and adequacy will be realized through the instrument of LACR. If these instruments were to work properly, it can be assumed that they would have a beneficial effect on the credibility of bail-in, as they eliminate both of the identified *ex ante* and *ex post* lacks (Part 3, A.I. – *The Potential of RRP to Enhance Credibility Ex Ante Resolution Decision;* and Part 4, A.II. – *The Potential of LACR to Enhance Credibility Ex Post Resolution Decision*).

The two main parts of the thesis (Part 3, A.II. – *Identification of Possible Impediments to the Potential of Recovery and Resolution Planning;* and Part 4, A.III. – *Identification of Possible Impediments to the Potential of Loss-Absorbing Capital Requirements*) therefore examine both instruments in detail, showing that neither the framework for recovery and resolution planning nor the concept of LACR are free from flaws. The detailed uncovering of inherent impediments in both instruments constitutes one of the main values of the thesis, as detailed knowledge about such impediments can prove useful for policy makers and legislators – especially in light of the ongoing legislative process – in their efforts to further enhance both instruments and tackle their current shortcomings.

In conclusion, with recourse to previous results, possible solutions to the identified impediments of RRP and LACR will be presented and assessed. Naturally, not all impediments can be cured by a one-size-fits-all approach. Despite presenting various tangible approaches, part 5 rather draws its strength from giving guidance and indicating courses of action for involved parties and legislators in charge (Part 5 – *Attempts to Find Solutions to the Identified Impediments*). Ultimately, it is hoped that the thesis contributes to an action plan to ameliorate both instruments, rendering them useful in enhancing the credibility of bail-in and resolution procedures in general. It will conclude with a summary of the found propositions (Part 6 – *Summary of Theses*).

PART 2 – CREDIBILITY OF RESOLUTION PROCEDURES AND CURRENT LACKS

This part explains why the thesis strives to enhance the credibility of resolution procedures at all, and why the credible prospect of resolution in general and bail-in in particular is a precondition for the efficient functioning of the entire European Banking Union project (I.). It will then point at the current lacks corroding the credibility of resolution procedures (II.) that can be distinguished into the following two categories: a lack *ex ante* resolution decision (II.1.); and a lack *ex post* resolution decision (II.2.). This part closes by outlining the factors necessary for the credible application of resolution procedures and proposes RRP and LACR as remedies to the identified lacks that simultaneously meet the factors necessary for a credible resolution framework (III.).

The Importance of Credible Resolution Procedures

To understand why credibility is the central aspect of this thesis, this section accounts for the political and economic importance of credibility as a meta-level in the discourse relating to banking resolution. In this respect, it is appropriate to indicate that even though the term is axiomatically used in the literature and in legislation, there is no official definition of credibility.[51] Furthermore, in light of the absence of a universal definition, it is understood that credibility cannot be measured, which means that only quantitative assessments are viable with respect to enhanced credibility.

---

51 Attempts in this direction were made, for example, in the Commission Delegated Regulation (EU) 2016/1075 on RTS of Recovery and Resolution Plans, where the credibility of normal insolvency proceedings or a specific resolution strategy is assessed by carrying out an impact assessment, see Arts. 24 and 32. However, even within European institutions, the term is not used consistently.

Why the Credibility of Resolution is So Important

With regard to the BRRD resolution framework, credibility has a much bigger role than only determining which legislation is given the status of soft law due to the lack of credible execution mechanisms. In the present case, credibility is not only a necessary component to ensure mandatory application of the legislation in the future and making it a "hard law", but it is also subject to a double burden. This is grounded in the fact that the regime in place pre-BRRD allowed behavioral devastation among financial market participants[52] that still lingers, imposing the additional task. It left behind a debauched group of potential addressees of which one half are accustomed to getting away scot-free without experiencing losses, and the other half are accustomed to being scapegoats for other people's transgressions. Credibility, therefore, has the additional task of correcting old habits and mindsets, paving way to an efficient application of the new rules.

So far, the alleged lack of credibility of resolution has already severely impacted financial markets, and has already been reflected in banks' funding costs and the consequent inconsistencies that have influenced their competitiveness.[53] Thus, credibility is of major importance and is recognized accordingly: the first recitals of the BRRD's preamble prominently refer to the credibility of the recovery and resolution framework and point out its importance.[54] This mantra is consistently repeated throughout the Directive and its accompanying documentation. However, not only in the legislative process and acts but also amongst academics and authors of legal and financial literature, a widespread consensus on the importance of the credibility of banking resolution can be found.[55]

---

52 Hüpkes states that "the financial crisis destroyed the credibility of economic policy and the reputation of the banking system of advanced economies", see E. Hüpkes, *Resolution: overcoming credibility gaps*, EFDI International Conference 2016 (Vilnius, 2016).

53 Yiatrou, *Bank Resolution Credibility and Economic Implications*, pp. 15 *et seq.*

54 "[...] credible recovery and resolution framework [...]" (recital (1) BRRD); "[...] the credibility of the internal market in die field of financial services" (recital (3) BRRD). One fundamental objective of the BRRD is to define 'a credible set of tools to intervene sufficiently early and quickly'; see preamble, recital (5) BRRD.

55 See, among many, emphasizing the importance of credibility: Armour, 'Making Bank Resolution Credible'; L. Donato, Z. Rotondi and A. Scognamiglio, 'From the Rescue of Banks to the Single Resolution Mechanism: Institutional and Empirical Analysis', *SSRN Electronic Journal* (2017) retrievable at SSRN https://ssrn.com/abstract=2892501 accessed 1 October 2022; Schäfer, Schnabel and Di Weder

Therefore, the first special task regarding credibility with respect to resolution rules is to 'clean up' the mess of longstanding bailout practice and to re-discipline the banking industry that, through years of excessive risk-taking, tax-funded bailouts, and a disregard for risk-adequate behavior, had got used to holding the helping hand of government.[56] Evidence of a massive lack of credibility when it comes to the application of bail-in can be found in market reactions and spreads of credit default swaps during bank restructurings in recent years in Europe.[57] For legislation to be credible, it must therefore be able to eradicate deeply ingrained behavior. Active users of the resolution legislation, such as stakeholders and other market participants, need to understand and genuinely believe that the implemented bail-in regime will apply by mandate, that the rules are credible and without any convenient gaps or loopholes, and that bailout is no longer acquiesced to.

Second, when it comes to the passive users of bank resolution rules, specifically taxpayers throughout Europe, credibility of legislation entails

---

Mauro, 'Bail-in expectations for European banks'; P. Honohan, *Management and Resolution of Banking Crises: Lessons from Recent European Experience*, Peterson Institute for International Economics Policy Brief (2017) retrievable at https://piie.com/publications/policy-briefs/management-and-resolution-banking-crises-lessons-recent-european accessed 1 October 2022; Yiatrou, *Bank Resolution Credibility and Economic Implications*, pp. 14 *et seq.*; stating the various aspects where credibility of effective resolution plays a crucial role see Hüpkes, *Resolution: overcoming credibility gaps*; G. Wihlborg, *Bail-ins - Issues of Credibility and Contagion*, SUERF Policy Note (2017), pp. 7 *et seq.* retrievable at https://www.suerf.org/docx/f_210f760a89db30aa72ca258a3483cc7f_883_suerf.pdf accessed 1 October 2022.

56 J.-H. Binder, 'Resolution: Concepts, Requirements, and Tools' in J.-H. Binder and D. Singh (eds.), *Bank Resolution: The European Regime* (Oxford: Oxford University Press, 2016), pp. 25–59, p. 26, recital 2.02; Yiatrou, *Bank Resolution Credibility and Economic Implications*, p. 2.

57 Indications have been found that bail-in expectations appear to depend on the sovereign's fiscal strength, which means that banks' reactions to bail-in are stronger in countries with limited fiscal space for bailout (such as Greece, Ireland, Italy, Portugal, or Spain), since the expectation of a bailout still remains higher for banks in fiscally stronger countries. Furthermore, actual bail-ins caused a much stronger market reaction than the mere implication of a process of banking resolution regimes, meaning that the legislative process of the SRM yields relatively little in terms of market reactions, which is suspected to be related to the uncertainty regarding the outcome of the resolution (*e.g.* the actual creditor involvement in case of distress). Both findings support the hypothesis that the new regime on bail-in is not yet taken seriously. For a detailed analysis of the findings, see Schäfer, Schnabel and Di Weder Mauro, 'Bail-in expectations for European banks'.

restoring the trust of people[58] under the BRRD's jurisdiction and reviving levels of fairth damaged by years of public bailout practice in most economies during the financial crisis since 2007.[59] Ergo, credibility of resolution is crucial in two directions: firstly, in obliterating the negative aftereffects of longstanding bailout practice by changing the habits of the industry; and, secondly, in soothing European society by reinstating trust in financial markets and by ensuring that taxpayers no longer bear the burden of bank failures. Both aspects of such credibility are crucial for a functioning resolution regime that, in turn, is essential for financial stability.[60]

Additionally, not only must both components of credibility be achieved, but they must be achieved as soon as possible. If not, the wrongly incentivized behavior of financial actors and the mistrust of the public, key legacies of the old bailout regime, will spill over not only into current and subsequent approaches and regimes, permanently destroying public belief that the new rules will be applied mandatorily. Credibility is needed here to assuage the still-existing market concerns, to facilitate a definitive exit from the recent crisis, and to enable the reintegration of banking markets in the euro area.[61] With these goals in mind, and despite the political challenges that are inevitably associated with banking resolution, it is important that any future resolution case accords with the new framework, cementing the approach and demonstrating its assertiveness for the future.[62] In this respect, the handling of recent EU resolution cases has been a letdown.[63] In terms of signaling effects, the success and credibility of

58 "Trust is the ingredient that makes a market economy work" states M. A. King, *The And of Alchemy: Money, banking and the future of the global economy*, First edition (London: Little Brown, 2016).

59 Binder, 'Resolution: Concepts, Requirements, and Tools', p. 25, recital 2.01.

60 Ibid., p. 25, recital 2.02.

61 Hadjiemmanuil, 'Bank Resolution Financing in the Banking Union', p. 203.

62 Honohan, *Management and Resolution of Banking Crises: Lessons from Recent European Experience*, p. 10.

63 Neither of the prominent resolution cases pre-BRRD were handled in an exemplary way, see World Bank Group, Financial Sector Advisory Center (FinSAC), *Bank Resolution and "Bail-In" in the EU: Selected Case Studies Pre and Post BRRD* (2016), which gives an overview of case studies from Austria, Cyprus, Denmark, Greece, Italy, the Netherlands, Portugal, Slovenia, Spain, and the UK. See also, T. Philippon and A. Salord, *Bail-ins and bank resolution in Europe: A progress report*, Geneva reports on the world economy Special report (Geneva, London: ICMB International Center for Monetary and Banking Studies; CEPR, 2017), vol. 4, part 2, pp. 27 *et seq.*, and B. Mesnard, *"Bail-ins" in recent banking resolution and State aid cases*, In-Depth Analysis for the Economics and Monetary Affairs Committee of the European Parliament (2016) retrievable at http://www.europar

the entire project depends heavily on the handling of the next resolution cases in Europe.[64] If the BRRD is not credibly applied to future resolution cases, its entire *raison d'être* might be called into question.

The Current Lack of Credibility in the Resolution Framework

Having highlighted the importance of credibility and the need for its swift enhancement, the following section tries to shed light on the current lacks in the resolution regime that render its credibility lacking. As will be shown, the current lacks can be broken down into two underlying factors: some can be grouped under unpredictability, over-complexity, and the absence of modification measures *ex ante* resolution action; and the others fall under the unavailability of sufficient, adequate, and easily-accessible non-public funding *ex post* resolution decision.[65]

Ex Ante: Lack of Predictability, Complexity, and Missing Modification Measures

Despite the hard work put in in setting up the Banking Union and the new BRRD resolution framework, certain lingering problems continue to hamper the swift and effective reorganization and resolution of institutions in distress. These include a lack of predictability, excessive complexity in institutions' structures, and the absence of modification measures with respect to such structures.[66] These three issues arise at the *ex ante* stage, prior to a potential resolution decision, but have an impact on the credi-

l.europa.eu/RegData/etudes/IDAN/2016/574395/IPOL_IDA(2016)574395_EN.pdf accessed 1 October 2022.

64 Schäfer, Schnabel and Di Weder Mauro, 'Bail-in expectations for European banks', p. 25.

65 A similar presentation of impediments to resolvability can be found in D. Schoenmaker, *The different legal and operational structures of banking groups in the euro area, and their impact on banks' resolvability*, In-Depth Analysis for the Economics and Monetary Affairs Committee of the European Parliament (2016), abstract, pp. 13 *et seq.* retrievable at http://www.europarl.europa.eu/RegData/etudes/IDAN/2016/587376/IPOL_IDA(2016)587376_EN.pdf accessed 1 October 2022 but with the addition of a third disruptive factor, which Schoenmaker determines to be the broad definition of critical functions. This third factor is left out in the following.

66 J.-H. Binder, 'Resolution Planning and Structural Bank Reform within the Banking Union' in J. E. Castañeda, D. G. Mayes and G. E. Wood (eds.), *European Banking Union: Prospects and challenges* (Routledge, 2016), pp. 129–56, pp. 130, 155, 156.

bility of the entire resolution procedure, as will be demonstrated in the following.

Lack of Predictability – Political Influence

The first point at which the credibility of resolution plays an important role is usually before a resolution decision is made and sometimes even before the institution gets into trouble (*i.e.* the feasibility of application *ex ante*). This applies both to the general initiation of resolution procedures as well as to the application of a particular resolution tool, in most cases the bail-in tool. If the application of BRRD resolution procedures or the chosen resolution tool is not plausible and probable, the mechanisms can appear impotent and this leaves room for conjecture and leeway as to whether the resolution regime or resolution tool will be applied at all. This is especially pertinent where resolution involves potential loss-participation by stakeholders through bail-in.

Causes of the Lack of Predictability

When looking at the BRRD and its supplementing legislation, it is striking how multipolar[67] the decision-making process is leading to a resolution decision or a specific resolution scheme. Even if an institution is struggling, it is difficult for investors, customers, and other market participants to predict if BRRD resolution procedures at all and if so, which resolution tool will be applied. Currently, if a bank is in distress, resolution with loss-participation through bail-in may or may not occur and is – in the eyes of investors, customers, and even the institutions themselves – at the discretion of a higher power. The factors and parameters of such influence appear unclear and opaque, especially for market participants. However, it seems that political considerations[68] and personal interests have influence on the process, which results in a lack of predictability.

Such influence is possible, for example, within the SRM and the Single Resolution Board (SRB). The decision-making structure for resolution decisions is complex and layered,[69] involving many stages at which influence

---

67 Tröger, 'Too complex to work', p. 17.

68 Papanikolaou states that authorities are more prone to provide support to a distressed bank, which is well-connected with politicians and political parties and less prone to let it go bankrupt. N. I. Papanikolaou, 'To be bailed out or to be left to fail? A dynamic competing risks hazard analysis', *Journal of Financial Stability* 34 (2018), 61–85, pp. 61 *et seq.*

69 See for example Arts. 7, 18, 30, 31, 32 SRMR.

can be exerted[70] and many actors including representatives of Member States. The latter, for example those within the Supervisory Board of the European Central Bank (ECB), are obliged to act in the common European interest. However, this might in practice give leeway to considerations, and even the pursuit, of national or internal interests,[71] especially when it comes to cross-border resolutions and their preparation in Resolution Colleges or similar fora.[72] As will be explained in due course, (political) influence can be exerted in various ways by various players at nearly every stage, either directly or indirectly.[73] It can be wielded, for example, by influencing the decision as to whether to enter into resolution at all,[74] whether to adopt the planned resolution action into a resolution scheme,[75] how to share the burden of losses in resolution,[76] or by indirect intervention in the wider context of resolution planning[77]. Such imponderables, especially with respect of the application of the bail-in tool in the first place, cause unwanted economic behavior on the part of market participants: if there is uncertainty surrounding loss-participations and the possibility exists that the institution might be supported with public money, some

70 V. de Serière and L. Milione, 'De-Politicizing Bail-in', *Journal of International Banking Law and Regulation* 34, Issue 2 (2019), pp. 71 *et seq.*

71 For a detailed analysis on Member States' potential (political) influence on decision-making processes in connection with the resolution of failing banks, see D. Busch, M. van Rijn and M. Louisse, 'How Single is the Single Resolution Mechanism?', *European Business Law Review* (2019), 30, Issue 4, pp. 577 et seq. For a general analysis that highlights how decision makers in public administration are driven by personal motives such as power and prestige, see W. A. Niskanen, *Bureaucracy and representative government* (Chicago: Aldine Atherton, 1971), pp. 36 *et seq.*

72 See *infra* under Part 3, A.II.1.a – *Potential Divergences between Authorities – Cross-Border Coordination.*

73 Serière and Milione, 'De-Politicizing Bail-in'.

74 See *infra* under Part 2, A.II.2.a. – *A Junction Before Resolution: Precautionary Recapitalization.*

75 See *infra* under Part 3, A.II.1.j. – *Gateway to Political Influence – Enforceability of Plans.*

76 See *infra* under Part 2, A.II.2.b.ii. – *Internal Private Funding – Bail-in.*

77 See *infra* under Part 3, A.II.1.j. – *Gateway to Political Influence – Enforceability of Plans.*

actors might consider it worthwhile to attempt to influence the process, thereby jeopardizing the credibility of resolution measures.[78]

Examples from Recent Cases

One example of the unpredictability in the initiation of resolution procedures is the Monte Paschi di Siena case[79], where the application of resolution procedures was uncertain[80] until the European Parliament's consultation and a subsequent agreement with Italy's government led to resolution being shunned in favor of precautionary recapitalization.[81] Since neither the initiation of BRRD resolution procedures nor specific resolution tools were predefined, the Italian government and the European Commission had the possibility of deciding discretionally[82] on how to deal with the case, presumably integrating political considerations[83] in the process and adjusting their decision accordingly. Nevertheless, despite the (alleged)

---

78 That is, because investors base their risk assessment on the foreseeability of bail-in action. Investors gather such information when monitoring competent authorities' administrative practice, which is a hard task because of the opaque decision-making structures in place. This may lead to distorted risk assessment with all of its damaging consequences, see Tröger, 'Too complex to work', p. 17.

79 For an extensive overview of the development of MPS in the last 10 years and an overview of how the current crisis in MPS evolved see C. Barbagallo, *Interventi - Banca Monte dei Paschi di Siena: Senato della Repubblica – Camera dei Deputati, Commissione Parlamentare di inchiesta sul sistema bancario e finanziario* (2017), p. 9 *et seq.*, 14 *et seq.* retrievable at https://www.bancaditalia.it/pubblicazioni/interventi-vari/int-var-2017/Barbagallo-22112017.pdf accessed 1 October 2022 (in Italian).

80 For an analysis of MPS's situation and the potential outcomes before the Commission's decision, which range from a full bail-in to a total deviation from prescribed burden-sharing mechanisms, see I. Triantafyllakis, 'Italienische Banken: Wenn nicht alle Wege zum Bail-in führen', *Zeitschrift für Wirtschafts- und Bankrecht* (2016), 2248–55, p. 2255.

81 See on this topic *supra* under Part 2, A.II.2.a. – *A Junction Before Resolution: Precautionary Recapitalization*.

82 The transferal of the decision-making powers on the resolution of failing banks to the European level was very fittingly compared with Odysseus tying himself to the mast of his ship and instructing his men not to release him, even if he begs and prays to be released, see Busch, van Rijn and Louisse, 'How Single is the Single Resolution Mechanism?'. However, it seems that in the recent European cases, Odysseus's proverbial ties were not as tight as they should have been or that his men did not obey his order not to release him.

83 For example, a considerable amount of potentially bail-inable debt was held as savings or by other small and private investors, who actually do not possess the required loss-bearing and risk-management capacity, which caused Italy and the Commission to shelter such unprofessional financial actors from the burden of

circumvention[84] of BRRD resolution procedures, the Commission and Italy cannot be accused of literally breaking the law by integrating political and economic interests into their decision. Therefore, the case left open the question of whether the Commission and Italy had bypassed the law by handling the MPS case in the way they did, or whether they had used an inherent loophole in the new legislative framework.[85] Either way, the case lacked predictability.

Another example of the unpredictability of resolution procedures is found in the case of two local Venetian banks, Veneto Banca[86] and Banca Popolare di Vicenza:[87] after struggling for months, the ECB declared both banks no longer viable because they repeatedly breached supervisory capital requirements and – due to a lack of a systemic dimension and public interest[88] established by the SRB – their 'bad parts' were wound-down according to national insolvency proceedings, with their 'good parts' taken over under a number of requirements by Italy's second largest bank, Intesa

---

bail-in, compare *supra* under Part 4, A.III.6. – *Potential Investors and Holders of MREL Eligible Instruments*.

84 The argument that a disrupted and NPL-flooded Italian financial market caused the problem long before the application of the new legislative framework and that different treatment of the situation would be adequate, can be considered invalid as transitional arrangements were explicitly not provided for in the BRRD.

85 J.-H. Binder, 'Systemkrisenbewältigung durch Bankenabwicklung? Aktuelle Bemerkungen zu unrealistischen Erwartungen', *Zeitschrift für Bankrecht und Bankwirtschaft* 29 (2017), 57–71, p. 71; M. R. Götz, J. P. Krahnen and T. H. Tröger, 'Testfall Monte dei Paschi, Frankfurter Allgemeine v. 3.2.2017', *Frankfurter Allgemeine Zeitung* (2017), 19.

86 Single Resolution Board, *Decision of the Single Resolution Board concerning the assessment of the conditions for resolution in respect of Veneto Banca S.p.A.* (2017), retrievable under https://srb.europa.eu/sites/srbsite/files/srb-ees-2017-11_non-confidential.pdf.

87 Single Resolution Board, *Decision of the Single Resolution Board concerning the assessment of the conditions for resolution in respect of Banca Popolare di Vicenza S.p.A.* (2017), retrievable under https://srb.europa.eu/sites/srbsite/files/srb-ees-2017-12_non-confidential.pdf.

88 S. Grünewald, 'Legal challenges of bail-in' in European Central Bank (ed.), *ECB Legal Conference 2017: shaping a new legal order for Europe: A tale of crises and opportunities: 4-5 September 2017* (Frankfurt am Main: Europäische Zentralbank, 2017), pp. 287–310, p. 299.

Sanpaolo,[89] for a symbolic fee of one euro.[90] Interestingly however, even if the two Venetian banks were not deemed systemically important to the EU, the Italian government decided that they most certainly were to Italy[91] and that the failure of both banks would disrupt the local economy in Venice.[92] Against this backdrop, the Italian government dressed a bailout as a rescue by Intesa in the context of national insolvency proceedings and injected over five billion euros of capital for the wind-down and transfer of the shares to Intesa and, additionally, provided 12 billion euros of gua-

89 G. Federico, 'Crisi delle banche venete ad "aiuti di Stato"', *Questione Giustizia* (2017), 212–20, p. 213; B. Mesnard, A. Margerit and M. Magnus, *The orderly liquidation of Veneto Banca and Banca Popolare di Vicenza*, Briefing of the European Parliament (2017) retrievable at http://www.europarl.europa.eu/RegData/etudes/BRIE/2017/602094/IPOL_BRI(2017)602094_EN.pdf accessed 1 October 2022.

90 This is reminiscent of Santander's recent acquisition of Banco Popular for 1 euro. However, contrary to the Italian case, Santander took full financial responsibility for Banco Popular. See for a tabular comparison between the cases (together with Veneto Banca and Banca Popolare di Vicenza) Sachverständigenrat zur Begutachtung der Gesamtwirtschaftlichen Entwicklung, *Für eine zukunftsorientierte Wirtschaftspolitik*, Jahresgutachten (Wiesbaden, 2017), 54.2017/18, ch. 5, table 19.

91 Andrea Enria noted that "two different definitions of 'public interest' have been applied, one at the EU level and another one by national authorities", see S. Sciorilli Borrelli, *Q and A with Andrea Enria of European Banking Authority*. https://www.politico.eu/pro/q-and-a-with-andrea-enria-of-european-banking-authority/ accessed 1 October 2022. A similar interpretation can be found in Grünewald, 'Legal challenges of bail-in', p. 308 and S. Merler, *Critical functions and public interest in banking services: Need for clarification?*, In-Depth Analysis for the Economics and Monetary Affairs Committee of the European Parliament (2017), p. 11.

92 The Italian government stated that in the absence of public support measures, the placement of the two banks into forced administrative liquidation would cause a "serious disturbance to the local economy", see Camera dei deputati ed il Senato della Repubblica, *Conversione in legge, con modificazioni, del decreto-legge 25 giugno 2017, n. 99, recante disposizioni urgenti per la liquidazione coatta amministrativa di Banca Popolare di Vicenza S.p.A. e di Veneto Banca S.p.A. (17G00133) (GU Serie Generale n.184 del 08-08-2017)* ; F. Coppola, 'Italy's Latest Bank Bailout Has Created A Two-Speed Eurozone', Forbes, 26 June 2017 retrievable at https://www.forbes.com/sites/francescoppola/2017/06/26/italys-latest-bank-bailout accessed 1 October 2022; Federico, 'Crisi delle banche venete ad "aiuti di Stato"', p. 218. See also Merler for a discussion about whether the specific case of the two Venetian banks calls for a clarification of the definition of "public interest" and "critical functions", see S. Merler, 'Bank liquidation in the European Union: clarification needed', *Bruegel Policy Contributions* Issue no. 1 (2017) retrievable at http://bruegel.org/wp-content/uploads/2018/01/PC-01_2018.pdf accessed 1 October 2022.

rantees to cover non-performing loans.[93] Unpredictability due to political influence thus occurred here in the following two ways: first, the Italian government used public funds during national insolvency proceedings, resulting in a de facto bailout; and, second, it tried to avoid the application of BRRD resolution to the 'good parts' of the banks, determining that they did not perform critical functions and that their services were substitutable. The political rationale behind this is clear: resolution would have affected savers with deposits of over 100 000 euros as well as junior and senior creditors,[94] as many of them are mom-and-pop investors, making up the vast majority of theVeneto region's businesses.[95] However, only a few weeks earlier, the SRB had established such public interest in the resolution of the likely-to-fail[96] Banco Popular Español (BPE)[97] as the bank was engaged in deposit-taking from households and non-financial corpora-

93 P. Cichy, Buchmüller and Igl, '§ 15 Sanierungs- und Abwicklungsplanung' in J.-H. Binder, A. Glos and J. Riepe (eds.), *Handbuch Bankenaufsicht* (Köln: RWS, 2017), p. 732; for a more detailed description of the MPS case, see Binder, 'Systemkrisenbewältigung durch Bankenabwicklung? Aktuelle Bemerkungen zu unrealistischen Erwartungen'.

94 Handelsblatt, 'Bankenrettung kostet Steuerzahler bis zu 17 Milliarden Euro', Handelsblatt, 25 June 2017, retrievable at http://www.handelsblatt.com/finanzen/banken-versicherungen/veneto-banca-banca-popolare-di-vicenza-bankenrettung-kostet-steuerzahler-bis-zu-17-milliarden-euro-/19977578.html accessed 1 October 2022.

95 S. Sirletti and A. Weber, *Italy Commits $19 Billion for Veneto Banks in Biggest Rescue*. https://www.bloomberg.com/news/articles/2017-06-25/italy-mobilizes-up-to-19-billion-to-keep-veneto-banks-afloat accessed 1 October 2022.

96 European Central Bank, *'Failing or Likely to Fail' Assessment of Banco Popular Espanol* , retrievable at https://www.bankingsupervision.europa.eu/ecb/pub/pdf/ssm.2017_FOLTF_ESPOP.en.pdf accessed 1 October 2022; Single Resolution Board, *Decision of the Single Resolution Board concerning the adoption of a resolution scheme in respect of Banco Popular Espanol, S.A.: Executive Session* (2017) retrievable at https://srb.europa.eu/sites/srbsite/files/srb_decision_srb_ees_2017_08_non-confidential_scanned.pdf accessed 1 October 2022.

97 The BPE case was frequently cited as one of the role model resolution cases under the BRRD. However, even if this case probably has come closest to the envisaged resolution procedures, it must be noted that the circumstances of Banco Popular were unusually favorable. It had a comparatively simple legal structure and only few comparatively small operations outside of Spain, plus there was a willing buyer, Banco Santander, available to take over BPE. For a detailed analysis of the case and why it cannot be seen as a blueprint for further resolution cases see J.-H. Binder, *Wunderkind is Walking? The Resolution of Banco Popular as a First Test for the Single Resolution Mechanism*. https://www.law.ox.ac.uk/business-law-blog/blog/2017/06/wunderkind-walking-resolution-banco-popular-first-test-single accessed 1 October 2022.

tions, lending to small and medium enterprises (SMEs) and payment and cash services – just like the two Venetian banks.[98] Therefore, in the Italian case, the SRB and the Commission wangled the application of resolution in a way that established insufficient public interest for the two banks to enter resolution, while at the same time establishing enough public interest for them to receive liquidation aid.[99] In light of the latter, it seems that the Commission applies double standards in certain cases.[100] The lesson to be drawn from this case is as follows: resolution could have been applied to the two Venetian banks, however the Italian government decided to resolve them partly under national resolution procedures that were specifically amended for this case. Neither customers, investors, nor stakeholders could have predicted the fate and fortune of Veneto Banca and Banca Popolare di Vicenza.

Thus, what happened in the MPS case was somewhat mirrored in the case of the Venetian banks: the application of resolution was not predefined, and Italy and the Commission were free to negotiate their way around the applicable resolution rules due to a political desideratum. In both cases, public money was involved. In neither case was anyone able to predict whether the institutions would enter resolution procedures or not, let alone the specific procedure to be used. Especially in the MPS case, a rational BRRD user might have assumed that resolution procedures would be applied but the reality was quite the opposite.

Lack of Predictability with Respect to the Liabilities Subject to Bail-in

Not only is predictability insufficient in relation to the initiation of resolution procedures in general or in their execution specifically, but it

---

98 Highlighting the similarity between the Italian and the Spanish cases, Merler, *Critical functions and public interest in banking services: Need for clarification?*, pp. 8 *et seq.*

99 Merler illustrates the history of SRB assessments with respect to the Venetian banks and points out that only in 2015 did the SRB deem liquidation under normal insolvency proceedings not credible for the same banks for which they would establish no public interest only two years later, see ibid., pp. 11 *et seq.*; Grünewald, 'Legal challenges of bail-in', p. 299.

100 Or, at least, that there is a double standard for countries such as Italy (or Germany and France) that can afford to bail-out their banks and that are 'too big to bully,' yielding them demureness and discretion from the Commission, while other countries (such as Greece or Portugal) cannot afford to bail-out their banks and are therefore forced to bail-in their senior creditors or unsecured depositors, and thus enter resolution procedures, see Coppola, 'Italy's Latest Bank Bailout Has Created A Two-Speed Eurozone'.

is also lacking with respect to the liabilities subject to bail-in.[101] Until the very last moment, statements on which asset or liability will be involved in the bail-in cannot be made and consequently cannot be predicted by their holders. This is owing to the characteristics of financial instruments potentially eligible for bail-in, since banks' business no longer consists merely of accepting deposits, paying interest, and granting loans[102]. Nowadays, sophisticated instruments comprise networks of claims in their own right, for example securitized debt,[103] credit default swaps, interbank transactions such as securities lending and repurchasing, collateralized debt obligations, and mortgage lending across multiple jurisdictions. These are but a few instruments that heighten the complexity of a modern banks' balance sheet.[104] By contrast, bail-inable liabilities need to be rather simple.[105] In this new era of banking business, it is particularly difficult to sort out the bail-inable instruments in the course of a resolution procedure. Moreover, as seen in the case of Italy, some simple liabilities that are potentially eligible for bail-in are spared due to political or economic considerations. Because of the potential influence of external interests, a reliable prediction of assets and liabilities used during loss-allocation in resolution is as unpredictable as resolution and bail-in itself.

Such a lack of predictability, on the one hand in relation to the initiation of bail-in-related resolution procedures in general, and on the other in relation to the liabilities subject to bail-in, disrupts the credibility of resolution. Reliable forecasting is essentially not possible, which prevents realistic risk analysis by market participants and diminishes the sense of

101 Tröger, 'Too complex to work', p. 4.

102 At a time when banks business was considered mainly deposit-taking and granting loans, bank executives were said to follow the "3–6–3 rule," meaning they would accept deposits at three percent interest, made loans at six percent interest, and would hit the golf course by 3pm, see J. R. Walter, 'The 3-6-3 rule: An urban myth?', *Economic quarterly* 92 (2006), 51–78.

103 Securitization is said to be one of the main increasers of the complexity and dimensionality of financial networks. Financial intersections have grown in size and interconnections have multiplied, making the source and location of the underlying claims anyone's guess, see A. G. Haldane, *Rethinking the Financial Network* (Financial Student Association, Amsterdam, 2009).

104 R. F. Weber, 'Structural regulation as antidote to complexity capture', *American business law journal: the official publication of the American Business Law Association* 49 (2012), 643–738, p. 674.

105 Although bail-in generally applies to all liabilities of an institution, Art. 44(1) BRRD, certain liabilities are excluded due to their complex characteristics, Art. 44(2) and (3) BRRD.

certainty and feelings of trust among customers and taxpayers alike. Additionally, it tempts the parties concerned to try to influence the process, as unpredictability fosters political interference. Each deviation from the rules stipulated by the BRRD renders their application more unpredictable, which currently renders the resolution framework lacking in credibility.

Complexity in Bank Structures

One objective of the BRRD resolution regime is to make resolution faster. Resolution should, in comparison with the normal national insolvency proceedings, be employable over one weekend in order to prevent unwanted systemic consequences and contagion. Considering the current banking landscape throughout Europe,[106] it is hard to believe that the new regime can deal with the present complexities.

Looking back at the last 100 years of banking history, banks have constantly become bigger, more interconnected, more ramified and have moved away from traditional depositary and lending business being their main activities.[107] Although this trend – after a significant increase in complexity before the crisis and until 2011[108] – may already be decreasing,

106 The overall euro area's financial sector was valued at about 76.2 trillion euros in March 2017 and continues to increase; see for an overview European Central Bank, *Report on financial structures* (2017), pp. 22 *et seq.* retrievable at https://www.ecb.europa.eu/pub/pdf/other/reportonfinancialstructures201710.en.pdf accessed 1 October 2022. There are 30 banks belonging to parent companies headquartered in the euro area that have assets in excess of 150 billion euros and are supervised by the ECB, including the eight globally systemically important banks (GSIBs), leaving 22 "European systemically important banks (ESIBs)" that together represent roughly 60 % of the total banking assets in the Banking Union. Furthermore, 19 of these 30 banks are considered financial conglomerates; see Schoenmaker D., Véron N., Gehrig T. P., Messori M., Leite A. P., Sapir A., Steffen S., Tibi P., Vegara Figueras D., Vries C. G. d. and Xafa M. (eds.), *European banking supervision: The first eighteen months*, Blueprint series (Brussels, Belgium: Bruegel, 2016).

107 S. Schelo, *Bank recovery and resolution*, International banking and finance law series (Alphen aan den Rijn: Kluwer Law Internat, 2015), vol. 26, § 1.01 – Evolution of size and shape of banks.

108 A detailed analysis of the historical evolution of bank complexity, starting right before the crisis in December 2007 until May 2013, may be found in J. Carmassi and R. Herring, 'Corporate Structures, Transparency and Resolvability of Global Systemically Important Banks', *Wharton School Working Papers* (2014), pp. 106 *et seq.* An even earlier description of the expansion of the financial sector

due to both the increasing realization that complexity may forestall plausible resolution action *and* an increase in regulatory capital requirements aligned with the risk posed by an institution,[109] most institutions (especially global systemically important banks (GSIBs)) still suffer from complexity.[110] Large mergers and acquisitions across institutions,[111] as seen often in recent times,[112] aggravate the existing intricacy of banks' structures alongside classic causes of complexity, such as asset size and the number of separately incorporated entities in a banking group.[113]

---

can be found in R. Herring and A. Santomero, 'The Corporate Structure of Financial Conglomerates' in M. H. Kosters and A. H. Meltzer (eds.), *International Competitiveness in Financial Services: A Special Issue of the Journal of Financial Services Research* (Dordrecht, s.l.: Springer Netherlands, 1991).

109 The systemic risk posed by an institution is determined, amongst other things, by indicators of its complexity. This means the more complex an institution is, the more systemic risk it poses and the higher the regulatory capital requirements it has to comply with, see J. Carmassi and R. Herring, 'The Corporate Complexity of Global Systemically Important Banks', *Journal of Financial Services Research* 49 (2016), 175–201, p. 195.

110 For a detailed econometric analysis of a set of panel data substantiating the current complexity and opaqueness of GSIBs, see ibid.

111 G. Karamichailidou and D. G. Mayes, 'Plausible recovery and resolution plans for cross-border financial institutions' in J. E. Castañeda, D. G. Mayes and G. E. Wood (eds.), *European Banking Union: Prospects and challenges* (Routledge, 2016), pp. 38–66, p. 40. Carmassi and Herring state that, besides merger activity and acquisitions, regulation and tax incentives may also lead GSIBs to adopt more complex structures, see Carmassi and Herring, 'The Corporate Complexity of Global Systemically Important Banks', pp. 175 *et seq.*

112 Most notably, such mergers and acquisitions in the financial sector can frequently be observed in the course of bank crises (*e.g.* when an institution in distress sells the whole or part of their business to other solvent institutions or merges with solvent institutions). This not only enhances complexity in the purchasing bank's structure but it also adds distressed balance sheet items such as non-performing loans to the balance sheet of the solvent bank. Therefore, such absorption often requires a capital increase by the purchasing bank. The most recent example is given by Santander who purchased the distressed Banco Popular for a symbolic one euro, see Handelsblatt vom 07.06.2017, "Santander rettet Banco Popular in letzter Minute", retrievable at http://www.handelsblatt.com/finanzen/banken-versicherungen/spanische-krisenbank-santander-rettet-banco-popular-in-letzter-minute/19900498.html accessed 1 October 2022.

113 Although Carmassi and Herring state that, setting aside regulatory and tax incentives and other factors that tend to evolve over time, asset size does not have a significant impact on the complexity of GSIBs, asset size is still considered one of the most prominent causes for complexity, see Carmassi and Herring, 'The Corporate Complexity of Global Systemically Important Banks', pp. 175, 178.

Although there is no universal definition of complexity, for many years and even before the financial crises of 2007 and 2009, bank complexity was and still is a major concern amongst scholars and in practice.[114] The frequently used term "too big to fail" can also be translated into "too complex to fail"[115] or "too complex to be resolved properly," meaning

---

114 See, for example, R. Herring and J. Carmassi, 'Complexity and Systemic Risk: What's Changed Since the Crisis?' in A. N. Berger (ed.), *The Oxford handbook of banking*, 2. ed. (Oxford: Oxford Univ. Press, 2015); E. Bauer, F. Mrusek, K. Metka and M. Schöll, *Complexity kills - How European banking models have to change in a complex world*, Results from zeb's European Banking Study 2015 (2015) retrievable at https://www.bankinghub.eu/banking/research-markets/complexity-kills-european-banking-models-change-complex-world accessed 1 October 2022; Carmassi and Herring, 'The Corporate Complexity of Global Systemically Important Banks'; W. P. de Groen, *The different legal and operational structures of banking groups in the euro area, and their impact on banks' resolvability*, In-Depth Analysis for the Economics and Monetary Affairs Committee of the European Parliament (2016) retrievable at http://www.europarl.europa.eu/RegData/etudes/IDAN/2016/587378/IPOL_IDA(2016)587378_EN.pdf accessed 1 October 2022; N. Cetorelli and L. Goldberg, 'Measures of Global Bank Complexity', *FRBNY Economic Policy Review* (2014), 107–26; R. Herring and J. Carmassi, 'The Corporate Structure of International Financial Conglomerates: Complexity and Its Implications for Safety and Soundness' in A. N. Berger (ed.), *The Oxford handbook of banking*, 2. ed. (Oxford: Oxford Univ. Press, 2015), p. 195; J. Oldfather, S. Gissler and D. Ruffino, *Bank Complexity: Is Size Everything?* https://www.federalreserve.gov/econresdata/notes/feds-notes/2016/bank-complexity-is-size-everything-20160715.html accessed 1 October 2022; Weber, 'Structural regulation as antidote to complexity capture'; R. Lastra, R. Ayadi, R. Olivares-Caminal and C. Russo, *The different legal and operational structures of banking groups in the euro area, and their impact on banks' resolvability*, In-Depth Analysis for the Economics and Monetary Affairs Committee of the European Parliament (2016) retrievable at http://www.europarl.europa.eu/RegData/etudes/IDAN/2016/587377/IPOL_IDA(2016)587377_EN.pdf accessed 1 October 2022; Schoenmaker, *The different legal and operational structures of banking groups in the euro area, and their impact on banks' resolvability*; H. James, *Keynote speech - Lehman in a Broader Perspective*, Lehman - 10 Years After (Goethe-Universität Frankfurt am Main, 2018); C. M. Stiefmüller, *Ten Years After - The 2017 Banking Package: One Step Forward, Two Steps Back*, Finance Watch Policy Brief (2017) retrievable at https://www.finance-watch.org/wp-content/uploads/2017/06/Finance-Watch-Policy-Brief-June-2017.pdf accessed 1 October 2022.

115 This term was originally coined to express that a "too complex to fail" bank would simply not be put into insolvency or resolution and would be bailed out. However, it can also be understood to mean that a bank is so complex that it is impossible to plan for its orderly resolution or to properly execute resolution measures.

that the institution can be so complex in its structures that it becomes unmanageable in terms of providing comprehensive, orderly, and undisrupted resolution, even though its actual size might be moderate. In this respect, complexity is the enemy of both reliability and security. The more complex a system is, the greater the chance of the unexpected interaction of components and the less the chance to fully comprehend the system.[116]

Evaluating the European banking landscape, there might at least be some European banks that are too complex for the envisaged resolution approach. This presumption has been confirmed by various cases in which the authorities struggled to deal with a failing bank in the space of one weekend. This is certainly due to, and correlates with, the sheer size of certain institutions, but it will be shown that complex legal and organizational structures and business models (*e.g.* the structure of assets and liabilities) within individual institutions are the more pertinent issue in this respect.[117] The following section, therefore, will shed light on contributors to complexity[118] in order to better assess at a later stage whether the proposed remedy is appropriate.

---

116 C. Perrow, *The Next Catastrophe: Reducing Our Vulnerabilities to Natural, Industrial, and Terrorist Disasters* (Princeton: Princeton University Press, 2011); Weber, 'Structural regulation as antidote to complexity capture', p. 643.

117 Binder, 'Resolution Planning and Structural Bank Reform within the Banking Union' pp. 129, 145. On the other hand, it is argued that no single accepted metric for complexity exists, see Cetorelli and Goldberg, 'Measures of Global Bank Complexity'. Nevertheless, in order to explain complexity, Cetorelli and Goldberg introduce an organizational-complexity metric and a business-complexity metric too.

118 The three components determining the complexity of a bank are chosen by the author particularly with regard to possible resolution action. This does not mean that these three indicators are the only components constituting complexity in banks. For example, another approach in determining the components constituting complexity is used by the Basel Committee of Banking Supervision (BCBS). The BCBS designated the following components as measures of complexity: (1) the amount of over-the-counter-derivatives; (2) the quantity of trading and available for sale securities; and (3) the amount of Level 3 assets, see Basel Committee on Banking Supervision, *The G-SIB assessment methodology: Score calculation* (Basel: Bank for International Settlements, 2014) and Basel Committee on Banking Supervision, *Global systemically important banks: Updated assessment methodology and the higher loss absorbency requirement: Updated assessment methodology and the higher loss absorbency requirement*, July 2013 (Basel: Bank for International Settlements, 2013).

Asset Size

Some academics opine that the complexity in banks derives primarily from the sheer size of an institution.[119] While doing so, the means used to measure bank size are not uniform but, most commonly, associated with the size of the balance sheet of the respective bank,[120] as for example used by the Basel Committee on Banking Supervision.[121] Although it is often denied that size alone creates complexity[122] it can be presumed that there is a natural correlation between the size of the balance sheet and increased complexity, since a big bank is, in the vast majority of cases, also a complex bank.[123] Empirical evidence can be found for this by looking at the ECB's list of supervised entities.[124] All listed entities have considerable total assets – all have assets amounting to more than 30 billion euros and some run into the hundreds of billions. Banco Santander, S.A., for example, has

---

119 The opposite view is presented by Caramassi and Herring, who state that asset size, once account is taken of regulatory and tax incentives or other factors that evolve over time, would not have any impact on the complexity of banks. This is because the bank, following a hypothetical assumption, would then grow organically and only as rapidly as market conditions would permit, without creating new legal entities or making acquisitions or offering new products, see Carmassi and Herring, 'The Corporate Complexity of Global Systemically Important Banks', p. 176. Also, Cetorelli and Goldberg are of the view that complexity cannot be equated with institution size and that no close relationship exists with complexity measures, see Cetorelli and Goldberg, 'Measures of Global Bank Complexity'.

120 Bauer, Mrusek, Metka and Schöll, *Complexity kills - How European banking models have to change in a complex world.*

121 The BCBS developed three measures of overall complexity, all of which are associated with balance sheet measures: Level 3 assets; trading and available-for-sale-securities; and the national amount of over-the-counter-derivatives, see Basel Committee on Banking Supervision, *Global systemically important banks: Updated assessment methodology and the higher loss absorbency requirement.*

122 Carmassi and Herring, 'The Corporate Complexity of Global Systemically Important Banks', p. 176; Cetorelli and Goldberg, 'Measures of Global Bank Complexity' L. Laeven, L. Ratnovski and H. Tong, *Bank Size and Systemic Risk* (2014); Oldfather, Gissler and Ruffino, *Bank Complexity: Is Size Everything?.*

123 And even if such a big asset-sized bank is not deemed complex, the problem of resolving an big asset-sized bank often derives from their sheer size. Even if simply structured, many of them surpass the GDP of a single Member State of the EU, see H. Chen Chen, 'The Recovery Framework in the BRRD and its Effectiveness', *International Company and Commercial Law Review* 10 (2015), 26..

124 European Central Bank, *List of supervised entities – cut-off date for significance decisions: 1 April 2017* (2017).

total assets above 1000 billion euros and 25 ECB-supervised subsidiaries with respective branches in Spain, Austria, Belgium, France, Germany, Italy, Luxembourg, and Portugal,[125] leaving aside non-bank and all non-EU entities. The sum of balance sheet assets of the 13 European GSIBs, which are unsurprisingly considered the most complex institutions, equals approximately 110 % of the aggregated GDP of the EU-28.[126] The bigger the total assets are, the more subsidiaries and branches the institution has in general. Therefore, even if not an imperative cause in itself, size can still be considered an indicator of complexity, and Europe hosts a number of very big banks.

Legal and Organizational Structures

The second contributor to complexity in bank structures is legal and organizational structures. It can be defined as the number of material legal entities[127] and subsidiaries under an institution,[128] banking group, or financial conglomerate and their distribution across different EU and non-EU jurisdictions.[129] Furthermore, their governance arrangement (i.e. whether they are government-controlled, commercial, or cooperative,[130] a public or a savings bank) has to be taken into account. Finally, technical equipment such as IT systems, telecommunication, and data management facilities all contribute to organizational diversity. The more extensive the-

---

125 See ibid., p. 3.

126 Stiefmüller, *Ten Years After - The 2017 Banking Package: One Step Forward, Two Steps Back*, p. 5.

127 Weber, 'Structural regulation as antidote to complexity capture', p. 662; E. Avgouleas, C. Goodhart and D. Schoenmaker, 'Bank Resolution Plans as a catalyst for global financial reform', *Journal of Financial Stability* 9 (2013), 210–8, pp. 214 *et seq.*

128 On the "too many to fail" problem, see V. V. Acharya and T. Yorulmazer, 'Too many to fail - An analysis of time-inconsistency in bank closure policies', *Journal of Financial Intermediation* 16 (2017), 1–31; C. Brown and S. Dinc, 'Too Many to Fail? Evidence of Regulatory Forebearance when the Banking Sector is Weak', *Review of Financial Studies* 24 (2011), 1378–405.

129 For cross-border complexity issues, see J. Carmassi and R. Herring, 'The Cross-Border Challenge in Resolving Global Systemically Important Banks' in K. E. Scott, T. H. Jackson and J. B. Taylor (eds.), *Making failure feasible: How bankruptcy reform can end "too big to fail"*, Hoover Institution Press publication (Stanford, California: Hoover Institution Press, Stanford University, 2015), pp. 249–75.

130 Schoenmaker, *The different legal and operational structures of banking groups in the euro area, and their impact on banks' resolvability*, p. 7.

se categories are in an institution, the more challenging is the resolution of such institutions.

Number of Legal Entities and Distribution of Banking Groups and Activities Across Jurisdictions

Most euro-area GSIBs have a larger-than-average number of legal entities[131] and a greater-than-average-cross-border activity,[132] not only within the eurozone or the Banking Union but also beyond European borders. The 129 ECB-supervised[133] banking institutions have 782 subsidiaries, of which 596 are located in the eurozone. These subsidiaries are spread across 39 countries, not all of which are in the eurozone. In addition, 105 of 129 institutions have branches of their own, adding to the 484 branches belonging to their respective subsidiaries.[134] This cross-border structure results in the interpositioning of a multilevel management structure for each entity in the banking group. On this matter, a former Citigroup risk manager stated that such management structures that were necessary for multi-entity banking groups "put[s] distance between data gatherers and users in senior management," and that as a result "information gets lost in the compression and transmission of the data."[135] As restructuring of institutions is likely to produce substantial transaction costs and extensive

131 For an overview and data of majority-owned subsidiaries of GSIBs, see Carmassi and Herring, 'The Corporate Complexity of Global Systemically Important Banks', table 1, p. 178.

132 For an overview of entities and outside-EU activity per institution, see Schoenmaker, *The different legal and operational structures of banking groups in the euro area, and their impact on banks' resolvability*, p. 8, figure 1; Groen, *The different legal and operational structures of banking groups in the euro area, and their impact on banks' resolvability*, p.1.

133 The data is taken from European Central Bank, *List of supervised entities - cut-off date for significance decisions: 1 April 2017* (2017). The most recent published list however is European Central Bank, *List of supervised entities - cut-off date for significance decisions: 1 July 2018* (2018) with only 119 significant entities.

134 Lastra, Ayadi, Olivares-Caminal and Russo, *The different legal and operational structures of banking groups in the euro area, and their impact on banks' resolvability*, p. 11.

135 R. Bookstaber, *A Demon of Our Own Design: Markets, Hedge Funds, and the Perils of Financial Innovation* (New York, NY: John Wiley & Sons, 2007), pp. 126–127.

management involvement, the structures are often left intact and superfluous legal entities are not shut down.[136]

Governance Arrangements

In addition, the European banking landscape comprises a blend of government-controlled banks (17 out of 129 ECB-supervised banks[137]) as well as commercial banks (38 out of 129), cooperative banks (22 out of 129), public banks (9 out of 129), or pure savings banks (19 out of 129), which can further complicate resolution. For example, cooperative banks are often part of financial conglomerates and are very difficult to handle in resolution, since managers are accountable to the members and clients, and such accounting can consume large quantities of precious resolution time. Commercial banks, on the other hand, are more investment-orientated and more involved in capital markets where they are exposed to more risky functions, such as in the bond market, the secondary market, and prime brokerage. Lastly, saving banks tend to be of crucial importance to the real economy and retail markets, and are therefore vulnerable to political and social considerations and influence, which can also be an impediment to resolvability.[138]

Discrepancies in Institutions' Technical Infrastructure

With respect to the technical particularities of entities, even if they are part of the same group or are held by the same parent holding company, entities frequently use different information technology in all kind of fiel-

136 R. Ayadi and W. P. de Groen, 'Banks' Business Models in Europe' in T. Beck and B. Casu (eds.), *The Palgrave Handbook of European Banking* (London: Palgrave Macmillan UK, 2016), pp. 81–102, pp. 84 *et seq.*; Carmassi and Herring, 'The Corporate Complexity of Global Systemically Important Banks', p. 188.

137 Data obtained from R. Ayadi, W. P. de Groen, I. Sassi, W. Mathlouthi, H. Rey and O. Aubry, *Banking Business Models Monitor 2015 Europe* (Montréal: International Research Centre on Cooperative Finance, 2016), pp. 19 *et seq.*, 103 *et seq.*, appendix II; Lastra, Ayadi, Olivares-Caminal and Russo, *The different legal and operational structures of banking groups in the euro area, and their impact on banks' resolvability*, p. 10.

138 Lastra, Ayadi, Olivares-Caminal and Russo, *The different legal and operational structures of banking groups in the euro area, and their impact on banks' resolvability*, p. 12.

ds. This can range from different data collection and procession systems[139] to discrepant internal communication systems.[140] The outdated IT systems of banks have frequently and recently been a hot topic in the banking industry, and are furiously discussed[141]. Often, such technical diversity has resulted from mergers and acquisitions over time. But far more often, technical infrastructure dates back further, leaving a legacy of data production, processing, and information technologies that were initially applied in the 1990s. Even the major banks nowadays operate a vast array of systems that have evolved over decades, layering new technologies and equipment on top of ancient systems[142]. This leads to problems regarding group-internal communication and data-gathering, as reliable information about group-wide financial data often cannot even be obtained at the top level of the group, let alone in the multiple subsidiaries in various jurisdictions. IT problems have grown in line with the increasing complexity of bank structures. As will be shown in the following discourse[143], this seemingly trivial issues amount to a severe impediment for the new resolution regime. Clear evidence can be derived from the past, namely the failure of Lehman Brothers[144], that difficulties arise in complex and opaque legal and

139 An associated problem is the existence of different IFRS application levels. Although largely implemented and binding in Europe, with certain exceptions for some countries and different kinds of corporations, the IFRS standard is not globally uniform. This issue is related to the problem of diverse data collection and procession systems and a further contributor to the complexity of banks' structures.

140 Stiefmüller, *Ten Years After - The 2017 Banking Package: One Step Forward, Two Steps Back*, p. 5.

141 See, among many, K. Flinders, 'Big banks' legacy IT systems could kill them', computerweekly.com, retrievable at https://www.computerweekly.com/news/2240212567/Big-banks-legacy-IT-systems-could-kill-them accessed 1 October 2022; S. Herrmann and U. Heinke, 'Kernbanksysteme müssen moderner werden', SpringerProfessional, 05 April 2017 retrievable at https://www.springerprofessional.de/bank-it/os/kernbanksysteme-muessen-moderner-werden/12197548 accessed 1 October 2022; S. Littmann, A. Welp and C. Welp, 'Computersysteme der Banken veraltet - Opa sitzt im Serverraum', Wirtschaftswoche, 19 April 2017, retrievable at https://www.wiwo.de/unternehmen/banken/computersysteme-der-banken-veraltet-opa-sitzt-im-serverraum/19661560.html accessed 1 October 2022.

142 Stiefmüller, *Ten Years After - The 2017 Banking Package: One Step Forward, Two Steps Back*, p. 5.

143 Part 3, A.II.1.h. – *Opaque Data Production and Collection Process.*

144 Carmassi and Herring, 'The Cross-Border Challenge in Resolving Global Systemically Important Banks', p. 251; E. Kapur, 'The Next Lehman Bankruptcy' in K. E. Scott, T. H. Jackson and J. B. Taylor (eds.), *Making failure feasible: How*

organizational structures that stretch across multiple national borders. In that high-profile case, over 100 bankruptcy proceedings in a multitude of jurisdictions were initiated. Additionally, because crucial data centers were sold together with one of the entities, other affiliates and their respective resolution authorities lost access to fundamental information about the ownership structure of the firm. The coordination of the numerous legal entities in various jurisdictions was nearly impossible, with information so fragmented that resolution could not achieve its intended aim.[145]

Institutional Structure: Business Models

In Europe, the prevailing model tends to be universal banking[146] (also referred to as commercial banking), as fewer sharp distinctions apply than in the models customarily applied in the United States or the UK. However, universal banks especially appear to be more complex than, for example, sheer retail banks or less complex wholesale banks.[147] Primarily, this is because diversification of the business model usually goes hand-in-hand with an increased number of subsidiaries and branches, resulting in more complex structures. Although diversification is in principle seen as risk-minimizing, diversified structures can accelerate contagion within a banking group.[148] In contrast, retail banks and wholesale structures are more mono-lined, avoiding the intra-group contagion risk but leaving themselves more exposed to sector-specific shocks than universal banks.[149] Since the vast majority of banks subject to the BRRD are part of the universal banking

---

bankruptcy reform can end "too big to fail", Hoover Institution Press publication (Stanford, California: Hoover Institution Press, Stanford University, 2015), pp. 175–241; James, *Keynote speech – Lehman in a Broader Perspective*.

145 Carmassi and Herring, 'The Corporate Complexity of Global Systemically Important Banks', p. 176; Weber, 'Structural regulation as antidote to complexity capture', p. 673.

146 For the different types of banks and their characteristics, see Schelo, *Bank recovery and resolution*, vol. 26, § 1.03 -Type of banks.

147 Bauer, Mrusek, Metka and Schöll, *Complexity kills - How European banking models have to change in a complex world.*

148 Compare for example the events in the course of the Fortis case, R. Wiggins, N. Tente and A. Metrick, *European Banking Union C: Cross-Border Resolution – Fortis Group*, Yale Program on Financial Stability Case Study 2014-5D-V1 (2015).

149 Lastra, Ayadi, Olivares-Caminal and Russo, *The different legal and operational structures of banking groups in the euro area, and their impact on banks' resolvability*, p. 15.

model, the chosen business model can be considered a third component contributing to the complexity in banks' structures.

Results

The above-identified factors – asset size, legal and organizational structures, and business model – broaden out understanding of the complexity in bank structures. Therefore, a potential remedy to *ex ante* complexity must tackle these three points, amongst others[150]. All three components can be observed in numerous European banks, especially those considered GSIBs or otherwise systemically important banks (OSIBs) (*i.e.* banks who are considered too important to be sent into national insolvency proceedings[151] and are therefore subject to the resolution framework).

No Adequate Modification Measures Ex Ante

The third factor that completes the tripartie compound is the lack of adequate modification mechanisms *ex ante*. Even if resolution authorities detect complex structures and their negative impact on potential resolution measures before an actual crisis scenario occurs, they currently cannot do much about it.[152] Therefore, an instrument to eliminate identified impediments to resolution or bail-in caused by the inherent complexity of institutions is needed. The absence of such measures to modify banks' structures invasively before resolution further demonstrates the lack of predictability and the over-complexity in banks' structures.

---

150 As already outlined, the entire dimension of complexity cannot be described or understood using these three factors alone, and there are dozens of definitions of complexity even within the academic community.

151 C. M. Stiefmüller, *Ten Years After: Back to Business as Usual: The Pit and the Pendulum – Post-Crisis Financial Regulation in Europe*, Finance Watch Report (2018), p. 26 retrievable at https://www.finance-watch.org/wp-content/uploads/2018/09/10YA-FW-report.pdf accessed 1 October 2022.

152 Stiefmüller identifies the lack of imposing structural changes upon specific institutions as one of the three categories that still need to be properly implemented in order to make the new resolution regime credible, see Stiefmüller, *Ten Years After - The 2017 Banking Package: One Step Forward, Two Steps Back*, p. 7.

Results of Ex Ante Evaluation

The above section set out current pre-resolution shortcomings with respect to the establishment of a credible resolution regime. Three factors were identified: the lack of predictability; excessive complexity in bank structures; and the absence of adequate modification measures *ex ante*. Moreover, it was also demonstrated that European banks are affected by those factors and that any potential remedy must therefore tackle at least these three aspects.

Ex Post: Lack of Sufficient Funding for Resolution

Continuing the analysis of the current lacks adversely affecting the credibility of resolution, the following sections will demonstrate that the deficient design of resolution financing hampers the credibility of the resolution process *ex post* resolution decision. As a starting point, a few general remarks about optimal BRRD resolution funding are made here.

When deciding to put a bank into resolution, one of the main questions to answer is how cost-intensive[153] resolution action will be financed. Additionally, if parts of the institution are supposed to survive resolution, such parts need to be recapitalized. This means that the institution is required to again meet the current bank capital levels set out in the CRR and the CRD IV. During this process, the focus is on compliance with the five resolution objectives[154] set out in Article 31(2) BRRD. One of those objectives is the protection of public funds.[155] To achieve this objective,

---

153 When resolving an institution, substantial financing needs to typically arise. Such funding requirements depend highly on the implemented resolution strategy and applied resolution tools, and emerge because of liquidity shortfalls such as depositor-fluctuation and withdrawals, refinancing of non-matching maturities, or the loss of existing sources of financing or capital shortfalls, see Cichy, Buchmüller and Igl, '§ 15 Sanierungs- und Abwicklungsplanung', p. 729; Groen, *Cash outflows in crisis scenarios*, pp. 17, 18.

154 The five resolution objectives laid down in Art. 31(2) BRRD are: (i) ensure the continuity of critical functions of the credit institution under resolution; (ii) avoid significant adverse effects on financial stability, in particular by preventing contagion and by maintaining market discipline; (iii) protect public funds by minimizing reliance on extraordinary public financial support; (iv) protect depositors and investors covered by deposit and investment guarantee schemes; and (v) protect client funds and client assets.

155 Art. 31(2)(c) BRRD.

the financial means for resolution and recapitalization need to derive from private (or at least sector-specific) sources and must be easily and quickly accessible. Additionally, they must be sufficient to cover the whole resolution and recapitalization process and, most importantly, their use must not entail further negative consequences. In that respect, the no-public-funds postulate seems to contrast with other resolution objectives: the protection of covered depositors[156] and in particular the protection of client funds and client assets[157]. Thus, the financial means to support resolution and recapitalization must be found somewhere between public and private funding.

Therefore, when assessing the currently available means of resolution financing in the following section, it is crucial to analyze where they come from. With the resolution objectives in mind, it is not sufficient that the financial needs of an institution in distress are covered one way or another; who bears the financial consequences of covering an institution's losses is of the utmost importance. Even if all resolution and recapitalization costs can be covered, there might be a lack of sufficient funding in the sense that some of the financing is derived from public or national government sources, entailing negative incentives and moral hazard reminiscent of the crisis years. Similar problems can crop up in the context of sector-funded financing. Moreover, the use of funding that derives from private sources within an institution is not always the optimal solution *per se*, if write-down or conversion would trigger further-reaching negative consequences.[158]

On the other hand, it is important to stress that even if the protection of public funds is embedded into the new legislative framework[159] and is subsequently affirmed multiple times by legislators and politicians, the BRRD does not prohibit the use of public funds entirely. On the contrary,

---

156 Art. 31(2)(d) BRRD.

157 Art. 31(2)(e) BRRD.

158 As seen in the MPS case, where a BRRD-compliant bail-in would have affected savers and clients of the firm that are incapable of bearing losses and would have suffered severe socio-economic consequences.

159 The aim of avoiding the use of public funds cannot only be found in the BRRD. The Commission's 2013 Banking Communication (*Communication from the Commission on the application, from 1 August 2013, of State aid rules to support measures in favour of banks in the context of the financial crisis ('Banking Communication'), 2013/C 216/01* (2013), henceforth Banking Communication 2013) also provides for clear burden-sharing and provides that any injection of public funds must be preceded by all possible measures to minimize the cost of remedying the identified capital shortfall.

the Directive allows for it in very exceptional cases. As will be elucidated in due course, this is done for various reasons and, to put it dramatically, sees the BRRD sacrifice its integrity for a greater cause.[160] Juxtaposing the BRRD's possibility of very exceptional public-funds use with the BRRD's paramount goal of avoiding public-funds use, however, it becomes apparent that resolution should, as a general rule, not entail the use of public funds. Therefore, the rules governing public-funds use must be rigid. Nevertheless, what will also be observed in the following sections is that the provided exceptions to using public funds are poorly designed and therefore open to frequent misuse and opportunistic application outside the stipulated very exceptional cases.

Against this backdrop, the preferred way to resolution and recapitalization of a bank would be privately funded.[161] However, private funding *per se* is not the 'holy grail.' Indeed, private funding must also meet certain requirements. The following sections will demonstrate that the current financing mechanisms incorporated in the BRRD do not promote optimal approaches and instead offer the wrong incentives.[162] The available private financing mechanisms seem too discretionary, insufficient, and sometimes inadequate, thereby encouraging actors to resort to public financing which is handled too leniently.[163] The assessment of industry-financed contributors to resolution funding here will show that the existing instruments are not optimal funding sources in resolution and that these should instead act as a backstop when private funding is lacking and as a liquidity-provider during or shortly after resolution. Nevertheless, it will also be found that the available sector-funded mechanisms do not fulfil this task.

---

160 See *infra* under Part 2, A.II.3. – *Excursus: Limits to the No-Bailout-Policy – The Role of Public Financing.*

161 Recital (5) *et seq.* BRRD; Hadjiemmanuil, 'Limits on State-Funded Bailouts in the EU Bank Resolution Regime', p. 91; Micossi, Bruzzone and Cassella, 'Fine-tuning the use of bail-in to promote a stronger EU financial system', p. 4.

162 T. F. Huertas, 'A Resolvable Bank' in K. E. Scott, T. H. Jackson and J. B. Taylor (eds.), *Making failure feasible: How bankruptcy reform can end "too big to fail"*, Hoover Institution Press publication (Stanford, California: Hoover Institution Press, Stanford University, 2015), pp. 129–74; Schoenmaker, *The different legal and operational structures of banking groups in the euro area, and their impact on banks' resolvability*, p. 15.

163 The current BRRD and bail-in rules allow for exceptions and substantial discretionary leeway, thus limiting its binding power, see Schäfer, Schnabel and Di Weder Mauro, 'Bail-in expectations for European banks' and German Council of Economic Experts, *Annual Economic Report 2014/2015: The Long Road to More Financial Stability in Germany and Europa* (2015).

The BRRD offers an opportunity to evade resolution procedures and private funding, and this will be elaborated on in the following section before the three sources of resolution funding are examined.

A Junction Before Resolution: Precautionary Recapitalization

In 2016, the European Banking Authority (EBA) detected a capital shortfall in Italy's oldest bank, Monte dei Paschi di Siena. The stress test revealed that, in an adverse scenario, the bank would have negative Common Equity Tier 1 (CET 1) capital.[164] Despite this shortfall being identified, the bank itself was not considered insolvent in the classical sense (*e.g.* balance-sheet insolvent, unable to repay debts or to meet other obligations) but only undercapitalized in the event of an adverse scenario. After an unsuccessful attempt to raise the bank's capital through the market at the end of 2016, the Italian government planned to bail-out the bank with state money, without sending the institution into resolution according to BRRD resolution procedures.[165]

While public-funds use during resolution procedures is consensually unwanted, the BRRD allows for the possibility of public-funds use by maneuvering certain cases out of resolution procedures, thereby softening the resolution regime and providing for an exemption that prevents the given institution from being declared failing or likely-to-fail. In Italy, despite the massive capital shortfall, MPS was pronounced solvent, paving the way for the application of an instrument that is only used on solvent institution, *instead* of resolution procedures. As the following discourse will show, it is questionable whether precautionary recapitalization was the correct approach to MPS's situation, and concerns were indeed raised that a 'courtesy solution' was applied in this case. If so, it can be assumed that the BRRD

---

164 EBA, *2016 EU-Wide Stress Test Results* (2016), p. 16, with an identified lack in the CET 1 capital from more than -2 % in an adverse scenario.

165 See already *supra* under Part 2, A.II.1.a. – *Lack of Predictability – Political Influence* for a more detailed description of the case. See also M. G. Götz, J. P. Krahnen and T. H. Tröger, 'Taking Bail-in Seriously - The Looming Risks for Banking Policy in the Rescue of Monte Paschi di Siena', *SAFE Policy Letter* No. 54 (2017) retrievable at https://safe-frankfurt.de/fileadmin/user_upload/editor_common/Policy_Center/SAFE_Policy_Letter_54.pdf accessed 1 October 2022; Triantafyllakis, 'Italienische Banken: Wenn nicht alle Wege zum Bail-in führen'; Busch, D., van Rijn, M. and Louisse, M., 'How Single is the Single Resolution Mechanism?', *European Business Law Review* (2019), 30, Issue 4, pp. 600 *et seq.*

suffers from structural weaknesses that encouraged the Commission and Italy's government to exploit the possibility of circumventing resolution procedures for the benefit of MPS's clients.[166] This would constitute an additional contributor to the lack of credibility in resolution financing, as it enables the avoidance of resolution procedures and their financing mechanisms entirely.

The Current Framework of Precautionary Recapitalization

Generally, the BRRD states that the mere need for state support sets off resolution procedures and is therefore considered one of the four triggers of a bank's placement into resolution (see Article 32(4)(1)(d) BRRD). This means that MPS ought to have been placed into resolution after the Italian government decided that the bank needed state money. However, the BRRD contains exceptions to the rule that the need for state money, also referred to as extraordinary public financial support (EPFS),[167] triggers a resolution procedure. Pertinently, resolution will not be triggered if EPFS is granted: (a) in order to remedy serious disturbance in a Member State's economy and preserve financial stability; and (b) when the state provides the support in a certain form (*e.g.* state guarantees to back liquidity facilities provided by the ECB, or for newly-issued liabilities, or through injections of own funds or purchases of capital instruments (precautionary recapitalization)), according to Article 32(4)(d) BRRD. Furthermore, in order to be classified as an exception, the support: (a) must be confined only to solvent institutions; (b) must be precautionary and temporary; (c) must be proportional to the consequences of the economic disturbance; and (d) must not be used to offset already incurred or likely-to-be-incurred

166 K. Lannoo, *Uneven progress in implementing cross-border bank resolution in the EU* (2017); Binder, 'Systemkrisenbewältigung durch Bankenabwicklung? Aktuelle Bemerkungen zu unrealistischen Erwartungen', p. 59.

167 Extraordinary public financial support is defined in Art. 2(1)(28) BRRD as state aid within the meaning of Art. 107(1) TFEU, or any other public financial support at supra-national level, which, if provided for at national level, would constitute state aid, that is provided in order to preserve or restore the viability, liquidity, or solvency of an institution or entity referred to in point (b), (c) or (d) of Art. 1(1), or of a group of which such an institution or entity forms part. This excludes explicitly Emergency Liquidity Assistance as defined in Art. 2(1)(29) BRRD. For a detailed differentiation of the two instruments, see Hadjiemmanuil, 'Limits on State-Funded Bailouts in the EU Bank Resolution Regime', p. 107.

losses and must only be for capital shortfalls revealed in hypothetical adverse scenarios used in stress testing, Articles 32(4)(d) and 32(4)(3) BRRD. When it comes to precautionary recapitalization, as envisaged in the case of MPS, the support must further be at prices and on terms that do not confer an advantage upon the institution, and the support must be limited to addressing the identified capital shortfall, Article 32(4)(d) third para. BRRD.[168]

Looking at the numerous elaborate requirements, it seems likely that precautionary recapitalization will hardly be used[169] except in extreme cases with completely exogenous shocks to systemically important banks, since application of the exemption requires the assessment of *all* systemic implications of hypothetical failure scenarios for institutions that are technically solvent but failed a stress test. Furthermore, in order to qualify as an exception, these institutions are required to be a going concern *despite* their inability to collect enough money on financial markets to reinforce their capital basis.[170] Lastly, the granting of any of the permitted forms (guarantees for facilities; guarantees for new issues; and precautionary recapitalization) is subject to the demanding provisions of the 2013 Banking Communication.[171]

---

168 B. Mesnard, A. Margerit and M. Magnus, *Precautionary recapitalisations under the Bank Recovery and Resolution Directive: conditionality and case practice*, Briefing of the European Parliament (2017), p. 2.

169 Binder, 'Systemkrisenbewältigung durch Bankenabwicklung? Aktuelle Bemerkungen zu unrealistischen Erwartungen', p. 70; Hadjiemmanuil, 'Limits on State-Funded Bailouts in the EU Bank Resolution Regime', p. 105.

170 Tröger, 'Too complex to work', p. 14.

171 Banking Communication 2013.

Application of Precautionary Recapitalization in Italy – Unveiling the Problems

Despite the restrictive framework,[172] the Italian government nevertheless managed to gain approval from the Commission[173] for the application of precautionary recapitalization, thereby avoiding resolution procedures. This development raised various issues as it seemed that MPS would rather fulfil the applicable requirements to be sent into resolution procedures. Looking at MPS at that time, one might harbor some reservations about MPS fulfilling all the necessary conditions for exceptional state support in the form of precautionary recapitalization.[174] This is primarily due to the amount of undefined terms and preconditions used in the legislative text. A few examples given below will help to illustrate the problematic use of such undefined terms.

First, it seems difficult to determine whether a specific supportive measure constitutes a remedy to 'a serious disturbance in the national economy' and whether it is necessary 'to preserve the financial stability'[175] of

172 Hadjiemmanuil, 'Limits on State-Funded Bailouts in the EU Bank Resolution Regime', p. 106; N. Véron, *Precautionary recapitalisation: time for a review?*, In-Depth Analysis for the Economics and Monetary Affairs Committee of the European Parliament (Brussels, 2017), p. 6 retrievable at http://www.europarl.europa.eu/RegData/etudes/IDAN/2017/602090/IPOL_IDA(2017)602090_EN.pdf accessed 1 October 2022.

173 This approval was not the first time the Commission allowed exceptional state support, bypassing the official resolution framework: two Greek banks, the National Bank of Greece and Piraeus Bank, received capital injections in the form of contingent convertible bonds (CoCo bonds) for three-quarters of the amount and of ordinary shares for the remaining quarter of 2.71 and 2.72 billion euros to cover capital shortfalls that were detected in the ECB's stress testing conducted in October 2015, see European Commission, *State Aid SA.43364 (2015/N) - Greece - Amendment of the restructuring plan approved in 2014 and granting of new aid to Piraeus Bank* (2015); European Commission, *State Aid SA.43365 (2015/N) - Greece - Amendment of the restructuring plan approved in 2014 and granting of new aid to National Bank of Greece C(2015) 8930 final* (2015); Véron, *Precautionary recapitalisation: time for a review?*, p. 2.

174 See for example Triantafyllakis, who – even before the Commission decided on the case – raised doubts as to whether MPS could still have been declared solvent, let alone whether MPS would not use the potential money to offset losses incurred because of the sale of NPLs, Triantafyllakis, 'Italienische Banken: Wenn nicht alle Wege zum Bail-in führen', p. 2250.

175 For more on the influence of the objective of financial stability on resolution planning, see N. Kleftouri, 'European Union Bank Resolution Framework: can the objective of financial stability ensure consistency in resolution authorities'

the specific institution.[176] A definition of 'serious disturbance' is not available nor can it be determined objectively. The wording is often described as ambiguous or confusing,[177] and leaves it at the discretion of arbitrary interpretation when setting the conditions necessary for EPFS to be given. Furthermore, in order to determine whether the measure is necessary to preserve financial stability in a specific institution, far-reaching and comprehensive analysis is required and it is questionable to what extent such analysis can be carried out. In addition, it is unclear whether MPS could really have been declared solvent[178] at the time of the support being granted, since it still held an enormous amount of non-performing loans (NPLs) and suffered losses from the sale of NPLs in the past.[179] The term 'Solvency' is not defined in Article 2 BRRD and seems at odds with the conditions of not meeting the circumstances mentioned in Article 32(4) (a) to (c), since those conditions are altogether more demanding than a plain solvency test.[180] Therefore, it seems that determining whether an institution qualifies as 'solvent' is left to the discretion of the respective decision-maker rather than being subject to objective criteria. Moreover, it is questionable whether the state support was not used to offset already-incurred losses or losses that were likely to be incurred in the near future, since the capital shortfall in an adverse scenario originated from long-standing NPLs.[181] The stipulation that precautionary recapitalization

decisions?', *Journal of the Academy of European Law - ERA Forum* 18 (2017), 263–79, pp. 266 *et seq.*

176 Götz *et al.* state that – although there is a lack of detailed data – the size of Monte Paschi di Siena does not suggest that its resolution would trigger a systemic event because of their relatively low total assets of about 170 billion euros (September 2017), representing only 4.5 % of the Italian banking sector, and because of their business mostly being in lending and standard deposit-taking, Götz, Krahnen and Tröger, 'Taking Bail-in Seriously - The Looming Risks for Banking Policy in the Rescue of Monte Paschi di Siena'.

177 Véron, *Precautionary recapitalisation: time for a review?*, p. 6.

178 Binder, 'Systemkrisenbewältigung durch Bankenabwicklung? Aktuelle Bemerkungen zu unrealistischen Erwartungen', p. 71.

179 In July 2016, the Italian private equity fund "Atlante," which is dedicated to recapitalizing banks through subscribing capital increases, buying their shares, and purchasing NPLs, signed a memorandum of understanding to buy notes of the securitized bad loan portfolio of MPS in the amount of 1.6 billion euros.

180 Véron, *Precautionary recapitalisation: time for a review?*, p. 6.

181 Hadjiemmanuil states that the requirements for precautionary recapitalization are designed in a way that makes this instrument unusable for the most vulnerable banks (*e.g.* banks that are already weakened by losses or carry substantial amounts of NPLs). This is interesting, as Monte dei Paschi di Siena carries a

'shall not be used to offset losses' is widely open to interpretation.[182] The same could also be said of the qualification of the measure as 'precautionary' and 'temporary'.[183]

Nevertheless, it has to be remarked that the state support in the MPS case was accompanied by cost cuts, a certain degree of investor bail-in, and deep restructuring of the bank,[184] even if the Commission was not required to do so. Paragraph 45 of the Banking Communication on State Aid[185] provides for the possibility of excluding burden-sharing for precautionary recapitalization if it would 'endanger financial stability or lead to disproportionate results.' Just like the opaque wording with respect to precautionary recapitalization, this formulation is also abstract and inconclusive. As a result, precautionary recapitalization can be applied without any burden-sharing, relying entirely on public financing. This opens the way for flexible interpretation and discretion, including with regard to Article 107(3)(b) TFEU,[186] leading to the justification of extensive precautio-

significant amount of NPLs and is therefore ineligible for precautionary recapitalization, Hadjiemmanuil, 'Limits on State-Funded Bailouts in the EU Bank Resolution Regime'.

182 Véron, *Precautionary recapitalisation: time for a review?*, p. 6.

183 Although the Commission tried to clarify the provision of 'precautionary' and 'temporary' in an explanatory document in June 2017, questions remain and the explanations are not legally binding, see European Commission, *State aid: How the EU rules apply to banks with a capital shortfall - Factsheet* (2017); Véron, *Precautionary recapitalisation: time for a review?*, p. 6; Sachverständigenrat zur Begutachtung der Gesamtwirtschaftlichen Entwicklung, *Für eine zukunftsorientierte Wirtschaftspolitik*, 54.2017/18, ch. 5, para. 435.

184 A. Barker and R. Sanderson, 'Brussels and Rome seal rescue deal for Monte dei Paschi: Investor bail-in and deep restructuring agreed for Italy's oldest bank', Financial Times, 01 June 2017.

185 Banking Communication 2013. Already, before the communication entered into force in mid-August 2013, Mario Draghi, President of the ECB, wrote a letter to Joaquín Almunia, Vice-President and Commissioner for Competition in the European Commission, stating that "forced conversions of debt into equity may not be warranted in certain situations where a bank after an asset quality review has a level of capital that is above the regulatory minimum, but below the hurdle rate in a stress test" and that he is "[...] convinced that in certain situations State aid should be possible for precautionary recapitalization without subordinated debtors being mandatorily converted", see M. Draghi to J. Almunia, 30 July 2013, 'Banking Communication - treatment of subordinated debt in precautionary recapitalisation', Letter.

186 Art. 107(3)(b) TEUF allows state aid in cases where this is necessary to remedy a serious disturbance in a Member State's economy.

nary recapitalization[187] of undercapitalized banks without burden-sharing according to the BRRD.[188] However, even with a limited bail-in in the MPS case, the BRRD's pre-described burden-sharing cascade was brushed off in the end and Italian taxpayers' money was used to rescue the bank.[189]

Meanwhile, as precautionary recapitalization in the MPS case was granted as a consequence of the conducted stress test and the results thereof, it must be noted that the involvement of stress test results or asset quality reviews performed by individual Member States and their national authorities in the scenario leading up to precautionary recapitalization increases the probability of resolution being delayed or even prevented. Although the EBA adopted Guidelines[190] on the type of tests which may lead to the provision of EPFS and precautionary recapitalization, national authorities are still allowed to conduct their own tests and reviews as they seem fit. Member States can therefore broaden the scope of application for precautionary recapitalization by detecting capital shortfalls in their own stress tests performed intra-state (instead of those conducted by the EBA[191] or the ECB[192]). This issue might gain importance within the Banking Union in cases where the Member State tries to circumvent the application of the

---

187 This casual and stretched application with respect to precautionary recapitalization can further expand on government guarantees with the latter then becoming customary and current in use, tearing down and destroying all incentives for adequate pricing of bank capital, see Tröger, 'Too complex to work', p. 14.

188 Micossi, Bruzzone and Cassella, 'Fine-tuning the use of bail-in to promote a stronger EU financial system', pp. 4 *et seq.*

189 Banca D'Italia, *La ricapitalizzazione precauzionale di MPS: domande e risposte* (2017), pp. 2–8 retrievable at http://www.bancaditalia.it/media/approfondimenti/2017/ricapitalizzazione-precauzionale-mps/ricapitalizzazione-precauzionale-MPS-31082017.pdf accessed 22 November 2019. Hadjiemmanuil, 'Limits on State-Funded Bailouts in the EU Bank Resolution Regime', p. 108.

190 EBA, *Guidelines on the types of tests, review or exercises that may lead to support measures under Article 32(d)(iii) of the Bank Recovery and Resolution Directive: EBA/GL/2014/09* (2014).

191 See Art. 32(2) of *Regulation (EU) No 1093/2010 of the European Parliament and of the Council of 24 November 2010 establishing a European Supervisory Authority (European Banking Authority), amending Decision No 716/2009/EC and repealing Commission Decision 2009/78/EC OJ L 331, 15.12.2010, p. 12–47: EBA Regulation* (2010). The EBA tested 51 banks in its 2016 EU-wide stress test, see http://www.eba.europa.eu/risk-analysis-and-data/eu-wide-stress-testing/2016/results.

192 Art. 4(1)(f) of *Regulation (EU) No 1022/2013 of the European Parliament and of the Council of 22 October 2013 amending Regulation (EU) No 1093/2010 establishing a European Supervisory Authority (European Banking Authority) as regards the conferral of specific tasks on the European Central Bank pursuant to Council Regulation (EU) No 1024/2013 OJ L 287, 29.10.2013, p. 5–14* (SSMR).

SRM by declaring the institution technically solvent and only in need of precautionary recapitalization, thereby avoiding resolution.[193]

The Use of Precautionary Recapitalization as a Symptom of Insufficient Resolution Funding

It became clear in the previous section that the application of the rules pertaining to precautionary recapitalization were applied to the MPS case in a questionable manner. But besides the finding that the framework for precautionary recapitalization is weak itself and allows for exploitation, another interesting conclusion can be drawn with respect to the current resolution-funding framework. Why did Italy try to avoid resolution procedures in the first place? It may be assumed that such avoidance derives from the lack of sufficient funding in resolution procedures. As Italy realized that an extensive bail-in of MPS's liabilities would have done more harm than good, they tried to avoid BRRD-compliant resolution procedures. However, if the available liabilities of MPS were suitable to bail-in and private loss-absorption would have caused no further damage, perhaps Italy would not have tried to avoid resolution.

One central issue might here be that many bonds were held not by adequate investors, but by small private retail investors,[194] which, in a resolution scenario, would have been subject to extensive bail-in. Although the BRRD provides for the general possibility of exempting certain liabilities from bail-in, such exemption is associated with problems (see *infra* Part 2, A.II.2.b.i.(b) – *Internal Private Funding Instruments – Bail-in*) and simply circumventing bail-in is certainly an easier course for the institution to take. To have devolved the full losses onto the bank's primarily domestic shareholders could have caused irreparable damage to Italy's economy and brought the whole banking sector to ruin.[195] Additionally, the bank feared that clients would panic as had been the case in a similar crisis

193 Micossi, Bruzzone and Cassella, 'Fine-tuning the use of bail-in to promote a stronger EU financial system', pp. 15, 16.

194 In the special case of Monte dei Paschi di Siena, an alleged mis-selling of bonds to private and small investors and savers occurred. Therefore, a lot of potentially bail-inable debt was held by private persons that invested their savings, see P.-H. Conac, *Subordinated debt and self-placement: Mis-selling of financial products*, Study requested by the ECON Committee (Brussels: European Parliament), pp. 25 *et seq.*

195 Hadjiemmanuil, 'Limits on State-Funded Bailouts in the EU Bank Resolution Regime', p. 112.

before.[196] It is understandable that – especially against the backdrop of the accused potential mis-selling of bonds to retail investors – Italy did not want to write-off small clients' savings. On the other hand, this situation certainly leads to the conclusion that there is a deficiency in the design of resolution-financing mechanisms, since the holdings of bail-inable capital must be restricted in the first place. In addition, there might be omissions in the design of the whole structure of bail-inable instruments. If designed poorly and therefore causing unbearable consequences when bail-in is applied, it comes as no surprise that the Italian government was reluctant to send MPS into resolution. If the BRRD now offers a loophole to avert an unpleasant bail-in, Italy is most certainly tempted to use it.[197]

Precautionary Recapitalization – Quo Vadis?

Yet, even leaving aside the questionable correctness of the application of exceptions, the use of EPFS in the MPS case in lieu of triggering an ordinary BRRD resolution procedure leaves a bitter aftertaste in the mouth of the proponents of the recently-implemented resolution regime[198]. Indeed, some have even demanded the abolition of the precautionary recapi-

196 In the course of the earlier resolution of four Italian banks, namely Banca Etruria and three other regional banks, a dramatic incident happened in Civitavecchia, where a 68-year old pensioner killed himself after he lost all of his savings amounting to 110 000 euros. A suicide note was found later on which he explained that the was willfully and intentionally defrauded by his bank: "Non mi hanno rimborsato le obbligazioni, la banca sta fallendo. Così ho perso tutti I risparmi", see R. Frignani, 'Choc a Civitavecchia – Salvabanche, il pensionato morto', Corriere Della Sera, 10 December 2015.

197 Paradoxically, precautionary recapitalization will most likely not help sustainably in the Monte dei Paschi di Siena case and will therefore be no more than a palliative remedy. Due to the prescribed form of precautionary recapitalization, namely the injection of own funds or the purchase of capital instruments at a realistic price, all NPL-related transactions are outside the scope of application, especially if they contain some kind of subsidization. The clean-up and absorption of bad assets such as the NPLs in the long run can only be performed under the resolution framework, granting Monte dei Paschi di Siena only a temporarily relief, see Hadjiemmanuil, 'Limits on State-Funded Bailouts in the EU Bank Resolution Regime', p. 114.

198 Binder, 'Systemkrisenbewältigung durch Bankenabwicklung? Aktuelle Bemerkungen zu unrealistischen Erwartungen'; Sachverständigenrat zur Begutachtung der Gesamtwirtschaftlichen Entwicklung, *Für eine zukunftsorientierte Wirtschaftspolitik*, 54.2017/18, ch. 5, para. 437.

talization clause in Article 32(4) BRRD.[199] Admittedly, the idea of granting precautionary recapitalization was driven by an endeavor to prevent market participants from losing trust in either the market or a specific institution purely as the consequence of a negative stress test,[200] and this might appear a reasonable desire in light of the economic importance of stress testing.[201] However, compared with the determination and passion with which legislators and policy makers announced the shift from publicly-funded bailouts to substantial or even entire private-sector resolution, the tool has been poorly applied. Therefore, the Commission, with its 2016 banking reform package[202], tried to relieve the burden and reliance on precautionary recapitalization as an instrument to compensate shortfalls exposed by the adverse scenario of a stress test by introducing the concept of "Pillar 2 guidance" (P2G, also known as "soft Pillar 2") into the CRD (new Article 104b CRD). Supervisors can formulate non-binding capital measures needed to counterbalance what would otherwise be balanced by precautionary recapitalization. However, as those provisions are not yet in force or binding, the capacity of such P2G capital measures to push back precautionary recapitalization is questionable.[203]

That the exploitation of the limited exception to use precautionary recapitalization is not exactly in the spirit of the BRRD is clear; and the legisla-

199 Stiefmüller, *Ten Years After - The 2017 Banking Package: One Step Forward, Two Steps Back*, p. 7.

200 Binder, 'Systemkrisenbewältigung durch Bankenabwicklung? Aktuelle Bemerkungen zu unrealistischen Erwartungen', p. 70.

201 Although arguing that the role of stress testing is overrated, has no legal or regulatory consequences under EU law, and that its results should not be relied upon to gauge the risk of an institution failing, Champsaur demonstrates that there is clearly the potential for stress-test results to trigger self-fulfilling prophecies by making struggling banks raise additional capital at a time when they will find it difficult to do so, see A. Champsaur, 'Stressed tests', *International Financial Law Review* 35 (2016), 43–4, p. 43. See for a similar reasoning A. Ebner, 'The Financial Stability Aspects of the EU-wide Stress Test', *Journal of Financial Regulation* 4 (2018); G. Petrella, 'The Interplay Between Banks and Markets: Supervisory Stress Test Results and Investor Reactions' in T. Beck and B. Casu (eds.), *The Palgrave Handbook of European Banking* (London: Palgrave Macmillan UK, 2016), pp. 409–47, p. 410.

202 European Commission, *Capital requirements (CRR/CRD IV) and resolution framework (BRRD/SRM) amendments*, Fact Sheet - Frequently Asked Questions (2016) retrievable at http://europa.eu/rapid/press-release_MEMO-16-3840_en.htm accessed 1 October 2022.

203 Stiefmüller, *Ten Years After - The 2017 Banking Package: One Step Forward, Two Steps Back*, p. 11.

tor anticipated that the availing of such an instrument must be reviewed closely. Therefore, Article 32(4)(d)(iii) BRRD required the Commission to carry out a review of whether there was a continuing need to allow precautionary recapitalization by 31 December 2015. So far,[204] no such review has been carried out though. Critics might be tempted to say that the Commission does not want to take a stand on the matter. Otherwise, the Commission would be forced to either state that precautionary recapitalization is no longer needed (thereby closing the door for convenient precautionary recapitalization forever) or it would need to explain why precautionary recapitalization is still needed. Both lines of approach seem inconvenient for the Commission at present. However, in a parliamentary question on 7 June 2017[205] that was answered by Vice-President Dombrovskis on behalf of the Commission, it was declared that due to the late transposition of the BRRD into Member States' national laws, there had been very little practical experience in the application of precautionary recapitalization. The Commission stated that it would carry out a review as soon as the necessary practical experience had been accumulated. Whether this means that more cases of precautionary recapitalization must first occur before such a review is finally conducted, remains an open question.

With the first symptoms of scarce resolution-financing design surfacing, it is to be feared now that Italy and the Commission have opened up Pandora's Box,[206] and that more governments will follow suit by try to rescue banks that are only solvent on paper with state money under precautionary recapitalization, instead of applying resolution and bail-in. A lack of sufficient financing is thus already apparent even before a particular resolution action is entered into.

---

204 C. M. Stiefmüller, *European Parliament ECON Public Hearing on the new banking legislation package*, European Parliament's ECON Committee Public Hearing (Brussels, 2017) retrievable at https://www.finance-watch.org/publication/public-hearing-at-econ-on-the-banking-legislation-package/ accessed 1 October 2022.

205 Written questions E-002235/17 and E-002368/17, see http://www.europarl.europa.eu/sides/getAllAnswers.do?reference=E-2017-002368&language=EN.

206 Surprisingly, an analysis of premiums on credit default swaps showed that the Italian cases did not have significant spillover effects on other Member States. Even though there is evidence that there was a rise in bailout expectations for senior debt, this expectation focusses on Italian local banks – Italy seems to be a 'special case', see Sachverständigenrat zur Begutachtung der Gesamtwirtschaftlichen Entwicklung, *Für eine zukunftsorientierte Wirtschaftspolitik*, 54.2017/18, ch. 5, para. 438 and box 13.

The Available Funding Sources and the BRRD's Burden-Sharing Cascade

The following sections will assess the current lack of sufficient resolution financing that erodes the credibility of resolution *ex post* resolution decision. The available resolution-funding mechanisms within the BRRD can generally be divided into the following three categories:[207] private funding; sector-specific funding; and public funding. Private funding or funding from institutions themselves is the desired funding mechanism. Therefore, the BRRD emphasizes its preference for this options. This is because stakeholders profit from holding stakes in the given institution and should therefore bear the corresponding risks. Banks themselves are responsible for their risk management and financial strategies, so it seems appropriate that the banking sector bears the financial consequences of possible mismanagement or bad investment strategies themselves. Negative effects should not be externalized and should remain with those actively seeking to profit from the given activity. Meanwhile, public funding in the form of taxpayers' money seems to be the least favorable option, since they hold no stake in the institution nor do they have any kind of influence over it.[208] Therefore, public funding within the BRRD is only available to a limited scale and within limited exceptions, and ideally should not be used.

However, due to the special nature of the services that banks perform and the crucial role they play in the economy,[209] the BRRD tried to esta-

---

207 The following discourse is partly based on Yiatrou, *Bank Resolution Credibility and Economic Implications*.

208 It is remarkable that this tenet seems to be evident for commercial companies other than banks and investment firms. However, there might be differences if the company is a state's major asset and 'biggest player' to the extent that the state might want to shield this company against a possible insolvency. See also Gleeson and Guynn, *Bank Resolution and Crisis Management*, p. 3, para. 1.01 *et seq.* who argue that banks and commercial companies cannot be treated the same way due to their different kinds of creditors. While a commercial company has commercial and financial creditors, and payments to the latter can be suspended in insolvency proceedings without stopping the commercial company from doing business, the distinction between commercial and financial creditors of a bank is not a meaningful one. A suspension of payment to commercial creditors is not possible, as commercial creditors are, by definition, financial creditors, and such a suspension would mean immediate cessation of their business.

209 See recital (4) BRRD. Banks and their Member States are generally more reluctant to pass losses onto their stakeholders. The main reason for this lies in banks' special and unique role in providing services to the market. While the insolvency of non-financial corporations normally does not entail serious

blish a burden-sharing cascade that both respects the prevailing dominance of private funding in resolution and also considers the special role of financial institutions in Europe's economy by allowing public financing in very exceptional cases. Nevertheless, recent resolution episodes[210] have shown that the BRRD's burden-sharing cascade is often disregarded, and is instead carefully manipulated, especially if bail-in is involved. The decision to bail-in has often been taken only after repeated bailouts and other public measures, and at a point where potential bail-inable instruments had already been substantially eroded.[211] Member States often resorted, and are still resorting, to the traditional tendency to publicly fund bank rescues in order to resolve and recapitalize their failing banks without, or with little participation of, the banks' stakeholders.[212] The reason behind such behavior persisting despite the new rules must lie in the rules themselves. Essentially, it can be assumed that the current BRRD rules are insufficient and that they do not provide for adequate private funding, and this triggers the demand for alternative funding sources. Together with a certain reluctance[213] towards private- or bank-funded financing, state money is too easily accessible within the current legal framework. The following section will show that the poor design of the current resolution funding system is the cause of repeated non-compliance. It does so by examining the consecutive steps prescribed by the burden-sharing cascade of the BRRD, dividing them bluntly into 'the good' (private funding), 'the bad' (public funding) and 'the ugly' (sector-specific funding).

---

consequences for the economy, the insolvency of a bank often does: negative socio-economic effects, bank runs, and contagion can be the result. In addition, economies often want to keep the bank alive as an entity for reputational or representational reasons, and do not want to liquidate it. However, if stakeholders are shielded from bearing losses and banks are not liquidated, someone else has to bear the costs. This is when governments used to step, or are still stepping, in with public money.

210 For an overview of the recent bank resolution cases in the EU pre- and post-BRRD, see World Bank Group, Financial Sector Advisory Center (FinSAC), *Bank Resolution and "Bail-In" in the EU: Selected Case Studies Pre and Post BRRD*.

211 Ibid., Introduction.

212 Stiefmüller, *Ten Years After: Back to Business as Usual*, p. 36, for example as seen only recently in the case of Monte dei Paschi di Siena.

213 Stiefmüller, *Ten Years After - The 2017 Banking Package: One Step Forward, Two Steps Back*, p. 7; A. Weber, 'Monte Paschi Bailout Plan Has Some ECB Supervisors Grumbling', Bloomberg retrievable at https://www.bloomberg.com/news/articles/2017-03-27/italy-s-monte-paschi-bailout-has-some-ecb-supervisors-grumbling accessed 1 October 2022.

The Good: Private Funding

Private funding, for the above-mentioned reasons, is the desired funding option. The BRRD provides for three different private funding possibilities in this respect: resolution within national insolvency proceedings; bail-in; and external private funding.

National Insolvency Proceedings

A struggling bank that is no longer deemed viable can be dealt with in two different ways:[214] either it can be liquidated according to national and normal insolvency proceedings[215]; or it can be resolved according to the BRRD.[216] Whether liquidation or resolution is pursued depends on the impact normal insolvency proceedings would have on the financial stability of the states' or regions' economy. The BRRD states that a failing institution should be liquidated under national insolvency proceedings and that insolvency should always be considered before resolution tools are applied.[217] Within normal insolvency proceedings, losses are regularly borne by stakeholders and customers of the institution. Since the BRRD entered into force, a number of institutions have been wound down using national insolvency proceedings, with one of the most recent examples being the liquidation of the Latvian ABLV Bank.[218] This applies except

---

214 D. R. Munoz, 'Bank resolution and insolvency ranking and priorities' in European Central Bank (ed), *ECB Legal Conference 2017: shaping a new legal order for Europe: A tale of crises and opportunities: 4-5 September 2017* (Frankfurt am Main: Europäische Zentralbank, 2017), pp. 256–86.

215 Normal insolvency proceedings means collective insolvency proceedings which entail the partial or total divestment of a debtor and the appointment of a liquidator or an administrator normally applicable to institutions under national law and either specific or those institutions or generally applicable to any natural or legal person, see Art. 2(1)(47) BRRD.

216 In some cases, a combination of resolution tools and national insolvency proceedings can occur, *e.g.* where the assets of an institution under resolution are partially transferred to a private purchaser or a bridge bank. The remaining parts should be wound up under normal insolvency proceedings, see recital (50) BRRD.

217 Recital (45) and (46) BRRD.

218 The bank experienced a bank run after the U.S. Treasury on February 2018 accused ABLV of money laundering. ABLV was therefore promptly denied U.S. dollar funding while depositors rushed to remove their money from the bank, F. Coppola, 'Why The U.S. Treasury Killed A Latvian Bank', Forbes, 28 February

when insolvency proceedings would jeopardize financial stability, interrupt the provisions of critical functions, and adversely affect the protection of depositors. If any of these exceptions are present, then resolution is needed to achieve the resolution objectives, and the initiation of BRRD resolution proceedings is in the 'public interest', see Article 32(5) BRRD.[219]

One objective of the BRRD resolution regime is to protect public funds by minimizing reliance on EPFS for failing institutions.[220] It is clear that the same must hold true for institutions that undergo normal insolvency proceedings according to national insolvency law. Both alternatives should therefore have one thing in common: the avoidance of the use of public funds to the greatest extent possible. This becomes evident when it is recalled that the only difference between resolution according to BRRD and national insolvency proceedings lies in the expected effects on financial stability. Since, according to that understanding, only smaller banks should undergo normal insolvency proceedings, it is to be expected that, especially in this case, public funding would not be necessary.

However, the scope of EU law regulating the use of public money in resolution and liquidation is broad and diverse and a substantially similar case conducted under these two different frameworks could arrive at very divergent outcomes for the bank, the bank's creditors, and the taxpayers.[221] The use of public funds in national insolvency proceedings is provided for, namely through Section 6, recital 66 of the Banking Communication on State Aid 2013. It states that "due to specificities of credit institutions […] it might not be feasible to liquidate a credit institution under ordinary insolvency proceedings. For that reason, State measures to support the liquidation of failing credit institutions may be considered as compatible aid […]" A recent example of this can be found in Italy, whe-

2018 retrievable at https://www.forbes.com/sites/francescoppola/2018/02/28/why-the-u-s-treasury-killed-a-latvian-bank/#153555257adc accessed 1 October 2022, ABLV Bank, *Voluntary Liquidation of ABLV Bank, AS to Protect the Interests of Clients and Creditors*. https://www.ablv.com/en/legal-latest-news/voluntary-liquidation-of-ablv-bank-as-to-protect-the-interests-of-clients-and-creditors accessed 1 October 2022; European Central Bank, *ECB determined ABLV Bank was failing or likely to fail*, Press Release retrievable at https://www.bankingsupervision.europa.eu/press/pr/date/2018/html/ssm.pr180224.en.html accessed 1 October 2022.

219 Compare also recital (45) BRRD.

220 Ibid.

221 Merler, *Critical functions and public interest in banking services: Need for clarification?*, p. 11.

re long-struggling[222] Veneto Banca[223] and Banca Popolare di Vicenza[224] were wound down according to national insolvency proceedings as the SRB did not find sufficient public interest for the application of BRRD resolution procedures. The SRB also dismissed the risk of a deposit run, claiming that national insolvency proceedings would offer the same level of protection for the parties involved.[225] Despite this claim, the Italian state feared negative consequences and provided nearly 5 billion euros in cash to break the bank down into pieces, and another 400 million euros in guarantees for Intesa Sanpaolo, who took over the banks' remaining viable parts.[226] The most remarkable feature of the case, however, was not the use of public funds in national insolvency proceedings but the fact that the Italian government altered national insolvency law shortly before applying it to the two Venetian banks by passing a specific decree that established a 'special insolvency proceeding.'[227]

If public money can be used to support national insolvencies and if such aid is granted easily, there is a chance that governments, or the institutions themselves, will develop a tendency to advocate for the application of national insolvency proceedings, rather than resolution under BRRD

---

222 Mesnard, Margerit and Magnus, *The orderly liquidation of Veneto Banca and Banca Popolare di Vicenza*, p. 4.

223 Single Resolution Board, *Decision of the Single Resolution Board concerning the assessment of the conditions for resolution in respect of Veneto Banca S.p.A.*

224 Single Resolution Board, *Decision of the Single Resolution Board concerning the assessment of the conditions for resolution in respect of Banca Popolare di Vicenza S.p.A.*

225 However, it is not clear whether the SRB, in coming to this conclusion, assumes that the liquidation of the banks under normal insolvency proceedings would necessarily involve recourse to public funds, see Mesnard, Margerit and Magnus, *The orderly liquidation of Veneto Banca and Banca Popolare di Vicenza*, p. 7.

226 For an overview of the case see ibid.

227 The government asked the chamber for a '*speciale procedura d'insolvenza*' within the 'Camera dei deputati ed il Senato della Repubblica, *Conversione in legge, con modificazioni, del decreto-legge 25 giugno 2017, n. 99, recante disposizioni urgenti per la liquidazione coatta amministrativa di Banca Popolare di Vicenza S.p.A. e di Veneto Banca S.p.A. (17G00133) (GU Serie Generale n.184 del 08-08-2017)* retrievable at http://www.gazzettaufficiale.it/eli/id/2017/08/08/17G00133/sg accessed 1 October 2022. For an overview see Banca D'Italia, *Informazioni sulla soluzione della crisi di Veneto Banca S.p.A. e Banca Popolare di Vicenza S.p.A.* (2017) retrievable at https://www.bancaditalia.it/media/notizie/2017/Nota-Venetobanca-e-BPV.pdf accessed 1 October 2022 (in Italian).

procedures.[228] This depends highly on the willingness and discretion of the SRB, the Commission, and their application of the Banking Communication on State Aid 2013.

Furthermore, it seems that different standards are applied from case to case, and that no clear-cut requirements exist. Especially in regard to the 'public interest' test, reservations have been raised. Since it seems that no uniform application of such test exists within the EU, it is unclear whether similar banks across Member States can expect predictable equal treatment in case of failure.[229] If the public interest test remains loosely defined[230] and public funds are easier to obtain under national insolvency proceedings, thereby sparing more stakeholders from losses than under BRRD resolution proceedings, national authorities might favor this option and go against the wishes of the SRB. In particular, where governments have the chance to alter existing insolvency rules ahead of insolvency proceedings being applied. Put in simpler terms: Member States can opt-out of resolution procedures and resort to a self-designed procedure, establishing a parallel regime. The multiplicity of national insolvency regimes in place across the different Member States adds further complications to the matter. Rumors have already spread that investors In the case of the two Venetian banks were better off in liquidation than in resolution.[231] As a result, unwanted bailouts – in the context and under the guise of insol-

228 This tendency and incentive was just recently stressed by I. Angeloni, *SRB Conference 2018 - 10 years after the crisis: are banks now resolvable?*, SRB Annual Conference (Brussels, 2018) Angeloni illustrates that this can be achieved by influencing the 'public interest' evaluation. On the other side, some consider the denial of a positive public interest test by the Commission to be a sign of the Commission's strength, J.-H. Binder, 'The Relevance of the Resolution Tools Within the SRM', *European Banking Institute Working Paper Series* (2018), p. 6. This view, however, is not shared.

229 J.-H. Binder, M. Krimminger, M. J. Nieto and D. Singh, 'The Choice between Judicial and Administrative Sanctioned Procedures to Manage Liquidation of Banks: A Transatlantic Perspective', *SSRN Electronic Journal* (2018), p. 19 retrievable at SSRN https://ssrn.com/abstract=3244334 accessed 1 October 2022; Merler argues that the Spanish case and the Italian case were rather similar, however, treated differently with respect to the public interest test, see Merler, *Critical functions and public interest in banking services: Need for clarification?*, p. 4.

230 Merler, *Critical functions and public interest in banking services: Need for clarification?*, pp. 11 *et seq.*

231 Sciorilli Borrelli, *Q and A with Andrea Enria of European Banking Authority* accessed 1 October 2022; Mesnard, Margerit and Magnus, *The orderly liquidation of Veneto Banca and Banca Popolare di Vicenza*, p. 7.

vency proceedings – occur, and BRRD resolution rules are circumvented, contributing further to the resolution framework's lack of credibility.

Internal Private Funding Instruments – Bail-In

The first and preferred[232] source of resolution financing is the bail-in tool,[233] Articles 43, 44 BRRD. As emphasized above, a viable bail-in regime is the key prerequisite of a functioning resolution framework. Nevertheless, the following discourse will reveal certain deficiencies within its current set-up. The starting point here is that all liabilities of the institution are in general subject to bail-in. Article 48 BRRD describes the sequence of write-down and conversion as follows: (a) CET1 capital; (b) additional Tier 1 capital (AT1); (c) Tier 2 capital instruments (T2); (d) subordinated debt that is not Tier 2 debt in accordance with the hierarchy of claims in normal insolvency proceedings; and (e) the rest of eligible liabilities in accordance with the hierarchy of claims in normal insolvency proceedings.[234]

---

232 Bail-in is the preferred source of resolution financing because it is the funding source which has the most adequate risk allocation and incentive structure and which best complies with the BRRD's resolution objectives, see Wojcik, 'Bail-in in the Banking Union', p. 98. Also, the bail-in tool seems to reduce the financing needs not absorbed by any available tool under the new resolution regime by about 60 %, indicating that the bail-in tool is the most important tool when it comes to avoiding public funds, see P. Benczur, G. Cannas, J. Cariboni, F. Di Girolamo, S. Maccaferri and M. Petracco Giudici, 'Evaluating the effectiveness of the new EU bank regulatory framework: A farewell to bail-out?', *Journal of Financial Stability* 33 (2017), 207–23, p. 18.

233 For a detailed description of the functioning of the bail-in tool in general, see World Bank Group, *Understanding Bank Recovery and Resolution in the EU: A Guidebook to the BRRD* (Vienna, 2017), ch. 15. Furthermore, bail-in can occur as the write-down and conversion of capital instruments independently of a specific resolution procedure and outside the scope of a resolution tool.

234 Art. 2(1)(47) BRRD states that 'normal insolvency proceedings' means collective insolvency proceedings which entail the partial or total divestment of a debtor and the appointment of a liquidator or an administrator normally applicable to institutions under national law and either specific to those institutions or generally applicable to any natural or legal person". This may give rise to interpretation difficulties, as resolution authorities must determine which proceedings they would apply in a hypothetical case. Due to the increasingly crowded field where traditional winding-up proceedings stand next to reorganization, voluntary arrangements, debt workouts and restructurings, this has become a difficult task, see Munoz, 'Bank resolution and insolvency ranking and priorities'.

Reducing the Pool of Bail-inable Instruments through Articles 44(2) and 44(3) BRRD

A range of liabilities such as covered deposits, secured liabilities, and certain other liabilities are exempted *per se*, Article 44(2) BRRD, and some can further be excluded or partially excluded by the resolution authority under certain circumstances and at their discretion, Article 44(3) BRRD[235]. These two provisions already narrow the pool of bail-inable liabilities significantly, though there are generally good reasons to exclude certain liabilities from the scope of the bail-in. This is mainly because the overall (social and financial) costs[236] of bailing-in such liabilities are higher than the benefits of bailing them in. Alternatively, the exemption is necessary to promote a sound banking and public policy, which becomes evident when looking, for example, at the exemption of secured deposits or liabilities of employees in Article 44(2) BRRD (protection of vulnerable creditors as a socio-political exemption). Nevertheless, even if it is assumed that every exemption in Article 44(2) BRRD is legitimate and that the legislator factored in the contrasting costs and benefits of a possible write-down or conversion, the *per se* exemption in Article (44)(2) BRRD still raises concerns about its clarity and firmness. Even though it is a *per se* exemption, which should in principle allow for the exact determination of exempted liabilities and claims, it leaves room for avoidance strategies,[237] which, even on the assumption that the exemptions are factored in, is not desired. One example here is the exemption of encumbered-assets claims, Article 44(2)(b) BRRD. Although collateralized claims should in general be easily recognizable, the regulator still has not determined whether a partial collateralization of a claim is sufficient to be excluded from bail-out.[238] If this

---

235 For a detailed description see C. Hadjiemmanuil, 'Bank stakeholders' mandatory contribution to resolution financing: principles and ambiguities of bail-in' in European Central Bank (ed.), *ECB Legal Conference 2015: From monetary union to banking union, on the way to capital markets union: new opportunities for European integration, 1-2 September 2015* (Frankfurt am Main: European Central Bank, 2015), pp. 225–49, pp. 236 *et seq.*

236 See Tröger, 'Too complex to work', pp. 21, 22, Table 1 and Table 2 outlining the various reasons for the exemption of liabilities from bail-in and Wojcik, 'Bail-in in the Banking Union', pp. 108 *et seq.*

237 G. Franke, J. P. Krahnen and T. von Lüpke, *Effective Resolution of Banks: Problems and Solutions*, White Paper Series (2014), p. 10 retrievable at https://safe-frankfurt.de/uploads/media/Franke_Krahnen_vonLuepke_Effective_Resolution.pdf accessed 1 October 2022.

238 Ibid., p. 10.

were the case, it might lead to the devising of avoidance strategies in which claims are in small parts collateralized just to keep them out of the scope of the bail-in. Given its ambiguity, this exemption in particular is subject to further queries. Although answers have been given to the questions of whether liabilities guaranteed by third parties or a state guarantee can be subject to bail-in, or whether securities guaranteed by an independent on-demand guarantee can be considered as "otherwise guaranteed" claims (recital (70) BRRD) and as such be excluded from bail-in,[239] the issue remains open to discretion.[240] Furthermore, for the resolution authority, the extent of partial collateralization may be very difficult to evaluate during a short pre-resolution timeframe.[241] The same applies to the exclusion of short-term liabilities with a maturity of less than seven days. Banks may be incentivized to revert to short-term borrowing in order to bypass bail-in. One last example can be drawn here from the *per se* exclusion in Article 44(2)(g)(ii) BRRD, where creditors for goods and services that are critical to the daily functioning of an institution's operations are spared. The potential number of subsequently excluded liabilities is limitless, since the failing institution continues to operate after resolution.

In relation to Article 44(3) BRRD, an exclusion can be ordered in situations where it is not possible to bail-in such liabilities within a reasonable timeframe or where the exclusion is strictly necessary and is appropriate to achieving the continuity of critical functions and core business lines. Further exclusion applies where the application of bail-in would cause significant devaluation, or to avoid the spreading of contagion and financial instability, which may cause serious disturbance in the economy.[242] The last exemption can be interpreted very widely given that bail-in *per se*

239 See for example Single Rulebook Q&A, *Question ID: 2015_1779* retrievable at http://www.eba.europa.eu/single-rule-book-qa/-/qna/view/publicId/2015_1779 accessed 1 October 2022; Single Rulebook Q&A, *Question ID: 2016_2951* retrievable at http://www.eba.europa.eu/single-rule-book-qa/-/qna/view/publicId/2016_2951 accessed 1 October 2022.

240 It is left open whether liabilities that are generally not excluded under Art. 44(2)(b) BRRD can be excluded under Art. 44(3) BRRD, Single Rulebook Q&A, *Question ID: 2016_2951*.

241 Franke, Krahnen and Lüpke, *Effective Resolution of Banks: Problems and Solutions*, p. 10.

242 For further clarification on the circumstances in which exclusion is necessary under Art. 44(3) BRRD, see *Commission Delegated Regulation (EU) 2016/860 of 4 February 2016 specifying further the circumstances where exclusion from the application of write-down or conversion powers is necessary under Article 44(3) of Directive 2014/59/EU of the European Parliament and of the Council establishing a framework*

always frightens the banking sector and the country as a whole, since it is associated with bank failure. Therefore, the mere application of bail-in could cause bank runs or may deter investments,[243] making it difficult for the resolution authority to determine whether the situation constitutes an extreme macroevonomiv event. It is also possible that creditors or respective lobbyists will attempt to influence the authorities by rent-seeking and will try to convince the resolution authority that bailing-in their claims would destabilize financial markets. If such a claim is made during a resolution process, it is almost impossible for the resolution authority to confirm or deny it in due time.[244] Also covered by the scope of Article 44(3) BRRD are such liabilities that are issued under foreign law or by an entity outside the EU. This exemption too leaves room for shifting liabilities out of the scope of bail-in. To narrow the applicability of bail-in further, authorities are obliged to consider the consequences of liabilities bailed-in when natural persons or micro-, small-, or medium-sized companies above the 100 000 euro coverage level for depositors are concerned. It is envisaged that the resolution fund[245] shall be able to make good the amount of excluded obligations that would have been generated if these obligations had been bailed-in.[246] However, even despite such a fallback, it has been suggested that for the purpose of avoiding rent-seeking attempts, the resolution authority should have no discretion over which specific liabilities and assets are to be bailed-in, and that its discretion should extend only to the amount of liabilities and assets.[247]

---

for the recovery and resolution of credit institutions and investment firms, OJ L 144, 1.6.2016, p. 11-20.

243 Recital (77) SRMR.

244 Franke, Krahnen and Lüpke, *Effective Resolution of Banks: Problems and Solutions*, p. 11.

245 See *infra* Part 2, A.II.2.b.ii.(b) – *Pre-Funded Funds – SRF and National Resolution Funds*.

246 This again only provided that at least 8 % of the total liabilities or 20 % of risk-weighted assets had been bailed-in by shareholders, holders of other relevant capital instruments, and other eligible liabilities, see Gleeson and Guynn, *Bank Resolution and Crisis Management*, p. 177, para. 9.62.

247 Franke, Krahnen and Lüpke, *Effective Resolution of Banks: Problems and Solutions*, p. 11.

An issue that was discussed in the context of recent resolution cases in Italy[248] and also in Portugal[249] was the exclusion of generally eligible debt from the scope of bail-in, because it was held by non-adequate investors. Presumably, such exclusion rests on Article 44(3)(b), where "exclusion is strictly necessary and proportionate to avoid giving rise to widespread contagion, in particular as regards eligible deposits held by natural persons and micro, small and medium sized enterprises, which would severely disrupt the functioning of financial markets, including of financial market infrastructures, in a manner that could cause a serious disturbance to the economy of a Member State or of the Union." This was the case in Italy, where, for years, risky debt with a high default probability was sold to retail investors and savers. In its current version, the rules pertaining to the bail-in tool do not provide for restrictions on holdings or other coping mechanisms regarding retail holdings of risky bail-in debt. Therefore, as long as holdings in bail-in debt are not regulated and controlled, Member States and authorities will be tempted to exclude respective liabilities at their discretion and without established procedures.

All of these exceptions are minimizing instead of maximizing the pool of bail-inable creditors.[250] With the described exemptions in place, non-exempted creditors are likely to be required to undergo an even more severe haircut with respect to their liabilities than they would have done if fewer exemptions were provided *ab initio*. This again triggers the No-Creditor-Worse-Off (NCWO) principle under which a creditor must not be placed in a worse position than they would have been under ordinary liquidation procedures.[251] The consequence of a breach of the NCWO principle is the entitlement to compensation for the excessive losses experienced. Although this compensation itself is said to not be public money,[252] such compensation claims do further increase the overall resolution costs and, as such, increase the risk of public financing being needed to stem the costs of resolution.

248 The issue of retail holdings in subordinated debt exposed to bail-in recurred in all recent cases such as Banca Marche, Banca Etruria, Carif, Carichieti, Banca Tercas, Veneto Banca, Banca Popolare die Vicenza, and Monte dei Paschi di Siena.

249 Also, in the Portuguese case, senior bonds were excluded from bail-in because they were mostly held by retail investors, Mesnard, *"Bail-ins" in recent banking resolution and State aid cases*, p. 2.

250 Yiatrou, *Bank Resolution Credibility and Economic Implications*, p. 5.

251 Ibid., p.5.

252 NCWO compensation claims are mainly funded by the Single Resolution Fund.

Exemption of Senior Debt Holders

On top of all the exemptions provided by the BRRD, what disrupts the credibility of the bail-in in particular is the treatment of senior debt holders.[253] Among all bank resolution cases in Europe in recent years, only very few cases,[254] such as Amagerbanken or Andelskassen[255] in Denmark, Laiki Bank in Cyprus[256], and HETA Asset Resolution AG (a resolution vehicle to continue Hypo Alpe-Adria-Bank International AG) in Austria,[257] incorporated the bail-in of senior debt, with Amagerbanken being under a national resolution scheme at that time (rather than BRRD regulation). In all other resolution cases where bail-in was used, such as SNS Reaal in the Netherlands, Banca Marche, Banca Etruria, Carif, Carichieti, Banca Tercas in Italy,[258] Greece, Spain or Portugal,[259] senior unsecured debt holders

---

253 For the treatment of senior unsecured liabilities in the context of MREL/TLAC see *infra* under Part 4, A.III.5. – *Debt Subordination – New Article 108 BRRD.*

254 H.-J. Dübel, *The capital structure of banks and practice of bank restructuring: Eight case studies on current bank restructurings in Europe ; final report*, CFS working paper series (2013), No. 2013,04, pp. 18 *et seq.* for Amagerbanken and pp. 43 *et seq.* retrievable at https://www.ifk-cfs.de/fileadmin/downloads/publications/wp/2013/CFS_WP_2013-4.pdf accessed 1 October 2022 for Laiki Bank; see also H.-J. Dübel, *Creditor Participation in Banking Crisis in the Eurozone - A Corner Turned?: Empirical analysis of current bank liability management and restructuring policies with conclusions for the European bank restructuring and resolution framework*, Study commissioned by Bundestagsfranktion Bündnis90/ Die Grünen (Berlin, 2013) retrievable at https://deutsche-wirtschafts-nachrichten.de/wp-content/uploads/2013/07/12-10-Bank-Creditor-Participation-Eurozone-Final-6_28_13.pdf accessed 1 October 2022; Mesnard, *"Bail-ins" in recent banking resolution and State aid cases*; World Bank Group, Financial Sector Advisory Center (FinSAC), *Bank Resolution and "Bail-In" in the EU: Selected Case Studies Pre and Post BRRD..*

255 Andersen, Lintner and Schroeder, World Bank Group, Financial Sector Advisory Center (FinSAC), *Bank Resolution and "Bail-In" in the EU: Selected Case Studies Pre and Post BRRD*, pp. 26 *et seq.*

256 Although Cyprus bailed-in senior unsecured debt and even haircutted and converted depositors, the country faced enormous costs during the BoC and Liaki crisis, see ibid., p. 23; Mesnard, *"Bail-ins" in recent banking resolution and State aid cases*, p. 1.

257 Lincoln and Lintner, World Bank Group, Financial Sector Advisory Center (FinSAC), *Bank Resolution and "Bail-In" in the EU: Selected Case Studies Pre and Post BRRD*, pp. 9 *et seq.*

258 Mesnard, *"Bail-ins" in recent banking resolution and State aid cases*, p. 2.

259 See the resolution of the Portuguese bad bank from which Banco Espirito Santo originated, where losses had to be borne only by junior creditors while senior debt was transferred to the good bank Novo Banco. Novo Banco received a capital injection of 4.9 billion euros, from which 400 million was drawn from

were spared.[260] This can most likely be attributed to suboptimal insolvency ranking and priorities[261] and the fact that senior unsecured creditors rank *pari passu* (*i.e.* all have the same rank and rights in insolvency proceedings). This means that – in line with the postulated NCWO principle – either all or no claims attributed to the senior unsecured asset class should be bailed-in. Otherwise, the risk of successful legal challenge against the resolution plan by unsecured creditors might be so high that it could discourage resolution authorities from using the bail-in tool at all.[262] As a result, resolution authorities may prefer not to apply bail-in on the respective senior unsecured claims, potentially leaving a funding gap that would have to be filled with other types of funding that might include, *inter alia*, public funds.

Interestingly, it was found that bail-ins involving no senior creditors led to much less pronounced market reactions: only a minor rise in credit-default-swap (CDS) spreads and only a slight drop in stock returns were observed, indicating that markets had a much reduced bail-in expectation in this case. Bailing-in senior creditors and even depositors, as happened in the Danish and Cypriot cases, sent a much stronger and more credible signal to markets and investors, causing a significant rise in CDS spreads and a material drop in stock returns. That demonstrated the intention of

the Portuguese deposit insurance funds and 4.5 billion was drawn from the euro rescue package ("Euro-Rettungsschirm"), granted by the Portuguese state as a loan to the Portuguese bank resolution fund. Consequently, senior debt holders did not face any haircuts while taxpayers' money was used to continue the good bank. Later, in December 2015, Novo Banco transferred senior bonds of almost 2 billion euros back to Banco Espirito Santo. These bonds were all held by institutional investors, while retail investors did not face any losses. This partial re-transfer was challenged by the institutional investors in April 2016 for the breach of the principle of equal treatment of creditors and the NCWO principle. There were, however, some cases of senior unsecured debt bail-in before the adoption of the Single Resolution Mechanism, for example in Cyprus, see Schäfer, Schnabel and Di Weder Mauro, 'Bail-in expectations for European banks'; Mesnard, *"Bail-ins" in recent banking resolution and State aid cases*, p. 2.

260 Schäfer, Schnabel and Di Weder Mauro, 'Bail-in expectations for European banks', p. 10.

261 Munoz, 'Bank resolution and insolvency ranking and priorities'.

262 Stiefmüller, *Ten Years After - The 2017 Banking Package: One Step Forward, Two Steps Back*, p. 13.

legislators and authorities to move away from bail-out towards bail-in.[263] Nevertheless, most recent cases also show that some kind of refrainment from bailing-in senior debt still exists: in June 2017, Italy recapitalized two Venetian banks, Veneto Banca and Banca Popolare di Vicenza, according to national insolvency proceedings but fully protected senior debt holders.[264] Considering the CDS spreads, sparing senior creditors communicates to the market that the resolution regime is not fully credible.

Bail-inable Instruments in the Cross-Border Context

The structure of institutions constitutes the last issue complicating the application of bail-in, in two specific regards: first, institutions, and especially the more important ones, operate supranationally and maintain branched third-country cross-border structures; and, second, even outside a cross-border context or only within the limited European Banking Union context, banking groups employ widely ramified structures (see also *supra* Part 2 A.II.1.b.ii. – *Legal and Organizational Structures*) with a variety of subsidiaries and branches possessing different business models and of fluctuating importance to the real economy. Looking at the first of these two aspects, most banks, and especially those considered important for the financial system, have subsidiaries in many jurisdictions inside as well as outside the scope of the BRRD. If a bail-in were to be applied to one of those cross-border institutions, foreign liabilities subject to the respective domestic law might not automatically respond to the applied BRRD resolution laws.[265] Foreign authorities and governments might try to shield their entities' assets and liabilities by not recognizing foreign resolution action, which is especially true for third countries and sometimes even applicable for Member States within the Banking Union. This complicates and narrows the application of bail-in in its current state. Turning to the second aspect, namely the branched and complex structures within the Banking Union, another problem arises. Until now, most banking

263 See, for detailed data and explanation of methodology employed, Schäfer, Schnabel and Di Weder Mauro, 'Bail-in expectations for European banks', pp. 10 *et seq.*

264 Handelsblatt, 'Bankenrettung kostet Steuerzahler bis zu 17 Milliarden Euro'.

265 For a detailed presentation of the 'clash of two regimes', namely private international law versus bank resolution law, see M. Lehmann, 'Bail-in and Private International Law: How to Make Bank Resolution Measures Effective Across Borders', *International & Comparative Law Quarterly* 66 (2017), 107–42.

groups under the BRRD have applied or – due to their internal structures – are have been forced to apply a multiple point of entry (MPE) resolution structure. If such a banking group enters resolution under the MPE approach, the struggling entity is resolved no matter where it sits in the group's structure. This has various disadvantages. First, it is impossible to tell upfront which entity in the banking group structure will be subject to financial distress and therefore resolution. This is crucial, as typically not every entity in a group's structure is equally important, either for the institution as a whole or for the financial market and its stability. Plans cannot be made to counter the failure of one of the groups entities hitting an important or a less important unit that is subsequently subject to resolution. Second, the specific entity under resolution will most likely only be able to provide bail-inable liabilities (which it holds itself) and capital (which is available on its own balance sheet) as – in most cases and leaving aside group financial support[266] – it cannot access other group capital or instruments. In a resolution case, it would vary from entity to entity as to what amount and quality of liabilities and assets could be bailed-in. An up-streaming or down-streaming of losses, as observed frequently within the single point of entry (SPE) resolution scenarios mostly found in US resolution cases, is not provided for in the BRRD, neither when it comes to the necessary structure nor when it comes to internal financing mechanisms for such kinds of resolution. This means that – ahead of a concrete case – a potential resolution case is hard to forecast and resolution will often target entities that are important for a group's structure or entities that, due to their business model, hold suboptimal bail-inable financial instruments. This can further narrow the pool of bail-inable instruments.

Conclusion

In conclusion, it can be noted that the legal framework for the bail-in tool under the BRRD provides for a vague approach with various restrictions, exemptions, and undefined legal terms that limit its scope, thereby tempting authorities to use their discretion in adressing private financing of resolution.[267] Furthermore, the inherent discretion might induce politi-

266 See Arts. 19 *et seq.* BRRD; EBA, *Guidelines specifying the conditions for group financial support under Article 23 of Directive 2014/59/EU* (2015).

267 Tröger, 'Too complex to work', pp. 4, 12 *et seq.*; T. H. Tröger, 'Regulatory Influence on Market Conditions in the Banking Union: the Cases of Macro-Pru-

cal or other financial actors to exercise influence on the bail-in decision. The cross-border and complexity problem amplifies said impediments and contributes to the finding that the rules governing the bail-in tool are not sufficient. Due to the insufficiency of bail-inable instruments, the most important private funding mechanisms fall short of expectations, thereby tempting banks, governments, and authorities to resort to other means.

External Private Funding Instruments

Besides bail-in, the only possibility of private financing within the BRRD is through the attraction of financing from the market. Even though the general possibility of funding privately through external sources is generally allowed, such funding will not in most cases play an important role, as it is hard to attract and therefore rarely used. The external private funding of struggling banks often goes awry, as can be observed in some recent cases. For example, in the run-up to the insolvency of two Venetian banks – Veneto Banca and Banca Popolare di Vicenza – the Italian government and the management of the two respective banks tried to collect the missing 6.4 billion euros through investors on the open market but failed.[268] This showed that private external funding, for example through market funding, proves difficult in times of resolution. Potential creditors might be deterred from investing in an institution under resolution since they fear the subsequent bail-in of their claims, see Article 32(1)(b) BRRD. Therefore, in order to attract market funding, creditors must be given guarantees that will shield them from bail-in. Moreover, in the case of a wider crisis, the financial means might be lacking in the market. Institutions in a struggling market might be more risk-averse, rearranging their balance sheets to meet capital requirements. In such a scenario, they will most likely not be willing to increase their leverage to provide external private funding to another struggling bank.[269] Therefore, external private funding in resolution is, in most cases, not prevalent.

---

dential Instruments and the Bail-in Tool', *European Business Organization Law Review* 16 (2015), 575–93, p. 590; Hadjiemmanuil, 'Bank stakeholders' mandatory contribution to resolution financing: principles and ambiguities of bail-in', p. 236.

268 Handelsblatt, 'Bankenrettung kostet Steuerzahler bis zu 17 Milliarden Euro', Handelsblatt, 25 June 2017; Mesnard, Margerit and Magnus, *The orderly liquidation of Veneto Banca and Banca Popolare di Vicenza*, p. 3.

269 Yiatrou, *Bank Resolution Credibility and Economic Implications*, p. 7.

The Ugly: Sector Funding

Having assessed normal insolvency proceedings, bail-in, and external funding, all possible private funding options have been evaluated. However, before resorting to the unwanted involvement of public funds, industry-funded financing might be of assistance if private funding is lacking. The costs of such industry-funded financing of resolution and recapitalization are borne by those responsible. However, on the downside, industry-financed options tend to socialize costs, and are therefore exposed to the dangers of moral hazard and risk-insensitive behavior.

Pre-Funded Funds – DGS and EDIS as Sector-Funded Financing

Deposits, whether insured or held by individuals or SMEs, are preferred under the BRRD and Deposit Guarantee Scheme Directive (DGSD).[270] The intention behind this feature is to protect weaker participants in the financial market from losses. This helps to limit negative repercussions for the real economy by keeping the financial means in the economic circle and by preventing bank runs.

However, Deposit Guarantee Scheme (DGS) contributions are unable to actually *finance* resolution or recapitalization action. That is because DGS contributions to a bank resolution are, in a literal sense, limited to compensating covered depositors and are further limited to the amount a creditor of a covered deposit would lose in normal insolvency proceedings, Article 109 BRRD.[271] However, the prospects for insured depositors in normal insolvency proceedings are quite optimistic, as a high or even total loss to the depository only occurs in extreme cases. This entails that Article 109 BRRD, which states that a DGS is not liable to contribute to a bank resolution to a greater extent than it would have done under normal insolvency proceedings, has the power of all but barring any recourse to the DGS in order to finance resolution or recapitalization.[272] In other words, a contribution by the DGS never goes beyond getting the institution back to zero. In fact, the only real usefulness of the DGS lies in its ability to

270 *Directive 2014/49/EU of the European Parliament and of the Council of 16 April 2014 on deposit guarantee schemes, OJ L 173, 12.6.2014, p. 149–178*, Section 3.1.

271 Hadjiemmanuil, 'Limits on State-Funded Bailouts in the EU Bank Resolution Regime', p. 102.

272 Gleeson and Guynn, *Bank Resolution and Crisis Management*, p. 173, para. 9.43.

provide liquidity in order to help meeting the target for paying out insured depositors in the event that a bank undergoes orderly insolvency proceedings rather than being placed in resolution.[273] If used to repay depositors, due to its weak target-level setting, which is set at around 0.8 % of covered deposits, a DGS does not prove a very strong and contributive tool when it comes to finance resolution actions and recapitalizations. Indeed, currently it would most likely fall short of the payout amount. Furthermore, as a DGS is solely national, it is vulnerable to large local shocks and does not prevent Member States' budgets from being exposed to risk in their banking sectors. Furthermore, the different sizes and funding levels of the existing 38 DGSs may, in the long term negatively affect depositors' confidence and the internal market.[274]

Additionally, a common European initiative, such as the European Deposit Insurance Scheme (EDIS) – a concept closely linked to the Member States' implementation of the DGS and with a higher insurance coverage – is still missing. Therefore, it is still not able to contribute its part in alleviating bank-sovereign risk and solving the problems pertaining to national DGSs. A conclusive agreement on the last features of the EDIS is likely to prove elusive, since not all Member States agree with the mutualization of the current banking sector risks.[275] According to the most recent reports, the proposal is still under discussion.[276]

Consequently, sector-specific pre-funded financing through a DGS does not provide a reliable supplement to private sector involvement.

Pre-Funded Funds – the SRF and National Resolution Funds

Another sector-specific funding option is the use of national resolution funds, or, for Member States of the Banking Union, the SRM's Single

273 Ibid., p. 173, para. 9.43.

274 See Explanatory Memorandum and section 3.1 of *Proposal for a Regulation of the European Parliament and of the Council amending Regulation (EU) 806/2014 in order to establish a European Deposit Insurance Scheme COM/2015/0586 final - 2015/0270 (COD)* (henceforth EDIS Proposal).

275 International Monetary Fund, *2016 Article IV Consultation - Press Release; Staff Report; and Statement by the Executive Director for the Euro Area*, IMF Country Report No. 16/219 (2016), para. 46 retrievable at https://www.imf.org/en/Publications/CR/Issues/2016/12/31/Euro-Area-Policies-2016-Aticle-IV-Consultation-Press-Release-Staff-Report-and-Statement-by-44067 accessed 1 October 2022.

276 Council of the European Union, *Presidency Progress Report on Work in the AHWP on strengthening the Banking Union 9819/1/18 REV 1* (2018), pp. 3 *et seq.* retrievable at http://data.consilium.europa.eu/doc/document/ST-9819-2018-REV-1/en/pdf accessed 1 October 2022.

Resolution Fund (SRF). After private funding, the resolution funds are intended to serve as the primary source of outside financing for resolution.[277] However, unlike private funding, the SRM assumes a special liquidity support role during resolution to prevent the bank from being forced to fire-sale assets and to bridge liquidity needs might arise.[278] Together with central bank liquidity, the SRF and the national resolution funds constitute two options for liquidity provisioning to banks that run short in liquidity. While Emergency Liquidity Assistance (ELA) was originally intended to provide liquidity only to solvent[279] institutions in exchange for collateral,[280] the SRF and the national resolution funds are intended to provide liquidity to institutions under resolution. Moreover, in contrast to ELA, the granting of which is at the discretion of the national central banks, the SRF is obliged to provide liquidity if the conditions for its application are met. This makes the SRF the *de facto* lender of last resort, at least under the resolution mechanism.[281]

These funds are pre-funded by bank contributions, which are raised at the Member States' national level in national resolution funds but are thereupon intended to be pooled at Union level into the SRF. Outside the eurozone, each Member State is required to set up its own domestic fund.[282] An exception to this requirement to fund is when Member States are part of a resolution-financing arrangement, which is funded through general industry contributions and has an amount raised equal to what a fund would have raised, such as, for example, the UK Bank Levy.[283] The need to pre-fund the SRF lies in its attempt to avoid pro-cyclical, destabilizing effects of *ex post* collection on banks, especially when the bank failure emerged in the course of a systemic crisis.[284] The target level of the SRF was set at 1 % of deposit-guarantee-covered deposits of all

277 Hadjiemmanuil, 'Bank Resolution Financing in the Banking Union', p. 206.

278 An overview of the impact of resolution tools on the liquidity position for each resolution tool may be found in Groen, *Cash outflows in crisis scenarios*, p. 10, table 1.

279 Either in a state in which the institution can still be considered solvent or after resolution, where the institution can again be considered solvent.

280 As will be demonstrated *infra* under Part 2, A.II.4. – *Quod Erat Demonstrandum: Emergency Liquidity Assistance*, the provision and granting of ELA is no longer limited to solvent institutions outside resolution.

281 Groen, *Cash outflows in crisis scenarios*, pp. 14 *et seq.*

282 Gleeson and Guynn, *Bank Resolution and Crisis Management*, p. 171, para. 9.35 *et seq.*

283 Sch 19 Finance Act 2011.

284 Recital (104) SRMR.

banks authorized in the Banking Union – about 55 billion euros (and with required increased *ex post* contributions stretching to 76 billion euros[285]) in total funds – to be reached during an eight-year period starting from January 2016.[286] If money is drawn out of the fund and the target level is undercut, the fund must be refilled by contributions of the institutions.

These funds are only available after stakeholders have contributed at least 8 % of total liabilities in order to absorb losses[287] and are limited to no more than 5 % of the bank's total liabilities.[288] Moreover, in addition to these two limitations, the SRF will always be limited by its total available resources (*e.g.* its target level). The SRF's initial target was set at only 1 % of the covered deposits of credit institutions within the European Banking Union, Article 69 SRMR, which will amount to 55 billion euros by the end of the transition period in January 2024. For states which are not members of the European Banking Union, the target level is set even lower, at about 0.8 % of the covered deposits.[289]

The limited financial power is said to be a major problem of the resolution fund. This becomes even clearer considering that more than 80 % of the support granted during the financial crisis and the euro area debt crisis consisted of loans and guarantees to strengthen the liquidity position of the struggling institutions.[290] Liquidity provision in crisis, therefore, cannot be underestimated. Although an intervention beyond the 5 % cap is possible after a full write-down of unsecured, non-preferred liabilities, the intervention will always be limited by the absolute maximum contribution set by the fund's total available resources. Furthermore, the available resources – even at the end of the transition period and even with the estimated additional funds taken out of borrowing[291] – are substantially less than the approximate 100 billion euros that some of the individual large banks required during the crisis years, and even less than the total 1.1

285 Groen, *Cash outflows in crisis scenarios*, p. 15, table 2.

286 Recital (101) and Art. 69(1) SRMR; Arts. 2, 5, and 6 DGSD.

287 Art. 44(5)(a) BRRD.

288 Art. 44(5)(b) BRRD.

289 Armour, 'Making Bank Resolution Credible', p. 482.

290 And despite the high amount of 80 % of the total support, liquidity has received much less attention in the legislative overhaul post-crisis than capital shortfalls through the introduction of higher capital requirements and the resolution framework. Only the CRR was completed with revised liquidity rations (Liquidity Coverage Ratio (LCR) and Net Stable Funding Ratio (NSFR)), see Groen, *Cash outflows in crisis scenarios*, pp. 5, 7 *et seq.*

291 For the maximum amount that the fund can potentially mobilize under the current legislation during the transition period, see table 2, p. 15 in ibid.

billion euros in liquidity support that was granted to the financial system during those years.[292]

This might lead to the conclusion that the targets of the resolution funds are likely to be insufficient[293] to react promptly, to use the resolution tools appropriately, and to deal with the effects of a systemic crisis or even with an individual crisis alone, given the fact that some institutions account for substantial portions of the given state's GDP.[294] Although the resolution funds are able to raise subsequent contributions and, in the event that the collected sums are still not sufficient, are able to borrow money from third parties,[295] the resolution fund's increased capacity to help finance a resolution depends heavily on the lending capacity of the market and the financial industry,[296] which might be disturbed in times of financial uncertainty.

Another critical characteristic of the resolution fund is that it cannot be used directly to absorb losses of the failed bank or to contribute equity to recapitalize it, Article 101(2) BRRD, but can only be used for the purposes

---

292 Ibid.

293 Yiatrou, *Bank Resolution Credibility and Economic Implications*, p. 9; M. Hellwig, *Yes Virginia, There is a European Banking Union! But It May Not Make Your Wishes Come True* (2014), p. 19; Hadjiemmanuil, 'Bank Resolution Financing in the Banking Union', p. 177; Groen, *Cash outflows in crisis scenarios*, p. 16. On the other hand, de Groen and Gros argue that, according to their estimates of the potential financing needs of the SRF based on the euro area bank resolutions that actually occurred between 2007 and 2014, the SRF would have been able to deal with these past crises under the assumption that its full financing capacity had been available, see W. P. de Groen and D. Gros, *Estimating the bridge financing needs of the Single Resolution Fund: How expensive is it to resolve a bank?*, In-Depth Analysis for the Economics and Monetary Affairs Committee of the European Parliament (Brussels, 2015) retrievable at http://www.europarl.europa.eu/RegData/etudes/IDAN/2015/542687/IPOL_IDA%282015%29542687_EN.pdf accessed 1 October 2022.

294 As, for example, BNP Paribas with a total assets of 1,994 billion euros, Deutsche Bank with assets in the amount of 1,629 billion euros and liabilities in an amount of over 2 trillion euros and Commerzbank with assets in an amount of 533 billion euros an amount of around 100 billion euros, see Hellwig, *Yes Virginia, There is a European Banking Union! But It May Not Make Your Wishes Come True*, p. 19 and Bruegel calculations in Schoenmaker, *The different legal and operational structures of banking groups in the euro area, and their impact on banks' resolvability*, p. 19.

295 Arts. 105 *et seq.* BRRD.

296 Yiatrou, *Bank Resolution Credibility and Economic Implications*, p. 10.

defined in Article 101(1) BRRD,[297] none of which target the absorption of direct losses or the recapitalization of the bank itself. Some scholars have raised concerns that this prohibition could be problematic because the NCWO principle acts as an *ex ante* limitation in the BRRD.[298]

What further weakens the position of the SRF is that the Commission must approve its financial intervention in a resolution procedure.[299] Such approval by the Commission can entail restrictions and conditions for the bank, which can include burden-sharing requirements, divided-payment restrictions, expansion restrictions, restructuring plans, and disclosure requirements. These restrictions may deter institutions from pursuing resolution fund financing.

However, even if the resolution funds are used to contribute to the resolution – despite their rather low target level, and despite their difficult application process and extensive restrictions that can be imposed on the institution – their application might still entail further difficulties and encourage unwanted behavior. That is because the financial risk of bank resolution is mutualized through the funds. Institutions that will most likely never use the fund, because they are diligent and risk-averse, are obliged to pay into such a fund, financing the resolution actions of institutions that are more venturesome. This means that, again, the creation of risk and the bearing of risk in not allocated proportionately. Such misalignment produces behavioral risks as can be observed in the context of bailouts.

As a final point, the SRF is said to lack an effective and common fiscal backstop[300] that kicks in when the SRF's immediately available resources become insufficient for capital or liquidity purposes. Although Member States have already committed to the creation of a backstop for the SRF in 2013, which should be fiscally neutral as it recoups contributions from the banking sector, this has not yet been set up.[301] Even the Commission has

297 Such purposes include but are not limited to short-term funding to a failed bank or a bridge entity, funding NCWO compensation payments to shareholders and creditors, the providing of guarantees to potential purchasers of a failed bank, or capital injections in a bridge entity.

298 Gleeson and Guynn, *Bank Resolution and Crisis Management*, p. 172, para. 9.38.

299 Recital (30) and (75), Arts. 18(9) and 19 SRMR.

300 Groen, *Cash outflows in crisis scenarios*, p. 17. On the general importance of a credible fiscal backstop, see D. Schoenmaker, 'A fiscal backstop to the banking system' in M. Haentjens and B. Wessels (eds), *Research Handbook on Crisis Management in the Banking Sector* (Edward Elgar Publishing, 2015), pp. 42–54..

301 However, the SRB states that there will be political consent on a backstop by the end of 2019, see König, *SRB Conference 2018 – 10 years after the crisis: are banks now resolvable?*.

stressed that this needs to be made operational urgently so as to reinforce the overall credibility of the bank resolution framework in the Banking Union and to underpin the SRB's actions.[302] Access to a last-resort common backstop would, it is hoped, serve to provide credibility to the entire resolution-financing system, and, if designed properly, would eventually become obsolete.

Consequently, it can be noted that financing through resolution funds may not be the optimal alternative, since they can also create unwanted behavior and therefore counteract the major objectives of the new supervisory and resolution regime. Additionally, its capacity is limited, and so too is its ability to contribute to loss-absorption or recapitalization. Moreover, the SRF lacks a robust backstop while, lastly, institutions could try to avoid the SRF's intervention because of the unattractive restrictions attached to its assistance.

The Bad: Public Funding

Public funding constitutes the least favorable option in resolution funding, and is therefore only provided for in the BRRD within limited exceptions. Unlike private and sector-specific funding, the emphasis of the following discourse is not placed on the sufficiency of the instruments but rather on the durability of their design and their exceptional nature. Having determined the possibility to engage in public funding through precautionary recapitalization and within national insolvency proceedings, public funding can further be obtained from the European Stability Mechanism (ESM) and through state support in the context of Government Financial Stabilization Tools (GFSTs).

---

302 The Commission proposed to establish a European Monetary Fund (EMF) that is anchored in the ESM and would provide the common backstop to the Single Resolution Fund and act as a last-resort lender in order to facilitate the orderly resolution of distressed banks, see European Commission, *Commission sets out Roadmap for deepening Europe's Economic and Monetary Union*, Press Release (2017) retrievable at http://europa.eu/rapid/press-release_IP-17-5005_en.htm accessed 1 October 2022. Also, either a credit line provided by the European Stability Mechanism or Member States to simultaneously provide either loans or guarantees for the Single Resolution Fund were identified as possible backstops, see European Commission, *Reflection Paper on the Deepening of the Economic and Monetary Union COM(2017) 291 of 31 May 2017* (2017), p. 20 retrievable at https://ec.europa.eu/commission/sites/beta-political/files/reflection-paper-emu_en.pdf accessed 1 October 2022.

European Stability Mechanism – Direct Recapitalization Instrument

The ESM[303] provides a potential financing instrument in relation to bank resolution. Originally created as a tool for the management of sovereign debt crises ('indirect bank recapitalization') and not financial crises, the ESM now[304] also provides for – at least theoretically – the possibility to recapitalize banks directly,[305] without bypassing a state's balance sheets, through the so-called Direct Recapitalization Instrument (DRI).[306] The direct bank recapitalization program is one of five possible support programs[307] offered under the ESM. Contributions to the ESM are made in accordance with percentages laid down in the treaty, so that it should hold an overall authorized capital of approximately 700 billion euros of which 80 billion is paid-in capital. As it stands, the DRI is subject to an overall cap of 60 billion euros of paid-in capital with only 500 billion euros of

303 A treaty set up the intragovernmental organization ESM on 27 September 2012 as a successor of the earlier European Financial Stability Facility (EFSF) and the European Financial Stability Mechanism (EFSM) in order to safeguard financial stability though breaking the link between banks and sovereigns and to provide instant access to financial assistance programs for eurozone Member States, see Council of the EU, *Treaty establishing the European Stability Mechanism between the Kingdom of Belgium, the Federal Republic of Germany, the Republic of Estonia, Ireland, the Hellenic Republic, the Kingdom of Spain, the French Republic, the Italian Republic, the Republic of Cyprus, the Republic of Latvia, the Republic of Lithuania, the Grand Duchy of Luxembourg, Malta, the Kingdom of the Netherlands, the Republic of Austria, the Portuguese Republic, the Republic of Slovenia, the Slovak Republic and the Republic of Finland*.

304 DRI was finally included in the toolkit of the ESM's financial assistance instruments on 8 December 2014, see ESM Board of Governors, *Resolution of the Meeting of 8 December 2014: Establishment of the instrument for the direct recapitalisation of institutions* (2014).

305 Council of the EU, *ESM Direct Bank Recapitalisation Instrument - Main Features of the Operational Framework and Way Forward* (2013) retrievable at https://www.consilium.europa.eu/uedocs/cms_data/docs/pressdata/en/ecofin/137569.pdf accessed 1 October 2022; Hadjiemmanuil, 'Bank Resolution Financing in the Banking Union', p. 206.

306 For a detailed overview of the features of the direct recapitalization instrument see, among many, D. Vovolinis, 'The European Stability Mechanism Direct Recapitalisation Instrument: An Element for a Complete European Banking Union', *ECEFIL Working Paper Series* (2015), pp. 43 *et seq.* retrievable at http://www.ecefil.eu/UplFiles/wps/wps2015-13.pdf accessed 1 October 2022.

307 The other support programs are the sovereign bailout loan, precautionary financial assistance, primary market support facility, and the secondary market support facility.

authorized capital.[308] Therefore, funding through the ESM is considered public funding. However, the following section will show that the risk of exploiting public-funds use through the DRI is basically non-existent.

The creation of the ESM as a mutualization of resolution costs in the euro area experienced some major resistance, especially from Germany, the Netherlands, and Finland – three of the most powerful lender countries in Europe. Accordingly, renegotiations about the conceptualization of the common fiscal backstop were influenced by the restrained attitude and suspiciousness of these three Member States. Eventually, that led to an ESM design that is no longer as easy and streamlined as previously envisaged in earlier stages, making direct recapitalization under the DRI an exception.[309] In fact, to date the DRI has never been used.

The first obstacle to the use of the DRI lies in the complicated legal framework enshrined in the ESM's DRI Guidelines.[310] Starting with the eligibility criteria in Article 3, the DRI is only available to institutions which "have systemic relevance or pose a serious threat to the financial stability of the euro area as a whole or of the requesting ESM Member" and financial assistance is deemed indispensable for this reason. Furthermore, Article 3 establishes the eligibility criteria that the institution "is, or is likely to be in the near future, in breach of the capital requirements established by the ECB [...], is unable to attract sufficient capital from private sector sources to resolve its capital problems and the bail-in [...] is not expected to address fully the capital shortfall."[311] Private-sector sources in this context mean the involvement of new market investors or existing shareholders. While this criteria is generally acceptable – since it only prevents precautionary measures that no longer apply in cases of initiated

308 This limitation was considered necessary in order to minimize risk associated with acquiring equity participations in weak banks and to retain the ESM's AAA rating.

309 S. Merler, *Comfortably numb: ESM direct recapitalization*, bruegel Blog Post (2014) retrievable at http://bruegel.org/2014/06/comfortably-numb-esm-direct-recapitalization/ accessed 1 October 2022.

310 European Stability Mechanism, *Guideline on Financial Assistance for the Direct Recapitalisation of Institutions* (2014) retrievable at https://www.esm.europa.eu/sites/default/files/20141208_guideline_on_financial_assistance_for_the_direct_recapitalisation_of_institutions.pdf accessed 1 October 2022; see for an analysis of the DRI Guidelines in general B. van Roosebeke, *The ESM's Direct Recapitalisation of Banks: Looking Forward in Backstop-Questions* (2014).

311 European Stability Mechanism, *Guideline on Financial Assistance for the Direct Recapitalisation of Institutions*, Art. 3 (1).

resolution procedures – the next criteria evidently complicate the use of the DRI.

The ESM will only contribute to the resolution via DRI if a contribution to loss absorption and recapitalization equal to an amount not less than 8 % of the total liabilities and own funds has been made through write-down or conversion, if a contribution of the resolution-financing arrangement of 5 % of the total liabilities and own funds has been made, and if all unsecured, non-preferred liabilities have been written down or converted in full, Article 8 para. 3 of the ESM Guideline on DRI.

A request for the application of the DRI must be submitted by an ESM Member State, which has to be "unable to provide financial assistance to the institutions in full without very adverse effects on its own fiscal sustainability, including via the instrument of an ESM loan for the recapitalization of financial institutions. [...]"[312] This provision has three serious consequences. First, the criterion of "inability to provide financial assistance" may mislead countries and dissuade them from making a request to the ESM. An admission of a country that it is unable to provide financial assistance and that it suffers from fiscal weakness could send negative signals to the market and trigger the vicious bank-sovereign circle[313] that legislators tried to avoid so hard when setting up the framework for the Banking Union and the ESM. Second, it is very hard to determine whether the requesting country is unable to provide financial assistance without *very* adversely affecting its fiscal sustainability. When is an impact *very* adverse and when is it considered only slightly adverse? This vague requirement leaves room for politically-, financially-, and lobbyist-motivated maneuvers and opens the eligibility process up to the discretion of certain people. The consequence of such discretionary treatment of eligibility provisions is the loss of credibility and predictability with respect to the application of the instrument. Third, Article 3(2)(a) explicitly brings into play the option of indirect bank recapitalization. This consists of a loan being issued to the requesting country, not to the bank itself. It is called *indirect* recapitalization, as the financing is provided to the bank by the requesting state who in turn borrowed the money from the ESM. Article 3(2)(a) states that DRI can only be used if the requesting member is unable to provide financial assistance to the institution without causing drastic impacts on the country's fiscal sustainability, or if alternative solutions could endanger

312 Ibid., Art. 3 (2) a.
313 Hadjiemmanuil, 'Bank Resolution Financing in the Banking Union', p. 208.

the continuous access to markets of the requesting ESM member.[314] It further states that said financial assistance would include the instrument of an ESM loan. This, in turn, leads to the conclusion that direct recapitalization is only available in a situation where the Member State is unable to finance the rescue of the institution from its own accounts with money from capital markets or with the use of the ESM loan, without wrecking its fiscal prospects.[315] In the majority of cases, requesting countries will be capable of taking a loan from the ESM without "very adverse effects on its own fiscal sustainability." This constitutes a rather striking inconsistency. If a state cannot convince the ESM's decision-makers that their finances or fiscal prospects are at risk (which it might not even try to do on account of a fear of negative repercussions in the market), the requesting state would probably be pushed down towards indirect recapitalization. The consequence of this construction is that the direct recap instrument will most likely never be granted. Then, by requesting indirect recapitalization, the state will be granted a loan from the ESM that will end up on the liability side of the state's balance sheet, potentially endangering public finances.[316] To put it concisely: apart from extreme cases, the ESM's DRI is subsidiary to the indirect recapitalization tool and will hardly be used in practice.

Even if a state requests direct recapitalization under the DRI, there are further hurdles to overcome. The decision as to whether a state can request direct recapitalization for a bank (*i.e.* whether it complies with the eligibility criteria) has to be adopted with the participation of various bodies entrusted with the assessment of eligibility, including amongst others the Commission, the ESM's Managing Director, the competent authority,[317] the ECB as supervisor, and, whenever appropriate, the International Monetary Fund (IMF). Eventually, the ESM's Board of Governors, which consists of the euro area's ministers of finance, grants the assistance based on the other parties' assessment through a unanimous decision. Having

314 Ibid., p. 208.

315 Ibid., p. 208.

316 S. Merler, *Comfortably numb: ESM direct recapitalization*, bruegel Blog Post (2014).

317 The 'competent authority' means a competent authority as defined in point (40) of Art. 4(1) of Regulation (EU) No 575/2013 (CRR), including the European Central Bank with regard to specific tasks conferred on it by Council Regulation (EU) No 1024/2013. The competent authority is the supervisory authority. The supervisory authority is either the relevant national or European competent authority.

the euro area's finance ministers sitting at the ESM's board grants each Member State an effective veto right, which further complicates the application process for direct recapitalization.[318]

Assuming that a state applied for direct recapitalization under the DRI and was eligible to do so, another paradoxical situation arises. Although the Member State was considered too weak and unable to stabilize the bank with private financing, it is obliged to make the first contribution to the recapitalization of the troubled bank upfront by injecting capital necessary to build-up the bank's shortfall on capital, precisely to an amount of 4.5 % of CET 1. Only after this threshold is passed or if the bank still has the 4.5 % CET 1 floor, will the ESM provide financial aid to the extent necessary to refill the ECB-prescribed level, but not without having the member contribute a certain amount up to 20 % of the total amount of the public contribution.[319] If a member is unable to provide the capital because of its fiscal position andanticipated significant effects upon market access,[320] the ESM's Board of Governors is able to mutually agree to partially or fully suspend the contribution requirement, but only on the condition that the country indemnifies the ESM for any loss incurred in connection with the country's non-participation. This is an additional hindrance to the use of the DRI as an instrument for financing resolutions as states might refrain from asking the ESM for financial help for the above reasons.

Another point that states might consider before approaching the ESM for help is that any use of the DRI entails conditionality for both the bank and the requesting Member State. For example, the bank will likely be restructured in order to ensure its success post-recapitalization and will further be subject to other institution-specific conditions such as limitations on remuneration and divided policy. Thus, the ESM, as a shareholder as well, will have great influence on key aspects of the institutions, which might not be desirable for the state or the troubled bank itself. In relation to the requesting Member State, memoranda of understanding will be concluded that impose conditions relating to financial-sector policy and macroeconomic implications.

---

318 Hadjiemmanuil, 'Bank Resolution Financing in the Banking Union', p. 208.

319 European Stability Mechanism, *Guideline on Financial Assistance for the Direct Recapitalisation of Institutions*, Article 9; Hadjiemmanuil, 'Bank Resolution Financing in the Banking Union', p. 209.

320 As happened in the Cyprus case, in which the state faced such severe fiscal pressure, that it was unable to fund any contribution whatsoever, see Gleeson and Guynn, *Bank Resolution and Crisis Management*, p. 176, para. 9.56.

All of the foregoing suggests that the ESM's DRI will barely be used,[321] whether it be due to restrictions imposed by the ESM itself or to refrainment on the part of the requesting state. Even the IMF has expressed doubts, stating that this centralized resolution resource might have overly onerous application requirements and might not be sufficient to handle stress in large banks.[322] Lastly, doubts have also been raised as to whether it is sufficiently capitalized with a paid-in amount of 60 billion euros.[323]

Further State Intervention and Government Financial Stabilization Tools

The BRRD as well as the Commission's norms on state aid[324] explicitly provide for alternative financing sources in the form of state aid and allow for government assistance[325] to ailing banks in resolution in exceptional circumstances, according to Articles 37(10), 56–58 BRRD.[326] Such GFSTs fall within the greater category of "extraordinary public financial support" and – unlike precautionary recapitalization (see *supra* Part 2, A.II.2.a. – *A Junction Before Resolution: Precautionary Recapitalization*) – are not considered an *aluid* to resolution but rather a source and supplement of the resolution-financing strategy.[327] They are generally only admissible in the

321 Hadjiemmanuil, 'Limits on State-Funded Bailouts in the EU Bank Resolution Regime', pp. 108 *et seq.*

322 International Monetary Fund, *2014 Article IV Consultation - Staff Report; Press Release; and Statement by the Executive Director*, IMF Country Report No. 14/198 (2014), paras. 20 and 51 retrievable at https://www.imf.org/en/Publications/CR/Issues/2016/12/31/Euro-Area-Policies-Staff-Report-for-the-2014-Article-IV-Consultation-With-Member-Countries-41741 accessed 1 October 2022.

323 Angeloni, *SRB Conference 2018 - 10 years after the crisis: are banks now resolvable?*.

324 Banking Communication 2013.

325 Or, as Gortsos puts it in familiar terms, GFSTs provide a special 'government bail-out regime', see C. V. Gortsos, *A Poisonous (?) Mix: Bail-Out of Credit Institutions Combined with Bail-In of Their Liabilities Under the BRRD - The Use of 'Government Financial Stabilisation Tools'* (2016), p. 21, paper presented at the Workshop of the Financial and Monetary Law Working Group of the European University Institute (EUI, Florence, 12 October 2016) retrievable at SSRN https://ssrn.com/abstract=2876508 accessed 1 October 2022; Busch, van Rijn and Louisse, 'How Single is the Single Resolution Mechanism?', p. 18.

326 It is up to Member States' discretion whether to incorporate Art. 56–58 BRRD into their national law ("Member States may provide (…)", see Art. 56(1) BRRD). Some Member States, such as Germany, have not incorporated the provisions into their national laws. Member States that did not incorporate Art. 56–58 BRRD cannot be forced by the SRM to provide public financial support.

327 A. Gardella, 'Bail-in and the Financing of the SRM' in D. Busch and G. Ferrarini (eds.), *European Banking Union* (Oxford: Oxford Univ Press, 2015), part III, ch.

very extraordinary situation of a systemic crisis, Article 37(10) BRRD, as a last resort, Article 56(3) BRRD, after all other[328] resolution tools have been exhaustively considered and used, and only after a contribution to loss absorption and recapitalization of bail-inable assets in an amount equal to not less than 8 % of total liabilities.[329] The Member State can either apply the "public equity support tool" in Articles 56(5)(a), 57 BRRD (which involves state capital injections in exchange for equity and other determined instruments[330]) or the "temporary public ownership tool" in Articles 56(5)(b), 58 BRRD (which means nationalization of the institution).

To restrict the application, GFSTs may only be used if "the competent ministry or government and the resolution authority, after consulting the central bank and the competent authority, determine that the application of the resolution tools would not suffice to avoid significant adverse effect on the financial system," according to Article 56(4)(a) BRRD, or "the competent ministry or government and the resolution authority determine that the application of the resolution tools would not suffice to protect the public interest, where extraordinary liquidity assistance from the central bank has previously been given to the institution," according to Article 56(4)(b) BRRD. With respect to the temporary public ownership tool, the competent ministry or government, after consulting the competent authority and the resolution authority, must determine that "the application of the resolution tools would not suffice to protect the public interest, where public equity support through the equity support tool has previously been given to the institution," according to Article 56(4)(c) BRRD. The Member State retains full discretion on the participation and organization, albeit it cooperates with the resolution authority to a certain degree.[331] Lastly,

11. However, the restriction of the use of GFSTs only after other financing mechanisms, such as the resolution funds, are depleted is not a 'hard' requirement for their application, leaving room for earlier application, see Binder, 'Systemkrisenbewältigung durch Bankenabwicklung? Aktuelle Bemerkungen zu unrealistischen Erwartungen', fn. 106.

328 The term 'other' resolution tools is somehow misleading in this case, as GFSTs do not constitute a resolution tool.

329 For details see Gortsos, *A Poisonous (?) Mix: Bail-Out of Credit Institutions Combined with Bail-In of Their Liabilities Under the BRRD - The Use of 'Government Financial Stabilisation Tools'*, p. 13.

330 "Equity and determined other instruments mean Common Equity Tier 1 instruments (Art. 28 CRR), Additional Tier 1 instruments (Art. 52 CRR) or Tier 2 instruments (Art. 63 CCR).

331 Hadjiemmanuil, 'Limits on State-Funded Bailouts in the EU Bank Resolution Regime', p. 106.

even if the design and structure of the concrete support measure is not laid down in the BRRD,[332] the granting thereof has to be in accordance with the Banking Union's state aid framework,[333] Article 37(10)(b) BRRD, that works in tandem[334] with the respective Banking Communication 2013 that binds the discretion of the Commission.

Taking into consideration all of the above, it seems that the likelihood of GFSTs being used is low. They are only admissible and should only be used in the "very extraordinary situation of a systemic crisis" and after other resolution solutions have been "assessed and exploited to the maximum extent practicable whilst maintaining financial stability,"[335] which seem to be demanding requirements. However, on closer inspection, setting up such high requirements not only lowers the probability of GFSTs being used but also makes its application more random and less transparent. The higher and the more abstract a requirement's design, the harder it becomes to retrace decisions concerning this requirement. This is evidenced by the requirement of a "very extraordinary situation of a systemic crisis." Whether this condition is met is determined by the Commission, which carries out the respective assessment. Although the term "systemic crisis" is defined in Article 2(1)(30) BRRD as a "disruption in the financial system with the potential to have serious negative consequences for the internal market and the real economy," it is evident that such an important assessment (the determination of the existence of a systemic crisis) cannot be achieved solely with the help of this narrow definition (let alone the extensive use of undefined legal and economic terms in this definition such as "serious negative consequences"). For example, it has been argued that the wording of this definition also covers structural crises triggered by economic crises that were not caused by unsound management or excessive risk-taking by institutions,[336] thus opening up the use of GFSTs in such situations.

332 Except for recitals 8 and 58 BRRD, according to which the resolution strategy and the application of the GFSTs shall be structured in such a way that the Member State is the beneficiary of potential restructuring profits and in such a way that leaves the financial support budgetary neutral in the medium term.

333 Art. 107(3)(b)(2) TFEU.

334 Hadjiemmanuil, 'Limits on State-Funded Bailouts in the EU Bank Resolution Regime', p. 95.

335 Recital (10) and Arts. 37(1) and 56(3) BRRD.

336 Gortsos, *A Poisonous (?) Mix: Bail-Out of Credit Institutions Combined with Bail-In of Their Liabilities Under the BRRD - The Use of 'Government Financial Stabilisation Tools'*, p. 12.

Despite the fact that the determination of the conditions for the use of GFSTs is subject to the review and assessment of a number of bodies,[337] such as the relevant government, the national ministry of finance, resolution authority, supervisory authority, and even the ECB, it remains unpredictable and leaves room for highly discretional and incomprehensible decisions. On one hand, GFSTs may be permitted and applied with difficulty because of these intangible conditions, while on the other hand decision-making bodies can easily and opaquely waive through their usage. In addition, the involvement of the Commission with respect to the compatibility with the state aid framework is no real assurance that GFSTs are used scarcely, as was seen in their lenient and patronizing treatment of the MPS case.[338] On the contrary, in recent crisis years, the Commission has approved[339] a high number of national programs that support institutions, including both individual banks and national banking systems.[340] Although this is generally thought to be a temporary response to overcome financial distress during the crisis years only, the Commission nonetheless continues to apply state aid permissions[341] and it seems that the Commission is willing to do so for the future.[342]

Although public intervention would now happen at a later stage, namely when resolution is already triggered and some bail-in or other non-public financing may have occurred, the availability of GFSTs is a retrodisplacement of the problem and the mix of bail-out with bail-in within the

337 For an overview of governance issues relating to the conditions for the provision of GFSTs and their application, see ibid., table 3, p. 24.

338 Götz, Krahnen and Tröger, 'Taking Bail-in Seriously – The Looming Risks for Banking Policy in the Rescue of Monte Paschi di Siena'.

339 For a comprehensive overview of the total amounts of state aid to banks approved and used in the EU over the period 2008–2016, see European Commission, *State Aid Scoreboard 2017: Aid in the context of the financial and economic crisis*.

340 Hadjiemmanuil, 'Limits on State-Funded Bailouts in the EU Bank Resolution Regime', p. 97.

341 See years 2015 and 2016 of the Commissions State Aid Scoreboard 2017, in which especially guarantees and other liquidity measures are still granted, European Commission, *State Aid Scoreboard 2017: Aid in the context of the financial and economic crisis* .

342 The Commission stated in its 2013 Communication that "[t]he stress in financial markets and the risk of wider negative spillover effects persist" and that state interventions may still be needed to stabilize the Eurozone, see Banking Communication 2013, paras. 4 and 6.

resolution framework may become “poisonous.”[343] Institutions and their stakeholders might conclude that, even if the prescribed burden-sharing cascade is insufficient to resolve the bank and keep its important functions alive, the government will also take care of the leaks in the resolution procedure; or, worse still, they might assume that the government will spare sensitive liabilities and assets of the institution during resolution and use public money to replenish consequent shortfalls.

Results of *Ex Post* Evaluation

Because it is hard to predict precise resolution-funding needs in advance, criticism of the current financing arrangements is difficult to substantiate. Nevertheless, the above section indicates some inadequacies in the design of current resolution financing. The first point to consider here is the possibility to circumvent resolution procedures through precautionary re-capitalization, where public funds can be used rather too discretionally. The second point pertains to the unclear conditions under which an institution is allowed to be liquidated under national insolvency proceedings and the possibility of public funds being employed uncontrollably. Third, public funding mechanisms and especially the bail-in tool lack substance and are too discretional. The multiple exceptions to bail-inable liabilities[344] push resolution costs further down the BRRD’s burden-sharing cascade. Fourth, sector-specific funding as a backstop to the use of private funding only plays a limited role or is unable to contribute a sufficient amount if needed. Lastly, with regard to public funding, only state aid with respect to GFSTs plays a role, while DRI is practically irrelevant. However, even if GFSTs is a public funding tool that can be potentially exploited to fund resolution, the real problem of public financing lies in precautionary resolution and national insolvency proceedings, and the numerous opportunities to alter loss allocation post resolution.[345]

However, even if the existing private funding mechanisms would ultimately prove to be sufficient after resolution, the current inconsistencies

343 Gortsos, *A Poisonous (?) Mix: Bail-Out of Credit Institutions Combined with Bail-In of Their Liabilities Under the BRRD - The Use of 'Government Financial Stabilisation Tools'*, p. 21.

344 Schäfer, Schnabel and Di Weder Mauro, ‘Bail-in expectations for European banks’, p. 4.

345 Hadjiemmanuil, ‘Limits on State-Funded Bailouts in the EU Bank Resolution Regime’, p. 110.

and margins of discretion in the resolution-financing system cause mistrust in the market and amongst investors.[346] As a result, feared lacks of sufficient private or sector-specific resolution funds disrupt the credibility of the resolution-financing regime. The promise to resolve the bank in private is no longer credible.[347]

Excursus: Limits to the No-Bailout Policy – The Role of Public Financing

Bearing in mind the discourse on the unwanted consequences of publicly-financed resolution, a question might arise as to why the use of public financial means in relation to ailing banks was not prohibited by law in general. The answer is that such a hardline approach is not practicable. Some scholars and policy makers, especially in the US,[348] point out that a bail-in, as a mandatory resolution tool, can aggravate the situation in some extreme cases, namely in situations of economic distress and system-wide banking weakness,[349] and that state aid and other public financing (even precautionary recapitalization[350]) should be allowed as *ultima ratio* during

346 Hadjiemmanuil, 'Bank Resolution Financing in the Banking Union', p. 209.

347 Yiatrou, *Bank Resolution Credibility and Economic Implications*, p. 2.

348 A. J. Levitin, 'In Defense of Bailouts', *Georgetown Law Journal* 99 (2011), 435–514, pp. 490 *et seq.*, R. K. Rasmussen and D. A. Skeel, 'Governmental Intervention in an Economic Crisis', *University of Pennsylvania Journal of Business Law* 19 (2016), 7–48; for a more optimistic view that considers bail-in applicable even during systemic crises, see Zhou, Rutledge, Bossu, Dobler and Jassaud, *From bail-out to bail-in*, 2012/3, pp. 22 *et seq.*

349 Tröger, 'Too complex to work', p. 9; Hadjiemmanuil, 'Limits on State-Funded Bailouts in the EU Bank Resolution Regime', p. 110; M. Dewatripont, 'European banking: Bailout, bail-in and state aid control', *International Journal of Industrial Organization* 34 (2014), 37–43, p. 43; Micossi, Bruzzone and Cassella, 'Fine-tuning the use of bail-in to promote a stronger EU financial system', p. 4; E. Avgouleas and C. Goodhart, 'Critical Reflections on Bank Bail-ins', *Journal of Financial Regulation* 1 (2015), 3–29; Binder in Binder, 'Resolution: Concepts, Requirements, and Tools' suggests that such extreme circumstances are rather cases of large and complex failures in volatile markets. However, what both scenarios have in common is that many unpredictable variables and unknown quantities are involved.

350 Véron, *Precautionary recapitalisation: time for a review?*, pp. 6 *et seq.*

systemic crises[351] or out of transitional or permanent considerations.[352] Financial history[353] shows that governments who refused to intervene in a financial system as a backstop during crises in fact aggravated the situation. To prove their point, proponents of state intervention validly point out that secondary European law does not forestall the application of EPFS or GFSTs *per se*,[354] although the BRRD prominently postulates the avoidance of public money use. It has been hypothesized that, if the financial system in a Member State finds itself in a particularly weak condition, the application of the resolution tools, especially bail-in, would have a contagious effect through market reactions to the microeconomic incident in question, with the contagious macroeconomic effects being worse than those deriving from the direct transmission of losses.[355] Bank runs might occur, even from investors of other banks that have no plausible reason to believe that their institutions are affected and that their claims are subject to bail-in. This market reaction would then cause claimholders of other institutions to make cross-border investments in other institutions, which increases the national bank's refinancing costs, deepening an already delicate financial situation.[356] In such cases, *ultima ratio* state aid and public financing would be allowed to prevent the unwanted incentive problems by creating strict terms of use.[357]

One example that seemed to support non-mandatory bail-in is the recent case of Monte dei Paschi di Siena, in which a sufficient volume of

351 Binder, 'Systemkrisenbewältigung durch Bankenabwicklung? Aktuelle Bemerkungen zu unrealistischen Erwartungen', pp. 59, 68; Avgouleas and Goodhart, *A Critical Evaluation of Bail-ins as Bank Recapitalisation Mechanisms*; Avgouleas and Goodhart, 'Critical Reflections on Bank Bail-ins', pp. 5, 10 *et seq.*

352 Even if in a US context, see for arguments J. Manns, 'Building Better Bailouts: The Case for a Long-Term Investment Approach', *Florida Law Review* 63 (2013), 1350–405, p. 404; E. A. Posner and A. Casey, 'A Framework for Bailout Regulation', *Notre Dame Law Review* 91 (2015), 479–536; for Europe see Véron, *Precautionary recapitalisation: time for a review?*, p. 4.

353 This reference is aimed at the Federal Reserve's policy mistakes during the Great Depression, see, with further references, Tröger, 'Optimal Bail-In Tools - Observations From A European Perspective' p. 8.

354 The BRRD itself opens the way for GFSTs in Arts. 56–58 BRRD and extraordinary financial support in Art. 32(4) BRRD; see also Véron, *Precautionary recapitalisation: time for a review?*, p. 11.

355 Hadjiemmanuil, 'Limits on State-Funded Bailouts in the EU Bank Resolution Regime', p. 111.

356 See also Part 3, A.II.1.i. – *Planning Capacity for Systemic Crises.*

357 Rasmussen and Skeel, 'Governmental Intervention in an Economic Crisis', pp. 47 *et seq.*

bail-inable junior debt was generally available to absorb losses. However, the Italian government instead refrained from applying bail-in and asked the Commission to allow precautionary recapitalization to remedy serious disturbances in the economy of a Member State and preserve financial stability, Article 32(4)(d) BRRD. Without knowing the exact justification for the assumption that a serious disturbance in the economy must be remedied and why financial stability would otherwise not be preserved, it would not be too far-fetched to believe that one rationale for not going down the hard bail-in path was that the Italian government wanted to avoid contagious effects through market reactions, since the entire Italian banking sector suffers from similar problems as those suffered by Monte dei Paschi di Siena (*e.g.* a crisis with a systemic dimension). A bail-in, in this case, could have signaled to other Italian bondholders that their savings were at risk, and thus probably triggering bank runs and investor flights.[358]

Meanwhile, the opponents of mandatory bail-in make the point that, since the monetary and banking landscape of the EU and the euro area is deeply fragmented, a uniform application of bail-in to fundamentally different situations in differently financially-positioned Member States is likely to deepen the current divergences and inequalities.[359]

Another macroeconomic argument that has been quite convincingly put forth is the following: the aim of minimizing taxpayers' costs in cases of bank resolution becomes void when the costs of bank resolution are shifted to them in different roles, namely as banks' costumers or counterparts.[360] In other words, if the costs for taxpayers are lower than the costs for society, it might make economic sense to impose a lower amount of costs directly on them rather than a higher amount through increased charges. Therefore, all bailouts that are "pie-increasing" for markets and taxpayers might be desirable.[361]

---

358 Hadjiemmanuil, 'Limits on State-Funded Bailouts in the EU Bank Resolution Regime', p. 111.

359 Ibid., p. 112.

360 G. Sjöberg, 'Banking Special Resolution Regimes as a Governance Tool' in W.-G. Ringe and P. M. Huber (eds.), *Legal challenges in the global financial crisis: Bail-outs, the euro and regulation*, Studies of the Oxford Institute of European and Comparative Law (Oxford: Hart, 2014), pp. 187–96, p. 195.

361 For an extensive discussion of the legitimacy of post-crisis bailouts within the EU, see M. A. Schillig, 'The (Il-)Legitimacy of the EU Post-Crisis Bailout System', *King's College London Law School Research Paper* 2018 (2018), pp. 37 *et seq.*

Such reservations about a mandatory, uniform bail-in, especially in the context of systemic crises, cannot be simply brushed aside, since it is hard to determine if it would have the predicted effects on the financial economy or not. There are too many variables, which cannot be calculated or anticipated upfront, as crises with systemic dimensions are extremely hard to predict and future conditions are hard to gauge. Maybe, in the MPS case, a mandatory bail-in, in the course of an orderly resolution, would have caused losses to only retail investors (*i.e.* there would have been no greater damages to the financial stability of Italy). But, on the other hand, it could just as easily have caused a greater crisis and brought more harm to the financial stability of Italy and even beyond its borders. Therefore, considering the difficulties the bail-in tool still suffers from, it might not be negative *per se* and might actually be helpful to have the possibility to limit the application of bail-in in certain cases.[362]

Despite realizing that public funding must be available as a credible solution in a systemic crisis, the current private funding opportunities must be enhanced. The current inadequacy, misuse, and bending of the exceptions[363] sap the BRRD's credibility massively.[364] Enhancement in relation to the application of the bail-in tool can, in the long run, lead to primarily private-funded resolutions being used with public funding serving as a backstop in case of a systemic crisis.

Quod Erat Demonstrandum: Emergency Liquidity Assistance

Supra assessments have demonstrated that the current resolution framework suffers from a lack of credibility. While the application of the resolution regime is unpredictable and faces a complex and resolution-unfriendly banking landscape *ex ante*, the available private financing mechanisms are poorly designed and encourage recourse to non-compliant approaches to resolution.

However, the majority of the market – like unsophisticated bank customers or small depositors – does not have a comprehensive understanding of the above-detected lacks. Even if they suspect that such lacks

362 Binder, 'Systemkrisenbewältigung durch Bankenabwicklung? Aktuelle Bemerkungen zu unrealistischen Erwartungen', p. 71.

363 Binder, 'Resolution: Concepts, Requirements, and Tools', recital 2.36.

364 Triantafyllakis, 'Italienische Banken: Wenn nicht alle Wege zum Bail-in führen', p. 2249.

exist, actual knowledge will probably never go farther than guesswork and hearsay. Despite the unawareness of specific shortcomings, the market still somehow finds the resolution regime lacking in credibility and we here add a third lack to the above discourse: the insufficient trust of market participants. Such a lack of trust exists regardless of the existence of actual crises, problems, and shortcomings and regardless of whether the resolution regime would work in the end or not. It is an irrationally driven fear,[365] which is the result of financial markets being inherently fragile[366] ("fragile" in this context means vulnerable to panics and runs)[367] paired with pre-BRRD handling of banking crises such as in Greece or Spain, which caused anxiety among market participants in an already delicate market. In addition, recent cases, such as the rescue of the Italian bank Monte dei Paschi di Siena and the respective media coverage, fuel such feelings of aversion and distrust.

Although the BRRD provides a legal framework for resolution that represents a major improvement compared with the preceding years of bailout practice, markets still do not fully trust the new regulations. In fact, bail-in still might trigger bank runs. If investors, however, were fully rational and the rules completely reliable, resolution and the application of bail-in would not trigger bank runs and wider crises, because it is explicitly aimed at limiting losses and contagion.[368] Such a lack of trust among

---

365 Avgouleas and Goodhart argue that creators of the bail-in mechanism seem to have underestimated the dynamics of a bank run *ex post*, even where creditors face no potential losses in the aftermath of a bailout or a rescue by the resolution fund, due, presumably, to reputation risks as well as the (irrational) fear of future risks E. Avgouleas and C. Goodhart, 'An Anatomy of Bank Bail-ins: Why the Eurozone Needs a Fiscal Backstop for the Banking Sector' in G. B. Navetti, G. Calzolari and A. F. Pozzolo (eds.), *European Economy: Banks, Regulation, and the Real Sector* (Rome: Europeye, 2016), pp. 75–91, pp. 83 *et seq.* For the phenomenon of irrational bank runs see M. A. Carlson and J. D. Rose, 'Can a Bank Run Be Stopped? Government Guarantees and the Run on Continental Illinois', *Finance and Economics Discussion Series* (2016), 1–44.

366 The source of fragility in the financial markets is the combination of the desire for safe money-like stores of value and the need for funding for long-term, illiquid, risky investments and purchases, creating the need for maturity transformation, see T. Geithner, *Are We Safer? The Case for Strengthening the Bagehot Arsenal*, Per Jacobsson Lectures (2016) p. 4 retrievable at http://www.perjacobsson.org/lectures/100816.pdf accessed 1 October 2022.

367 Ibid., p. 4.

368 Tröger, 'Optimal Bail-In Tools - Observations From A European Perspective' p. 10.

market participants debilitates – to the same extent as the discussed *ex ante* and *ex post* lacks – the credibility of the current resolution regime.

An example that illustrates the market's reluctance to trust in the new resolution framework can be found in the recent use of ELA, a topic that has attracted much public interest.[369] The following sections will give a brief overview of the functioning of ELA, its application principles, recent ELA cases, and will close by outlining why the prevalendce of ELA is an illustration of the problem of a lack of trust in the new resolution regime.

Emergency Liquidity Assistance for Solvent Institutions – An Overview

According to the ECB's ELA Agreement,[370] ELA occurs when a Eurosystem national central bank provides either (i) central bank money or (ii) any other assistance that may lead to an increase in the flow of central bank money to a financial institution or a group of financial institutions facing liquidity problems. ELA was therefore designed to bridge temporary liquidity problems by granting money or assistance against collateral.[371] Together with the SRF and the resolution funds (see *supra* Part 2, A.II.2.b.ii.(b) – *Pre-Funded Funds – SRF and National Resolution Funds*), ELA constitutes one of the two main options for providing assistance to banks that are short on liquidity. In the past, ELA was applied either in single institution scenarios or during wider systemic crises in order to cushion liquidity outflows that could have collided with the short-term borrowing and long-term lending of the institution (*e.g.* the maturity transformation). Besides that, there are no specific criteria determining when and to whom ELA is to be granted; indeed, some national central banks have decided not to set out applicable criteria and have instead followed the concept of "constructive ambiguity."[372] This is intended to prevent banks from moral hazard as they cannot calculate the granting

369 Y. Mersch, *The limits of central bank financing in resolution*, IMFS Distinguished Lecture Series (Goethe-Universität Frankfurt am Main, 2018) retrievable at https://www.ecb.europa.eu/press/key/date/2018/html/ecb.sp180130.en.html accessed 1 October 2022; Philippon and Salord, *Bail-ins and bank resolution in Europe*, vol. 4, p. 48.

370 European Central Bank, *Agreement on emergency liquidity assistance* (2017) (henceforth ELA Agreement).

371 Groen, *Cash outflows in crisis scenarios*, pp. 11, 17.

372 European Parliament, *Emergency Liquidity Assistance - moving away from "constructive ambiguity"?*, Briefing of the European Parliament (2017), p. 1 re-

of ELA credits in their decisions.[373] This also implies that the national central banks are generally not obliged to provide funds to the bank, as this is instead left at their discretion. The party financially responsible for granting ELA is the respective Member State alone; no redistribution of any kind – as is common in relation to the ECB – is applied. If losses owing to ELA occur, such losses are incurred directly by the national central bank, burdening the national budget in the process.

The provision of ELA does not have to be disclosed before the public[374] and is often kept concealed in order to shield institutions. Such shielding might become necessary in certain cases, as ELA application always implies that the applying institution faces – at least – a liquidity problem, sending corresponding signals to the market. This can lead to a paradoxical situation, in which the application for ELA and the making public of its granting causes depositors and customers to withdraw money from the bank, even though ELA is intended to protect depositors and their access to liquidity. However, there is little evidence for this to be gleaned from the procedures of past and recent ELA cases. Even if a number of ELA cases[375] were leaked, there is an information asymmetry between the public and central banks regarding the use of such credits.

When approaching the problem, it must be understood that ELA is not the same as the general opportunity of institutions to draw standing facilities in exchange for respective collateral in case they need extra money urgently. Institutions will only apply for ELA if its standing facilities are exhausted and it cannot apply for more. This should not necessarily lead to the assumption that the requesting institution, rather than having only

---

trievable at http://www.europarl.europa.eu/RegData/etudes/BRIE/2017/587395/IPOL_BRI(2017)587395_EN.pdf accessed 1 October 2022.

373 Mersch, *The limits of central bank financing in resolution*.

374 The ECB states that national central banks will from now on have the option of communicating publicly about the provision of Emergency Liquidity Assistance (ELA) to the banks in their country, in cases where they deem that such communication is necessary, see European Central Bank, *Communication on Emergency Liquidity Assistance*, Press Release (2015) retrievable at https://www.ecb.europa.eu/press/pr/date/2015/html/pr150916.en.html accessed 1 October 2022.

375 For example Norther Rock in 2007, to a number of institutions in Germany (Hypo Real Estate), Belgium (Fortis) and the Netherlands in September and October 2008, to RBS and Lloyds also in September 2008 as well as to certain banks in Cyprus and Greece in 2011 and 2012.

a liquidity problem, has a solvency problem, but it does suggest[376] this to a certain extent and demonstrates the thin line between the two conditions.[377] Insolvency matters, however, fall within the competence of the national supervisory and resolution authorities and not within the competence of the national central bank. The ECB has repeatedly stated that the financing by central banks of insolvent institutions is incompatible with the monetary financing prohibition and that resolution planning should not assume that central bank liquidity would fill-in any gaps.[378] The ECB states further that resolution financing is primarily left to the banks and, if necessary, to the government, and liquidity provision during resolution is actually a job for the SRF.[379] Even during the time until the SRF is fully operationalized,[380] the provision of ELA by the central bank cannot and should not constitute a backstop or alternative. This is because if ELA is granted in cases where the applying institution is not just illiquid but actually insolvent, it opens up the possibility for Member States to prolong a solvency problem[381] and to drop it off on the shoulders of their national

---

376 Paul Fisher from the UK's Prudential Regulation authority stated that "If a central bank lends enough money to a firm where solvency is inherently uncertain – and it always is for a bank in a liquidity crisis – then however well collateralized the loan, there is a risk of losing money – public money.", see P. Fisher, 'Practical issues for the lender of last resort' in European Central Bank (ed.), *ECB Legal Conference 2015: From monetary union to banking union, on the way to capital markets union: new opportunities for European integration, 1-2 September 2015* (Frankfurt am Main: European Central Bank, 2015), pp. 86–9, p. 88.

377 Liu even states that a strict solvency requirement is not only difficult to implement but also unnecessary or even counterproductive during a crisis, see X. Liu, 'Some Comments on Central Banks' Lender of Last Resort Function in the Post-Crisis World' in European Central Bank (ed.), *ECB Legal Conference 2015: From monetary union to banking union, on the way to capital markets union: new opportunities for European integration, 1-2 September 2015* (Frankfurt am Main: European Central Bank, 2015), pp. 90–7, p. 92.

378 Groen, *Cash outflows in crisis scenarios*, pp. 11 *et seq.*

379 Mersch, *The limits of central bank financing in resolution*.

380 The SRF will gradually be built over a period of eight years with a target level of at least 1 % of the amount of covered deposits of all credit institutions within the banking union by the end of 2023, see Part 2, A.II.2.b.ii.(b) – *Pre-Funded Funds – SRF and National Resolution Funds*.

381 M. R. Götz, R. Haselmann, J. P. Krahnen and S. Steffen, *Did emergency liquidity assistance (ELA) of the ECB delay the bankruptcy of Greek banks?*, SAFE Policy Letter (2015), pp. 3 *et seq.* retrievable at https://safe-frankfurt.de/fileadmin/user_upload/editor_common/Policy_Center/Goetz_et_al_Did_ELA_delay_bankruptcy.pdf accessed 1 October 2022.

central bank, which is then tasked with fulfilling quasi-fiscal tasks. This is particularly relevant where resolution would be extremely cost-intensive. However, since it is nearly impossible to distinguish between illiquidity and insolvency, the misuse of ELA for monetary financing might occur but be hard to prove. ELA, however, can only be granted to illiquid but *solvent* credit institutions, para. 4 of the ELA Agreement. As described above, this illustrates the following quandary: where does illiquidity stop and where does insolvency begin?[382] The ELA Agreement has a specific view of what the solvency criteria entail. Namely, it states that a credit institution is considered solvent for ELA purposes if its harmonized minimum regulatory capital levels, according to CRR, are met, or if there is a credible prospect of recapitalization in the event that it does not comply with the minimum regulatory capital levels. However, this "prospect period" can extend up to 48 weeks. ELA to insolvent institutions and institutions for which insolvency proceedings have been initiated, according to national laws, is not allowed and violates the prohibition of monetary financing, at least according to the ELA Agreement. Therefore, as such misuse is hard to prove, it can be assumed that some ELA credits that might have been granted over a long term do not only bridge liquidity restraints but also finance insolvent institutions. This phenomenon, however, is directly at odds with the fundamental rule of ELA.

The Bagehot Doctrine

Whenever it comes to central banks lending out money, as is the case with ELA, it is conventionally accepted that in times of financial crisis central banks should follow the Bagehot rule. In the absence of specific rules for the provision of ELA, especially when, how, and to whom it should be lent, the Bagehot rule gives good guidance. This rule can be summarized as "lend without limit, to solvent firms, against good collateral, at high rates."[383] By lending liberally, it is less likely that central bank money will be needed. The good collateral can help the central bank to distinguish

---

382 European Parliament, *Emergency Liquidity Assistance - moving away from "constructive ambiguity"?*, p. 5.

383 Walter Bagehot formulated this rule in his 1873 account of the money market's "Lombard Street", where he urged the Bank of England to stave off panics in the financial market by lending "quickly, freely and readily" at a penalty rate of interest to banks that can offer "good securities" as collateral, see W. Bagehot, *Lombard Street: A description of the money market*, Wiley investment classics (New York: Wiley, 1999); The Economist, 'What would Bagehot do?: Should central banks act as buyers of last resort?', The Economist, 16 August 2007.

insolvent banks from illiquid ones, and the penalty rate of interest ensures that the central bank remains the lender of last resort.[384] Consequently, ELA should only be given to solvent institutions, against sufficient collateral at discouragingly punitive rates. However, looking at the few known past and recent ELA provisions, one might conclude that the Bagehot rule is not obeyed in every case. Indeed, some have even demanded that the Bagehot toolkit for financial crises in modern financial systems needs to be updated to include the ability to provide funding across the financial system, wherever there are runnable liabilities, and to also include the ability to recapitalize the financial system, including with public resources if necessary.[385]

Recent History of ELA Provision

The recent history of ELA provision started with Northern Rock,[386] where the disclosure of ELA led to depositor panic and long queues outside the branches. After Lehman, where liquidity assistance was not granted, sizable ELA provisions by larger European central banks in Belgium, the Netherlands, Germany, and the United Kingdom were granted but not disclosed to the public. This concealment was attributable to prior experience with the bank run on Northern Rock in 2007. Moreover, during the Irish and Icelandic crises, a reluctance to ELA can be retraced to the fear that its granting might have worsened the liquidity position. In the Greek[387] and Cypriote[388] crises, national central banks provided national institutions with (capped[389]) ELA. Indeed, even the German Bundesbank granted such credits.

However, even if specific ELA cases are known to the public, until 20 April 2012, the ECB did not specifically disclose the beneficiaries or amount of granted (and still outstanding) ELA to the public. Information about ELA provision was somehow hidden between the "Other Securities" and "Other Assets" sections in the Eurosystems Central Bank's consolida-

---

384 The Economist, 'What would Bagehot do?'.

385 Geithner, *Are We Safer? The Case for Strengthening the Bagehot Arsenal*, p. 19.

386 Honohan, *Management and Resolution of Banking Crises: Lessons from Recent European Experience*, p. 6.

387 Götz, Haselmann, Krahnen and Steffen, *Did emergency liquidity assistance (ELA) of the ECB delay the bankruptcy of Greek banks?*, p. 2.

388 C. Xiouros, *Handling of the Emergency Liquidity Assistance of Laiki Bank in the Bailout Package of Cyprus* (2013), retrievable at SSRN https://ssrn.com/abstract=2254499, accessed 1 October 2022.

389 The provision of ELA to Cyprus was capped in 2013, to Greece in 2015.

ted financial statements. As the ECB relocated ELA into a separate section called "Other Claims on Euro Area Credit Institutions Denominated in Euros," it revealed that a single total amount, namely 121.14 billion euros, of ELA had been granted in the eurozone as of that date. Since then, the section has been updated regularly, but as it is a consolidated position, the exact amount of ELA cannot be separated from the other components of the section entitled "Other Claims on Euro Area Credit Institutions Denominated in Euro."[390] As for the issue of who exactly benefits from ELA credits, the ECB remains silent. Furthermore, national central banks are not keen to provide detailed information about ELA amounts, recipients, requirements for granting, collateral, interest rates, or maturity. This is because of a fear that the disclosure would have negative impacts on both the financial market and the confidence of its participants. Because authorities are so secretive about the provision of ELA, many details and even entire cases remain unclear or unknown.

Due to this lack of publicly available information on ELA, it is hard to verify how ELA is actually issued and used. However, there is evidence[391] that a major shift in the postulated Bagehot doctrine, and therefore in the provision of ELA, has occurred as a reaction to evolving market conditions. The long-standing credo of the central bank's function as lender of last resort (LoLR) might have been altered in recent years[392] and there has been a general tendency to widen the application space of ELA significantly; that is, to provide ELA to institutions that are on the verge of being declared "failing or likely to fail," that *have* been declared "failing or likely to fail," or that have already undergone resolution procedures.[393]

---

390 European Central Bank, *Consolidated financial statement of the Eurosystem as at 20 April 2012* (2012) retrievable at https://www.ecb.europa.eu/press/pr/wfs/2012/html/fs120424.en.html accessed 1 October 2022, European Central Bank, *Annual Report 2012* (2013) retrievable at https://www.ecb.europa.eu/pub/pdf/annrep/ar2012en.pdf accessed 1 October 2022.

391 I. Plenderleith, *Review of the Bank of England's Provision of Emergency Liquidity Assistance in 2008-09: Presented to the Court of the Bank of England* (2012) pp. 48 *et seq.*, recitals 181 *et seq.* retrievable at https://www.bankofengland.co.uk/-/media/boe/files/news/2012/november/the-provision-of-emergency-liquidity-assistance-in-2008-9 accessed 1 October 2022, European Parliament, *Emergency Liquidity Assistance - moving away from "constructive ambiguity"?*, p. 5.

392 Plenderleith, *Review of the Bank of England's Provision of Emergency Liquidity Assistance in 2008-09*, ch. 9, recital 280.

393 Mersch, *The limits of central bank financing in resolution*.

The Current Problem

With the foregoing in mind – the Bagehot doctrine on the one hand and the recent developments in ELA provision on the other – there is reason to believe that the ELA regime has changed its character significantly. The paradigm of lending only against good collateral and only to solvent institutions has been softened by lending central-bank money to institutions just before entering, or even after undergoing, resolution procedures.

This became necessary for two reasons. First, liquidity problems are traditionally considered a concern for central banks as lenders of last resort and sentinels of the monetary policy framework, not for governments and authorities faced with a struggling institution, since failing liquidity requirements normally does not trigger resolution. Therefore, liquidity provision, except for the SRF, was not provided for outside central banking in substantial amounts. However, as the liquidity need proved to be particularly high during crisis years,[394] the demand for liquidity provision in the context of banking failures exceeded the provided resources (and still does). This explains the increasing popularity of recourse to central bank liquidity in resolution times, even though this was designed for outside-resolution scenarios. The second reason is that liquidity was withdrawn from near-to-resolution or resolved institutions despite the application of BRRD procedures. Why did clients and depositors withdraw their funds and deposits from a bank whose failure, even if it occurred, would have no impact on their savings?[395] Simply put, because they lacked trust in the regulatory framework. This is paradoxical as resolution procedures according to BRRD are explicitly designed to shield creditors, depositors, and customers of the bank and to safeguard their liquidity. Furthermore, if the application of BRRD resolution procedures is in sight, the surviving critical functions and parts of the institution can be considered solvent again after the application of the resolution tools. Nevertheless, and despite the prospect of the market having access to liquidity at all times and to a solvent bank after resolution, bank-run-like scenarios have pressured institutions to ask for ELA from their national central bank. As a consequence, the provision of ELA in such cases has even worsened the situation

394 80 % of the total support provided during the global financial crisis and the euro area debt crisis consisted of loans and guarantees to strengthen the liquidity position of banks, see Groen, *Cash outflows in crisis scenarios*, p. 5.

395 At least in the end, where deposits are reimbursed by the DGS.

further by signaling to the market that the just-resolved and recapitalized institution is short on liquidity – again.

Does that mean that the Eurosystem of central banks would be prevented from providing liquidity in the narrow context of resolution?[396] This is not necessarily the case if the provision of ELA was to comply with the Bagehot doctrine. However, when granting ELA to pre-resolution or post-resolution banks, the requesting institutions at this point in time are either insolvent but still in possession of certain amounts of good collateral (immediately pre-resolution), or solvent but no longer in possession of good collateral[397] since this was consumed during the resolution procedures (post-resolution). Additionally, even if some good collateral is still left after resolution, a significant amount of time will have to pass before the now-resolved bank is declared solvent by the competent authority again.[398] This means that lending to an institution in one of these states automatically violates the Bagehot rules and therefore the concept of ELA. Consequently, lending to institutions just before, during, or shortly after resolution can never comply with Bagehot and therefore should not be allowed.

The reality, however, is quite different. Central banks have become more and more generous in granting ELA outside the scope of the Bagehot

396 For a discussion about whether ELA should be available to finance banks in resolution, see J. Deslandes and M. Magnus, *Banking Union: Towards new arrangements to finance banks under resolution?*, Briefing of the European Parliament (2018), pp. 2 *et seq.* retrievable at http://www.europarl.europa.eu/RegData/etudes/BRIE/2018/624402/IPOL_BRI(2018)624402_EN.pdf accessed 1 October 2022.

397 A standalone guarantee that can be issued even in post-resolution times is under no circumstances adequate collateral under the ELA framework. Such adequate collateral rather consists of a pledge or repurchase agreement adequately secured by assets capable of being transferred and/or sold at first notice. However, such a guarantee often is the only notable 'collateral' that a post-resolution institution can issue in order to 'cure' the lack of adequate collateral, see Mersch, *The limits of central bank financing in resolution*.

398 To be considered solvent, the post-resolved bank needs to comply with capital requirements and have a sound business plan again. The latter requirement especially will significantly delay the bank's declaration of being solvent again, as the first resolution conducted by the SRB in the Banco Popular case has shown. It took several months before the business plan was finalized and considered 'sound,' and the potential ELA could not have been used until that point. In the Banco Popular case, Banco Santander, which acquired Banco Popular, provided liquidity and capital, see Groen, *Cash outflows in crisis scenarios*, pp. 11 *et seq.*

doctrine.[399] ELA is necessary in those situations, because bank runs occur despite the new resolution framework: markets are suspicious and anxious about resolution and want to test the capacity and reliability of the recapitalized bank on Mondays post-resolution. This is a clear sign that the new resolution framework, as provided by the BRRD, has failed to gain credibility among market participants in its now nearly four-year existence. The market participants' lack of trust as a third evidential component of the lack of credibility of the resolution framework finds its formulation in the provision of, and demand for, ELA in times when the BRRD's new provision should forestall such provision and demand.

As a reaction to the above, the ECB proposed[400] the introduction of special resolution facilities (Eurosystem Resolution Liquidity), which are not subject to the long-standing restrictions of regular ELA.[401] However, such resolution facilities have encountered resistance. Some argue that providing liquidity to a bank that is in the process of resolution is a task for the SRF, not for a central bank.[402] Without the ECB providing further information on these special resolution facilities, an impression is given that the ECB has chosen the easy option by simply relabeling what was called ELA for decades to justify its use in these situations.

Results

It was found that the European banking landscape comprises complex institutions, which make resolution action and especially the application of bail-in unpredictable. In addition, complex structures cannot be altered before resolution as there is no adequate modification procedure. This leads to a lack of credibility *ex ante* resolution. Furthermore, it was found

---

399 Even the European Parliament, in a recent briefing, outlined that ELA can be used "before and in resolution," Deslandes and Magnus, *Banking Union: Towards new arrangements to finance banks under resolution?*, p. 9, table 2. See also Liu, 'Some Comments on Central Banks' Lender of Last Resort Function in the Post-Crisis World', pp. 92 *et seq.*

400 A. Weber and A. Speciale, 'ECB Weighs Emergency Cash Injections to Smooth Bank Rescues', Bloomberg, 09 April 2018 retrievable at https://www.bloomberg.com/news/articles/2018-04-09/ecb-considers-proposal-for-new-cash-line-to-aid-bank-rescues accessed 1 October 2022.

401 Deslandes and Magnus, *Banking Union: Towards new arrangements to finance banks under resolution?*, pp. 10 *et seq.*

402 See ibid., p. 11 for a discussion of if and how such resolution liquidity can be designed; Mersch, *The limits of central bank financing in resolution*.

that the current BRRD regulations do not provide for a resolution-financing regime that is sufficient in terms of private sector involvement and that prevents exploitation of necessary but exceptional public-funds use. This leads to a lack of credibility *ex post* resolution decision. Both shortcomings contribute to the current lack of credibility in the resolution framework. Proof of such a shortage of credibility was then presented from the recent use of ELA by institutions and central banks. Ultimately, it was conclusively found that the resolution framework in its current state is not credible.

When is Resolution Credible?

With the current shortcomings in mind, it will be assesed under which conditions the resolution framework can be considered credible. It is argued that, in order to achieve a credible framework, current credibility lacks *ex ante* and *ex post* must be remedied. In this respect, an assessment will be undertaken as to whether the already-mentioned instruments, recovery and resolution planning on the one hand and loss-absorbing capital requirements on the other, can serve as potential remedies to the diminished credibility of the resolution regime.

Credibility Ex Ante: Recovery and Resolution Planning

During the process of setting up special bank-resolution mechanisms, there has been a growing realization[403] that complexity in banks' structures cannot be dealt with by only organizing resolution *ad hoc* and that most of the impediments to resolution stem from banks' complicated, intertwined structures.[404] Resolution was intended to be swift, with time scarce to

---

403 Binder even states that the development of harmonized concepts for the reorganization and resolution of large, complex, internationally active institutions is one of the most important aspects of the new Banking Resolution regime, see Binder, 'Resolution Planning and Structural Bank Reform within the Banking Union', p. 130.

404 D. Singh, 'Recovery and Resolution Planning: Reconfiguring Financial Regulation and Supervision' in J.-H. Binder and D. Singh (eds.), *Bank Resolution: The European Regime* (Oxford: Oxford University Press, 2016), pp. 1–24, recital 1.14; Binder, 'Resolution Planning and Structural Bank Reform within the Banking Union', p. 129; Carmassi and Herring, 'The Corporate Complexity of

dissolve impediments to resolution, to organize the resolution of various legal entities in different jurisdictions, to locate the bail-inable financial instruments, to find their holders, and to sort out the bail-in process of such instruments.[405] Therefore, resolution procedures were often unpredictable. If complexity in banks' structures was detected before financial distress arose, authorities were unable to properly address this problem with the institutions.

Remedy of the aforementioned lacks could be found in the concept of recovery and resolution planning according to the BRRD.[406] Recovery plans[407] (which are drawn up by the institutions themselves and are assessed by the competent authority) are intended to help avoiding insolvency or resolution *a priori* while resolutions plans[408] (which are drawn up by

---

Global Systemically Important Banks', p. 195; Weber, 'Structural regulation as antidote to complexity capture', p. 710.

405 Or, as was the case in the Monte dei Paschi di Siena recapitalization, there was an unwillingness to bail-in specific liabilities for political reasons.

406 The BRRD's provisions on recovery and resolution planning are a blueprint for the corresponding regime under the SSM and the SRM regulations, all activated by Section 11 with Annex III of the Financial Stability Board's Key Attribute to Effective Resolution Regimes for Financial Institutions, originally from October 2011 and revised October 2014. Furthermore, even if not directly applicable to the authorities and institutions, the BRRD's provisions on recovery and resolution plans provide interpretation aid with respect to the transposing national laws, such as the SAG (Sanierungs- und Abwicklungsgesetz) in Germany. These applicable national laws are supplemented by technical standards, issued in the way of Commission-delegated regulations, see Arts. 290 and 291 TFEU. EBA Guidelines complement the system of regulation.

407 Art. 5–9 and Section A of Annex to the BRRD. The provisions of the BRRD need to be transposed into national law. In Germany, for example, the SAG (Sanierungs- und Abwicklungsgesetz) was established and covers recovery planning in §§ 12 to 21a SAG. Furthermore, regulatory technical standards such as the Commission Delegated Regulation (EU) 2016/1075 provide the legal basis for recovery planning (Art. 3–21). For further guidance, the EBA issued various guidelines (EBA/GL/2015/16 Guidelines on the application of simplified obligations under Art. 4(5) of Directive 2014/59/EU; EBA/GL/2015/02 Guidelines on the minimum list of qualitative and quantitative recovery plan indicators; EBA/GL/2014/06 Guidelines on the range of scenarios to be used in recovery plans) in order to guarantee the consistent interpretation of Union law. Lastly, statements issued by supervisory bodies can contribute to a better understanding of the application of the recovery plan framework.

408 Art. 10–14 and Section B of Annex to the BRRD. As of 1.1.2016, the European legislator enacted the SRMR, which, besides establishing the SRB, regulates the preparation of resolution plans (Art. 8–11). The SRMR created a double regime where national legislators already transposed the BRRD into national

the resolution authority[409]) are designed to predict possible crisis situations and resolution scenarios, and to prepare resolution measures so that banks and authorities can rely on a certain kind of preparedness in case such crisis situations actually occur.

The features of RRP imply that recovery and resolution planning could help to tackle the current lacks of the resolution framework *ex ante* a potential resolution decision. Planning in advance could enhance the credibility of resolution, as it renders resolution procedures and resolution actions more predictable and the complex institution more transparent. Moreover, it eliminates room for spontaneous acts out of necessity because resolution action is pre-planned and pre-defined. Additionally, within RRP, authorities will be granted the power to make changes to the institutions, thereby reducing complexity with adequate measures *ex ante*. Hence, RRP has the general potential of serving as a credibility-enhancing instrument, as it responds to the identified lack of *ex ante* credibility of resolution.[410]

---

law, such as in Germany. However, the European SRMR overrides national law. Furthermore, regulatory technical standards, such as the Commission Delegated Regulation (EU) 2016/1075 on RTS of Recovery and Resolution Plans, provide the legal basis for resolution planning (Art. 22–32). In 2016, the Commission issued *Commission Implementing Regulation (EU) 2016/1066 of 17 June 2016 laying down implementing technical standards with regard to procedures, standard forms and templates for the provision of information for the purpose of resolution plans for credit institutions and investment firms pursuant to Directive 2014/59/EU of the European Parliament and of the Council OJ L 181, 6.7.2016, p. 1–38*) (henceforth: Commission Implementing Regulation (EU) 2016/1066 on ITS on Resolution Plans) that transposed EBA, *Final Report - Draft implementing technical standards on procedures, forms and templates for the provision of information for resolution plans under Article 11(3) of Directive 2014/59/EU of the European Parliament and the Council EBA/ITS/2015/06* (2015) (henceforth: EBA Draft ITS on Resolution Plans).

409 The SRB will be in charge of drafting resolution plans for credit institutions in participating Member States, parent undertakings that are subject to consolidated supervision by the ECB in participating Member States, investment firms and financial institutions established in a Member State and subject to consolidated supervision by the ECB, and groups in accordance with Art. 6(4) of the SSM Regulation. The role of national resolution authorities (NRAs) in participating Member States remains the responsibility for all other institutions and groups under national laws, see for an overview Binder, 'Resolution Planning and Structural Bank Reform within the Banking Union', pp. 137 *et seq.*

410 For a detailed examination outlining the remedial features of RRP, see *infra* Part 3, A.I. – *The Potential of RRP to Enhance Credibility Ex Ante Resolution Decision.*

Credibility *Ex Post:* Loss-Absorbing Capital Requirements

The analysis of the current resolution-funding design revealed different shortcomings in the legal framework that ultimately lead to the loss of credibility in resolution financing. The main findings suggest that, due to a lack of sufficient private funding – induced by weak legislative design – and the possibility of exploiting exceptions for public-funds use, the pre-described burden-sharing cascade of the BRRD is channeled according to political considerations or personal interests.

A desideratum is to lower the incentives to resort to public funding in any form by increasing the success of the pre-determined burden-sharing mechanism laid down in the BRRD. This relates in particular to the enhancement of the bail-in tool that was identified as the key requirement for a viable resolution-financing framework. Current reservations about the bail-in tool could be countervailed if the consequences of sending an institution into resolution and the feared consequences associated with bail-in were to be eliminated or, at least, reduced to a level that would result in governments assigning more weight to the benefits of resolution than its negative consequences. The prerequisite for this, however, is the sufficiency of available bail-inable material.

A remedy for the aforementioned problem can be found in the newly-introduced instrument of LACRs. These are intended to bolster the available bail-inable instruments with explicit liabilities that can be easily bailed-in without causing undesirable consequences that would go beyond the mere loss of the respective claim. Furthermore, such liabilities, since they were openly designated as LACRs, would help investors to better price the risk associated with said liabilities, as they can better forecast the possibility and the extent to which such liabilities would be subject to bail-in. As a result, sparing these liabilities from bail-in is no longer needed or desired, resulting in a refrainment from public-funds exploitation. This can have a credibility-enhancing impact on the entire resolution framework in general and on the bail-in tool in particular, as it precisely targets and combats the identified *ex post* lacks.[411]

---

411 For a detailed examination outlining the remedial features of LACR, see *infra* Part 4, A.II. – *The Potential of LACR to Enhance Credibility Ex Post Resolution Decision*.

Result of Part 2

The preceding part has identified two problems that linger within the current bank resolution set-up, thereby deteriorating the credibility of the current resolution framework. To illustrate how the identified lacks have already impaired the credibility of the regime, it was outlined how the use of, and demand for, ELA has changed in recent years. The results serve as evidence supporting the initial hypothesis that the resolution regime itself is not credible and that the regime is also perceived to be lacking in credibility among market participants. Therefore, it has only served demonstrational purposes and will not be examined any further.

Regarding the two identified lacks, two potential remedies were discovered: recovery and resolution planning as an antidote to the *ex ante* problem; and boosting loss-absorbing capacities as an antidote to the *ex post* problem. It was found that, theoretically, both instruments serve their purpose of remedying the identified lacks. In the following parts, both instruments will be examined, detecting eventual shortcomings and problems inherent in both instruments. Part 3 deals with recovery and resolution planning, while Part 4 turns towards loss-absorbing capacities.

PART 3 – RECOVERY AND RESOLUTION PLANNING – IMPACTS ON CREDIBILITY

The Impact of Recovery and Resolution Planning on the Credibility of Bail-In

The following part tries to promote the idea of recovery and resolution planning as an antidote to the discussed *ex ante* problems and examines its impact on the credibility of resolution in general, and bail-in in particular. After briefly explaining the remedial character of recovery and resolution planning (I.), this section turns towards the possible shortcomings of recovery and resolution planning itself (II.).

The Potential of RRP to Enhance Credibility Ex Ante Resolution Decision

The following section will briefly outline the remedial character of recovery and resolution planning by pointing out selected features thereof based on their legal frameworks set out in Articles 5–14 BRRD. The following list is not exhaustive, but instead tries to indicate the remedial character of such planning.

Remedy for the Lack of Predictability

It was found that predictability lacks with respect to the initiation of resolution action, with respect to the application of resolution tools (especially bail-in), and with respect to the liabilities eligible for bail-in. Even though the resolution plan is not disclosed to the public – and therefore avoids consultation with market participants which might yield greater predictability – and also does not cover the decision as to whether an institution will be sent into resolution, it nevertheless does enhance predictability by introducing an institutional framework and by infusing the resolution process with specific underlying assumptions.

For example, Article 10(3) BRRD states that resolution planning shall not take for granted extraordinary public financial support, nor shall it assume any central bank emergency liquidity assistance, nor any other central-bank liquidity assistance provided under non-standard collateralization, tenor, and interest-rate terms. In addition, resolution authorities must stipulate in the plan how the resolution options could be financed without such support, Article 10(7)(i) BRRD. Moreover, the plan shall set out the amount required in terms of own funds and eligible liabilities to finance the application of the bail-in tool, Article 10(7)(o) BRRD.

These provisions prevent the unplanned use of public money as they provide a financing concept, thereby enhancing the probability of bail-in application. If a plan with pre-arranged financing concepts is available at a time when an institution is actually due to be resolved and the provided financing concept is reliable and reasonably bearable for all affected parties, resolution authorities, governments, and other decision-makers might be less reluctant to trigger resolution and apply resolution tools (especially loss-participation within the bail-in). Furthermore, for markets and stakeholders of the institution, the prospect of BRRD-compliant resolution procedures is more likely in the knowledge that a compliant plan exists, despite being uninformed explicitly about its content.

Regarding external influence, even though RRP might not eliminate the problem of political influence on resolution decisions, it can make the prospect of applying resolution procedures more palatable to decision-makers, as it illustrates the resolution process and sets out "what could happen in the worst case." Moreover, as the plan sets out the bail-inable liabilities, it can contribute to predictability with respect to the liabilities used for bail-in. If only suitable and non-controversial liabilities are considered, it would reduce *ad-hoc* deviation and discretion due to political interference after the resolution decision is taken. Consequently, recovery and resolution planning would enhance predictability.

Remedy for Complexity

Recovery planning, with regard to the complexity of banks' structures, can help to overcome opaqueness by including a range of scenarios of macroeconomic and financial stress relevant to the institution's specific conditions into the recovery plans, Article 5(6) BRRD. This measure can help employees and management to understand the institution's specific situation, thereby clarifying its structures.[412] In addition, through giving competent authorities the power to require an institution to maintain detailed records of financial contracts, Article 5(8) BRRD, institutions and

412 Cichy, Buchmüller and Igl, '§ 15 Sanierungs- und Abwicklungsplanung', p. 689.

authorities can disentangle parts of the bank's interconnectedness and sophistication with respect to its financial instruments. The competent authorities shall, when assessing the appropriateness of the recovery plans, take into consideration the appropriateness of the institution's capital and funding structure with regard to the level of complexity of the organizational structure and the risk profile of the institution, Article 6(3) BRRD. By implementing this provision, not only do the institutions gain an expanded insight into their structures, but the competent authority also benefits from the enlightening effect of setting up recovery plans. Furthermore, the possibility of delivering group recovery plans – which must include arrangements to ensure the coordination and consistency of measures to be taken at the level of the Union parent undertaking, the entitie's level, as well as measures to be taken at the level of subsidiaries and, where applicable, at the level of significant branches, Article 7(4) BRRD – helps understanding of the organizational structure of the group and might incentivize institutions to reduce the complexity caused by the involvement of numerous subsidiaries and branches. The requirement of identifying whether there are obstacles to the implementation of recovery measures within the group also enhances this effect, Article 7(6) BRRD.

In addition, resolution planning provides for complexity-reducing features. Article 10(7) BRRD, for example, states that the resolution plan shall set out the options for applying the resolution tools and resolution powers, and shall include a demonstration of how critical functions and core business lines could be legally and economically separated from other functions, Article 10(7)(c) BRRD; an assessment of resolvability, Article 10(7)(e) BRRD; a description of arrangements to ensure that the information required is up-to-date and accessible to resolution authorities at all times, Article 10(7)(h) BRRD; a detailed description of the different resolution strategies and critical interdependencies, Article 10(7)(j) and (k) BRRD; and a description of essential operations and systems to maintain the continuous functioning of the institution's operational process, Article 10(7)(q) BRRD. All of these features contribute to a better understanding of existing complex structures and might incentivize institutions to reduce complexity. Lastly, according to Article 10(8) BRRD, resolution authorities shall have the power to require institutions and their entities to maintain detailed records of financial contracts to which they are a party. This can be helpful in terms of sorting the financial obligations by which the institution is bound. By obliging the institution to maintain records of their financial contracts, an understanding of their complexity can be fostered. Having the possibility of setting up group resolution plans with the same requirements, Article 12 BRRD, also helps to understand the institution's specific structures. Additionally, group-wide cross-border resolution planning creates a window of opportunity for the introduction of a consistent legal regime for the coordinated resolution of cross-border institutions across jurisdictions, but especially within Europe,[413] thereby soothing jurisdictional differences and disparate approaches.

Overall, it can be said that both the particular features of recovery and resolution planning *and* the process of planning have a positive effect on institutions' complexity, as they gain a better understanding of their business and might be incentivized to take measures to reduce complexity on their own. Indeed, the positive side-effects of the planning process are frequently highlighted as one of the most valuable features of recovery and resolution planning.[414] In summary, RRP constitutes a viable remedy for current complexity issues.

Remedy for Missing Modification Measures

Some have been critical of no modification measures being at hand to alter complex structures before resolution procedures are initiated. This problem was redressed by recovery and resolution planning by the granting of powers to the competent and resolution authority to require changes within the institution with respect to, for example, existing business models, funding arrangements, and corporate or group structures. Therefore, the supervisory and resolution authorities could eventually decide to enforce greater consistency of business models, funding arrangements, and legal structures of individual firms and groups,[415] thus reducing complexity.

Already, during recovery planning, the competent authority can order changes in the institutions[416] by directing them to take measures (such

413 Avgouleas, Goodhart and Schoenmaker, 'Bank Resolution Plans as a catalyst for global financial reform', p. 214.

414 S. Dimova, *Resolution Planning: Too Complex to Work or Cornerstone of a Stable Financial Architecture?: The Perspective of Regulators*, SAFE/BaFin Conference (House of Finance, 2018); Weber, 'Structural regulation as antidote to complexity capture'.

415 Binder, 'Resolution Planning and Structural Bank Reform within the Banking Union', p. 140.

416 This approach was criticized by Philipp, who pointed out that shareholders might be deprived of the ability to exercise their rights over the management board and the supervisory board by having the competent and supervisory aut-

as reducing the risk profile, enabling recapitalization measures, reviewing strategy and structure, or making changes to funding strategy or to the governance structure) to remedy deficiencies or potential impediments identified in the recovery plan, Article 6(6) BRRD. Member States can further allow their competent authorities to take additional measures under national law.

Resolution planning, in turn, provides that the resolution authority shall identify any material impediments to resolvability and outline relevant actions for how those impediments could be addressed, Article 10(2) BRRD. If impediments are identified and the institution fails to propose adequate measures to address or remove the impediments, the resolution authority can require the institution to take alternative measures that may achieve the objective. These powers include, *inter alia*, measures such as: requiring the institution to revise intragroup financing arrangements or to review the absence thereof; the drawing-up of service agreements to cover critical functions, Article 17(5)(a) BRRD; requiring the institution to limit its maximum exposures, Article 17(5)(b) BRRD; requiring the institution to divest specific assets, Article 17(5)(d) BRRD; requiring the institution to limit or cease the carrying out of specific activities, Article 17(5)(e) BRRD; or restricting or preventing the development of new business lines or sales of products, Article 17(5)(f) BRRD. The most relevant provision in this respect, however, is Article 17(5)(g) to (k) BRRD, according to which the resolution authority is granted the power to re-arrange the institution's structure in different ways. The resolution authority, for example, can require changes to legal or operational structures of the institution, or any directly or indirectly controlled group entity, so as to reduce complexity when applying resolution tools, Article 17(5)(g) BRRD, or require the institution or parent undertaking to set up a parent financial holding company[417] in a Member State or a Union parent financial holding company,[418] Article 17(5)(h) BRRD.

---

hority establish its own management-board-like position, see W. Philipp, 'Systemänderung: Amputiertes Aktienrecht für Banken - Das Sanierungs- und Abwicklungsgesetz (SAG)', *Die Aktiengesellschaft* (2015), 77–82, p. 80.

417 Parent financial holding company in a Member State means a parent financial holding company in a Member State as defined in point (30) of Art. 4(1) of Regulation (EU) No 575/2013 (CRR).

418 Union parent financial holding company means an EU parent financial holding company as defined in point (31) of Art. 4(1) or Regulation (EU) No 575/2013 (CRR).

Consequently, the RRP provides powerful mechanisms for altering existing complex structures within institutions and, therefore, constitutes a remedy for the lack of modification measures *ex ante* resolution decision.

Identification of Possible Impediments to the Potential of Recovery and Resolution Planning

It has been demonstrated that recovery and resolution planning includes features that are potentially suitable for tackling the identified lacks pre-resolution. However, an enhancement of credibility through said instrument can only be credibly expected if the provisions of recovery and resolution planning are suitable, not only in theory but also in practice, and if recovery and resolution planning does not suffer from its own inherent impediments.

The following section, therefore, tries to shed light on impediments inherent in recovery and resolution planning. In doing so, it will precisely point out the individual impediments rather than offer only general criticism, thereby eventually contributing to finding suitable solutions afterwards.

Impediments Concerning Recovery and Resolution Planning

Both recovery and resolution plans are drawn up at the same stage and under similar circumstances, namely in a pre-crisis and pre-resolution environment. Consequently, they suffer to some extent from the same problems. Moreover, although the plans are drawn up by different parties, both the institution and the authorities find themselves in the same tenuous situation: while planning, the actual crisis is outside the range of vision and the institution in particular is encumbered with ongoing day-to-day tasks and business that requires most of their attention, resources, and workforce. In addition, both plans ultimately depend upon the information that the institution provides,[419] both in terms of quantity and quality. This is complemented by the fact that RRP was only recently

419 Cichy *et al.* even stated that in the context of resolution planning, the institution predominantly assumes the role of a sole information provider for the resolution authority, see Cichy, Buchmüller and Igl, '§ 15 Sanierungs- und Abwicklungsplanung', p. 719.

introduced among institutions and authorities,[420] hence the lack of experience and routine. As a result, recovery and resolution planning is prone to impediments, some of which are outlined in the following section.

Potential Divergences Between Authorities – Cross-Border Coordination

In the cross-border and multi-authority environment that characterizes financial markets, coordination is the key element of collective movements and joint projects. Consequently, as institutions usually operate across borders and are always under the remit of a number of authorities, coordination is also central to recovery and resolution planning.[421] Specifically, coordination is therefore required in the following two dimensions: vertically – between different authorities of the same jurisdiction (*e.g.* supervisory and resolution authorities);[422] and horizontally – between authorities in different jurisdictions (*e.g.* supervisory and resolution authorities across states).[423]

420 2019 is the first year in which the SRB had resolution plans for all banking groups under its remit, see König, *SRB Conference 2018 - 10 years after the crisis: are banks now resolvable?*

421 The strengthening of cross-border coordination and the reluctance of certain authorities to properly engage in the process were among the main topics at this year's annual SRB conference, see A. Enria, *SRB Conference 2018 - 10 years after the crisis: are banks now resolvable?*, SRB Annual Conference (Brussels, 2018) See also J.-H. Binder, 'Cross-border coordination of bank resolution in the EU: All problems resolved?', *European Company and Financial Review* 13 (2016), 575–98, pp. 580 *et seq.*; EBA, *EBA Final Draft Regulatory Technical Standards on the content of resolution plans and the assessment of resolvability EBA/RTS/2014/15* (2014), section 4.1.2.

422 Sometimes, other players such as ministries or central banks can be involved in vertical coordination as well.

423 *Commission Delegated Regulation (EU) 2016/1075 of 23 March 2016 supplementing Directive 2014/59/EU of the European Parliament and of the Council with regard to regulatory technical standards specifying the content of recovery plans, resolution plans and group resolution plans, the minimum criteria that the competent authority is to assess as regards recovery plans and group recovery plans, the conditions for group financial support, the requirements for independent valuers, the contractual recognition of write-down and conversion powers, the procedures and contents of notification requirements and of notice of suspension and the operational functioning of the resolution colleges OJ L 184, 8.7.2016, p. 1–71* (2016), Arts. 50 *et seq.* (henceforth: Commission Delegated Regulation (EU) 2016/1075 on RTS of Recovery and Resolution Plans).

In terms of vertical coordination, the planning process is distributed between at least two different parties.[424] While recovery planning is the responsibility of the institution and is supervised by the competent authority, resolution planning is assigned to the resolution authorities, Articles 5(1) and 10(1) BRRD. However, even if both authorities have their own area(s) of responsibility, both are obliged and encouraged to cooperate with each other while carrying out their tasks. For example, Article 6(4) BRRD states that the competent authority shall provide the recovery plan to the resolution authority, which the latter may examine and make recommendations to be re-laid to the competent authority regarding actions to remove impediments to resolution. Furthermore, the resolution authority shall consult the competent authority to draw up the resolution plan, Articles 8(2)(1), 9(2) SRMR. Such an approach is helpful, as it assists the resolution authority in laying the foundations for its own tasks, either by influencing the institution's organization, risk management, or business model during the recovery planning phase,[425] or by enabling institution-specific information to be reused and knowledge to be shared, thus saving resources. However, having two authorities acting in the process, conflicting opinions and interests can crop up[426] and consistency of planning could be hindered by contradictory views among the authorities, delaying the process or leading to semi-optimal compromises and trade-offs.

This situation is even more severe in the case of horizontal coordination, particularly in recovery and resolution planning for cross-border groups, where a large number of authorities and bodies at the national, EU, and non-EU level complicate the process.[427] Even though the main problem of cross-border coordination lies within the resolution planning process, coordination issues already arise in the course of recovery planning. With regard to recovery planning for groups, only the union parent undertaking

---

424 For an overview of resolution-related tasks and the division of responsibilities between supervision and resolution authorities based on the current BRRD framework, see World Bank Group, *Understanding Bank Recovery and Resolution in the EU: A Guidebook to the BRRD*, ch. 5, p. 48.

425 The even farther-reaching problem of authorities coordinating and agreeing on imposing changes to the institutions in the process of resolution, and especially recovery planning, is covered in a separate section, see *infra* under Part 3, A.II.3. – *The Problem with Modification Measures*.

426 For a general analysis that highlights how decision-makers in public administration are driven by personal motives such as power and prestige, see Niskanen, *Bureaucracy and representative government*, pp. 36 *et seq.*

427 Chen Chen, 'The Recovery Framework in the BRRD and its Effectiveness', p. 13.

is required to set up a plan,[428] with no subsidiaries of the group being subject to individual planning obligations. However, Article 8(1) BRRD requires the consolidated supervisor to review the submitted group recovery plan, together with the competent authorities of subsidiaries and significant branches. Furthermore, competent authorities emerging from the colleges of supervisors according to Article 116 CRD IV[429] shall be consulted. The parties must then reach a joint decision over the plan's adoption. Article 8 BRRD itself already provides for procedures and solutions for when a joint decision cannot be agreed upon. The problem here can be demonstrated by looking at the example of a cross-border group, namely Nordea.[430] Nordea is an integrated banking group with entities in, amongst other countries, Norway, Finland, Sweden, and Denmark. Each state has its own currency, while Finland is the only one that is part of the euro area. Norway is not part of the euro area but is part of the European Economic Area (EEA). Meanwhile, Sweden hosts the group's headquarters.[431] Even if the Nordic countries are among the most integrated groups internationally, they still have strongly diverging opinions on what tools should be applied in a crisis scenario or if government guarantees should be used.[432] Furthermore, competent authorities can take the view that a submitted recovery plan is insufficient because it is not substantiated by the provided information[433] or that a recovery plan on an individual basis

---

428 'Union parent' means an EU parent financial holding company as defined in point (31) of Art. 4(1) of Regulation (EU) No 575/2013 (CRR) or an EU parent mixed financial holding company as defined in point (33) of Art. 4(1) of Regulation (EU) No 575/2013.

429 European, *Directive 2013/36/EU of the European Parliament and of the Council of 26 June 2013 on access to the activity of credit institutions and the prudential supervision of credit institutions and investment firms, amending Directive 2002/87/EC and repealing Directives 2006/48/EC and 2006/49/EC, OJ L 176, 27.6.2013, p. 338–436.*

430 A similar scenario can be found with Erste Group, a banking group active in Central and Eastern Europe, comprising SSM countries such as Austria, Slovenia, or Slovakia, non-participating Member States such as Czech Republic, Hungary, Croatia, or Romania, and third countries such as Serbia.

431 Karamichailidou and Mayes, 'Plausible recovery and resolution plans for cross-border financial institutions', p. 40.

432 D. G. Mayes, 'Top-down restructuring of markets and institutions: The Nordic banking crises', *Journal of Banking Regulation* 18 (2017), 213–32.

433 The EBA, however, intends to redress the problem, that national competent or resolution authorities are dissatisfied and in doubt about the group-level competent or resolution authorities' information procurement, by introducing templates that constitute a minimum set of harmonized information to be shared by group-level authorities with the relevant national EU authorities,

shall be drawn up for some of the group's institutions. In the event of such a disagreement, and in the absence of a joint decision,[434] the consolidating supervisor is allowed to make its own decision with regard to the relevant matters, Article 8(3) BRRD. Even if it is obliged to take into account the views and reservations of the other competent authorities, at this point it will act and take decisions most likely in its own best interests according to what it deems appropriate. The competent authorities that fail to reach a joint decision can take their own decisions on that matter, either alone or in a joint decision on a group recovery plan covering only the group entities under their jurisdiction.[435]

Nevertheless, recovery planning poses less difficulties in this respect, mainly because the plan is drawn up in the institution and is only assessed by the authorities. In addition, inconsistent or deficient coordination at the recovery stage has less serious consequences for stakeholders and the economy, since recovery action has less impact on capital positions. As already indicated, cross-border coordination for resolution planning represents the core problem here. In resolution planning, coordination takes place in different fora according to the involved parties, such as Inter-

---

see EBA, *Consultation Paper for Draft Implementing Standards on the provision of information for the purpose of resolution plans under Article 11(3) of Directive 2014/59/EU EBA/CP/2017/15* , p. 6 retrievable at https://www.eba.europa.eu/documents/10180/2186621/Draft+ITS+on+the+provision+of+information+for+the+purpose+of+resolution+plans+%28EBA-ITS-2018-02%29.pdf accessed 1 October 2022.

434 Only after a four-month decision period between the consolidating supervisor and the competent authorities, and if the matter is not referred to the EBA by one of the competent authorities.

435 World Bank Group, *Understanding Bank Recovery and Resolution in the EU: A Guidebook to the BRRD*, p. 77.

nal Resolution Teams (ITRs), (European) Resolution Colleges, or Crisis Management Groups (CMGs)[436].[437]

The process for the assessment of recovery plans (*e.g.* joint decisions, mutual information and consideration) similarly applies to the adoption of group resolution plans, for example in Resolution Colleges. However, the process is more complex[438] and its outcome has a deeper impact. Disagreement, where joint decisions are required, could result in a banking group being fragmented under the scope of application of different resolution plans, depending on the discretion and willingness to cooperate among the different authorities involved. Disagreement can be reflected in the different changes that the respective authority can impose on the group's institutions under its jurisdiction during the recovery and resolution planning process, leaving behind a banking group that is a country-specific patchwork of differing exercises of powers by different authorities. Coordination problems, asset-allocation problems, and problems arising from applying different recovery or resolution measures within the same group are further consequences to bear in mind. In light of the interconnectedness of today's banking groups and the underlying endeavor to attain banking supervision and resolution at a superordinate level, fragmented recovery and resolution plans for the same group are not beneficial.

---

436 Home and key host authorities of all G-SIFIs should maintain CMGs with the objective of enhancing preparedness for, and facilitating the management and resolution of, a cross-border financial crisis affecting the firm. CMGs should include the supervisory authorities, central banks, resolution authorities, finance ministries, and the public authorities responsible for guarantee schemes of jurisdictions that are home or host to entities of the group that are material to its resolution, and should cooperate closely with authorities in other jurisdictions where firms have a systemic presence, see 8.1 of the FSBs *Key Attributes of Effective Resolution Regimes for Financial Institutions* (2014) retrievable at http://www.fsb.org/wp-content/uploads/r_141015.pdf accessed 1 October 2022.

437 When acting only within the Banking Union, the body responsible for resolution planning of a specific bank or group is the Internal Resolution Team (IRT). For resolution outside the Banking Union but within the European Union, such units are called Resolution Colleges. If only subsidiaries are located within the Banking Union and/or the European Union but the headquarters are located in a third country, the body responsible for resolution plan coordination is the European Resolution College. If a group has GSIBs inside the Banking Union and/or European Union as well as in a third country, the body responsible for resolution planning is the Crisis Management Group (CMG).

438 See, for example, the complicated process for joint decisions laid down in Arts. 61 – 96 of Commission Delegated Regulation (EU) 2016/1075 on RTS of Recovery and Resolution Plans.

But even leaving aside the extreme scenario of having dissenting views on resolution plans within a Resolution College resulting in different resolution plans for the same group, less extreme problems can arise out of impaired cross-border resolution planning that could impede the quality of the agreed plan. Besides current shortfalls in organizational aspects of Resolution College work and the level and quality of interaction within these colleges, massive impediments were detected regarding the deliverables a Resolution College has to present.[439] This might be traced back to the different 'mind-sets' of jurisdictions when it comes to resolution planning. While the attitude of certain jurisdictions towards resolution planning is aligned and ambitious (for example in most Central European Member States), peripheral[440] Member States or third countries participating in Resolution Colleges can conduct themselves differently with regard to resolution planning.[441] The EBA only recently recommended that all plans arising out of Resolution Colleges require improvements in key operational areas to implement the preferred resolution strategy (with respect to bail-in execution, funding and liquidity) and that such a lack can be traced back to participating host authorities not properly engaging in the process.[442] Further underlining this argument, the EBA figured that home and host authorities frequently presented different views on the assessment of critical functions within the same institution. This indicates that home authorities may not adequately consider both the specificities of host countries and their authorities' judgment in such matters, as a specific function can be critical in the country of the host authority not in the country of the home authority. Moreover, it seems that host authorities do not attach enough importance to their proper participation and involvement in the decision-making process, either because they feel like being passed over, or because they do not consider cross-border planning to be an essential task. Consequently, resolution plans of Resolution Colleges often

---

439 EBA, *EBA Report on the Functioning of Resolution Colleges in 2017*, Resolution Colleges Annual Report (2018) retrievable at https://www.eba.europa.eu/documents/10180/2087449/EBA+Report+on+the+functioning+of+resolution+colleges+-+July+2018.pdf accessed 1 October 2022.

440 A distinction between core, peripheral and neighborhood countries can be found in R. Haas, 'Recent Trends in Cross-Border Banking' in T. Beck and B. Casu (eds.), *The Palgrave Handbook of European Banking* (London: Palgrave Macmillan UK, 2016), pp. 475–97, p. 476.

441 Dimova, *Resolution Planning: Too Complex to Work or Cornerstone of a Stable Financial Architecture?*

442 EBA, *EBA Report on the Functioning of Resolution Colleges in 2017*, p. 11.

only focus on home country issues, frequently leaving material subsidiaries in host countries outside the scope of the plan.[443] The results presented by the EBA suggest that – even though they were only conducted in relation to Resolution College work – coordination at the horizontal level across borders, be it in IRTs, (European) Resolution Colleges, or CMGs, is still deficient under the current framework and leaves room for pursuing national interests, shirking, and passing over. Presumably, coordination worsens as the number of involved parties increases and as the number of parties located outside the EU increases too. A mechanism for information-sharing and proper inclusion of all parties within such fora is still not available.

With the above in mind, home competent authorities or home resolution authorities will always tend to influence decision in line with their own interests. Host authorities will block or dissent from decisions that would not give an advantage to the group's entities under their remit. In other cases, they might just shirk the issue and reduce their participation to a minimum. The presence of instruments such as Resolution Colleges, Cross-Border Stability Groups,[444] CMGs or institution-specific Cross-Border Cooperation Agreements (COAGs)[445] can help in setting-up uniform und conflict-free recovery and resolution plans through mutual information, cooperation, and consultation. However, it can be assumed that as long as authorities do not understand that cooperation in the interests of the group is also in their interests, and refrain from pursuing their own national interests, they will be less likely to act cooperatively.[446]

---

443 Ibid., p. 11.

444 A Cross-Border Stability Group is a group which involves all relevant parties from different Member States with the objective of enhancing preparedness in normal times and which may facilitate the management and resolution of a cross-border financial crisis, see *Memorandum of Understanding on Cooperation between the Financial Supervisory Authorities, Central Banks and Finance Ministries of the European Union on Cross-Border Financial Stability* , p. 3 retrievable at https://www.ecb.europa.eu/pub/pdf/other/mou-financialstability2008en.pdf accessed 1 October 2022.

445 For all G-SIFIs, at a minimum, institution-specific cooperation agreements, containing the essential elements set out in Annex I of the Key Attributes of Effective Resolution Regimes for Financial Institutions, should be in place between the home and relevant host authorities that need to be involved in the planning and crisis resolution stages, see 9.1 of the FSBs *Key Attributes of Effective Resolution Regimes for Financial Institutions*.

446 E. Hüpkes, 'Lines of defense against systemic crises: Resolution.' in G. Caprio and P. Bacchetta (eds.), *Handbook of safeguarding global financial stability: Politi-*

Protection of Own Markets, Market Players and Depositors

The above discourse is a direct outflow of the problem that national governments, authorities, and institutions are naturally inclined to protect what is closest to them: their own financial market, resident market participants, and domestic depositors. When setting up recovery and resolution plans, this could become a problematic issue. In particular, when planning for groups, the diverging interests of involved players might impede effective drafting.[447] This tendency can appear in different forms. In some cases, a single institution could pursue its own interests by furnishing the recovery plan with beneficial information in order to protect its own investors or clients. The competent authority in charge of assessing the plan might not be in a position to detect influence in this respect. In other cases, national competent authorities or resolution authorities can follow such intentions when negotiating and setting up group recovery and resolution plans in Resolution Colleges, and thus protect their national entities. Although authorities are obliged to take into account the possible repercussions of their policy decisions, a natural bias towards protecting their own markets, resident market players, and depositors could prove persistent in the actual planning reality.[448] Tendencies in this respect have been observed during the insolvency proceedings of Dexia[449] and Fortis[450] groups.

---

cal, social, cultural, and economic theories and models (London, Waltham, MA: Academic Press, 2013).

447 J.-H. Binder, 'Gleichung mit (zu?) vielen Unbekannten: Nachhaltige Bankenstrukturen durch Sanierungs- und Abwicklungsplanung?', *Zeitschrift für Bankrecht und Bankwirtschaft* 27 (2015), 153–65, p. 156; P. Cavelaars, J. de Haan, P. Hilbers and B. Stellinga, *Key Challenges for Financial Supervision after the Crisis* (2013), p. 19, retrievable under https://www.wrr.nl/publicaties/publicaties/2013/06/12/key-challenges-for-financial-supervision-after-the-crisis-71; also in the context of supervision T. H. Tröger, 'Effective Supervision of Transnational Financial Institutions', *Texas International Law Journal* 48 (2012), 177–221, pp. 214 *et seq.*; G. B. Navetti, G. Calzolari and A. F. Pozzolo, 'Bail-in, up to a point' in G. B. Navetti, G. Calzolari and A. F. Pozzolo (eds.), *European Economy: Banks, Regulation, and the Real Sector* (Rome: Europeye, 2016), pp. 9–33, p. 25.

448 Binder, 'Resolution Planning and Structural Bank Reform within the Banking Union', p. 138.

449 For the Dexia case see R. Wiggins, N. Tente and A. Metrick, *European Banking Union D: Cross-Border Resolution – Dexia Group*, Yale Program on Financial Stability Case Study 2014-5D-V1 (2015).

450 For the Fortis case see Wiggins, Tente and Metrick, *European Banking Union C: Cross-Border Resolution – Fortis Group*.

Planning as an Inconvenient Standard Exercise – Adding More Complexity

One considerable feature of recovery and resolution planning is that the planning process is extremely challenging, both for the institutions and for the authorities in charge. It requires extensive paperwork, tremendous internal organizational efforts, and a massive amount of information.[451] This is unsurprising considering the demands placed by recovery and resolution planning on the institution and the exhaustive and elaborate character of the plans. Such enormous demands could overstrain and thereby dull competent planners in institutions and authorities. Planning could be regarded as a necessary but burdensome deliverable that will not be scrutinized. Confirmation of such a presumption amongst planners could be derived from the frequency with which recovery and resolution plans are utilized: the ratio of plans actually used to the ones prepared is small.[452] Together with the underestimation of their importance, as recovery and resolution plans are relatively new and therefore not entirely present in the minds of industry players, the scarce use of plans might induce planners to allocate less care and value to the planning process.

Even though this might apply to resolution-authority employees too, the main problem lies in the drafting of recovery plans and the provision of information for the resolution plan by the institution's employees. For the most part, employees entrusted with recovery planning are not hired for the special purpose of setting up recovery plans, but are imposed with an extra task alongside their regular work.[453] Even though the core team[454] that is operationally responsible for drafting the recovery plan and providing the information for the resolution plan in its capacity as 'contact person' to the authorities is usually small, a number of other departments and employees are involved in information-providing, information-gathering, and other ancillary tasks. As the information for both recovery and resolution planning originate in the institutions themselves, it is of

---

451 EBA Draft ITS on Resolution Plans, p. 11.

452 Recently, there was only one prominent case in which the resolution plan was – partly – used and transposed into a resolution concept. After the ECB declared Banco Popular as 'failing or likely to fail' on 6 June 2017, the SRB decided on a resolution concept on 7 June 2017, which was approved by the European Commission on the same day.

453 Cichy, Buchmüller and Igl, '§ 15 Sanierungs- und Abwicklungsplanung'.

454 In the German context, such core teams are referred to as "Sanierungsplan-Kernteams", see ibid., p. 707.

the utmost importance that the initially generated information is correct and conscientiously generated. However, it appears that an institution's internal planners, due to the highly demanding nature of requests, might be inaccurate and opportunistic[455] when accumulating information and incorporating it into the recovery plan, thereby possibly underestimating the relevance of the plans.

This behavior is intensified by the sheer magnitude of recovery plans demanded by the competent authority. In terms of the size of a standard recovery plan for smaller institutions that do not fall under the scope of simplified obligations according to Article 4 BRRD, the volume tends to comfortably surpass 100 pages. Meanwhile, bigger and systemically important institutions or groups are expected to deliver a volume exceeding 1000 pages.[456] This can lead to planners losing track of the process and the inadequate accumulation of information, that is rather thoughtlessly processed into the recovery plan. When the time comes to update the recovery plan, such information might simply be recycled by the planners in charge without actually assessing which information is (still) relevant or up-to-date. Hoarding massive amounts of partially irrelevant or old information and exposing this in the recovery plans may actually add to complexity in recovery scenarios instead of reducing it.[457]

---

455 One backstop to institutions' employees excessively providing wrong information can be found in the RTS's specifying of the content of recovery plans, where it is required that the information on governance shall contain a detailed description of how the recovery plan was developed, as well as the role and function of persons responsible for preparing, implementing, and updating each section of the plan, and the identity of the person who has the overall responsibility for the plan, see Art. 5 of Commission Delegated Regulation (EU) 2016/1075 on RTS of Recovery and Resolution Plans. Such documentation shall be carried out via Word, Excel, or through the use of an IT-Tool, see ibid., p. 708. The requirement that incorporates a "name-and-shame" element into the planning process might entice biased or opportunistic behavior on the part of employees.

456 Ibid., p. 707.

457 See Thole, 'Bank Crisis Management and Resolution', p. 8. Thole even stated that it is rumored that the corresponding American counterpart, the living wills of some American institutions, "could fill a shipping container." The same is said of UK recovery plans, which could easily fill thousands of pages, see Cichy, Buchmüller and Igl, '§ 15 Sanierungs- und Abwicklungsplanung', pp. 707 *et seq.* If this is true, one can imagine how unwieldly the application of a recovery plan in distress will be and how such an extensive plan may actually add to complexity, rather than reduce it. Thomas M. Hoenig, Vice Chairman of the Federal Deposit Insurance Corporation (FDIC), makes the same observation:

Furthermore, the resolution authority sometimes obliges institutions to deliver information for, or set up parts of, the resolution plan themselves.[458] In doing so, the resolution authority 'outsources' parts of the resolution planning. The procedure is then comparable with the situation during the setting-up of recovery plans.[459] Consequently, as both plans are directly edited by the institution, they both suffer from the same planning inadequacies. The problem is aggravated by the extraordinary nature of information that is requested for the resolution plan.[460]

If, then, the recovery or resolution plan is needed in times of distress or crisis, what may be worse than having no plan at all would be having all responsible parties confidently rely on an incorrect plan that does not accurately reflect the institution's reality. The possibilities for authorities to counteract internal planning inadequacies and thereby prevent the spillover of superfluous, old, or falsely-generated information into the resolution plan, are limited. Recovery plans are among the main sources

"Unfortunately, based on the material so far submitted, in my view each plan being discussed today is deficient and fails to convincingly demonstrate how, in failure, any one of these firms could overcome obstacles to entering bankruptcy without precipitating a financial crisis. Despite the thousands of pages of material these firms submitted, the plan provide no credible or clear path through bankruptcy that doesn't require unrealistic assumptions and direct or indirect public support", see statement by T. M. Hoenig, *Credibility of the 2013 Living Wills Submitted by First Wave Filers* (2014) retrievable at https://www.fdic.gov/news/news/speeches/spaug0514a.html accessed 1 October 2022; P. Lippe, J. Putnis, D. M. Katz and I. Hurst, *How smart resolution planning can help banks improve transparency, increase profitability and reduce risk* (2015), retrievable at SSRN https://ssrn.com/abstract=2623027 accessed 1 October 2022.

458 S. Schelo and A. Steck, 'Das Trennbankengesetz: Prävention durch Bankentestamente und Risikoabschirmung', *Zeitschrift für Bankrecht und Bankwirtschaft* (2013), 227–43, p. 234; Cichy, Buchmüller and Igl, '§ 15 Sanierungs- und Abwicklungsplanung', p. 723. On the other hand, Engelbach/Friedrich are of the opinion that the duty of cooperation and provision of information is limited to already-existing information and analysis. This, in turn, would limit the impact of the institution to almost only the recovery plan and its information, see S. Engelbach and T. Friedrich, 'Die Umsetzung der BRRD in Deutschland: WM 2015 Heft 14, 662', *Zeitschrift für Wirtschafts- und Bankrecht* (2015), 662–71.

459 This approach is similar to the one applied in the US, where the resolution plan (or living will) is always drafted by the institution, see Schelo and Steck, 'Das Trennbankengesetz: Prävention durch Bankentestamente und Risikoabschirmung', p. 235.

460 In contrast with recovery plan information, which is frequently already available within the institution due to supervisory reporting or internal controlling, resolution plan information must be specially retrieved.

of information for the authorities, and due to the prevailing information asymmetry between institutions and authorities, the latter cannot do much to guarantee the appropriateness of information.

Moreover, monitoring of any kind is not provided for in either the BRRD or in the recovery plan RTS.[461] Besides Article 6 BRRD, the only review mechanism is presented in Articles 16 to 19 of the recovery plan RTS, which deals with the assessment of recovery plans by the competent authority.[462] While Article 16 is about the assessment of the completeness of recovery plans, Article 17 covers the quality of recovery plans. It is noticeable that the assessment is predominantly of a formal rather than a material nature, as the review process does not assess the correctness of the provided information. The assessment described in Article 18 (adequacy of recovery options to sustainably overcome a crisis) and Article 19 (swift and effective application of the recovery plan in financial distress) are to some extent of a material nature, however, since they only consider the delivered data, they do not contribute to verifying data at source. To the ensure that a material, qualitative examination is carried out, the competent authority is set a massive analytical task.[463] Therefore, the assessment primarily consists of an analysis to determine whether the provided information is complete, clear, understandable, relevant, comprehensive, and consistent. Such assessment, however, is carried out only with respect to the present information provided by the institution and only with regard to the submitted Excel templates,[464] but never with respect to all available information within the institution. The provided information can be incorrect in each of these elements (*i.e.* even when information is complete, clear, understandable, relevant, comprehensive, and consistent, it can still be incorrect) and can still pass the assessment process. Therefore, resolution plans and especially recovery plans run the danger of adding more complexity to the system.

---

461 Commission Delegated Regulation (EU) 2016/1075 on RTS of Recovery and Resolution Plans.

462 As part of the assessment by the competent authority, the recovery plan is further examined by the internal auditing unit of the institution as well as by the institution's external auditors as part of their annual review.

463 Cichy, Buchmüller and Igl, '§ 15 Sanierungs- und Abwicklungsplanung', p. 714.

464 Since 2016, the ECB uses Excel templates for their directly supervised institutions when assessing the recovery plan. Therefore, the ECB will only examine whether the information provided in the templates (formally) fulfils the assessment criteria.

Drawing-up of Plans Takes Place in Times of Stability – Optimism Bias

Another problem that obstructs optimal planning *ex ante* is optimism bias. Recovery plans, as well as resolution plans, are drawn up in times of financial stability. That means that relevant choices must be made *ex ante*, and that crucial and fundamental strategies and relevant policy decisions will have to be made at the pre-crisis stage rather than at the point when the institution or group is at the edge of resolution or even in resolution.[465] It is possible that, in such a situation, future crisis scenarios will be underestimated and, in turn, the effect of resolution measures will be overestimated.

Institutions in particular might be affected by such optimism bias and will be reserved when setting up a recovery plan. It is possible that institutions will be inclined to paint an overly optimistic picture of their current condition, either because they do not believe that they will ever get into financial distress or because they do not want to reveal an unflattering reality. If their own assessment turns out to be too negative and the controlling supervisory authority finds the proposed, often low-impact measures inadequate in terms of achieving recovery of a bank in a potential situation of distress, it might impose instructions and requirements[466] on the institution. Furthermore, by disclosing weaknesses of the institution in recovery plans, it could be interpreted that its management is performing badly, which is why the management might opt to be optimistic in recovery planning. In addition, if an institution is subject to measures taken by the supervisory or resolution authority, this might send negative signals to the market.

Determining whether information is not excessively optimistic and whether the submitted plan is accurate can prove difficult for the authorities, and deviations from reality cannot be detected in most cases.[467] Therefore,

465 Binder, 'Resolution Planning and Structural Bank Reform within the Banking Union', pp. 132 *et seq.*

466 The competent authority may "take any measures it considers to be necessary and proportionate, taking into account the seriousness of the deficiencies and impediments and the effect of the measures on the institution's business", Art. 6(6) BRRD. Although a list of possible measures is attached to that paragraph, it is clearly stated that this list is without prejudice and that any measure can be taken. Such measures could therefore also, *inter alia*, affect management positions. For another reason for refraining from delivering too pessimistic recovery plans, see Thole, 'Bank Crisis Management and Resolution', p. 8.

467 Ibid., p. 8.

recovery plans run the risk of being too optimistic and, in an actual crisis scenario, being inadequate to recover the institution. As information from the recovery plan and the biased information from institutions constitute major parts of resolution planning information, the optimism bias problem carries over to the resolution plan.

Costliness of Recovery and Resolution Plans

Recovery and resolution plans are costly to prepare both for the institutions[468] and the authorities[469] and, to a certain extent, the costs vary in relation to the complexity of the underlying legal and operational structures.[470] The costs stem mostly from the additional workforce needed to find, collect, prepare, process, and deliver necessary information and data. This includes the creation and maintenance of IT systems, the operation of information flows through the institution, the gathering and composition of information and data, and various other internal processes. However, substantial costs are also expected during the implementation phase that is still ongoing.[471] While parts of the information and data needed for re-

---

468 The EBA expects the industry to cover costs only for resolution planning processes in a range between 600 000 euros and 29 million euros, with an expected average between 1.8 and 17.9 million euros, see EBA Draft ITS on Resolution Plans. The large differences in the estimated costs show that even the EBA is incapable of foretelling the actual costs that the industry is obliged to bear while providing the resolution authorities with the needed information for resolution planning.

469 Data published in Germany indicate that the costs incurred by authorities in drawing up a resolution plan can be estimated at over 34 000 euros per firm, plus costs for *ex ante* resolvability assessments and annual *ex post* resolvability assessments of 14 500 euros. Additional costs associated with colleges' activities for an institution are about 6 500 euros, see *Gesetzesentwurf der Bundesregierung - Entwurf eines Gesetzes zur Abschirmung von Risiken und zur Planung der Sanierung und Abwicklung von Kreditinstituten und Finanzgruppen, Drucksache 17/12601 vom 04. 03. 2013* . For data regarding other Member States see table 1 .and 2, pp. 34, 36 of EBA, *EBA Final Draft Regulatory Technical Standards on the content of resolution plans and the assessment of resolvability EBA/RTS/2014/15* In light of the increasing demands on resolution planning, the costs may be higher than estimated in 2014.

470 EBA, *Guidelines on the range of scenarios to be used in recovery plans EBA/GL/2014/06* (2014), p. 14.

471 The costs arise from the "new processes and, in consideration to this, compliance costs could arise for both institutions and resolution authorities. However,

covery planning already exist because of supervisory reporting or internal bank governance and auditing, the data and information requested by the resolution authorities in the context of resolution planning are extremely specific and therefore not easily available. As the institution grows and becomes more complex, the task of collecting the needed resolution data becomes more difficult and more expensive.

An example of such costliness is the description and simulation of different crisis scenarios and the measures to be taken in case of the respective scenarios. Not only does this specific task require the procurement of various information and data, it also requires the simulation and analysis of an unknown future. The perception of data and information pertaining to future scenarios is even more difficult and costly than the already-complex analysis and provision of available data and information. Furthermore, although there are a number of pre-defined scenarios that must be covered,[472] due to the costliness of simulation and the decision to transfer the responsibility for selection of relevant crisis scenarios to the institutions,[473] the modeling and design of sub-scenarios will be limited[474] and selected scenarios will probably not be tested exhaustively (known as "walkthrough"[475]). This may result in sub-scenarios being left out. If, however, the omitted scenario happens to occur or if the actual scenario differs from those included in the plan, the usefulness of the plan is questionable.[476]

---

most of the costs would be one-off costs resulting from the implementation of the new reporting processes", see EBA, *Draft final report - Draft Implementing Standards on the provision of information for the purpose of resolution plans under Article 11(3) of Directive 2014/59/EU EBA/ITS/2018/02* (2018), p. 32.

472 The Guidelines require the description of at least three scenarios of severe macroeconomic and financial distress to ensure the coverage of a system-wide event, an idiosyncratic event, and a combination of system-wide and idiosyncratic events. G-SIIs and other systemically important institutions (O-SIIs) should include at least four scenarios, see EBA, *Guidelines on the range of scenarios to be used in recovery plans EBA/GL/2014/06*.

473 Ibid., p. 13.

474 Franke, Krahnen and Lüpke, *Effective Resolution of Banks: Problems and Solutions*, p. 8.

475 A "walkthrough" or stress analysis is considered to be the calculation and description of consequences of the different options for actions in the respective scenarios, see Cichy, Buchmüller and Igl, '§ 15 Sanierungs- und Abwicklungsplanung', p. 709.

476 Even respondents to the consultation in the run-up to the RTS on recovery planning proposed not to stick to certain supervisor-defined scenarios that are unlikely to be the real scenario that the institution would actually face, see *EBA*

The same is true for the selection of recovery plan indicators, Article 9 BRRD, and the corresponding options for action. While the average number of delivered indicators during the first round of recovery planning was around five (and the average options for action amounted to 21), the authorities today require institutions to provide at least 15 recovery plan indicators,[477] proportionally raising the amount of options for action. This again triggers costs and consumes resources, perhaps leading institutions to try to avoid such costs through shirking or sloppy planning. As long as the costs for preparing recovery and resolution plans are higher than the experienced benefits for the financial institution, a danger persists that the institution will try to cut costs by delivering information and data of inferior quality.

Predictability of the Actual Crisis Scenario at Some Future Date

Another issue in the process of RRP is the unpredictability of the actual crisis scenario.[478] Even if the institution or group itself can draw up an appropriate plan with reasonable crisis scenarios, the dynamic nature of financial markets will inevitably make it impossible to cover every feature of any possible crisis scenario[479]. Scenarios that do not seem very likely at the time of planning may actually occur because of unforeseen developments in the financial market or other global developments. Such a disparity between the planned and the actual crisis scenario was observed in the resolution case of Banco Popular Español, S.A., which was resolved in the

---

final draft Regulatory Technical Standards on the content of recovery plans under Article 5(10) of Directive 2014/59/EU establishing a framework for the recovery and resolution of credit institutions and investment firms: EBA/RTS/2014/11 (2014), p. 38, response (4).

477 The raised amount of recovery plan indicators is not necessarily accompanied by increased quality in the recovery plan. Critics have claimed that the selection of indicators is insufficient and without reference to the specific institution. Furthermore, indicators are not qualitative and forward-orientated, see Cichy, Buchmüller and Igl, '§ 15 Sanierungs- und Abwicklungsplanung', p. 711.

478 It has even been suggested that it is doubtful whether large cross-border banks could produce recovery and resolution plans that are credible and do not require public support, as they relate to periods of great stress that were not adequately predicted, see Karamichailidou and Mayes, 'Plausible recovery and resolution plans for cross-border financial institutions', p. 39.

479 World Bank Group, *Understanding Bank Recovery and Resolution in the EU: A Guidebook to the BRRD*, p. 76.

summer of 2017. The resolution procedure that was finally adopted varied significantly from the one initially planned. The 2016 resolution plan[480] assumed that the institution's failure would be associated with a deterioration of its capital position. However, the situation evolved differently and the events leading to its failure were not related to its capital position but instead to its inability to pay its debts or other liabilities in the future (*i.e.* to its liquidity position).[481] The initially planned application of the bail-in tool, as provided by the 2016 resolution plan, was rejected, as the resolution authority was unsure if it would effectively address the liquidity situation of the institution like it would have done in a scenario where the institution's capital position did indeed decline.[482]

Even though extreme 'black swan' events rarely happen, minor changes and deviations from the predicted crisis scenario can also have a major effect on the plans if the change is radical enough, such as the collapse of a certain market, a specific country, or a connected institution. Therefore, no matter how well-prepared and thought-out these plans are upfront, they most likely can never be considered 'blueprints' for future action.[483]

Besides the problem of predicting the actual crisis scenario at some future date, recovery and especially resolution planning require a massive legal analytical effort. Given the example of the resolution authorities' determination of resolution strategies, the identification of the preferred resolution strategy requires a prospective assessment and prognosis of all legal issues (*e.g.* if and how the legally-prescribed resolution instruments can be applied to the respective institution in a permitted and appropriate way in times of crisis). This means that all legal problems in the context of the application of the respective resolution instrument and strategy to the respective institution must be anticipated, weighted, assessed, and sometimes resolved well in advance, namely at the time of the plan being

480 Single Resolution Board, *Banco Popular Group Resolution Plan* (2016) retrievable at https://srb.europa.eu/sites/srbsite/files/bpe_2016_resolution_plan_updated_on_30_10_2018.pdf accessed 1 October 2022.

481 The case of Spain's Banco Popular demonstrates perfectly why liquidity in resolution is such a major component in an effective resolution regime and why ELA – even though originally designed for solvent institutions – is repeatedly considered in relation to resolution, see *supra* Part 2, A.II.4. – *Quod Erat Demonstrandum: Emergency Liquidity Assistance.*

482 Single Resolution Board, *Decision of the Single Resolution Board concerning the adoption of a resolution scheme in respect of Banco Popular Espanol, S.A.*, p. 9.

483 Binder, 'Resolution Planning and Structural Bank Reform within the Banking Union', p. 130.

prepared.[484] Thinking about the quickly-changing legal environment in the finance and banking field, combined with the equally quickly-changing institutions' structures and activities, such legal analysis, conducted months or even years before application, contributes to the problem of the predictability of the actual crisis scenario.[485]

Impermanence of Banks' Structures and the Topicality of Recovery and Resolution Plans

In addition to the unpredictability of the actual crisis scenario owing to the development and dynamics of financial markets, a similar problem emerges within institutions. Not only is the financial market volatile, but the institutions also find themselves in constant movement. This can be exemplified by looking at the far-reaching and nested structure of banking groups and their subsidiaries, branches, and other non-financial entities. Such structures are less of a static formation and more of a moving construction, with entities being shut down or established for tax reasons and due to the development and rise of new markets or new business models. In addition, assets can be moved around within the group.[486]

Especially in the days before a recovery plan or resolution plan kicks in, there is a rush of reorganization as the group tries to avoid entering the recovery or resolution.[487] Although the institution or group is required to update the recovery plan after a change to the legal or organizational structure of the institution, or its business or financial situation, Article 5(2) BRRD, and although the authority should review the resolution plan after being promptly notified by the institution and the competent authorities that any material changes to the legal or organizational structure of the institution or to its business or financial position has occurred,

484 Cichy, Buchmüller and Igl, '§ 15 Sanierungs- und Abwicklungsplanung', p. 728.

485 On the other side, it is argued that an approximate plan – be it with regard to the crisis scenario or legal issues – is still better than no plan at all. For further discussion of this view, see *infra* under Part 5, A.I. – *Is Improvement of Recovery and Resolution Planning Necessary at All?*

486 V. de Serière, 'Recovery and Resolution Plans of Banks in the Context of the BRRD and the SRM: Some Fundamental Issues' in D. Busch and G. Ferrarini (eds.), *European Banking Union* (Oxford: Oxford Univ Press, 2015), part III, ch. 10, chs. 10.03, 10.23.

487 Karamichailidou and Mayes, 'Plausible recovery and resolution plans for cross-border financial institutions', p. 49.

Article 10(6) BRRD, it seems unlikely that short-term changes and hectic reorganization would be accommodated in the recovery and resolution plans.

Opaque Data Production and Collection Process – Templates

Perhaps the most fundamental problem lingering around recovery and resolution planning is the difficulty related to the gathering of requested data to equip the plans with information. The availability and accuracy of data is the most relevant key prerequisite for the success of planning endeavors.[488] Unlike problems concerning the behavior of planners, the present issue is a factual problem that has its roots in the complexity of institutions, their outdated IT infrastructure (see *supra* Part 2, A.II.1.b. *Complexity in Bank Structures*) and the unstable recovery and resolution data-collection mechanisms currently in place. Recent inititatives to tackle the existing problems, such as the EBA's draft ITS of the provision of information for the purpose of resolution plans,[489] imply that much work remains to be done in this field.[490]

In this respect, it is crucial to understand that all information, whether for the recovery plan or the resolution plan, originates from the institution itself.[491] The institution decides which information is revealed to the market and how;[492] it is nearest to the necessary data and most familiar with it and its particularities. In addition, owing to already-existing structures and databases, it is cheapest for the institution to obtain the necessary da-

488 The EBA states that "collecting relevant and accurate information on institutions is crucial in order for resolution authorities to draw up resolution plans, substantiate their resolvability assessment and their resolution strategy", see EBA, *Draft final report - Draft Implementing Standards on the provision of information for the purpose of resolution plans under Article 11(3) of Directive 2014/59/EU EBA/ITS/2018/02*, p. 3, Executive Summary.

489 EBA, *Draft final report – Draft Implementing Standards on the provision of information for the purpose of resolution plans under Article 11(3) of Directive 2014/59/EU EBA/ITS/2018/02* (2018)..

490 See the extensive responses to the consultation by respondents, ibid., pp. 36–48.

491 This fact and associated problems were just recently acknowledged and stressed by König, *SRB Conference 2018 - 10 years after the crisis: are banks now resolvable?*.

492 Even though there are various reporting requirements such as annual financial statements or regulatory reporting, the information is only disclosed by the institution as the primary source of information itself and not 'taken out' by an investigating authority.

ta.[493] Therefore, resolution authorities, as provided by Article 10(5) BRRD, require institutions to assist them in the drawing-up and updating of the resolution plans.[494] This means that the institution is primarily responsible for providing information both in recovery as well as in resolution planning. While for recovery planning the institutions can be built on lessons learned during the crisis years, earlier times of difficulty, or existing supervisory reporting requirements, institutions often enter unknown territory when preparing the deliverables for the resolution authorities to support the development of a resolution plan.[495] Deliverables to the resolution authority represent a new kind of information that is not readily available at the institution. Moreover, the institution might be lacking the necessary technical means to collect and process the respective data.[496] This means that the institution might be overburdened by the requirements of resolution planning,[497] not only within the institution, but also in the context of the resolution authorities.[498]

493 Cichy, Buchmüller and Igl, '§ 15 Sanierungs- und Abwicklungsplanung', p. 710.

494 EBA, *Consultation Paper for Draft Implementing Standards on the provision of information for the purpose of resolution plans under Article 11(3) of Directive 2014/59/EU EBA/CP/2017/15*, p. 4.

495 See, for example, the EBA complaining that the quality of presentations by banks in Resolution Colleges is too low, as the bank's representatives could not answer the relevant questions of Resolution College participants and that banks often use only generic investor information to present to Resolution Colleges, see EBA, *EBA Report on the Functioning of Resolution Colleges in 2017*, p. 10; see also speech of Richard van Tilborgh, *Managing Information and Data Requests for Recovery & Resolution*, European Recovery and Resolution Plan Summit (Frankfurt am Main, 2016).

496 Only recently, the SRB stressed that "banks should ensure that they have the necessary IT processes in place to facilitate a timely, controlled and robust reporting process generating consistent and reliable results", see https://srb.europa.eu/en/content/liability-data-report accessed 1 October 2022.

497 An EBA survey conducted in the spring of 2017 amongst resolution authorities revealed that they had trouble with, or had been alerted by, the institutions under their jurisdiction whereby the requested templates were too difficult to be filled-in by banks. It was reported that banks were not really in a position to, for example, identify critical functions or critical counterparties as part of the respective template without further guidance, see EBA, *Consultation Paper for Draft Implementing Standards on the provision of information for the purpose of resolution plans under Article 11(3) of Directive 2014/59/EU EBA/CP/2017/15*, p. 28.

498 Richard van Tilborgh, *Managing Information and Data Requests for Recovery & Resolution*.

This 'new-kind-of-information' problem can be illustrated by considering the methods and internal schedules for planning and planning assistance within institutions[499] that give insight into what information is sought and how the institutions react to such requests. In this regard, the methods and internal schedules for recovery and resolution planning differ significantly.

Recovery Planning Process – Building Blocks

An institution's recovery planning process is divided into several building blocks. These include, *inter alia*, an analysis section (with a strategic analysis of the business model and strategy, the operational and legal structure, and a scenario analysis), different plans (the recovery plan itself, a monitoring plan, and a maintenance plan), and a tooling section (containing the description of recovery options, communication measures, monitoring metrics, and operational stability measures). The information and data required for the development and maintenance of the different building blocks is frequently present in the institution, as the main parts of the needed input are common data used also for regulatory reporting and everyday activities. In addition, data and procedures might already be known from earlier times of crisis or even as part of other, existing, internal crisis and contingency plans. This creates synergies, reduces maintenance efforts, and prevents inconsistencies. Considering that recovery data and information are not only needed and produced to meet recovery planning requirements but sometimes already exist, the chances are that such information and data are of a higher quality.

Resolution Planning Process – Building Blocks

In contrast, the resolution planning building blocks are more specific. These include, besides a strategic analysis of critical functions and material

499 The following section is based on ING's internal recovery and resolution planning processes as presented by Richard van Tilborgh on the Recovery and Resolution Plan Summit in Frankfurt am Main in June 2016, see ibid. Although schemes for recovery and resolution planning might vary to a certain extent from institution to institution, the present framework for the internal planning process can be deemed representative, as each institution must fulfil similar requirements.

entities, the preferred resolution strategy (SPE or MPE, hybrid approach, and initial impediments to the preferred resolution strategy), continuity considerations (development of processes to ensure continuity of critical functions during resolution; bail-in, funding and liquidity requirements implied by the resolution strategy; and access to financial market infrastructures), and a resolvability assessment.[500] Such information is highly specific and usually not readily available at the institution. Firstly, such information and data depend largely on future scenarios that must be simulated first; consequently, no reliable underlying assumptions are available. Secondly, in the majority of institutions, resolution with application of resolution tools was not an option in the past, as they only made plans for insolvency or bail-out. Therefore, existing plans and data focused on the two options that were the exact opposite of today's resolution concept. Thirdly, the special requirements for drawing up resolution plans, such as those defined in Annex 4 of the FSB's Key Attributes,[501] only emerged in the last few years and included information requirements that are so resolution-specific that they have no other significant use (*e.g.* data concerning resolution funding, critical interdependencies, and the impact of resolution action on business lines and legal entities).[502]

---

500 The EBA developed new templates for resolution plan reporting, which include three blocks of templates (B1 – B3). The first block, B1, consists of general information about the organizational structure. The second block, B2, entails financial information about the liability structure, own funds requirements, intragroup financial connectedness, major counterparties, and deposit insurance. The last block, B3, contains templates for assessing critical functions and core business lines, critical services, FMIs, and critical information systems. Although this structure is slightly different from the internal resolution planning building blocks described above, the information requirements and the increasing information magnitude are the same. The first blocks are general information that is present in the institution, while the second block contains both existing and special resolution information. The third block almost exclusively provides information that must specially be obtained for resolution purposes, see EBA, *Consultation Paper for Draft Implementing Standards on the provision of information for the purpose of resolution plans under Article 11(3) of Directive 2014/59/EU EBA/CP/2017/15*, p. 12.

501 *Key Attributes of Effective Resolution Regimes for Financial Institutions.*

502 EBA, *Draft final report - Draft Implementing Standards on the provision of information for the purpose of resolution plans under Article 11(3) of Directive 2014/59/EU EBA/ITS/2018/02*, recital 32 and table 1.

Evidence from Institutions Undertaking Planning

However, even if institutions develop an internal stepwise approach towards handling resolution data requests, the obtained data might not have the same quality and rigor as data involved in recovery planning, as the responsibility for resolution planning rests with the legislator and the resolution authorities. Since the concept of resolution planning is innovative both for institutions and resolution authorities, the optimal approach has not yet been found. This assumption is underlined by the reaction of institutions that receive resolution planning information requests from their competent resolution authority.

For example, some institutions criticized the fact that the requested data are often at a solo- or sub-coordinated level or at branch level, and are therefore not in line with the existing regulatory reporting scope.[503] Such data frequently must be acquired at entity level first, especially when cross-border group information is collected, which poses coordination and processing challenges for the group's Union parent undertaking. The responsible contact person or department acting as an intermediary between the resolution authority and the institution must organize the received data, with only limited capacity to verify it. Here, some requests by the resolution authority are so complex and overarching that the information can only be obtained by involving a large number of departments and by merging parts of the acquired information into the relevant dataset. An example of this is requests for information needed to analyze the resolvability of the institution. To obtain the needed information, such as group-, ownership-, and governance-structure, business model, core business lines, critical functions, key financial figures, internal and external interconnectedness, critical systems and infrastructures, loss-absorbing capacities and separability, a variety of departments must provide input. These include, amongst others, the risk and capital integration department, the regulatory reporting department, the capital management department, the bank treasury department, the IT department, the credit and market risk department, the non-financial risk department, the legal department, the procurement department, the communications department, the regulatory affairs department, and the HR department.

503 Stiefmüller, *Ten Years After - The 2017 Banking Package: One Step Forward, Two Steps Back*, p. 8.

Templates

Most criticism is directed toward the vehicles used to collect information at the institution. Information and data are collected using Excel sheet templates. As of now, the documentation concerning resolution plan information consists of 12[504] or 18[505] templates, with each template being more convoluted and crowded than the next. The regular size of one Excel template covers several pages with hundreds of rows and columns. Some have claimed that definitions, instructions, and templates used for data and information requests are incomplete or need further clarification.[506] Due to the different data management systems, structures, and accounting standards,[507] unclear definitions[508] or instructions can result in institutions interpreting the requirements differently and therefore delivering distinct information, thus distorting comparability and credibility.[509] Institutions

---

504 The European Commission laid down a minimum set of twelve templates to cover a core of information relating to an institution to be provided to the resolution authority, see Art. 3 of Commission Implementing Regulation (EU) 2016/1066 on ITS on resolution plans.

505 Even though the EBA Consultation Paper list only 10 templates and declares that "the templates have been calibrated with a view to avoiding any unnecessary or duplicate reporting, and in some cases whole templates or fields have been deleted", see EBA, *Consultation Paper for Draft Implementing Standards on the provision of information for the purpose of resolution plans under Article 11(3) of Directive 2014/59/EU EBA/CP/2017/15*, p. 8, the Annexes to the Consultation show an entirely different picture. Annex 1 consists of an Excel sheet showing the 18 different templates and Annex 2 also lists all 18 separate Excel templates.

506 Ibid., p. 7; European Banking Federation, *EBF response to EBA Consultation on Draft ITS on the provision of information for the purpose of resolution plans under Article 11(3) of Directive 2014/59/EU* (2017), pp. 5, 8.

507 For example, some especially big banks are allowed to use internal ratings-based approaches (IRB) to calculate capital requirements for credit risk, while smaller banks are required to use the standardized approach (SA), leading to different and sometimes advantageous results for capital requirements.

508 For example, it is criticized that some terms used in the templates are not terms commonly used in bank practice, which means that there is no industry-wide standard nor a commonly-accepted definition that can be referred to, see European Banking Federation, *EBF response to EBA Consultation on Draft ITS on the provision of information for the purpose of resolution plans under Article 11(3) of Directive 2014/59/EU*, p. 12.

509 A survey conducted by the EBA in spring 2017 amongst resolution authorities revealed difficulties they had experienced or to which they had been alerted by the institutions under their jurisdiction. One of them was the problem of insufficient information, where, for example, template I, which deals with 'Organizational Structure', needed to include size indicators, or Template V,

further deprecate the fact that the relevance of certain data and the requested level of detail is not always clear, and that requested data do not always match the objectives described. Another issue that can confound institutions in assisting the resolution authority is that some information requests by the authority are linked with familiar EBA Financial Reporting (FINREP) templates, while some templates differ substantially from the EBA templates or are completely new. In addition, in several cases, the instructions that were provided are not in line with the EBA's instructions. Departments entrusted with processing the resolution authorities' requests might find it difficult to distinguish which information request resembles those made by the EBA, and therefore might already be available, and those which do not resemble the templates at all or do so only in some parts, meaning that the data must be produced first.[510] There is also some discrepancy between the concepts and categories used in the SSM framework. A pertinent example here is the newly-established concept of liability by the BRRD, which does not correspond with the one used in the SRM. Even the SRB has acknowledged[511] that this poses administrative challenges for banks[512] and has adopted a gradual approach to the collection of data in

---

dealing with the 'Structure of Liability', was considered to be insufficiently granular, see EBA, *Consultation Paper for Draft Implementing Standards on the provision of information for the purpose of resolution plans under Article 11(3) of Directive 2014/59/EU EBA/CP/2017/15*, p. 28; see further EBA, *Draft final report - Draft Implementing Standards on the provision of information for the purpose of resolution plans under Article 11(3) of Directive 2014/59/EU EBA/ITS/2018/02*, recital (25), indicating that "the collection, quality control, treatment and exchange of large quantities of data on institutions cannot be meaningfully conducted solely based on a visual layout and legal definitions. It requires defining business and IT specifications allowing for automated collection and quality control. In turn, data thus collected enables users (banks and authorities) to produce standard reports and comparisons".

510 Deutsche Bank, *Deutsche Bank response to the European Banking Authority's consultation paper of the Draft ITS on the provision of information for the purpose of resolution plans under Article 11(3) of Directive 2014/59/EU* (2017), p. 3.

511 Press release of the Single Resolution Board, *Data collection for resolution planning and the determination of the Minimum Requirement for own funds and Eligible Liabilities (MREL)* (2016) retrievable at https://srb.europa.eu/en/node/52 accessed 1 October 2022.

512 Which is further demonstrated by the 30-page long explanatory document that was issued together with the new template, see Single Resolution Board, *Guidance to the Completion of the SRB's Liability Data Template for 2016* retrievable at https://srb.europa.eu/sites/srbsite/files/ldt_guidance_-_updated_29042016.pdf accessed 1 October 2022. The guidance document for the 2019 LDR even

its new Liability Data Template.[513] Owing to expected queries, mandatory data requests in this respect have been kept to a minimum, while some data only needed to be provided on a 'priority or best efforts basis.'[514]

Furthermore, requested data frequently differs substantially from the previous data request, in terms of both format and content. This can confuse institutions and complicate the acquisition of data and information, as old information and procedures cannot be reused and need to be revised. Another observation made by institutions on data and information requests was that certain data or information are more qualitative than quantitative and cannot be described numerically (for example, the support functions or the interconnectedness of entities and functions). As the information requests are submitted in the form of Excel sheets, information that cannot be displayed in figures and numbers poses a problem. Excel templates, at least in this regard, are not suitable for providing qualitative information. Filling in such information in a template, if it is even possible at all, would probably not provide the desired insight or would distort the actual significance of the information.[515] The same applies when authorities considered it necessary to require additional information not foreseen in the current templates. Such requests where included as a part of the current templates in some cases but included as part of separate templates or non-formal inquiries in others. This led to duplicate reporting and vary-

amounts to 54 pages, see Single Resolution Board, *Guidance on the 2019 Liability Data Report* (2018).

513 The banks are obliged to submit information via the templates annexed to the EC Implementing regulation; secondly banks must populate the Liability Data Template developed by the SRB, in cooperation with NRAs, the ECB and the EBA, to provide information regarding the bank's liability structure and for the determination of the MREL quote, see Single Resolution Board, *The Single Resolution Mechanism - Introduction to Resolution Planning* (2016), p. 21. The SRBs Liability Data Template may be obtained at https://srb.europa.eu/en/node/52.

514 Single Resolution Board, *Data collection for resolution planning and the determination of the Minimum Requirement for own funds and Eligible Liabilities (MREL)* (2016).

515 For instance, template R 07.01 requires institutions to list critical functions on the basis of a defined set of economic functions. As this might be understandable in light of comparability of critical functions assessments across banks, a defined set of economic functions cannot sufficiently capture the variety of activities of a bank, for example in capital markets, see Deutsche Bank, *Deutsche Bank response to the European Banking Authority's consultation paper of the Draft ITS on the provision of information for the purpose of resolution plans under Article 11(3) of Directive 2014/59/EU* (2017), p. 4.

ing administrative practices.[516] Lastly, and related to the previous point, certain data and information need expert judgment on a case-by-case basis, such as the presentation and explanation of legal contracts, and cannot be automated or converted into a figure.

Planning Capacity for Systemic Crises

As experience has shown, and along with the *too-big-to-fail* or *too-complex-to-fail* problem, the real issue with failing banks is not so much a likely crisis resulting from an idiosyncratic event, but more that it is 'part of a wider malaise.'[517] The main problem – be it for small, medium, or large banks – is contagion through an external systemic crisis.[518] Systemic crises are often unpredictable, uncontrollable, and cannot be influenced or steered, either by the institution under distress or in most cases by the respective state or government. As the last decades of crisis research has consistently shown,[519] a systemic crisis occurs because no-one was able to predict it and no-one expected it to evolve in the specific way that it did. That is the crux of the matter: all of the potential systemic crisis scenarios

---

516 EBA, *Consultation Paper for Draft Implementing Standards on the provision of information for the purpose of resolution plans under Article 11(3) of Directive 2014/59/EU EBA/CP/2017/15*, p. 7.

517 Karamichailidou and Mayes, 'Plausible recovery and resolution plans for cross-border financial institutions', p. 39.

518 For an attempt at defining the term 'systemic crisis' and further explanatory approaches on an economic and political definition see Levitin, 'In Defense of Bailouts', p. 443.

519 H. Ba, 'The systemic causes of financial crises in the long nineteenth century', *Business and Politics* 20 (2018), 208–38; L. Black, R. Correa, X. Huang and H. Zhou, 'The systemic risk of European banks during the financial and sovereign debt crises', *Journal of Banking & Finance* 63 (2016), 107–25; J. Cai, F. Eidam, A. Saunders and S. Steffen, 'Syndication, interconnectedness, and systemic risk', *Journal of Financial Stability* 34 (2018), 105–20; L. Laeven and F. Valencia, *IMF Working Paper - Systemic Banking Crises Revisited*, IMF Working Paper (2018) retrievable at https://www.imf.org/en/Publications/WP/Issues/2018/09/14/Systemic-Banking-Crises-Revisited-46232 accessed 1 October 2022; G. N.F. Weiß, D. Bostandzic and S. Neumann, 'What factors drive systemic risk during international financial crises?', *Journal of Banking & Finance* 41 (2014), 78–96; R. P. Buckley, E. Avgouleas and D. W. Arner, 'Three Major Financial Crises: What Have We Learned' in D. Arner, D. Busch, E. Avgouleas and S. Schwarcz (eds), *Systemic Risk in the Financial Sector: Ten Years After the Great Crash* (Centre for International Governance Innovation, 2019).

now considered in the recovery and resolution plans will most likely never become severe systemic crises, but rather only sectoral crunches that were predicted and can be dealt with in some way. Recovery and resolution planning for real and unforeseen systemic crises can, by definition, not be performed. Even if the institution under distress has a good recovery or resolution strategy that might help it in a real systemic crisis scenario, successful implementation might be difficult due to the financial market being violated.

One recent example of a crisis that was part of such a 'wider malaise' is said to be the Italian MPS case, where macroeconomic difficulties rather than individual mistakes caused financial woes that led to a massive increase in the number of non-performing loans throughout Italy,[520] involving numerous banks. In the end, the Italian government, with the consent of the European Commission, saved the bank.[521] It is questionable whether a resolution plan would have really solved the situation, for two main reasons. First, MPS's situation was precipitated by a crisis of the entire Italian banking sector, namely the dominance of NPLs in nearly every balance sheet of the country's bank.[522] Resolution plans of individual institutions, however, are powerless with respect to system-wide problems. Secondly, it appeared that the current instruments available in recovery and resolution plans were not suitable to satisfactorily solve a problem of a systemic nature.[523]

This raises questions about the practicability of the resolution tools that are used in resolution plans and, consequently, the practicability of the resolution plan itself. If the existing tools were incapable of dealing with a failing bank during a systemic crisis,[524] preparing resolution plans, including resolution tools, would not make much sense and would explain Italy's resistance towards their application. While the sale of business tool and the bridge institution tool are quite obviously problematic during systemic crises (as they require a suitable and solvent acquirer in times of

520 Binder, 'Systemkrisenbewältigung durch Bankenabwicklung? Aktuelle Bemerkungen zu unrealistischen Erwartungen', p. 58.

521 See *supra* under Part 2, A.II.2.a. – *A Junction Before Resolution: Precautionary Recapitalization*.

522 S. Bonfatti, 'Crisi bancarie in Italia 2015-2017', *Rivista di Diritto Bancario* (2018) retrievable at http://www.dirittobancario.it/rivista/crisi-bancarie-italia-2015-2017 accessed 1 October 2022 (in Italian).

523 Binder, 'Systemkrisenbewältigung durch Bankenabwicklung? Aktuelle Bemerkungen zu unrealistischen Erwartungen', p. 59.

524 Binder, 'The Relevance of the Resolution Tools Within the SRM', p. 16.

system-wide distress that often cannot be found without giving extensive and costly indemnities,[525] or they burden the already distressed state with considerable financial expenditures[526]), the asset separation tool and the bail-in tool *prima facie* seem to be means of resolving banks during systemic crises. Asset separation in asset management companies helps to foster market shakeouts even in times of distressed market prices for certain assets; adjusting the balance sheet of the institution[527] and bail-in eases the balance sheet by allocating losses to holders of debt and equity.

When put under some scrutiny, both instruments do have their weaknesses in systemic crisis too. Asset separation can only be expected to be successful if it is accompanied by at least preliminary substantial public investments to restructure the financial sector. If this is not possible, owing to a debt crisis in the public sector, as is often seen in larger systemic crises, the tool is likely to be structurally overburdened.[528] The application of the bail-in tool during a systemic crisis is said to suffer from similar problems to the application of the asset separation tool, because it does not provide liquidity for the institution but only adjusts the balance sheet (and also because there is little to no experience with the *ad hoc* sovereignly-enforced application of bail-in in an amount set by the resolution authority

---

525 See, for example, the difficulties in identifying and evaluating financial risk in the books of big, struggling banks during the 2008 to 2009 crisis in the US, which prevented government-organized takeovers such as in the case of Bear Stearns, see T. Geithner, *Stress test: Reflections on financial crises*, First paperback edition (New York: Broadway Books, 2014), pp. 147 *et seq.*; Binder, 'Systemkrisenbewältigung durch Bankenabwicklung? Aktuelle Bemerkungen zu unrealistischen Erwartungen', p. 62. On the other hand, it does not mean that – if such a suitable and solvent acquirer can be found during crisis – said instruments cannot help to overcome a crisis, as was demonstrated from 2012 to 2015 in Greece, see C. V. Gortsos, *The Impact of the Current Fiscal Crisis in the Euro Area on the Greek Banking System and the Measures Adopted to Safeguard its Stability: An Institutional, Supervisory and Regulatory Perspective* (2016), retrievable at SSRN https://ssrn.com/abstract=2769795 accessed 1 October 2022.

526 For a more detailed analysis of why the bridge institution tool is not suitable in times of systemic crisis, see Binder, 'Systemkrisenbewältigung durch Bankenabwicklung? Aktuelle Bemerkungen zu unrealistischen Erwartungen', p. 63.

527 As seen during the Scandinavian banking crisis at the beginning of 1990 as well as during the US Savings & Loans crisis at the end of 1980, see, among many, J.-H. Binder, 'Institutionalisierte Krisenbewältigung bei Kreditinstituten: Ausländische Gestaltungsvorbilder und mögliche Konsequenzen für die Weiterentwicklung des deutschen Aufsichtsrechts', *Zeitschrift für Bankrecht und Bankwirtschaft* (2009), 19–32, pp. 23 *et seq.*, 27 *et seq.*

528 Binder, 'Systemkrisenbewältigung durch Bankenabwicklung? Aktuelle Bemerkungen zu unrealistischen Erwartungen', p. 64.

according to an approximate need for restructuring).[529] Lastly, the actual enforcement of bail-in measures in a crisis could deepen the dilemma by sending frightening signals to market participants[530] who are fearful about their investments and who would make extensive controls of capital movement necessary. In addition, in the case of MPS in Italy, a bail-in could have worsened the NPL crisis in the financial market. Some scholars are even of the opinion that resolution with the use of BRRD resolution tools, and especially with the application of the bail-in tool, is applicable only in cases of failures of non-global or non-systemically important European banks outside systemic crises.[531]

Considering what has been discussed above, reservations about the capability of recovery and resolution planning for banks that struggle under a systemic crisis might be legitimate. Neither the available resolution tools nor the forecasting function of recovery and resolution planning are entirely convincing in their current configuration in times of system-wide distress. The available resolution tools for planning all face legal, economic, or practical difficulties that might sometimes even be counter-productive in systemic crises.[532] Since the occurrence of a systemic crisis cannot be ruled out, this raises some doubt about the efficiency of recovery and resolution planning.

Gateway to Political Influence – Enforceability of Plans

A notable characteristic of the new regime of recovery and resolution planning is the plans' lack of legal force. Under the BRRD, there is no legal certainty that a resolution plan will be enacted as planned and that

529 For a more detailed analysis of the shortcomings of bail-in during systemic crises, with examples referring to the Cypriote banking crisis and Hypo Alpe Adria, see, among many, ibid., p. 65.

530 See on this aspect *supra* Part 2, A.II.3. – *Excursus: Limits to the No-Bailout Policy – The Role of Public Financing.*

531 And that the failure of such smaller or local banks can be absorbed by normal and less costly insolvency proceedings, see Binder, 'Systemkrisenbewältigung durch Bankenabwicklung? Aktuelle Bemerkungen zu unrealistischen Erwartungen', p. 68; Gortsos, *A Poisonous (?) Mix: Bail-Out of Credit Institutions Combined with Bail-In of Their Liabilities Under the BRRD – The Use of 'Government Financial Stabilisation Tools'.*

532 Binder, 'Systemkrisenbewältigung durch Bankenabwicklung? Aktuelle Bemerkungen zu unrealistischen Erwartungen', p. 67.

the pre-determined resolution strategy will be applied[533] and transposed in the final resolution scheme. Under a recovery scenario, deviation from the foreseen plan might not have a strong impact on customers and stakeholders, while deviation from the resolution plan has wider consequences and, most importantly, offers wrong incentives for national resolution authorities and their governments to exert political influence in favor of national interests, which can impinge on the outcome of the resolution process. Deviation from the resolution plan's initial content signals that such plans are not much more than non-binding recommendations and that influencing resolution outcomes, even though already determined, is not futile. When a crisis is ongoing and the resolution plan threatens to bail-in considerable amounts of liabilities, some of which may be held by inadequate holders,[534] resolution authorities and governments can change their minds, using their influence to navigate their way around the adopted resolution plan and eventually bailing out the institution to protect national welfare.[535] As plans are not enforceable and as their non-compliance is not penalized, this may become the rule rather than the exception.[536]

Impediments Concerning Resolution Plans

The above section covered the impediments pertaining to both kinds of plans, while the following section discusses the problems that specifically concern resolution planning. The reason that a whole section is dedicated to resolution planning is because it operates in a delicate situation in which time, resources, and financial means are scarce commodities. In such situations, any action taken with respect to the institution under distress comes under public scrutiny. Therefore, preparatory work for resolution in resolution plans requires detailed attention.

---

533 World Bank Group, *Understanding Bank Recovery and Resolution in the EU: A Guidebook to the BRRD*, p. 109.

534 For the problem of adequate holders of bail-inable instruments see *supra* under Part 4, A.III.6. – *Potential Investors and Holders of MREL Eligible Instruments.*

535 On the tension and interplay of flexibility for resolution authorities and certainty when it comes to resolution planning, see Kleftouri, 'European Union Bank Resolution Framework: can the objective of financial stability ensure consistency in resolution authorities' decisions?', p. 278.

536 As happened in the Banco Popular case, where the initial resolution plan was dismissed or in the Italian cases, where resolution was tailored according to the needs of the government.

The starting point for each resolution-planning process is the bank's recovery plan, meaning that resolution plans are built on the configuration of the recovery plan[537], more or less, the following three ways. First, the resolution plan is based on the recovery plan's basic data and general information.[538] Besides basic data and general information pertaining to the institution, the resolution plan can consider the scenarios developed in the recovery plan as a starting-point for their own scenario.[539] Second, it is at the mercy of the competent authority's policy decisions and the outcomes of institution-authority interaction during the recovery planning process. This holds particularly true when the competent authority uses its powers to impose changes on business models, funding arrangements, or organizational legal structures of the institution undertaking planning,[540] as such changes will have a direct impact on the resolution assessment. Lastly, missing resolution-plan information is requested by the resolution authority at the institution via data templates.[541] In addition, on certain occasions, the resolution authority[542] may require the institution to provide

537 Single Resolution Board, *The Single Resolution Mechanism - Introduction to Resolution Planning* (2016), p. 21.

538 See Art. 8(1) of the Draft ITS, which states that "Competent and resolution authorities shall jointly verify whether part of all of the information to be provided to the resolution authority in order to draw up and implement the resolution plan is already available at the competent authority." Art. 8(2) states that information ready at the competent authority shall be provided to the resolution authority, and Art. 8(3) concludes that, where additional information is considered necessary and not available to the competent authority, the resolution authority shall directly request the institution or Union parent undertaking to provide the information, see EBA, *Consultation Paper for Draft Implementing Standards on the provision of information for the purpose of resolution plans under Article 11(3) of Directive 2014/59/EU EBA/CP/2017/15*, p. 25. The same requirements are now laid down in Commission Implementing Regulation (EU) 2016/1066 on ITS on resolution plans.

539 Single Resolution Board, *The Single Resolution Mechanism - Introduction to Resolution Planning* (2016)., p. 30.

540 Binder, 'Resolution Planning and Structural Bank Reform within the Banking Union', pp. 138 *et seq.*

541 Single Resolution Board, *The Single Resolution Mechanism - Introduction to Resolution Planning* (2016), p. 21.

542 When only acting within the Banking Union, the body responsible for the resolution of a specific bank or group is the Internal Resolution Team (IRT). For resolution outside the Banking Union but within the European Union, such units are called Resolution Colleges. If only subsidiaries are located within the Banking Union and/or the European Union but the headquarters are located in a third country, the body responsible for resolution plan coordination is the

additional information necessary to draft the resolution plan. Such additional requests for information outside the templates can entail information about the bank's structure, critical functions, or interconnectedness, as well as an analysis of the operational consequences of a resolution strategy or a description of the process and arrangements necessary to effectively provide information in resolution.[543] As a consequence, the information for the resolution plan originates, or is provided by, the institution, either directly or by relying on recovery plan information.

Considering the approach to resolution planning, a conflict becomes evident:[544] institutions possess the power to influence plans that are not drawn up by themselves but by a third, autonomous authority. Consequently, the information gathering process is only *de jure* allocated with the resolution authority but is *de facto* carried out by the institutions. In addition to the shortcomings of recovery planning laid out in the last section which diminish the accuracy of the recovery plan, further information production processes and internal data-collection procedures for resolution planning are often opaque. Not all data produced are undoubtedly accurate, although some data might already exist somewhere within the firm. Owing to the reliance of the resolution plan on 'recovery level information,' the transfer of incorrect information can occur at each of the following three stages of resolution-plan information gathering: first, the resolution plan base extracted from the recovery plans can be incorrect, because the basic data initially provided and general information were wrong; second, the policy decisions and outcomes of institution-authority interaction during the recovery planning process could be premised on incorrect information obtained by the competent authority; and, lastly, incorrect information can interlace the resolution plan if information request templates are filled out incorrectly or additional extra-template information requests are answered wrongly.

European Resolution College. If a group has GSIBs inside the Banking Union and/or European Union as well as in a third country, the body responsible for resolution planning is the Crisis Management Group (CMG). However, for the ease of reference, all bodies are referred to as resolution groups.

543 Single Resolution Board, *The Single Resolution Mechanism - Introduction to Resolution Planning*, p. 22.

544 For example recognized in part 4.1.2 (Problem definition) of EBA, *EBA Final Draft Regulatory Technical Standards on the content of resolution plans and the assessment of resolvability EBA/RTS/2014/15*.

Principal-Agent Conflict

The two-step planning process can be identified as a principal-agent[545] scenario, or as two separate principal-agent scenarios, merged in accordance with the recovery and resolution planning process of the BRRD. In the first step, the institution, acting as an agent, collects information for its principal, the monitoring competent authority. In the second step, the resolution authority, as a second principal, receives information collected by its two agents, the institution and the competent authority. The institution, as an agent, possesses the most information, while the principals at the top of the hierarchy (i.e. the competent and the resolution authority) possess the least. This creates information asymmetry between the planners in charge and the agent, as neither the competent authority nor the resolution authority has the time or financial resources to verify[546] the information of their agent. Agency costs for monitoring are in this case excessively high and the principal authorities have to rely on information given by the institution. This is true for each form of resolution-plan information gathering, either in relation to the underlying basis data from the recovery plan or the imposed changes in the run-up to resolution planning or the information request templates. The institution, as an agent, has incentives to take advantage of the situation and exploit the information asymmetry. For instance, the institution could disclose information incomprehensively or incorrectly. Furthermore, it can provide modified information for its own benefit. Apart from advantages such as saving money, time, and effort, the institution might be cautious in revealing critical information that could potentially lead the competent or resolution authority to impose changes on the institution's structure, financial arrangements, or management. Such changes entail costs and efforts that the institution would want to avoid.

The principal-agent conflict, especially between the resolution authority and the institution, is known to the resolution authorities and is recognized as such. Evidence for this can be found in the SRB's endeavors to find a more reliable agent than the institutions themselves, one that is

545 See M. C. Jensen and W. H. Meckling, 'Theory of the Firm: Managerial Behavior, Agency Costs and Ownership Structure', *Journal of Financial Economics* 3 (1976), 305–60 for general explanations regarding principal-agent theory.

546 Despite the limited assessment mechanisms laid out in Art. 6 BRRD and Arts. 16 *et seq.* Commission Delegated Regulation (EU) 2016/1075 on RTS of Recovery and Resolution Plans.

devoid of biases, contradictory interests, and incentives. For this purpose, in 2018, the SRB launched a call for tenders for a service contract for a "highly qualified financial data vendor to provide the Agency with access to financial data on banking institutions."[547] It can be assumed that, by engaging a neutral third party, the SRB hopes to eradicate the problems and gain uninfluenced access to information such as "[...] access to in-depth financial statements data, regulatory data, market analytics for banking institutions, extensive coverage of the banking and financial services sector, new feeds and updates on a great variety of topics at entity, sector and country level [...]."[548] Until now, a data vendor contract has not been concluded.[549]

Issues with Resolution Plans Relying on Institution-Provided Information

Despite the detected principal-agent conflict, resolution authorities need to rely on institution-provided data for their resolution planning. First, because this constitutes the most cost-efficient option and, second, because the institution is still the best-informed and cheapest information provider. The needed data and information for setting up the resolution plan comprise a mixture of basic information, changes the authorities imposed on the institution during the recovery planning stage, and for the most part information is requested by sending out templates or through non-formal requests made by the resolution authority. Except for parts of the data requested by sending out the templates or specific requests, some required information already exists[550] in the institution or competent

547 Single Resolution Board, *Ex ante publicity notice - negotiated procurement procedure: Call for Tender for the Provision of Access to Financial Data through a Data Vendor* (2018), retrievable at https://srb.europa.eu/en/content/provision-access-financial-data-through-data-vendor-0 accessed 1 October 2022.

548 Ibid., p. 2.

549 Even though such a data vendor would assume parts of the resolution authorities' data-collection process, the data vendor would most likely face similar problems as the resolution authority, at least in some parts. Moreover, in terms of a potential operator of such data, the institution might transmit influenced information where the vendor cannot obtain its data in the open market or other openly accessible data systems.

550 See, for overlapping information in recovery and resolution planning, Annex II of EBA, *Consultation Paper for Draft Implementing Standards on the provision of information for the purpose of resolution plans under Article 11(3) of Directive*

authority[551] because of recovery planning or supervisory reporting. If such information already exists, competent as well as supervisory authorities are obliged to provide such information to the resolution authority before approaching the institution.[552] Such information, for example, covers block 1 of the resolution plan (general information with an overview of the organizational structure of the group and entities, distribution of assets, and risk exposure)[553] which is comparable to the recovery plan's section on strategic analysis and the description of entities covered by the recovery plan (general description of entities, overall global business and risk strategy, business model, core business lines and critical functions, material legal entities mapping, interconnectedness, legal and financial structures, etc.).[554] Looking further into the agreed content of recovery and resolution plans, one can see a number of such overlaps.

Where information is already generated in the context of recovery planning or supervisory reporting, for economic and efficiency reasons it would be best for the resolution authority to resort to the available information and re-use it to prepare the resolution plan. In such cases, the institution's employees have already produced the information and have it readily available. In addition, the competent authority has received and to some extent already reviewed the incoming information in the form of the institution-drafted recovery plan. This suggests that close cooperation between the planners is generally desirable, as the resolution authority can benefit from information that has already been collected, processed, and

---

2014/59/EU EBA/CP/2017/15 in comparison to the Recovery and Resolution Plan RTS.

551 Binder, 'Resolution Planning and Structural Bank Reform within the Banking Union', p. 139.

552 Art. 2 of Commission Implementing Regulation (EU) 2016/1066 on ITS on resolution plans.

553 Annex II 1.2 (2) of EBA, *Consultation Paper for Draft Implementing Standards on the provision of information for the purpose of resolution plans under Article 11(3) of Directive 2014/59/EU EBA/CP/2017/15* or Art. 22(1) of the Recovery and Resolution Plan RTS.

554 Arts. 6 and 7 of *EBA final draft Regulatory Technical Standards on the content of recovery plans under Article 5(10) of Directive 2014/59/EU establishing a framework for the recovery and resolution of credit institutions and investment firms* or Art. 7 of the Recovery and Resolution Plan RTS.

reconditioned instead of requesting 'raw' information from the institution. The European Commission also reccomends this approach.[555]

However, even if data and information overlaps do exist, recovery and resolution planning processes are very different in their characteristics and focus, and they require different planning skills. This becomes clear when looking at the quality of reusable information and the quality of new information that the resolution authority requests in its templates. Even if information is still available, such information is of a more generic nature while the needed resolution information is extremely specific. Furthermore, even if a dataset is already available, it might be in an unusable form for resolution planning, or competent authorities may value the data or information differently, assigning them different levels of importance or using them in different contexts. In addition, the mindsets of planners on both the recovery side and the resolution side are diametrical, as one party is focused on protecting the institution while the other party is determined to protect markets, market players, and states while planning for the resolution of the institution. Therefore, even if some synergy between recovery experts in the banks and resolution experts in the resolution authority can be achieved, it may be less than expected.[556]

The resolution planning process is therefore caught between efficiency and cost considerations on the one hand, and the potential exploitation of information asymmetries on the other. The process of ultimately having the institutions under resolution planning in charge of preparing plans, collecting the crucial information, and providing all other necessary data is said to jeopardize the likelihood of the instrument's success.[557] To substantiate this concern, the following section explains different potential pertinent problematic situations.

Unintentionally Incorrect Information

Resolution plan information can sometimes be unintentionally incorrect. The reasons for this stem almost exclusively from complexity and opacity,

555 Art. 2 of Commission Implementing Regulation (EU) 2016/1066 on ITS on resolution plans that sets out the procedure of how information for the purpose of resolution plans should be collected.

556 Franke, Krahnen and Lüpke, *Effective Resolution of Banks: Problems and Solutions*, p. 15.

557 Weber, 'Structural regulation as antidote to complexity capture', p. 647.

either in the institution's structures or the way in which information is requested. This can occur when drawing information from the recovery plan as well as when requesting information directly from the institution through templates.

In the first case, the institution has already provided a flawed recovery plan because it was unable to provide a correct plan. Moreover, incorrect recovery-plan information can be traced back to the shirking behavior of employees because of excessive demands, laziness, or unwillingness to deal with complex matter[558] (see *supra* Part 3, A.II.1.c. and d.). In this case, incorrect information is provided unintentionally to the competent authority, affecting the recovery plan. In addition, there are cases where the institution's structure has changed and the recovery plan is not readjusted (see Part 3, A.II.1.g. – *Impermanence of Banks' Structures and the Topicality of Recovery and Resolution Plans*). Meanwhile, there are several ways in which a resolution authority can rely on unintentionally incorrect recovery-plan information.

In the second case, the institution provides unintentionally incorrect information at the request of the resolution authority. Reasons for this can be found in the complexity and opacity of the institution (see *supra* Part 2, A.II.1.b. – *Complexity in Bank Structures*) as well as in the complicated templates used to collect such information (see Part 3, A.II.1.h. – *Opaque Data Production and Collection Process – Templates*). Persons in charge of assembling the requested information might be overwhelmed by the complexity of the institution and therefore unable to produce the information as requested. Alternatively, even if those responsible have a good overview of the institution's structure and are potentially capable of producing information correctly, the request itself might be complicated or incomprehensible. In both cases, despite best efforts being made to the contrary, incorrect information is passed on to the resolution authority.

558 When describing crisis scenarios, the resolution authority is allowed to resort to the scenarios already described in the recovery plan, considering mainly (or even only) the said scenarios. If the initial scenario selection was influenced by unwillingness, laziness, shirking, or any other incorrect behavior, therefore leaving out possible scenarios, this error will persist in the recovery plan, see Single Resolution Board, *The Single Resolution Mechanism - Introduction to Resolution Planning*, p. 30.

Faulty Processing or Valuation of Information

In cases of faulty processing or valuation of data, the recovery-plan information as well as the information provided upon request are accurate, but the resolution authority fails to interpret them correctly. The reasons for this include, amongst countless others, the use of different parameters and standards to describe numbers, indicators, and figures, or the lack of space in the provided templates to describe the indicated information fully, resulting in miscommunication. Alternatively, resolution authorities might consider some of the provided information irrelevant when in actual fact it is crucial for the given institution's business model (see Part 3, A.II.1.h. – *Opaque Data Production and Collection Process – Templates*). There are several scenarios in which such misevaluation or faulty processing can take place, leading to resolution-plan errors.

Intentionally Incorrect Information

It is crucial to understand that the resolution authority pursues divergent interests to the institution. The resolution authorities' interests are primarily preserving financial stability in the market, preventing contagion, and protecting values, public money, and market players. Apart from this, the authority has no special interest in the institution itself. Writing-down of capital instruments, selling a bank's important parts to competitors or transferring them into bridge institutions while winding-down the remainder are options that the resolution authority is willing to take in order to achieve its resolution objectives. When the situation is serious and time is scarce, the preservation of the institution itself is a minor consideration, if indeed it is considered at all. On the contrary, the institution itself does of course aspire to 'stay alive.' It aims to protect its employees, retain its clients and business partners for further profit, and strives to preserve the company and its (good) name. Moreover, as resolution also means replacing the management of the institution, high-ranking bank employees try to protect their jobs. These antagonistic interests prove to be interesting when it comes to setting up two plans that – even though they serve the same greater purpose – arise from contrary interests. Therefore, the institution might be compromised when giving information to the resolution authority.[559]

An example of how incorrect information can positively affect an institution's future can be found in the first and third block of the recovery planning process[560] that is reflected in the first chapter of the resolution plan. This section deals with the strategic business analysis of the institution (*i.e.* its legal structure, business model, business lines, core business lines, and critical functions). The decision on whether or not to resolve a bank, and which functions or business units to preserve, will depend on the bank's characteristics. Within this section, such characteristics are assessed in detail to inform the determination of the preferred resolution strategy and resolvability assessment.[561] The institution might provide wrong or incomplete information in order to improve its position in a potential resolution, saving business units and functions or trying to delay resolution action. Besides that, the institution has numerous opportunities to alter its position by exercising influence through the provision of information and data.

The institution can pursue this objective either by already equipping the recovery plan with scarce information, as described in the section above, thus preventing measures to remove adverse impacts on its resolvability,[562] or by giving manipulated information when requested by the resolution authority. Such interference is certainly possible when filling out the standard templates or answering additional special information requests by the authority; however, such exertion of influence is even more exceptional when the resolution authority decides to outsource parts of the resolution planning to the institution. While the resolution authority can control the submitted information to a limited extent in the case of templates or additional information requests, it is far more difficult to control entire

559 One backstop to institutions' employees excessively providing wrong information can be found in the RTS specifying the content of recovery plans, where it is required that the information on governance shall contain a detailed description of how the recovery plan was developed, the role and function of persons responsible for preparing, implementing and updating each section of the plan and the identity of the person who has the overall responsibility for the plan, see Art. 5 of Recovery and Resolution Plan TRS. The requirement that incorporates a "name-and-shame" element into the planning process might prevent some blatant or obvious exertion of influence.

560 Cichy, Buchmüller and Igl, '§ 15 Sanierungs- und Abwicklungsplanung', p. 698.

561 Single Resolution Board, *The Single Resolution Mechanism - Introduction to Resolution Planning*, p. 22.

562 Ibid., p. 30.

completed parts of the resolution plan. Information has already been merged and processed, and punctual control of specific figures and numbers is not as possible as it is in the case of templates.

Outlook: Determination of MREL Quote

In anticipation of the following discourses, one aspect that is worth mentioning in this respect is the determination of the MREL quota. Article 10(7)(o) BRRD requires the resolution authority to include in the resolution plan "the minimum requirements for own funds and eligible liabilities required pursuant to Article 45(a) and a deadline to reach that level, where applicable." Referring to the exemplifications of information procurement of resolution authorities above, this fragment of the resolution plan might also be subject to interference by the institutions. Likewise, other resolution plan determinations, fulfilling a high MREL quota, are inconvenient and costly for the institutions.

Gateways for influencing the MREL decision can be found in Article 45 BRRD, which sets out the framework for the application of the minimum requirements. According to paragraph 6, the minimum requirements for own funds and eligible liabilities shall be determined by the resolution authority on the basis of at least, *inter alia*, the size, the business model, the funding model, and the risk profile of the institution,[563] and the extent to which the failure of the institution would have adverse effects on wider financial stability, taking into account its interconnectedness with other institutions or with the rest of the financial system.[564] As demonstrated above, such information is provided by the institution, either directly via data templates[565] or indirectly through the recovery plan, in the knowledge that such information will constitute the basis of the resolution authorities MREL determination process. Therefore, by giving unintentionally incorrect or intentionally overly-optimistic information and data, the institution might try to lower the MREL quota or calibrate it in a more convenient way.

563 Art. 45(6)(d) BRRD.

564 Art. 45(6)(f) BRRD.

565 In this context of determining MREL, banks are required to fill out the rather complex Liability Data Template, LDT. The LDT can be retrieved at https://srb.europa.eu/en/content/liability-data-report.

Conclusion

In summary, it can be noted that the information asymmetry[566] between institutions, competent authorities, and resolution authorities culminates in a classical principal-agent conflict. Due to the absence of alternatives, resolution authorities have to rely on the industry-provided information and data, either directly from the institutions or by requesting such data from the competent authority. Therefore, the problem of information provision at institutions vulnerable to complexity captures, misconduct, shirking, and other vulnerabilities is inherent. Some scholars have even stated that resolution plans are only as effective as the industry wants them to be.[567]

The Problems with Modification Measures

Now that the problems pertaining to recovery and resolution planning (the instruments identified as remedies for the lack of predictability and complexity in banks' structures) have been demonstrated, the following section turns to the potential problems of the third remedy: the possibility of competent or resolution authorities imposing measures and changes on institutions in the course of recovery[568] or resolution[569] planning. This tool solves one fundamental problem pre-resolution: unwanted conditions in institutions, such as impediments to resolvability, high risk, or impeding complexity, which can be eliminated during recovery planning and up-front resolution and – ideally – do not need to be dealt with in the plans. Such powers of the competent and resolution authority to substantially modify existing structures and models of single institutions or even entire

566 EBA Draft ITS on Resolution Plans, p. 11.

567 Weber, 'Structural regulation as antidote to complexity capture', p. 710.

568 Under certain conditions, Art. 6(6) BRRD gives the competent authority the power to direct the institution to take any measures it considers necessary and proportionate. Such measures include, but are not limited to: reducing the risk profile of the institution, including liquidity risks; enabling recapitalization measures; reviewing institutions' strategy and structure; and making changes to the funding strategy, or governance structure of the institution.

569 Art. 17 BRRD and EBA, *Guidelines on the specification of measures to reduce or remove impediments to resolvability and the circumstances in which each measure may be applied under Directive 2014/59/EU* (2014).

groups cannot be overestimated,[570] both in terms of their positive and negative impacts. Despite its clear intention to support viable and effective recovery and resolution planning, it also threatens to interfere with internal management and corporate governance decisions where boundaries of areas of competence become fluid.[571] Even if we assume that all forced changes by the competent or resolution authority have the best intentions and are intended solely to enhance recovery and resolution planning outcomes, institutions will probably be reluctant to adopt the imposed authorial modification measures. All forms of forced change to the existing organizational, funding, and legal structures will inevitably come with substantial implications for a firm's or group's profitability, both in terms of short-term cost (adjusting and reorganization costs) and long-term cost (reduced efficiency, high costs of adopting imposed measures). This is why institutions might try to influence the recovery or resolution planning process by infusing the planning process with redacted information, see *supra* Part 3, A.II.2.b.iii. – *Intentionally Incorrect Information*. Another example is the regionalization of banking activities, which could follow from the forced separation of existing groups along jurisdictional borders, which could in turn eventually reduce market liquidity and may be detrimental, especially in distressed markets.[572] Generally, it can be stated that modifications in that framework might cause problems for the institution, even if the objectives of such modifications are generally good in a recovery- and resolution-enhancing sense. However, this might not be the most relevant issue here.

A much greater problem lies in the conceptual division between recovery and resolution planning, which requires both authorities to synchronize the respective decisions made by involved parties at the other level. Forced modifications in the organizational, financial, or legal structure of the institution at the supervisory level affect the planning of resolution authorities while changes made obligatorily by resolution authorities will entail necessary adjustments in the recovery plans.

This is particularly evident when the power to impose changes on the competent authority or the resolution authority is applied in the context of different group-recovery or group-resolution scenarios. Although the

570 Binder, 'Gleichung mit (zu?) vielen Unbekannten: Nachhaltige Bankenstrukturen durch Sanierungs- und Abwicklungsplanung?', p. 155.

571 Ibid., p. 165.

572 Binder, 'Resolution Planning and Structural Bank Reform within the Banking Union', p. 141.

power of imposing changes on institutions and groups does help to overcome resolvability and complexity issues, it could produce imbalances too. This is because of the double-barreled competencies pertaining to recovery and resolution planning and because modification measures at the supervisory level will always have implications for resolution planning and vice versa.[573] While the competent authority is responsible for assessing the recovery plan and the resolution authority is responsible for drawing up the resolution plan, these authorities can take different on different forms. The competent authority could either be the supervisory authority as defined in Article 4(1)(40) CRR (a 'competent authority' means a public authority or body officially recognized by national law, which is empowered by national law to supervise institutions as part of the supervisory system in operation in the Member State concerned), or it could be the ECB when it comes to specific tasks conferred on it by Council Regulation (EU) No 1024/2013. The resolution authority can be either the national resolution authority, which is an administrative authority or authorities entrusted with public administrative powers according to Article 3(2) and (3) BRRD, or the SRB[574] can be the resolution authority if the institution is considered significant or is one over which the ECB has decided to directly exercise all of the relevant supervisory powers, or in relation to other cross-border groups where both the parent and at least one subsidiary are established in two different participating Member States of the Banking Union.

Owing to this determination, different group scenarios will be treated differently. Looking at a number of highly stylized group scenarios will illustrate this problem further. Such a group scenario under recovery or resolution can either be: (a) a pure Banking Union scenario with all individual entities and the whole group within the eurozone and supervised by the ECB; (b) a mixed European scenario with the ECB acting as consolidating supervisor for a group with branches and subsidiaries located within and outside participating Member States; (c) a mixed European scenario with the ECB acting as the competent authority for a subsidiary or a group that is under the supervision of home authorities in another EU Member

573 Binder, 'Gleichung mit (zu?) vielen Unbekannten: Nachhaltige Bankenstrukturen durch Sanierungs- und Abwicklungsplanung?', p. 163.

574 As of June 1, 2016, the SRB's remit covers 142 banks, including 129 banking groups of which 14 are significant banking groups (including all 8 Banking Union GSIBs) and 15 other cross-border banking groups.

State; or (d) a third-country scenario with the ECB acting as supervisor for a subsidiary of a foreign group.[575]

In scenario (a), the competent authority for assessing individual as well as group recovery plans would be the ECB, while the SRB would be the resolution authority assuming all tasks related to resolution planning at the individual firm level as well as at group level. Both the ECB and the SRM would be in a position to enforce and determine recovery and resolution policies and modification measures such as reallocation, separation or consolidation of business and service functions, or simplifying legal structures in a considerably autonomous way with little influence over national authorities, national policy, and national markets. In a recovery or resolution case, due to the autonomous exercising of modulation powers upfront, a high degree of consistency can be expected, and recovery and resolution might be more successful.[576] Although scenario (b) does not look very different to scenario (a), the potential for conflicts and tensions with the foreign-authority home supervisor of group entities licensed in non-participating Member States, or branches in non-participating Member States of institutions licensed within the Banking Union, will be higher than in the institutional hierarchy established within the Banking Union. The ECB and the SRB might follow a different approach in dealing with such non-participating Member State subsidiaries or branches by using their powers under the recovery and resolution planning framework to enforce changes that will benefit the systemic stability inside the Banking Union (such as the concentrating of all group business conducted within the eurozone into legal entities under their control) but that are undesirable for the non-participating Member State. This could lead to tensions and conflicts that could make recovery and resolution in this case less successful than in scenario (a). In scenario (c), a completely different setting arises. The ECB would only assume the role of the home supervisor for subsidiaries or a significant branch of a firm that is supervised by the authorities of a non-participating Member State. Although the Banking Union authorities would still be in charge of recovery and resolution planning for the individual under their remit, they would not have any control over the group itself, including over its legal or organizational structure. Imposing changes in favor of resolvability inside the Banking Union or any attempt to exert influence on the group resolution strate-

575 The group scenarios are taken from Binder, 'Resolution Planning and Structural Bank Reform within the Banking Union', pp. 142 *et seq.*

576 Ibid., p. 143.

gy could lead to conflicts with their counterparts in non-participating Member States.[577] In scenario (d), however, the influence of the ECB and the SRM is limited with regard to the deviation from their powers from the recovery and resolution framework. Although such powers could be exercised on the subsidiary whose parent is located in a third country, a group reorganization, separation, or consolidation (as seen in scenario (a) and partly in scenario (b)) cannot be expected, making recovery and resolution as envisaged by Banking Union authorities less balanced and less successful, as changes upfront were not exercised on the entirety or majority of the group.[578] Scenario (d) would most likely not differ much from scenario (c), which is mixed. Although a framework for cooperation has been established, Banking Union authorities would not have much impact on the group, but would have more on the subsidiaries under their supervision. Most likely, they would force such subsidiaries to revise their legal, financial and operational independence from the remainder of the group, enhancing resolvability at least for Banking Union subsidiaries. Nevertheless, if a crisis occurs that requires action from the entire group, uniform application of recovery or resolution procedures will be more difficult than in scenario (a) or (b), encouraging disintegration between participating and non-participating Member States.[579]

It can be assumed that modification measures taken ahead of resolution will hardly be used. Especially in Resolution Colleges or other cross-border fora, where a joint decision on the application of actions to remove substantive impediments must be reached, it is highly doubtful that frequent and consistent action to modify the institution in the course of the recovery or resolution planning process will be taken. Indeed, in 2017, no joint decision by a Resolution College to remove substantive impediments was taken,[580] despite the claim made by regulators that one of the most

---

577 Binder states that, even though the ECB and the SRB are not the consolidated supervisor or resolution authority for the group, the chances are that the relative influence of Banking Union authorities could be considerable, allowing the ECB and the SRB to effectively use their powers under the recovery and resolution planning regime in a way that could lead to a concentration of eurozone business in a subsidiary under direct ECB supervision, see ibid., p. 147.

578 See ibid., pp. 146 *et seq.* for a detailed explanation.

579 See for a similar excursus ibid., p. 147.

580 EBA, *EBA Report on the Functioning of Resolution Colleges in 2017*, p. 21; also indicated as a problem by the EBA in EBA, *Guidelines on the specification of measures to reduce or remove impediments to resolvability and the circumstances in which each measure may be applied under Directive 2014/59/EU*, p. 20.

valuable benefits of recovery and resolution planning does not lie in the final plan itself, but rather in the process of setting up the plan and the accompanying possibility of making adjustments and modifications to institutions during planning.[581]

Result of Part 3

This part has examined the instrument of recovery and resolution planning as a remedy for identified *ex ante* problems of the credibility of resolution. After confirming the general potential of the instrument to serve as an antidote, the part elaborated on the its inherent impediments. The analysis showed that the current framework for recovery and resolution planning suffers from an array of problems that might have a negative impact on its remedial character. At a later stage, the detailed outline of impediments will serve as the starting point for proposals to improve recovery and resolution planning in order to preserve their general potential to enhance the credibility of the resolution process.

581 Dimova, *Resolution Planning: Too Complex to Work or Cornerstone of a Stable Financial Architecture?* However, Dimova stated that a valuable asset of recovery and resolution planning lies in the institution's own intentions and endeavors to adjust in a way that removes impediments without an authority's intervention.

PART 4 – LOSS-ABSORBING CAPITAL REQUIREMENTS – IMPACTS ON CREDIBILITY

In Part 2, a lack of sufficient and adequate funding for resolution was identified as the second factor corroding the credibility of resolution as a reliable alternative to bailout or national insolvency proceedings. Available private funding mechanisms in the BRRD were found to be too discretionary (bail-in) or not applicable (external private funding). It has also been found that industry-funded financing is insufficient and incomplete (DGS and SRF), and therefore unable to provide a credible backstop before resorting to publicly-funded financing of resolution. Despite the public funding provided within the BRRD proving to be irrelevant to a certain extent (DRI), some instruments are actively used (state aid and GFST). Nevertheless, the most important observation is that the current framework itself contains easy-to-use loopholes. Circumventing resolution procedures, they provide for the possibility of precautionary recapitalization and liquidation under normal insolvency regimes. In both cases, as seen in recent resolution episodes in Europe, massive amounts of public funds were used. As a result, public financing has again become a focal point for struggling banks. However, the real root of recent developments lies in the poor design of private loss-participation through bail-in and a certain unpreparedness with respect to bail-inable capacities. This has led to the exploitation of exemptions as alternatives and the demand for another alternative, namely public financing.

Accordingly, the enhancement of bail-inable capacities through loss-absorbing capital requirements was proposed as a potential remedy to said lack, which would have a positive influence on private resolution funding and therefore the credibility of the resolution process.

The Impact of Loss-Absorbing Capital Requirements on the Credibility of Bail-In

The following part addresses the newly-introduced instrument of loss-absorbing capital requirements as an antidote to the detected *ex post* lack. After briefly explaining the instrument (I.) and remedial character of loss-absorbing capital requirements (II.), this section turns towards impediments inherent in the framework for loss-absorbing capital requirements (III.).

Convergence of MREL and TLAC – the European Proposal

The concept of loss-absorbing capital requirements is approached on two levels[582]: the European level; and the global level. Through Article 45 BRRD, the European legislator introduced the Minimum Requirements for Own Funds and Eligible Liabilities (MREL),[583] while the Financial Stability Board (FSB) together with the Basel Committee on Banking Supervision (BCBS) proposed the concept of Total Loss-Absorbing Capacity (TLAC)[584] that was adopted at the G20 summit in Turkey in 2015. Although these two concepts are set up for, and serve, the same purpose[585] – providing banks with enough loss-absorbing capital to ensure effective and credible application of the bail-in tool – discrepancies between them appear when examined more closely. While the MREL derives from the BRRD and is therefore applicable to all institutions under its remit,[586] TLAC only applies to the roughly 30 existing GSIBs worldwide, of which 13 are banking groups within the EU.[587] Moreover, because the latter was issued by the FSB, TLAC standards need to be transposed into European law to come into effect.

582 A third proposed regulation consists in the Federal Reserve proposal for a minimum TLAC and a separate GLAC (Gone Concern Loss Absorbing Capacity) requirement in the form of long-term unsecured debt requirements.

583 See Art. 45 BRRD and *Commission Delegated Regulation (EU) 2016/1450 of 23.05.2016 supplementing Directive 2014/59/EU of the European Parliament and of the Council with regard to regulatory technical standards specifying the criteria relating to the methodology for setting the minimum requirements for own funds and eligible liabilities OJ L 237, 3.9.2016, p. 1–9* (henceforth RTS on MREL).

584 Financial Stability Board, *Principles on Loss-absorbing and Recapitalisation Capacity of G-SIBs in Resolution: Total Loss-absorbing Capacity (TLAC) Term Sheet* (2015).

585 European Commission, *Capital requirements (CRR/CRD IV) and resolution framework (BRRD/SRM) amendments*, Fact Sheet - Frequently Asked Questions (2016).; B. Mesnard, *Loss absorbing capacity in the Banking Union: TLAC implementation and MREL review*, Briefing of the European Parliament (2016) retrievable at http://www.europarl.europa.eu/RegData/etudes/BRIE/2016/574408/IPOL_BRI(2016)574408_EN.pdf accessed 1 October 2022.

586 Binding MREL targets will not be set immediately but within bank-specific transition periods up to a maximum of four years.

587 European Parliament, *Global Systemically Important Banks in Europe*, Briefing of the European Parliament (2017) retrievable at http://www.europarl.europa.eu/RegData/etudes/BRIE/2016/574406/IPOL_BRI%282016%29574406_EN.pdf accessed 1 October 2022.

For this purpose, in the course of the launch of a broader banking reform package,[588] the Commission issued a proposal[589] in November 2016 to integrate the TLAC requirement into[590] the existing European MREL system. The amendments established, *inter alia*, the new Articles 45 to

---

588 The Commission submitted and referred five proposals for reforming the banking legislation to the European Parliament. The five proposals introduced key prudential as well as resolution-related issues and amended the CRR, the CRD, the SRMS, and the BRRD. See, for an overview, European Parliament, *Banking Reform Package - Impact Assessment (SWD(2016)377) of five European Commission proposals amending EU banking legislation*, Briefing of the European Parliament (2017) retrievable at http://www.europarl.europa.eu/RegData/etudes/BRIE/2017/603251/EPRS_BRI%282017%29603251_EN.pdf accessed 1 October 2022. The legislative texts are currently being finalized during the trilogue phase and are expected to be definite by the end of 2018 or beginning of 2019 at the earliest. The following discourse will refer to the initial proposals made by the Commission, if not indicated otherwise. As regards the CRR amendments, it will refer to the presidency compromise from 22 May 2018, *Proposal for a Regulation of the European Parliament and of the Council amending Regulation (EU) No 575/2013 as regards the leverage ratio, the net stable funding ratio, requirements for own funds and eligible liabilities, counterparty credit risk, market risk, exposures to central counterparties, exposures to collective investment undertakings, large exposures, reporting and disclosure requirements and amending Regulation (EU) No 648/2012 - Presidency compromise* (2018). As regards the BRRD amendments, it will only refer to the presidency compromise of 22 May 2018 if specifically indicated, *Proposal for a Directive of the European Parliament and of the Council amending Directive 2014/59/EU on loss-absorbing and recapitalisation capacity of credit institutions and investment firms and amending Directive 98/26/EC, Directive 2002/47/EC, Directive 2012/30/EU, Directive 2011/35/EU, Directive 2005/56/EC, Directive 2004/25/EC and Directive 2007/36/EC - Presidency compromise* (2018). For a full overview of the legislative proposal with respect to the here-examined TLAC Implementation Proposal see European Parliament, Legal Observatory, available at https://oeil.secure.europarl.europa.eu/oeil/popups/ficheprocedure.do?lang=en&reference=2016/0362(OLP).

589 *Proposal for a Directive of the European Parliament and of the Council amending Directive 2014/59/EU on loss-absorbing and recapitalisation capacity of credit institutions and investment firms and amending Directive 98/26/EC, Directive 2002/47/EC, Directive 2012/30/EU, Directive 2011/35/EU, Directive 2005/56/EC, Directive 2004/25/EC and Directive 2007/36/EC, COM(2016) 852 final* (TLAC Implementation Proposal).

590 The integration of the TLAC standard for GSIBs into the existing resolution framework, while the framework was amended as appropriate to ensure full comparability with the TLAC standard, was option two out of three proposed policy options for implementing the TLAC standard in the Union. Option one (BRRD would continue to apply in its current form) and option three (extending the scope of the TLAC minimum level to other systemically-important institutions in the Union other than GSIBs) were discarded.

45l BRRD, which were to regulate the integrated approach. Considering the initial different designs of both instruments, it is apparent that all difficulties in the proposal might not yet have all been ironed-out,[591] as will be demonstrated in the subsequent sections. Indeed, the following two sections will briefly outline key aspects of both concepts in order to understand their different origins, followed by the Commission's proposal for an integrated approach in Europe.

Minimum Requirements for Own Funds and Eligible Liabilities

MREL, as introduced by Article 45 BRRD and according to the RTS on MREL, sets bank-specific binding targets for all banks under the remit of the BRRD. Once fully implemented, MREL targets shall be determined individually for each institution on a case-by-case basis. In 2017, MREL targets were set for the majority of the largest and complex banks including GSIBs, while other smaller banks are still subject to initial default targets, which were non-binding, non-enforceable, and non-challengeable.[592]

591 Although some of the topics covered here are considered less uncontroversial and are therefore not covered, or covered only in minimal depth, by the European Parliament, it recognizes that some points might pose problems (such as the weaknesses in the regulatory framework for loss-absorption and recapitalization capacity or the insolvency ranking) and actively searches for solutions, see European Parliament, *Banking Reform Package - Impact Assessment (SWD(2016)377) of five European Commission proposals amending EU banking legislation*; European Commission, *Impact Assessment accompanying the document Proposal amending Regulation (EU) No 575/2013 on prudential requirements for credit institutions and investment firms; - Directive 2013/36/EU on access to the activity of credit institutions and the prudential supervision of credit institutions and investment firms; - Directive 2014/59/EU establishing a framework for the recovery and resolution of credit institutions and investment firms; - Regulation (EU) No 806/2014 of the European Parliament and of the Council of 15 July 2014 establishing uniform rules and a uniform procedure for the resolution of credit institutions and certain investment firms in the framework of a Single Resolution Mechanism and a Single Resolution Fund SWD(2016) 377 final*, Commission Staff Working Document (henceforth Impact Assessment on Banking Package) retrievable at https://ec.europa.eu/info/system/files/161123-impact-assessment_en.pdf accessed 1 October 2022.

592 B. Mesnard and C. Katopodi, *Hearing with Mrs Elke König, Chair of the Single Resolution Board*, Briefing of the European Parliament (2017) retrievable at http://www.europarl.europa.eu/RegData/etudes/BRIE/2017/587403/IPOL_BRI(2017)587403_EN.pdf accessed 1 October 2022.

However, reaching the final individual MREL targets for all banks encompasses a multi-year timeframe with bank-specific transposition periods.[593] Generally, MREL targets are calculated according to the default formula set out in the RTS on MREL as the amount of own funds and eligible liabilities expressed as a percentage of the total liabilities of own funds of the institution. The target MREL consists of two components: a default loss-absorption amount (LAA),[594] reflecting the losses a bank will incur in resolution; and a recapitalization amount (RCA),[595] reflecting the capital needs to meet the prudential capital requirements after resolution. The targets are thereupon tailored with bank-specific adjustments made to the RCA by using a different basis for risk-weighted assets (RWA), while taking into account any potential involvement of a deposit guarantee scheme and certain other factors.

Since each target shall be calculated individually, MREL levels are set by the resolution authority on a case-by-case basis, Article 45(6) BRRD. When setting the MREL, the resolution authority has certain discretions in assessing the MREL needs of a specific institution, taking into consideration of certain criteria that might lead the resolution authority to set higher or lower levels than the default formula would account for in specific cases.[596] In general, the MREL will set a sufficiently prudent level around an 8 % benchmark to allow access, if necessary, to financing arrangements such as the SRF.[597]

Instruments counting towards the MREL must meet the following eligibility criteria: eligible liabilities must be issued and fully paid up; the liability must not be owed to, secured by, or guaranteed by the institution itself; the purchase of the instrument must not have been funded directly or indirectly by the institution; the liability must have a remaining maturi-

593 See for the recent development of the MREL implementation under the remit of the SRB Single Resolution Board, *Minimum Requirements for Own Funds and Eligible Liabilities (MREL) - SRB Policy for 2017 and Next Steps* (2017).

594 SRB Default Loss Absorption Amount (LAA) = Max (P1+P2R+CBR; Basel 1 floor). The default LAA is considered to be the higher of either the sum of a bank's minimum capital requirements (Pillar 1), its Pillar 2 requirements (P2R) and its fully-loaded combined buffer requirements (CBR) or the amount required to meet Basel 1 floor, see ibid.

595 SRB Default Recapitalization Amount = Max (P1+P2R; Basel 1 floor) plus SRB Default Market Confidence Charge = CRB – 125 basis points, see ibid., p.11.

596 Mesnard, *Loss absorbing capacity in the Banking Union: TLAC implementation and MREL review*., p. 2.

597 Single Resolution Board, *Minimum Requirements for Own Funds and Eligible Liabilities (MREL) - SRB Policy for 2017 and Next Steps*..

ty of at least one year; the liability must not arise from a derivative; and the liability must not arise from a deposit which benefits from preference in the national insolvency hierarchy, see Article 45(4) BRRD. Liabilities governed by the law of a third country also require special attention when determining their eligibility for the MREL.[598]

Total Loss-Absorbing Capacity

TLAC differs from the approach taken by the MREL insofar as it sets a standard minimum level for highly loss-absorbent instruments to be held only by all GSIBs, meaning that it sets a mandatory Pillar 1 requirement. The minimum TLAC requirements apply to each resolution entity[599] within a GSIB. In contrast to the BRRD's discretionary approach consisting of individual requirements on a case-by-case basis, considered collectively as the "Pillar 2" requirement, each GSIB is required to hold a minimum level of eligible TLAC instruments. Beyond that, GSIBs may additionally be subject to additional firm-specific requirements that home authorities of resolution entities, in consultation with the Crisis Management Groups and subject to review in the Resolvability Assessment Process (RAP), can apply above the minimum TLAC if they consider it necessary and appropriate in terms of orderly resolution procedures, financial stability, critical functions, and the avoidance of public funds.[600]

Instruments eligible for fulfilling the TLAC minimum differ from those eligible for the MREL. According to the TLAC principles, a "TLAC-eligible instrument" refers to “any capital instrument, debt instrument, liability or other item that is eligible as TLAC under the term sheet.”[601] Such an

598 For a comprehensive overview of MREL and its features before the integrated approach, see N. G. Maragopoulos, *Minimum Requirements for own Funds and Eligible Liabilities (MREL): A Comprehensive Analysis of the New Prudential Requirement for Credit Institutions*, ECEFIL Working Paper Series (2016) retrievable at SSRN https://ssrn.com/abstract=2836530 accessed 1 October 2022.

599 A resolution entity is an entity to which resolution tools will be applied in accordance with the resolution strategy for the GSIBs. Depending on the resolution strategy, the resolution entity may be a parent company, in an intermediate or ultimate holding company, or an operating subsidiary. A GSIB may have more than one resolution entity. See Financial Stability Board, *Principles on Loss-absorbing and Recapitalisation Capacity of G-SIBs in Resolution*, term sheet point 3.

600 Ibid., term sheet points 3 and 4.

601 Ibid., recital (viii).

instrument must: be fully paid-in; be unsecured; not be subject to any set-off or netting rights that would undermine their loss-absorbing capacity; be subject to a maturity restriction; not be redeemable by the holder prior to maturity; and not be funded directly or indirectly by the resolution entity or a related party of the resolution entity.[602] The following are excluded: insured deposits; sight and short-term deposits; liabilities arising from derivatives; derivative-linked debt instruments such as structured notes; liabilities arising other than through a contract; liabilities which are preferred to senior unsecured creditors; or any liabilities that are excluded from bail-in under the laws governing the issuing country.[603] One of the biggest differences is that TLAC instruments need to be subordinated in a contractual, statutory, or structural way with only limited exceptions, while the MREL does not require a statutory subordination.

TLAC will come into effect as of 1 January 2019,[604] when all GSIBs will have to comply with a minimum amount equal to the higher of 16 % of risk weighted assets (RWA) or 6 % of leverage ratio exposure (LRE[605]), with a rise in the minimum thresholds in 2022 to 18 % and 6.75 % respectively.[606] As this TLAC quota only constitutes a minimum, authorities may add an individual surplus amount on a case-by-case basis.

In contrast to the MREL, TLAC also provides for internal TLAC within banking groups. As a first step, TLAC is applied at the level of the resolution entity, irrespective of whether there are one (SPE approach) or several (MPE approach) resolution entities. As a second step, a minimum amount of 75 % to 90 % of the initial external TLAC must be allocated to the

602 Ibid., term sheet point 9.

603 Ibid., term sheet point 10.

604 On 6 June 2018, the FSB called for public feedback on the technical implementation on its TLAC Standard, see Financial Stability Board, *Monitoring the Technical Implementation of the FSB Total Loss-absorbing Capacity (TLAC) Standard - Call for public feedback* (2018) retrievable at http://www.fsb.org/wp-content/uploads/P060618.pdf accessed 1 October 2022. So far, only institutions from Switzerland and Japan have responded, see http://www.fsb.org/2018/08/public-responses-to-the-call-for-public-feedback-on-monitoring-the-technical-implementation-of-the-fsb-total-loss-absorbing-capacity-tlac-standard/ accessed 1 October 2022.

605 Leverage ratio exposure (LRE) is the denominator of the leverage ratio according to the Basel III standard.

606 On the optimal size and composition of banks' total loss-absorbing capacity see C. Mendicino, K. Nikolov and J. Suarez, *Equity Versus Bail-In Debt in Banking: An Agency Perspective*, CEPR Discussion Paper (2017) retrievable at SSRN https://ssrn.com/abstract=2992534 accessed 1 October 2022.

subsidiaries for each material subgroup[607] within the resolution group. If losses at sub-group level occur, they can be up-streamed to the resolution entity in accordance with the pre-defined resolution strategy. Instruments eligible for internal TLAC are the same as those for eligible external TLAC, except with regard to the issuing entity and permitted holder.[608]

Integrated Approach – Commission Proposal

As TLAC is a global standard that needs to be integrated into European legislation for it to enter into force, the Commission issued the TLAC Implementation Proposal describing what an integrated approach, in accordance with the European MREL requirements, would look like. A pure adoption of the FSB's TLAC standard would have created a misalignment with the existing MREL conditions and would have established a parallel standard and duplication for GSIBs in the EU. Once the initial different designs above have been examined, it becomes apparent that an integrated approach would have been difficult[609] to come up with. Therefore, a consistent and in-depth integrated approach became necessary, and this required adjustments to the existing MREL provisions to ensure technical consistency with the structure of any GSIB requirement.[610] Operationally, the proposal introduced TLAC's minimum level (Pillar 1) into the MREL regulation through amendments to the CRR and CRD, while the additional institution-specific requirements (Pillar 2) for GSIBs and the

607 A sub-group of a resolution entity is considered "material" for purposes of applying the internal TLAC requirement if the subsidiary alone, or the subsidiaries forming the sub-group on a sub-consolidated basis at the level of the sub-group, meet at least one of the following criteria: (a) have more than 5 % of the consolidated risk-weighted assets of the GSIB group; or (b) generate more than 5 % of the total operating income of the G-SIB group; or (c) have a total leverage exposure measure larger than 5 % of the G-SIB group's consolidated leverage exposure measure; or (d) have been identified by the firm's CMG as material to the exercise of the firm's critical functions (irrespective of whether any other criteria of this section are met), see section 17 of the TLAC Term Sheet.

608 Mesnard, *Loss absorbing capacity in the Banking Union: TLAC implementation and MREL review*, p. 4; Financial Stability Board, *Guiding Principles on the Internal Total Loss-absorbing Capacity of G-SIBs ('Internal TLAC')* (2017).

609 A critical analysis of the Commission's banking package can be found in Stiefmüller, *Ten Years After – The 2017 Banking Package: One Step Forward, Two Steps Back*..

610 Context of the TLAC Implementation Proposal.

institution-specific MREL for non-GSIBs are covered by amendments to the BRRD and the SRMR.

Under the integrated approach, for the clarification of terminology issues, a minimum Pillar 1 MREL applies to GSIBs, while an individual Pillar 2 MREL applies to all non-GSIBs. An additional Pillar 2 MREL can be placed on GSIBs and non-GSIBs if necessary. If reference is made to a provision of the new integrated approach in the following part (either CRR, CRD, BRRD or SRMR), it is identified as "new Article [x]."

The integrated approach already solved some of the initial alignment problems, such as a common calculation base or the scope of application, and thereby lightened implementation difficulties. However, some of the initial issues have not been solved by the proposed integrated approach, while some issues are not even addressed in the proposal. The neglected points are outlined below. Conclusively, it has to be noted that no final agreement has been reached yet with regard to the integrated approach, especially on the proposals to amend the BRRD and the CRR.[611]

The Potential of LACRs to Enhance Credibility Ex Post Resolution Decision

Before entering into an analysis of impediments inherent in the new integrated approach, this paragraph intends to outline the potential of LACRs to enhance the credibility of bail-in. Above, under Part 2, A.III., loss-absorbing capital requirements (LACRs) were proposed as a potential antidote to current *ex post* problems harming the credibility of resolution. These encompass, primarily, the lack of sufficient and adequate private resolution financing. By adding a material component to the resolution pro-

611 See the recent presidency compromises on BRRD and CRR amendments, *Proposal for a Directive of the European Parliament and of the Council amending Directive 2014/59/EU on loss-absorbing and recapitalisation capacity of credit institutions and investment firms and amending Directive 98/26/EC, Directive 2002/47/EC, Directive 2012/30/EU, Directive 2011/35/EU, Directive 2005/56/EC, Directive 2004/25/EC and Directive 2007/36/EC - Presidency compromise*; *Proposal for a Regulation of the European Parliament and of the Council amending Regulation (EU) No 575/2013 as regards the leverage ratio, the net stable funding ratio, requirements for own funds and eligible liabilities, counterparty credit risk, market risk, exposures to central counterparties, exposures to collective investment undertakings, large exposures, reporting and disclosure requirements and amending Regulation (EU) No 648/2012 – Presidency compromise*.

cess, a contextual filling for the application of the bail-in tool, LACRs have the potential to significantly enhance the resolution-financing mechanism and thereby the credibility of resolution measures. The following section points out the remedial features of LACRs based on their current legal framework.[612]

The potential of loss-absorbing capacities lies in their ability to underpin private resolution-funding mechanisms or, more precisely, the bail-in instrument in such a way that public funding and – optimally – even sector-specific funding is no longer required. If loss-absorbing capacities were well set up, even loopholes such as precautionary recapitalization or fleeing into national insolvency proceedings would no longer be as appealing as they are now.[613] With sufficient and adequate loss-absorbing capacities in place, as envisaged, the resolution-funding procedure for a bank that is considered to be failing or likely to fail would be the following: without shirking resolution procedures by applying for precautionary recapitalization outside resolution, an uninfluenced decision is made as to whether the institution can be put under national insolvency proceedings or whether it needs to be resolved. As the path towards resolution is now paved with sufficient resolution funding, resorting to national insolvency proceedings in order to pass helter-skelter insolvency laws that permit public financing, as happened in Italy,[614] is no longer desirable. If the

612 It is referred to the framework as at the end of 2018. The Commission proposed a banking reform package with an extensive overhaul of key legislation pieces such as the CRR, CRD, BRRD, and SRMR in November 2016. The relevant reform was the integration of FSB's global TLAC standard into European MREL legislation, see European Commission, *EU Banking Reform: Strong banks to support growth and restore confidence*, Press Release (2016) retrievable at http://europa.eu/rapid/press-release_IP-16-3731_en.pdf accessed 1 October 2022. However, adoption is still pending. Therefore, pre-proposal legislation is still applicable, see Art. 45 BRRD for MREL; Financial Stability Board, *Principles on Loss-absorbing and Recapitalisation Capacity of G-SIBs in Resolution* for TLAC.

613 D. Laboureix and V. Decroocq, 'Enhancing the Capacity to Apply a Bail-in Through the MREL Setting' in G. B. Navetti, G. Calzolari and A. F. Pozzolo (eds.), *European Economy: Banks, Regulation, and the Real Sector* (Rome: Europeye, 2016), pp. 117–30, p. 128.

614 Camera dei deputati ed il Senato della Repubblica, *Conversione in legge, con modificazioni, del decreto-legge 25 giugno 2017, n. 99, recante disposizioni urgenti per la liquidazione coatta amministrativa di Banca Popolare di Vicenza S.p.A. e di Veneto Banca S.p.A. (17G00133) (GU Serie Generale n.184 del 08-08-2017)*; Banca D'Italia, *Informazioni sulla soluzione della crisi di Veneto Banca S.p.A. e Banca Popolare di Vicenza S.p.A.* retrievable at https://www.bancaditalia.it/media/notizie/2017/Nota-Venetobanca-e-BPV.pdf accessed 1 October 2022.

institution is determined to be sent into resolution, potential resolution-financing needs would primarily be covered by private funding (*e.g.* the mandatory bail-in). Such a mandatory bail-in, irrespective of the exact resolution plan and the applicable instruments, would ideally cover all resolution-funding needs – loss-absorption and recapitalization – that arise from or during the application of the envisaged resolution plan, which was designed to include the new loss-absorption requirements. If LACRs build up sufficient and adequate loss-absorbing capacity before resolution, problems such as discretional exemptions of certain liabilities, socio-economic repercussions of bail-in, or NCWO issues would have no impact on the likely outcome of the resolution. As a result, policy considerations would be weakened, rendering resolution more predictable.[615] Therefore, LAC is not only a remedy for the identified *ex post* lacks but would also enhance recovery and resolution planning. Additionally, when an institution was able to build up sufficient LAC in advance of a resolution case, it will be more capable of attracting other private market funding shortly after resolution,[616] thereby reducing the likelihood of ELA requests. Moreover, LACRs would install market discipline *ex ante*, and investors would price bank capital without considering implicit government guarantees, but only with respect to their default risk.[617] All successive steps of the pre-described BRRD burden-sharing cascade would no longer be necessary to actually finance the resolution procedure and could be put aside to serve as a backstop.

However, both MREL and TLAC, as well as the new integrated approach based on them, are new and hence suffer from teething difficulties and impediments. Therefore, the following section tries to shed some light on those impediments that might reduce the remedial potential of LACRs to enhance the credibility of resolution action *ex post*.

---

615 T. H. Tröger, 'Why MREL won't help much: Minimum requirements for bail-in capital as insufficient remedy for defunct private sector involvement under the European bank resolution framework', *SAFE Working Paper* no. 180 (2018), p. 2 retrievable at SSRN https://ssrn.com/abstract=3023185 accessed 1 October 2022.

616 The enhancement of LAC for the sake of attracting private market funding after resolution was recently stressed by B. Balz, *SRB Conference 2018 – 10 years after the crisis: are banks now resolvable?*, SRB Annual Conference (Brussels, 2018).

617 Tröger, 'Optimal Bail-In Tools - Observations From A European Perspective', p. 2.

Identification of Possible Impediments to the Potential of Loss-Absorbing Capital Requirements

It has been demonstrated that LACRs include features that are potentially suitable for tackling the identified post-resolution lacks. However, an enhancement of credibility through said instrument can only be reasonably expected if the provisions of LACRs are suitable not only in theory but in practice as well, and if the integrated approach does not suffer from its own impediments that might mitigate the enhancing potential of LACRs.

With this in mind, the following section will shed light on potential impediments. It does so by precisely pointing out the individual impediments rather than by offering only general criticism. Only though an accurate designation can we properly contribute to finding suitable solutions at a later stage. The focus of the research presented in the following paragraphs is the integrated approach enshrined in the Commission's proposed banking package (as indicated above), even though it is still not binding and will not be finalized before the end of 2018.

Implementation, Monitoring, and Maintenance Costs

When looking at the proposed concept of an integrated approach, it becomes clear that the implementation, monitoring, and maintenance of a functioning loss-absorbing system according to the proposed rules will most likely trigger massive administrative costs. This is particularly the case for non-GSIB MREL, as its Pillar 2 requirement needs to be determined by the resolution authority on an individual basis, while GSIB MREL is a Pillar 1 requirement, the determination for which requires less effort. The costs will materialize both initially and continually, and will consist of expensive manpower on both sides (institutions and authorities), time, resources, and actual equipment or software expenses. This can be demonstrated by considering the collection mechanisms required for MREL-relevant information. As well as the more general information that is drawn out of the institution-made recovery plan and certain templates annexed to the European Commission's Implementing Regulation,[618]

618 Commission Implementing Regulation (EU) 2016/1066 on ITS on resolution plans; for a detailed description of the templates used for resolution planning see *supra* Part 3, A.II.1.h.iv. – *Templates*.

standard forms, and other templates,[619] the competent resolution authority will collect the MREL-relevant information via the Liability Data Report (LDR).[620] The LDR is a complex multi-page Excel template that requests and collects a bundle of information by means of opaque abbreviations, ratios, indicators, and numbers. It is explained in a 54-page-long guidance document,[621] indicating that the understanding, completion, and submission of the LDR requires considerable effort. For both authorities and institutions, requests must be understood, approaches must be found, and information must be generated, processed and recorded. All such activities are time-consuming and costly. Furthermore, as it proved to be insufficient to collect the required LDR information via the provided Excel sheets, the SRB set up automated data collection, storage, and analysis using XBRL (eXtensible Business Reporting Language),[622] introducing and implementing a new format that required, and still requires, implementation, software, and learning from those concerned in the resolution-planning process.[623] That is extremely problematic in terms of the fragmented, outdated, and sometimes ancient IT structures still in place in institutions.[624] Once implemented, the process needs to be assessed regularly, and data collection and data renewing will both be ongoing tasks. This is also true for the monitoring and supervision of the institutions while they provide the data.

It is widely understood that the introduction of new regulation or instruments always triggers costs to a greater or lesser extent, however the costs associated with the implementation of LACRs appear to be exceptionally high, mainly because LACRs need to be updated perpetually and

---

619 Single Resolution Board, *The Single Resolution Mechanism - Introduction to Resolution Planning*, p. 21.

620 The latest version of the LDR Excel sheet (v2.7.1) can be downloaded at https://srb.europa.eu/en/content/liability-data-report accessed 1 October 2022.

621 Single Resolution Board, *Guidance on the 2019 Liability Data Report* retrievable at https://srb.europa.eu/sites/srbsite/files/2019_draft_guidance_on_the_liability_data_report_v2.3clean.pdf accessed 1 October 2022.

622 Liability Data Report, https://srb.europa.eu/en/content/liability-data-report (last retrieved on 04.09.2018).

623 The SRB recently demanded that "banks should ensure that they have the necessary IT processes in place to facilitate a timely, controlled and robust reporting process generating consistent and reliable results", see https://srb.europa.eu/en/content/liability-data-report accessed 1 October 2022.

624 See on this *supra* Part 2, A.II.1.b.ii. – *Legal and Organizational Structures.*

compliance thereto must be checked.[625] Moreover, the costs for individual institutions in implementing systems can be high. A statement, in the sense of a cost-benefit analysis, cannot be made. Nevertheless, high costs, not only initially but continually, might expose the LACRs to cost-avoidance attempts, thereby weakening the instrument, and raising doubts about its economic benefit.

Implementation of Integrated LACRs is Complex and Difficult to Understand

The second reservation that can be raised in connection with LACRs has several facets attributable to the complexity[626] of the instrument.[627] Against the MREL's rationale for creating clear-cut conditions for bail-inable instruments, one of the main problems is still that MREL specifications extend over different legislations and proposals and are too detailed and discretionary to achieve the intended rationale.[628]

The first problem concerns the understanding of international investors. TLAC – although itself already a complex regulation – is well-known to most international investors, as it is a global standard and applies to all GSIBs around the world. However, since the European Commission introduced the related concept of the MREL and subsequently merged the two concepts in its integrated approach, international non-EU investors might be confronted with an unknown and divergent concept of LACRs. Though international investors might understand TLAC and the consequences of investing in TLAC instruments, such investors might refrain from investing in the new integrated MREL instruments, where TLAC is implemen-

---

625 Although 2 out of 3 checks (level 1 for technical checks and level 2 for consistency checks) run automatically, the level 3 check that involves further consistency checks cannot be automated during the collection process, see Single Resolution Board, *Guidance on the 2018 Liability Data Report* (2017), p. 49.

626 In its impact assessment, the Commission as well as the European Parliament admitted that the current legislative framework is complex. Moreover, consultations amongst stakeholders obtained the same result, see European Parliament, *Banking Reform Package – Impact Assessment (SWD(2016)377) of five European Commission proposals amending EU banking legislation*.

627 Tröger, 'Why MREL won't help much', p. 2.

628 K. Lannoo, *Pursuing Multiple Objectives with the Banking Reform Package: Who can still follow?*, CEPS Commentary (Brussels, 2017), p. 3; Tröger, 'Why MREL won't help much', p. 3.

ted as a Pillar 1 MREL through amendments to both the regulatory capital and the resolution regulation.

Although investors might be confused about the 'relabeled' TLAC as Pillar 1 MREL, the problem affects mainly non-GSIBs that are subject to the discretionary Pillar 2 MREL, carrying implications on the institution's ability to issue and sell sufficient liabilities applicable for the MREL. As a consequence, institutions might be forced to discount on MREL instruments in order to sell sufficient instruments and fulfil the necessary quota.

Furthermore, in connection with the globally applicable TLAC, reservations about its transparency remain. The FSB's principles set out that "investors, creditors, counterparties, customers and depositors should have clarity about the order in which they will absorb losses in resolution."[629] The principles therefore concretize that “disclosure of information on the hierarchy of liabilities on a legal entity basis for, at a minimum, all resolution entities and each legal entity that forms party of a material sub-group is required so that there is as much clarity as possible *ex ante* about how losses are absorbed and recapitalization is effected in the resolution of cross-border groups.”[630] However questionable it is that every investor – even smaller and unsophisticated ones – has a full understanding of the hierarchy and structuring of each of their financial positions, it is even more doubtful that all kinds of counterparties, creditors, depositors, and especially the average customer fully understand the hierarchy of their investments and the accompanying consequences of such a hierarchy, particularly in light of the integrated European approach.

Eligibility of Instruments – Qualitative Requirements

One of the key issues in the new loss-absorbing regime is the definition of liabilities, which can be used to comply with the requirements of the new integrated approach to LACRs. Instruments must be of such a high quality that their conversion or write-down facilitates the loss-absorption and recapitalization of the institution's balance sheet and does not create liquidity constraints, or affect vulnerable creditors (*i.e.* must not entail

629 Financial Stability Board, *Principles on Loss-absorbing and Recapitalisation Capacity of G-SIBs in Resolution*, recital (xi).

630 Ibid., recital (xi).

negative consequences).[631] Initially, both instruments considered only certain liabilities to be eligible to satisfy the respective envisaged targets, and institutions started issuing eligible instruments either for the MREL or TLAC[632] prior to the proposed aligned and integrated exclusion and eligibility criteria under new Articles 72a, 72b CRR and 45b BRRD. To be clear, even if certain liabilities of an institution do not count towards LACRs, ineligible instruments are not necessarily excluded from bail-in. Such instruments might as well absorb losses in line with their ranking in the hierarchy of creditors.[633]

Under the original MREL approach, eligible instruments needed to be issued and fully paid-up, not owned, secured, or guaranteed by the institution, and the purchase of the instrument must not be funded directly or indirectly by the institution. The liability must not arise from a derivative or from a preferred deposit. To be considered eligible, the instruments do not need to be subordinated, however the resolution authorities can require that part of the MREL be met with contractual bail-in instruments, see Article 45(4) (a)-(c) BRRD. Excluded liabilities here comprise: covered bonds; mortgage bonds; securitizations; structured notes by default; non-covered and non-preferred deposits breakable below one year; liabilities issued under third-country law and most liabilities issued by entities located outside the EU; or liabilities governed by the laws of a country outside the EU. Compliance with binding targets will be assessed against eligible liabilities and own funds at the consolidated level: the SRB will consider those instruments issued by the parent undertaking and all other entities in the prudential scope of consolidation to be MREL-eligible, provided that they meet the other eligibility criteria.

In contrast, the initial TLAC term sheet considered liabilities unsecured and formally subordinated to excluded liabilities to be eligible, with only a

---

631 Tröger, 'Optimal Bail-In Tools - Observations From A European Perspective', p. 6.

632 This is why grandfathering rules or transitional arrangements are demanded in order to ensure the continued eligibility of such issuances and to provide clarity for banks on their shortfall and over their issuance needs in the future, see Association for Financial Markets in Europe, *Resolution aspects of the EU Risk Reduction Measures Package: Recommendation for effective implementation of TLAC, MREL and related reforms* (2017), p. 2 retrievable at https://www.afme.eu/globalassets/downloads/publications/afme-rrn-resolution-aspects-of-the-eu-rrm-package.pdf accessed 1 October 2022.

633 See Mesnard, *Loss absorbing capacity in the Banking Union: TLAC implementation and MREL review*, p. 3 and Annex A, where the eligibility of various classes of financial instruments for bail-in, the MREL, and TLAC is displayed.

few exceptions such as the option to allow non-subordinated instruments to count toward TLAC for an amount up to 2.5 %/3.5 % of RWA. Generally, TLAC-eligible liabilities are obliged to have a residual maturity of at least one year and need to be fully paid-up. Excluded here are structured notes, derivatives, and insured deposits, Section 9 (d) to (e) TLAC Term Sheet.

As both initial eligibility concepts diverge and would have produced inconsistencies when applied to European GSIBs, the Commission recognized the need for an integrated approach to the eligibility criteria for the instruments and items that could count toward meeting the integrated MREL by aligning them closely[634] to the eligibility criteria provided in the TLAC standard.[635] However, even if the criteria converge after the alignment, a certain disparity persists.[636] That disparity, even though it will contribute to some initial overall uncertainty, is said to have only a limited impact on practical results and will most likely disappear after the implementation of the integrated approach.[637] With respect to the alignment of the MREL with TLAC, the Commission has made significant progress.

Nevertheless, there seems to be a problem in terms of the new eligibility criteria of the integrated MREL being too loosely defined, leaving room for interpretation[638] and impairing the predictability of investors' loss exposure and risk pricing.[639] Some of these ambiguities are legacies from the initial single concepts, but some have emerged only recently in the wake of the introduction of the integrated approach. For example, under the integrated approach, derivative instruments, such as structured

---

634 Even if the alignment of the MREL eligibility criteria with the FSB's eligibility criteria for TLAC was partly pulled through, reservations remain about whether the proposed MREL eligibility criteria derive from the internationally agreed standard, see Bundesverband Öffentlicher Banken Deutschlands, VÖB, e.V., *Aktuelle Positionen zur Banken- und Finanzmarktregulierung, 2. Quartal 2018*, p. 14 retrievable at https://www.voeb.de/de/publikationen/voeb-positionen accessed 1 October 2022.

635 New eligibility criteria in chapter 5a of the CRR amendment proposal, especially Art. 72 (a) to (c) and (f) CRR amendment proposal (TLAC implementation) as well as Art. 45b (1) BRRD TLAC implementation proposal.

636 TLAC Implementation Proposal, explanatory memorandum, p. 9.

637 Tröger, 'Why MREL won't help much', p. 7.

638 See Impact Assessment on Banking Package.

639 Tröger, 'Why MREL won't help much', p. 7.

notes,[640] might be considered eligible in terms of meeting the MREL on a case-by-case basis[641] as long as they have a fixed principal amount repayable at maturity with only an additional return, because they could be sufficiently loss-absorbent in resolution and only the additional return is linked to a derivative and depends on the performance of a referenced asset, new Article 45b(2) BRRD. This new feature contradicts the notion that, generally, no derivatives are eligible in the fulfilment of either the MREL or the implemented TLAC standard. However, by allowing their eligibility on a discretional case-by-case basis, they are neither eligible nor excluded, thereby producing uncertainty.

Another notable example here can be found in the requirement that the now integrated TLAC in the form of the Pillar 1 minimum MREL should be largely met with subordinated debt instruments ranking below senior liabilities, such as covered deposits, derivatives, tax, or other public-law-related liabilities, which are explicitly excluded. Nevertheless, in exceptional cases, it can partly be met using non-subordinated debt instruments, new Article 72b(3) CRR. That contributes to uncertainty in relation to the current eligibility criteria.

In light of the two examples of the problem presented above, it is unsurprising that a consensus prevails that the design of the new eligibility criteria within the integrated approach has indeed eliminated initial alignment problems fully but has not succeeded in providing clarification and certainty in the market with respect to new integrated eligibility criteria for LACRs in Europe. This again contributes to the biggest (and underlying) problem of loss-absorbing instruments in the market in Europe: investors are unable to confidently handle the instruments as they lack predictability, transparency, and a sound referential framework.

Pricing of LAC Instruments

The points made in the last two paragraphs lead to a further problem: the correct and adequate pricing of loss-absorbing instruments by the market

640 Structured notes are debt obligations with an embedded derivative component. Their return is adjusted according to the performance of reference assets such as single equity, indices, funds, interest rates, commodities or currencies, see TLAC Implementation Proposal, explanatory memorandum, p. 9.

641 Single Resolution Board, *Minimum Requirements for Own Funds and Eligible Liabilities (MREL) - SRB Policy for 2017 and Next Steps*, pp. 15, 16.

in light of their complicatedness, complexity, and discretional character. Only if (at least sophisticated[642]) investors are capable of pricing integrated MREL instruments adequately, can LACRs play an efficient role in enhancing resolution and eliminating the option of public financing.[643] However, such adequate pricing can only be achieved if investors are able to understand *ex ante* what the risk and default probability of their investment is, meaning they must be able to predict outcomes of resolution and loss-allocation with certainty. Therefore, besides the elimination of political influence on bank failure, the accompanying implicit guarantees that result from such political interference[644] and the status of the intervening Member State,[645] a comprehensive understanding of the LACRs' underlying functioning and legal framework is of the utmost importance in ensuring that potential investors engage in adequate pricing.[646] Ideally, investors would only have to gauge the likelihood of the failure of the issuing bank for their pricing decision,[647] as the designated debt instruments would unexceptionally and constantly be bailed-in. Reservations about the European bail-in regime were expressed, and scholars have raised a concern that the new integrated approach to the rules concerning LACRs is highly detailed but at the same time fairly discretionary.[648] This makes it

642 As will be demonstrated below under Part 4, A.III.6. – *Potential Investors and Holders of MREL Eligible Instruments*, the investment in and holding of MREL-eligible debt instruments is only recommended to mainly sophisticated investors.

643 Although only in the context of general bail-in considerations, this was already stated by Tröger, 'Regulatory Influence on Market Conditions in the Banking Union: the Cases of Macro-Prudential Instruments and the Bail-in Tool', p. 585.

644 Tröger, 'Optimal Bail-In Tools - Observations From A European Perspective', p. 9.

645 88 % of investors think that the state, in which the institution they intend to invest in is incorporated, has a significant influence on the risk of their investment, W. Ervin, *SRB Conference 2018 – 10 years after the crisis: are banks now resolvable?*, SRB Annual Conference (Brussels, 2018).

646 Indeed, investors are concerned that there is a 'lack of overall consensus over the pricing of risk', see Tim Skeet to Thomas Jorgensen (ECB), 20 December 2016, 'Bail-in Working Group of the AMIC -International Capital Markets Association (ICMA)', Letter retrievable at https://www.icmagroup.org/assets/documents/Regulatory/Bank_Capital/BIWG-Letter-ECB-20-December-2016-201216.pdf accessed 1 October 2022.

647 Jensen and Meckling, 'Theory of the Firm: Managerial Behavior, Agency Costs and Ownership Structure', p. 49.

648 See Impact Assessment on Banking Package pp. 127 *et seq.*; Tröger, 'Why MREL won't help much', p. 6.

hard for potential investors in bail-in debt to correctly price the risk of their investment being involved in a potential bail-in. Indeed, currently only 10 % of European investors in debt instruments would say they have a comprehensive understanding of what happens with their investment in a resolution, or where they stand in the hierarchy. Three years ago, at least 30 % would have been satisfied with the transparency of their investment.[649] Thus, the new LAC rules might have actually reduced transparency.

The consequences of incorrect pricing are visible and far-reaching: each deviation from the optimal price produces either moral hazard (underpricing) or causes higher refinancing costs and impairs banks' lending capacity (overpricing).[650]

Given the eligibility criteria for debt to be suitable to count towards the MREL, specifically that it has to be long-term debt, another problem arises. Even if investors are somehow capable of correctly valuing the risk and price of the instrument at the time of investment, subsequent adjustments of authorities within the wide administrative discretion pertaining to the MREL arrangement may change the risk and price of the instruments, thereby rendering initial pricing decisions incorrect.[651] That is because the loss-participation of holders of MREL instruments might change[652], leaving the initially calculated risk-adjusted interest rate void and leading almost inevitably to initial overpricing or underpricing of MREL instruments, with respective implications for market discipline, moral hazard, and refinancing costs of the issuing banks.

Lastly, at least for a certain period of time prior to transition, markets will be swamped with bail-inable and MREL-suitable debt instruments when banks start to fulfil the quotas, especially when the envisaged stricter eligibility requirements in proposed Article 72b(2) CRR are confirmed.[653] The oversupply of MREL, besides causing massive issuance costs, will reduce the market depth for such instruments and might ultimately have

---

649 Ervin, *SRB Conference 2018 - 10 years after the crisis: are banks now resolvable?*.

650 For a numerical example, see Tröger, 'Why MREL won't help much', p. 3.

651 Ibid., p. 3.

652 See on why the loss-participation of MREL holders might change *supra* under Part 4, A.III.10. – *Calculation Process.*

653 Bundesverband der Deutschen Volksbanken und Raiffeisenbanken e.V. and Die Deutsche Kreditwirtschaft, *Stellungnahme zum Vorschlag der Kommission für Änderungen der BRRD/CRR im Zusammenhang mit MREL/TLAC Vorgaben* (2017), p. 2.

an additional distortionary influence on pricing until the market evens out. However, such a process could take several years.

Debt Subordination – New Article 108 BRRD

Another issue regarding the new integrated loss-absorbing capacities is the much-discussed problem of creditor hierarchies across EU Member States. In that respect, it is crucial to understand the difference between the concepts of eligibility for general bail-in and eligibility for integrated MREL.[654] Liabilities that are suitable for bail-in might not be eligible for LACRs, as the latter are aimed at defining and quantifying distinct categories of liabilities that can be bailed-in with a high degree of certainty, without interfering with the *pari passu* claims of others and therefore without triggering litigation risks.[655] Therefore, liabilities eligible for integrated MREL sometimes need to be subordinated to a certain extent. Such subordination can be achieved in three main ways: structural subordination;[656] contractual subordination;[657] or statutory subordination[658].

---

654 Stiefmüller, *Ten Years After - The 2017 Banking Package: One Step Forward, Two Steps Back*, p. 12.

655 In particular, subordination in relation to the MREL addresses risks stemming from having bail-inable instruments ranking *pari passu* with operational liabilities and any other excluded liabilities prescribed by Art. 44(2) BRRD or the discretionary power of the resolution authority to exclude some liabilities under exceptional circumstances, Art. 44(3) BRRD, see Single Resolution Board, *Minimum Requirements for Own Funds and Eligible Liabilities (MREL) - SRB Policy for 2017 and Next Steps*. In relation to the Pillar 1 requirement, subordination reduces the risk associated with the bail-in of senior securities ranking *pari passu* with other senior liabilities that are not bailed-in, such as covered bonds and derivatives, see Stiefmüller, *Ten Years After - The 2017 Banking Package: One Step Forward, Two Steps Back*, p. 12.

656 The eligible instruments are issued by a resolution entity which does not have any excluded liabilities ranking *pari passu* or is junior to the TLAC eligible instruments.

657 A contractual clause makes the instrument junior to excluded liabilities on the balance sheet of the resolution authority.

658 The eligible instrument is by law (statutory creditor hierarchy) junior to excluded liabilities on the balance sheet of the resolution entity.

On 23 November 2016, the Commission proposed[659] to amend Article 108 BRRD by partially harmonizing the insolvency hierarchies as regards priority of senior unsecured debt, which is generally eligible for both the MREL and the now-integrated TLAC standard. After implementation, two senior unsecured debt instruments would be available: preferred and non-preferred senior unsecured debt. However, only the latter would be eligible for the integrated minimum Pillar 1 MREL requirement for GSIBs or any subordination requirement that can be imposed by the resolution authorities on an individual basis. Some Member States, as a reaction to the TLAC and potential MREL subordination requirement and even before the proposal was issued, assessed and amended their insolvency ranking of certain bank creditors under national insolvency law – though not homogeneously.[660] According to the diverging national approaches, the existing amount of unsecured senior debt was subordinated with immediate effect, while others will need to issue new debt instruments to then meet the subordination requirement. Consequently, at the current stage, senior unsecured debt holders can be treated differently from one Member State to another. The significantly diverging national rules and the resulting uncertainty for issuers and investors, and the distorted cross-border application of bail-in, thus encouraged the European legislator to put forward a common approach for a harmonized national ranking of unsecured debt instruments in insolvency proceedings[661] that was adopted on 8 December 2017.[662] Now, throughout the EU, non-preferred senior

---

659 *Proposal for a Directive of the European Parliament and of the Council on amending Directive 2014/59/EU of the European Parliament and of the Council as regards the ranking of unsecured debt instruments in insolvency hierarchy, COM(2016) 853 final.*

660 Initially, France and Spain opted for contractual subordination, while the UK and Switzerland preferred structural subordination. Germany decided to alter the legislation and went for statutory subordination, see European Parliament, *Ranking of unsecured debt instruments in insolvency hierarchy*, Briefing of the European Parliament (2017) retrievable at http://www.europarl.europa.eu/RegData/etudes/BRIE/2017/599335/EPRS_BRI(2017)599335_EN.pdf accessed 1 October 2022.

661 *Proposal for a Directive of the European Parliament and of the Council on amending Directive 2014/59/EU of the European Parliament and of the Council as regards the ranking of unsecured debt instruments in insolvency hierarchy, COM(2016) 853 final*, context of the proposal.

662 *Directive (EU) 2017/2399 of the European Parliament and of the Council of 12 December 2017 amending Directive 2014/59/EU as regards the ranking of unsecured debt instruments in insolvency hierarchy, OJ L 345, 27.12.2017, p. 96–101: Insolvency Hierarchy Directive* (2017); see http://www.europarl.europa.eu/oeil/popups/summary.do?id=1514557&t=d&l=en accessed 1 October 2022.

unsecured debt must be a debt instrument such as a bond with no derivative-linked features. It must have an original contractual maturity of more than one year and must have a lower ranking than that of unsecured debt and a higher ranking than that of subordinated debt, new Article 108 BRRD. Most importantly, the subordination must be contractually agreed upon or such subordination must emerge from the prospectus.[663]

In response to the Commission's harmonized approach to national insolvency rankings, Member States have started to design their national insolvency laws accordingly, creating a new class of non-preferred senior instruments between subordinated debt and senior unsecured debt (*i.e.* the preferred senior debt). In line with the Commission's approach, Member States should opt for contractual subordination, whereby MREL eligibility requirements can be fulfilled by issuing debt subject to an express subordination clause. Germany[664] has already opted for a statutory subordination by changing the national insolvency laws at the beginning of 2017, where senior unsecured bonds were statutorily subordinated to operational liabilities like derivatives.[665] This approach largely conformed to the new approach, except for the absence of a requirement to contractually agree on the subordination. Starting from 21 July 2018, institutions were required to indicate the subordination of newly-issued non-preferred senior instruments either in the contract or in the prospectus. Other countries, such as France, Italy, Belgium, and Spain have already widely complied with the approach as they have chosen a mixed strategy, creating a new category of non-preferred senior unsecured debt mostly in the form of specific, contractual "non-preferred" Tier 3 debt, which is subordinated to operational debt.[666]

663 European Parliament, *Banking Reform Package – Impact Assessment (SWD(2016)377) of five European Commission proposals amending EU banking legislation*.

664 Germany changed its insolvency ranking by revising § 46f KWG (Kreditwesengesetz), which entered into force on 21 July 2018. German banks can now issue preferred senior unsecured debt; senior unsecured debt issued before 21 July 2018 remains non-preferred, even if not explicitly specified in the bond conditions, see S. E. Knips, *Bankenanleihen in Deutschland: Neue Preferred Senior Anleihen vor dem Start*, Helaba Volkswirtschaft/Research Credit Special (2018) retrievable at https://www.helaba.de/blob/helaba/467982/b4abee15218ed22c27c2b6dad70fab2b/cs-20180625-data.pdf accessed 1 October 2022.

665 BaFin, *Übersicht über die Haftungskaskade im Rahmen der Bankenabwicklung*. https://www.bafin.de/SharedDocs/Veroeffentlichungen/DE/Merkblatt/BA/mb_haftungskaskade_bankenabwicklung.html, accessed 1 October 2022.

666 Munoz, 'Bank resolution and insolvency ranking and priorities', pp. 271 *et seq.*

While, under the new integrated approach, GSIBs are largely required to comply with the subordination criterion for the Pillar 1 MREL minimum levels,[667] resolution authorities can decide on a case-by-case basis whether and to what extent the Pillar 2 MREL requirement is to be met with subordinated liabilities in order to "ensure that the resolution entity can be resolved in a manner suitable to achieve the resolution objectives," new Article 45b (3) BRRD.[668] In other words, only the transposed minimum Pillar 1 MREL instruments need to be subordinated (*e.g.* all GSIBs and some other systemically important institutions (OSIB)), while Pillar 2 MREL instruments do not need to be subordinated at all.[669]

Although the developments presented above make it sound like Europe is en route to finding an ultimate solution to the subordination problem, which was furiously discussed ahead of the recent proposal, the new approach still leaves room for criticism. What must be acknowledged is that the subordination requirement for the minimum Pillar 1 MREL for GSIBs[670] is still not set in stone and will most likely accommodate exceptions. Although eligible Pillar 1 instruments must generally absorb

667 European Commission, *Capital requirements (CRR/CRD IV) and resolution framework (BRRD/SRM) amendments*; Mesnard, *Loss absorbing capacity in the Banking Union: TLAC implementation and MREL review*, p. 4.

668 GSIBs will be expected to fulfil a minimum percentage of subordinated instruments (13.5 % RWA plus the CBR, pending further assessment of NCWO risks), while OSIBs will be set at a benchmark of 12 % of RWA plus CBR. The requirement of other institutions to subordinate will be determined on a case-by-case basis, European Parliament, *Amending the bank resolution framework - BRRD and SRMR*, Briefing of the European Parliament (2017) retrievable at http://www.europarl.europa.eu/RegData/etudes/BRIE/2017/603958/EPRS_BRI(2017)603958_EN.pdf accessed 1 October 2022.

669 Besides this 'light' scenario based on the EBA and the Parliament's recommendations, where only a minimum subordination requirement of 14.5 % of RWA for GSIBs, 12 % of RWA for OSIBs, and no requirement for the rest of the banks apply, two other scenarios are possible. A 'medium' scenario, according to the Council's minimum subordination requirement of 8 % of Total Liabilities and Own Funds for "top tier" banks, or a 'hard' scenario, with full subordination in which banks have to comply with MREL using only subordinated instruments, Presidency of the Council of the European Union, *Note to the Council; Subject: Banking package - General approach* (2018); J. García and M. Rocamora, *How prepared are European banks to comply with MREL?: The importance of the subordination requirement*, BBVA Research , p. 4 retrievable at https://www.bbvaresearch.com/wp-content/uploads/2018/08/2018-08-The-position-of-EU-banks-to-comply-with-MREL_Final.pdf accessed 1 October 2022.

670 Even the subordination requirement for non-GSIB MREL is not definite yet, see below at the end of this paragraph.

losses prior to liabilities excluded from minimum Pillar 1 MREL, subordination of eligible external Pillar 1 MREL to excluded liabilities is not required in certain cases,[671] as was incorporated in the newly-proposed Article 72b(3)-(6) CRR. This exemption has been addressed as a problematic issue and demands to be reconsidered. The line of argument in this respect is twofold. First, it assumes that it is difficult to see how including certain claims that are not subordinated, and therefore potentially give rise to "material risk of successful legal challenge or valid compensation claims" if bailed-in, would not also "have a material adverse impact on the resolvability of the institution," see new Article 72b (3)(c) CRR.[672] Second, and more importantly, authorities have discretion in requiring subordination both for Pillar 1, concerning exceptions from the mandatory subordination requirement, as well as for Pillar 2 concerning the general discretion as to whether instruments must be subordinated at all. In line with the above paragraphs, this complicates pricing by investors, as they have to resort to guesswork on the authorities' exercise of discretion and have to anticipate the supervisory or resolution authorities' comportment towards exceptions. Consequently, market discipline evolving from risk-adequate pricing of MREL/TLAC eligible debt is adversely affected.[673]

In conclusion, it must be noted that the final design of the subordination requirement has not been decided upon yet. Whereas the Council supports a tougher approach compared to the Commission's initial proposal, the Parliament seeks to stick to international principles.[674] Three

671 Financial Stability Board, *Principles on Loss-absorbing and Recapitalisation Capacity of G-SIBs in Resolution*, section 11.

672 For example, GSIBs are not required to subordinate certain amounts of their MREL (3.5 % of their RWA) if the instruments rank *pari passu* with only the lowest-ranking ineligible instrument and their inclusion "does not have a material adverse effect on the resolvability of the institution," Art. 72b (3) CRR amendment proposal. For another possible exception, see Art. 72b (4) CRR amendment proposal. Stiefmüller, *Ten Years After - The 2017 Banking Package: One Step Forward, Two Steps Back*, p. 13; Tröger, 'Why MREL won't help much', p. 8.

673 For examples illustrating how different discretional authority decisions can influence the loss-participation of investors MREL/TLAC debt, see Tröger, 'Why MREL won't help much', pp. 8 *et seq.*

674 The Parliament's version of the subordination requirement is similar to the one that may be found in the FSB's TLAC Term sheet, although its scope is expanded to include banks other than GSIBs.

possible scenarios could emerge, ranging from a light,[675] to a medium[676] to a hard[677] scenario. Depending on the scenario that ultimately materializes, massive shortfalls are to be expected[678] (see below Part 4, A.III.12. – *Current Shortfall and Transposition)* that would further weaken the situation of investors in estimating pricing and guessing the risk of MREL instruments.

Potential Investors and Holders of MREL-Eligible Instruments

The fate of loss-absorbing capital instruments is another issue here: in a bail-in, they can be written-off or converted into equity, resulting in their holders being either left empty-handed or their claims being converted into equity in a struggling institution in an amount most likely lower than the nominal value of the initial claim. Both scenarios have an impact on the financial situations of the holders of these instruments. Recalling the overreaching objective of the new resolution regime – enabling each bank to exit the market without contagion and threat to the financial markets or the real economy – it should be clear that such a burden can only be placed on the shoulders of those who can actually absorb such deep-cutting impacts.[679]

Holders of integrated MREL instruments must therefore be able to survive a potential bail-in of their holdings on their own, and either must

675 A light scenario would be based on the recommendations of the EBA, similar to the one proposed by the Parliament, that is, a minimum subordination requirement of 14.5 % of RWA for GSIBs; 13.5 % of RWA for O-SIIs and no requirement for the rest of the banks, see García and Rocamora, *How prepared are European banks to comply with MREL?*, p. 4.

676 A medium scenario would be based on the Council's minimum subordination requirement of 8 % of total liabilities and own funds, see ibid., p. 4.

677 A hard scenario would be based on full subordination, in which banks would have to comply with MREL using subordinated instruments only without any allowance to compute other instruments such as senior preferred debt, see ibid., p. 4.

678 Ibid., p. 5.

679 This feature is of the utmost importance, see Zhou, Rutledge, Bossu, Dobler and Jassaud, *From bail-out to bail-in*, 2012/3, p. 22; Krahnen and Moretti, 'Bail-In Clauses', p. 140; M. R. Götz and T. H. Tröger, *Should the marketing of subordinated debt be restricted/different in one way or the other?: What to do in the case of mis-selling?*, In-Depth Analysis for the Economics and Monetary Affairs Committee of the European Parliament (2016), p. 6 retrievable at http://www.europarl.europa.eu/RegData/etudes/IDAN/2016/497723/IPOL_IDA(2016)497723_EN.pdf accessed 1 October 2022.

be resilient enough not to pass on the negative effects to other market participants, or must not be affiliated to other market participants, in order to prevent contagion.[680] In addition, considering that recent banking crises have revealed the strong political influence of governments and bureaucrats on resolution, holders of potential MREL instruments must not only be equipped to bear losses and be resilient, but they must also be 'uninteresting' enough for politicians not to exert influence on or shield them. Given that this already leaves only a limited group of potential investors, it must be kept in mind that the use of loss-absorbing capital should not trigger systemic risk. Ideally, the potential investors must not be too few in number, as diversification of market participants generally reduces the risk of systemic effects.[681]

Possible Investors

Bearing in mind the features of optimal investors in MREL instruments – resilient, non-systemic and 'uninteresting' on the one hand, and diversified across the market on the other hand – the group of possible holders of MREL instruments is constantly evolving. However, before going into detail about the possible investors, it would be useful to first rule out all investors that are not suitable to hold loss-absorbing debt and to examine whether MREL instruments are currently held by any such unsuitable holders.[682]

Retail Investors – Households – SMEs

The most obvious exclusions from the pool of potential MREL holders are retail investors, households, and small or medium enterprises (SMEs). The main reason for their exclusion is not merely that smaller investors usually absorb losses less comfortably than bigger investors who are probably more diversified and capitalized, but it is rather primarily due to their lack of experience in researching and understanding the risk of their

680 Tröger, 'Optimal Bail-In Tools - Observations From A European Perspective', p. 10.
681 For a detailed list of an ideal investor's properties, see ibid., pp. 14 *et seq.*
682 Götz and Tröger, *Should the marketing of subordinated debt be restricted/different in one way or the other?*, pp. 10 *et seq.*

investments.[683] Furthermore, if these groups of people invest in bail-inable debt, losses could lead to adverse social effects that, in turn, may induce politicians to shield these people from losses, preventing wide-spread consequences, panic in the market, and impediments for the real economy. The anticipation of such interventions in resolution could again weaken credibility.[684] Additionally, the risk of litigation brought by retail investors might endanger the bank's future viability.[685] Therefore, investors belonging to the aforementioned group cannot be considered adequate holders of MREL-eligible instruments.[686] Evidence from Italy can be used again to demonstrate the importance of restricting holdings of MREL/TLAC eligible capital. In both Italian cases – Monte dei Paschi di Siena and the case of the two Venetian banks – political influence, because of 'wrong' holders of potentially bail-inable capital, was exerted and this influenced the loss-participation of such holders. In both cases, retail investors, savers, and SMEs were the designated 'wrong' holders. To be sure, other motivations such as shielding a 'national champion'[687] may also have played a role in tempting the Italian government to bail out the institutions, especially in the MPS

683 Furthermore, being uninformed and therefore not rational in their investments, they undermine the financial markets' role in allocating resources efficiently. In times of financial distress, they trade uncontrollably and unreasonably and cause panic selling. Retail investors are more prone to behavioral biases and external influences than sophisticated investors.

684 Tröger, 'Optimal Bail-In Tools - Observations From A European Perspective', p. 11.

685 Single Resolution Board, *Minimum Requirements for Own Funds and Eligible Liabilities (MREL) - SRB Policy for 2017 and Next Steps*, recital 43.

686 Although in the context of recent resolution cases and current holdings by unsophisticated investors, the SRB stated that it does not see any legal basis for resolution authorities to exclude *ex ante* and uniformly eligible liabilities held by natural persons or SMEs from MREL or from bail-in. It states that EU legislation includes many safeguards to ensure that financial products are sold to suitable investors only. Implementation and supervision is the responsibility of Member States' market authorities, and failure to comply is no argument for excluding these liabilities, see ibid. The EBA and the ESMA, however, take a more moderate view by stating that retail hold liabilities may, under specific and exceptional circumstances, be exempted from bail-in, even at the resolution planning stage, effectively rendering investment in retail debt riskless, see the EBA and ESMA, *Statement of the EBA and ESMA on the treatment of retail holdings of debt financial instruments subject to the Bank Recovery and Resolution Directive* (2018), p. 17.

687 MPS was not a 'national champion' in the classical sense, however, it was Italy's oldest bank and therefore prestigious. Letting MPS slip into insolvency would have destroyed over 500 years of successful banking history.

case. Nevertheless, the identity of the banks' creditors (*i.e.* the holders of bail-inable debt) significantly influenced the futures of the struggling institutions.

Notwithstanding both the above and common knowledge about retail investors holding bail-inable debt, retail investors still hold an important proportion of EU debt securities[688] and debt is still sold to retail investors. However, even if the negative consequences of selling loss-absorbing debt instruments to retail investors or other non-qualified investors are obvious and well-known, the new integrated approach fails to address this problem. Legislators did not interfere by imposing a restriction on selling instruments to retail investors, and instead left the problem to be regulated *ex post* by governments, as was the case in Italy, by securities regulation[689] or by supervisory authorities.[690] Indeed, even the SRB argues that the general EU legislation includes sufficient safeguards[691] to ensure that financial products are sold only to suitable investors.[692] However, it is highly doubtful that information and "a robust investor protection regime," as envisaged by the SRB or the EBA,[693] can mitigate the negative effects of selling core bail-in debt to retail investors. Just because retail investors are aware of the risk associated with financial products, negative

688 As of the third quarter of 2017, retail investors of the euro area held 262.4 billion euros or 12.7 % of the EU bank debt securities issued to euro area investors, see EBA and ESMA, *Statement of the EBA and ESMA on the treatment of retail holdings of debt financial instruments subject to the Bank Recovery and Resolution Directive*, pp. 2, 5. Especially in Italy (132.3 billion euros), Germany (49.4 billion euros) and France (31.7 billion euros), high amounts are held by retail investors. The distribution of retail debt is highly fragmented and becomes insignificantly small beyond the five countries with the biggest retail holdings.

689 Ibid., pp. 2 *et seq*.

690 Tröger, 'Why MREL won't help much', p. 20; Götz and Tröger, *Should the marketing of subordinated debt be restricted/different in one way or the other?*, p. 14.

691 For example, investor protection through information to retail clients according to Art. 24 MiFID II; Arts. 44, 46 and 48 MiFID II Delegated Regulation. For a detailed discussion of potential regulatory tools mitigating against mis-selling of bail-in instruments to unsophisticated investors, see Götz and Tröger, *Should the marketing of subordinated debt be restricted/different in one way or the other?*, pp. 13 *et seq.*

692 Single Resolution Board, *Minimum Requirements for Own Funds and Eligible Liabilities (MREL) - SRB Policy for 2017 and Next Steps*; EBA and ESMA, *Statement of the EBA and ESMA on the treatment of retail holdings of debt financial instruments subject to the Bank Recovery and Resolution Directive*, p. 16.

693 EBA and ESMA, *Statement of the EBA and ESMA on the treatment of retail holdings of debt financial instruments subject to the Bank Recovery and Resolution Directive*, p. 16.

consequences in cases of bail-in to retail debt liabilities are not softened. Contagion effects, financial instability, as well as damaged overall confidence in financial markets and negative impacts on economic situations are most likely the consequences of bailing-in retail customers. Moreover, just because retail investors *ex ante* know how risky their investment is, they will most likely still lack the necessary loss-bearing capacity, and governments will not be discouraged to bail-out or support the institution in question to protect retail investors and to prevent a deluge of negative consequences for their real economy.

Assertions and protestations by the SRB that retail holdings can be reduced during recovery and resolution planning as part of the resolvability assessment and the analysis of discretionary exclusions of certain liabilities from bail-in through analysis of the bank's exposure to retail holdings[694] imply that such assessment processes can be performed accurately and that banks are aware of the nature of their creditors, which is debatable. Furthermore, it would require that measures to remove substantive impediments are carried out[695] and it would take time to enforce the removal of the impediments to resolution (*e.g.* the selling of retail-held instruments to more adequate holders or their redemption). Eliminating inappropriate holdings only *ex post* might be like shutting the barn door after the horse has bolted.

Banks and Other Financial Institutions

Although banks generally qualify as potential investors insofar as they are in the best position to understand the risk of bail-in, and therefore the risk associated with an investment in loss-absorbing debt instruments, they disqualify themselves by not being 'storm-resilient.'[696] If MREL instruments

---

694 Single Resolution Board, *Minimum Requirements for Own Funds and Eligible Liabilities (MREL) - SRB Policy for 2017 and Next Steps*, recital 43.

695 The EBA discovered that, in 2017, no Resolution College issued a joint decision on actions to remove impediments to resolvability. Even if this can be traced back to internal problems of the colleges to agree on a joint decision, it has implications for the SRB's claim that inadequate holdings can be eliminated *ex post* in the course of removing impediments to resolvability. If no such actions are performed, this alternative measure becomes implausible, see EBA, *EBA Report on the Functioning of Resolution Colleges in 2017*, p. 12.

696 Tröger, 'Optimal Bail-In Tools - Observations From A European Perspective', p. 14.

are written-down or converted, holders of such instruments must be in a position where they do not face the threat of a run on their other liabilities, potentially triggering contagion and systemic effects. As banks are typically most affected by runs, they are disqualified from becoming a potential eligible holder of MREL debt. Therefore, loss-absorbing debt must be held outside the banking sector. However, banks hold considerable amounts of MREL-eligible debt, as it is part of their everyday business.[697] The legislator anticipated intra-bank holdings of MREL-eligible debt and required that if banks hold loss-absorbing capital instruments, they must be deducted from the institution's own regulatory capital.[698]

Deduction of Cross-Holdings

Even if the last paragraph suggests that banks are unsuitable holders of loss-absorbing instruments, the reality is quite different: institutions do hold other institutions' core bail-in capital. Initially,[699] the BCBS confronted the problem of cross-holdings by deducting them from the institution's own regulatory capital. This mechanism was also adopted for the GSIBs' minimum MREL requirements under the integrated approach,[700] and financially incentivized institutions not to hold massive amounts of bail-inable debt in other institutions. However, when one recalls that this applies only to the minimum Pillar 1 MREL under the new approach, and

---

697 Even though Hüser *et al.* argue that due to low levels of securities cross-holdings in the interbank network, there is no direct contagion in terms of creditor banks failing as a result of another bank being bailed-in. Moreover, certain holdings still exist and despite there perhaps not being direct contagion, financial distress can occur nevertheless, depending on the institution's financial situation, A.-C. Hüser, G. Hałaj, C. Kok, C. Perales and A. van der Kraaij, 'The systemic implications of bail-in: A multi-layered network approach', *Journal of Financial Stability* 38 (2018), 81–97, p. 81.

698 Financial Stability Board, *Principles on Loss-absorbing and Recapitalisation Capacity of G-SIBs in Resolution*, section 15; Gleeson and Guynn, *Bank Resolution and Crisis Management*, para. 4.56.

699 Financial Stability Board, *Principles on Loss-absorbing and Recapitalisation Capacity of G-SIBs in Resolution*, section 15.

700 Section 2 of the new chapter 5a (new Arts. 72e to 72j CRR) provides for the deduction rules applicable to determine the amount of liabilities that may count towards MREL. Institutions are obliged to deduct holdings of their own eligible liabilities instruments (new Art. 72f CRR), and holdings of eligible liabilities of other G-SIIs (new Arts. 72h and 72i CRR).

therefore only to the few GSIBs in Europe, questions about deductions of institution-specific GSIB MREL and non-GSIB MREL capital arises.

Contrary to the TLAC equivalent minimum Pillar 1 MREL, the integrated approach to institution-specific GSIB MREL and general non-GSIB MREL (*e.g.* each MREL requirement not arising out of the CRR) does not currently arrange for the deduction of cross-holdings.[701] Even if the BRRD grants resolution authorities the power to disallow investment in other banks' MREL instruments if they pose a threat to the institutions resolvability, Article 44(2)(5) BRRD, no automated deduction mechanism exists and banks can freely invest in other banks' core bail-in capital.[702] That is a shortcoming of the legislation, since if all loss-absorbing instruments were held by other banks, then bailing-in those instruments could trigger contagion of financial instability, potentially giving rise to political or lobbyist intervention.

Risk Transportation from the Banks to the Market – Who Remains?

Considering the above, the question arises as to who remains as potential investors in loss-absorbing capital. Retail investors, SMEs, other unsophisticated investors, and banks all still invest in core bail-inable debt, as this has not been prohibited. However, such investments are considered inadequate insofar as their treatment in resolution produces too many negative externalities that can ultimately distort smooth bail-in application. Therefore, it would be desirable to shift most (if not all) MREL investments to more adequate investors. In order to do so, adequate investors must be found.

First, such investors need to be sophisticated and able to understand the risk of bail-in, charge adequate risk premiums, and thus exert purposeful debt governance *vis-à-vis* banks. Secondly, they must be located outside the banking sector.[703] Third, they must dispose of sufficient capital to absorb

---

701 European Parliament, *Amending the bank resolution framework – BRRD and SRMR*.

702 Even GSIBs can invest in other GSIBs' MREL instruments in an amount equal to the institution-specific additional MREL requirement that was imposed on them by the resolution authority, see Tröger, 'Why MREL won't help much', p. 20.

703 Götz/Tröger argued that besides those two factors, debt holders of bail-in able debt shall additionally not be subject to an asset-liability mismatch due to their investment strategy, which is here already comprised in the definition of

losses when debt is bailed-in. When their claims are not bailed-in but rather converted, the same applies. As conversion occurs during periods of distress, new equity holdings will initially be of a substantially lower value than the nominal value of prior debt holdings. Where households invest a large portion of their wealth in banks' bail-inable capital, losses incurred potentially lead to adverse social and/or psychological consequences that, in turn, may induce politicians to spare their constituents and bail-out banks instead, as happened in the MPS case, thus triggering credibility loss.[704]

Therefore, ideal investors include insurance companies, pension funds, sophisticated high-net-worth individuals, or hedge funds.[705] All of these investors combine the necessary characteristics. However, the pool of remaining potential investors still seems rather limited. The small size of this group appears insufficient to accommodate the considerable amount of MREL debt that needs to be issued before the transposition date. If only said investors were allowed to invest in newly-issued MREL-eligible debt, this might have a destabilizing effect on the eligible investors' sector.

Imposition of Losses on Specific Classes of Creditors Could Give Rise to Adverse Systemic Effects

If only certain investor groups come into consideration when looking for adequate holders of loss-absorbing debt, the circle of potential investors appears to be relatively small. Does the imposition of all of an institution's bail-in-related losses on a specific group of investors give rise to potentially adverse systemic effects, either within the specific investor's sector or even throughout the financial market as a whole? That proposition is not too far-fetched considering the concerns already raised about banks holding considerable amounts of MREL-qualified debt. Therefore, if MREL-eligible debt is also shifted and sold mainly to the identified adequate holders, attention must be paid to whether this would or would not give rise to

---

being a 'sophisticated investor,' see Götz and Tröger, *Should the marketing of subordinated debt be restricted/different in one way or the other?*, p. 6.

704 Tröger, 'Too complex to work', p. 29.

705 Ibid., p. 11; Tröger, 'Optimal Bail-In Tools - Observations From A European Perspective' p. 10; Zhou, Rutledge, Bossu, Dobler and Jassaud, *From bail-out to bail-in*, 2012/3, p. 33; Krahnen and Moretti, 'Bail-In Clauses'; Götz and Tröger, *Should the marketing of subordinated debt be restricted/different in one way or the other?*, p. 6.

systemic effects within the specific sector and whether distress in a specific sector can be contagious for others.

Problem of Certain Banks in Complying with Loss-Absorbing Requirements

Under the integrated approach to MREL, only certain instruments are available and suitable to fulfil the eligibility requirements. Amongst others, covered and most uncovered deposits will not be eligible for the integrated MREL, and eligible liabilities must be issued. This complicates compliance with MREL standards for two particular kinds of banks: first, significant medium-sized institutions that follow a more traditional business model[706] and are mostly financed by capital and deposits; and, second, most of the banks in Eastern Europe whose business model consists mainly of deposit-taking and credit-granting.[707] Both kinds of institutions generally have limited recourse to capital-market financing.[708] For such institutions, fulfilling the MREL quota with eligible instruments can represent a serious struggle. This is especially true when considering that around 70 % of significant banks under direct SSM supervision are not listed, meaning there will be no quick access to capital. Furthermore, the majority of those institutions have never issued convertible instruments or subordinated debt.[709] As a consequence, this could produce a 'three-class-system' in which the top- and bottom-class institutions would be the following: systemic financial institutions actively participating in capital markets and the possibility of fulfilling MREL requirements, and which therefore qualify for resolution procedures; and truly non-systemic institutions without access to capital markets that – due to the lack of MREL debt

706 See for an overview of business models in Europe M. Farnè and A. Vouldis, *Business models of the banks in the euro area*, ECB Working Paper (2017) retrievable at https://www.ecb.europa.eu/pub/pdf/scpwps/ecb.wp2070.en.pdf?ee58f8028aa3d7b55dd977292218b268 accessed 1 October 2022.

707 See country-by-country analysis by European Banking Federation, *Facts and Figures - Banking in Europe 2018* (2018), retrievable at https://www.ebf.eu/facts-and-figures/country-by-country-overview/ accessed 1 October 2022.

708 F. Restoy, *Bail-in in the new bank resolution framework: is there an issue with the middle class?*, IADI-ERC International Conference: "Resolution and deposit guarantee schemes in Europe: incomplete processes and uncertain outcomes" (Naples, 2018).

709 See for a simplified calculation example in the case of a fully capital- and deposit-financed institution ibid.

– would only be subject to national insolvency procedures. The 'middle class' of institutions, for which failure would have (domestic) systemic consequences but whose business models prohibit active participation in the market for MREL instruments, and therefore compliance with the MREL requirements, would be faced with a problem. Distress would either result in regular insolvency proceedings,[710] possibly jeopardizing financial stability, or such institutions would have to be forced to raise MREL-eligible debt without proper involvement in capital markets.[711] Alternatively, such institutions can bail-in what they have in a potential resolution scenario, namely deposits. However, as deposits are to some extent protected by the deposit guarantee scheme (DGS), questions emerge as to who will then fund the DGS if it is extensively used in such cases. Either way, no clear solution for banks that have business-model and activity-related struggles in fulfilling MREL requirements is in sight.

Scope and Level of Application

While the TLAC only applies to GSIBs at the outset, MREL was intended to generally apply to every institution under the remit of the BRRD. As some of the European institutions are also GSIBs, the overlap necessitated an integrated approach, combining the TLAC and MREL, for said institutions. In the integrated approach, the Commission decided to draw a distinctive line between institutions that are systemically important and those that are not, treating GSIBs and non-GSIBs differently. At present, a harmonized minimum (Pillar 1) MREL applies to all GSIBs, as envisaged under the TLAC. While the minimum level is set out in the CRR, possible institution-specific add-ons for GSIBs are included in the BRRD and SRMR as Pillar 2 requirements. Non-GSIBs, however, are not subject to a minimum level or an exact ratio of MREL and are burdened with a discretionary Pillar 2 requirement on a case-by-case basis, set out in the BRRD and the SRMR. While the calculation process for both requirements were

710 This again would call for revision and improvement of national insolvency proceedings within the European Union.

711 Restoy, *Bail-in in the new bank resolution framework: is there an issue with the middle class?*

aligned and harmonized in the Commission's proposal – RWA and LRE apply[712] – some problems do remain.

One concern that has been raised in this context is whether the strict distinction between GSIBs and non-GSIBs is appropriate.[713] The TLAC, now in the form of a minimum Pillar 1 MREL requirement, which applies only to the – in comparison with the entire banking landscape -few GSIBs, generally is the higher, more rigid, and therefore possibly safer loss-absorbing capital requirement of both Pillar 2 MREL for non-GSIBs and the minimum Pillar 1 MREL requirement for GSIBs. Furthermore, Pillar 2 non-GSIB MREL is highly discretional and potentially error-pro-

712 A major element of discussion before the integrated approach was issued was the role of risk weighting in determining the amounts for MREL and TLAC, *e.g.* the denomination base. The European Parliament ordered four research papers dealing with the denomination basis. Ayadi/Ferri support a full alignment of MREL with TLAC, and recommend 'to keep the two metrics RWA and LRE and apply the maximum in each case'. Hellwig finds that neither RWA nor total assets provide proper guidance for determining MREL. In particular, risk weighting seems less suited for determining MREL, since 'capital regulation focuses on the probability of bad results, while MREL is concerned with the extent of losses conditional on results being bad'. Berger et al find the use of RWA more convincing, though they admit this method comes at a cost for smaller banks. In a similar vein, de Groen notes (on a sample of 90 banks) that the ratio of RWA to total assets turns out to be higher for smaller and retail-oriented banks, see R. Ayadi and G. Ferri, *"Total Assets" versus "Risk Weighted Assets": does it matter for MREL requirements?*, In-Depth Analysis for the Economics and Monetary Affairs Committee of the European Parliament (2016) retrievable at http://www.europarl.europa.eu/RegData/etudes/IDAN/2016/574412/IPOL_IDA(2016)574412_EN.pdf accessed 1 October 2022; M. Hellwig, *"Total Assets" versus "Risk Weighted Assets": does it matter for MREL requirements?*, In-Depth Analysis for the Economics and Monetary Affairs Committee of the European Parliament (2016) retrievable at http://www.europarl.europa.eu/RegData/etudes/IDAN/2016/574413/IPOL_IDA(2016)574413_EN.pdf accessed 1 October 2022; W. P. de Groen, *"Total Assets" versus "Risk Weighted Assets": does it matter for MREL requirements?*, In-Depth Analysis for the Economics and Monetary Affairs Committee of the European Parliament (2016) retrievable at http://www.europarl.europa.eu/RegData/etudes/IDAN/2016/574415/IPOL_IDA(2016)574415_EN.pdf accessed 1 October 2022; B. Berger, P. Hüttl and S. Merler, *"Total Assets" versus "Risk Weighted Assets": does it matter for MREL requirements*, In-Depth Analysis for the Economics and Monetary Affairs Committee of the European Parliament (2016) retrievable at http://www.europarl.europa.eu/RegData/etudes/IDAN/2016/574414/IPOL_IDA(2016)574414_EN.pdf accessed 1 October 2022.

713 Stiefmüller, *European Parliament ECON Public Hearing on the new banking legislation package*; Tröger, 'Why MREL won't help much', p. 11.

ne,[714] while Pillar 1 MREL for GSIBs permits little to no discretion. Instruments eligible for Pillar 1 MREL – as Pillar 1 MREL is basically only a rebranded TLAC for which the FSB's TLAC eligibility requirements were assumed – are subject to much more stringent requirements than Pillar 2 MREL-eligible instruments, such as the strict subordination requirement. Furthermore, internal TLAC requirements are much more developed than internal MREL[715] which has only been proposed so far and will take time to develop. But even its proposal has raised concerns about the adequacy of its scope, calibration, and eligibility criteria, especially when compared with the agreed internal TLAC standard.[716]

That only GSIBs are subject to the stricter and safer Pillar 1 MREL requirements may pose a problem insofar as other large banks that fall just below the thresholds, and are not GSIBs but are systemically important in one or several Member States (OSIBs or DSIBs – other/domestic systemically important banks), might pose at least as much of a threat to financial markets and financial stability as the GSIBs themselves.[717] An argument has been put forward that – when imagining the ranking of banks in the EU – the institution right behind the last GSIB is most likely not much different from the latter in terms of size, risk, interconnectedness, and business model.[718] Proof of this can also be gleaned from the comparative analysis of the characteristics of EU GSIBs and OSIBs.[719] OSIBs are highly heterogenic, and it can be observed that some OSIBs do resemble GSIBs in terms of size or activity. Therefore, it should be discussed whether a MREL minimum Pillar 1 threshold should also apply for other domestic systemically important institutions,[720] since other systemically important banks are currently only subject to the flexible and less strict Pillar 2

714 For potential errors of the resolution authority in setting the MREL amount for non-GSIBs, see *infra* under Part 4, A.III.10.b. – *The Impact of Recovery and Resolution Planning – First Step of Uncertainty*.

715 The integrated approach intends to introduce internal MREL requirements based on the concept devised by the FSB's internal TLAC.

716 Association for Financial Markets in Europe, *Resolution aspects of the EU Risk Reduction Measures Package*, p. 2.

717 Stiefmüller, *Ten Years After - The 2017 Banking Package: One Step Forward, Two Steps Back*, p. 6.

718 Tröger presents this using the example of the European Union's 13th largest institution that may not differ from the 14th largest institution, see Tröger, 'Why MREL won't help much', p. 11.

719 See Annex 3.13. to Impact Assessment on Banking Package.

720 Stiefmüller, *Ten Years After - The 2017 Banking Package: One Step Forward, Two Steps Back*, p. 12.

MREL requirement. If such an extended scope is to be applied, then according to which criteria (significance, size, business model, or governance) should the institutions be selected, and would a shifted threshold for the application of the more rigid minimum Pillar 1 MREL requirements not be discretional and random as well? with this in mind, the banking industry itself, especially, argues that minimum Pillar 1 MREL shall only be applicable to GSIBs and that fundamental differences of GSIBs and other institutions must not be thwarted. Corresponding to banking supervision, crisis management and resolution shall also be influenced by the principle of proportionality in order to respect different business models and structures of institutions.[721] However, it must be kept in mind that this position comes out of the banking industry itself and might therefore be influenced or even biased by industry concerns, which try to avoid additional effort or costs. Therefore, proponents of an extended minimum Pillar 1 MREL requirement for OSIBS do appear to have a point.

MREL Guidance – New Article 45e BRRD

The integrated approach provides for a new concept, namely that of guidance. Guidance is a discretional instrument that allows resolution authorities to request additional high-quality bail-in capital instruments that can be used in unforeseen resolution scenarios while addressing breaches of those levels in a more flexible manner and without directly referring to sanctions such as limitations of the Maximum Distributable Amounts (MDA), Article 45e BRRD TLAC implementation proposal.

At first glance, it seems odd that MREL guidance is cited as a possible impediment to the potential of LACRs, as it generally contributes to the availability of MREL instruments within a reasonable and limited framework. However, in accordance with the line of arguments presented in this section, it contributes to the looming and overarching problem of MREL: the struggle of investors to understand and price MREL instruments and their risk adequately. Under MREL guidance, potential holders of MREL instruments are not in a position to gauge *ex ante* the correct default probability of their present investment, as MREL guidance requirements can vary and are imposed discretionally. Under MREL guidance, the instruments an institution is required to hold depend on a complicated

721 Bundesverband Öffentlicher Banken Deutschlands, VÖB, e.V., *Aktuelle Positionen zur Banken- und Finanzmarktregulierung, 2. Quartal 2018*, p. 14.

interplay between resolution and supervisory authorities' decisions on complex and non-linear factual issues.[722] MREL guidance by resolution authorities is strongly linked to regulatory capital prescriptions, which are set by the supervisory authority in the form of capital guidance (Pillar 2 guidance). This constitutes a restriction on resolution authorities' calibration of MREL guidance, as the proposed wording imposes a cap ("shall not exceed") and ties the resolution authorities' assessment of the loss absorption and recapitalization amounts for MREL guidance to the supervisory authorities' calibration of Pillar 2 (new Articles 104n and 128 CRD). Therefore, the resolution authority is bound by the supervisory authority's judgment, thus constituting an institutional hierarchy.[723] The process of setting MREL guidance therefore always entails the decisions of at least two different authorities at their own discretion. Even if the level of MREL is finally determined (for example, the GSIB's minimum amount or specific add-on), supervisory authorities, by giving the leading capital guidance, can offer an opportunity to resolution authorities to require more high-quality bail-in capital for the institution.[724] However, resolution authorities are not obliged to follow the supervisory authority in their capital guidance and can decide not to impose any additional amounts. Indeed, they can sometimes even exceed the amounts set by the supervisory authority.[725] As a result, and alongside the mere complication of having a 'hard' and a 'soft' MREL component that are both designed identically (loss-absorption and recapitalization component) but determined differently, initial default risk considerations and subsequent pricing decisions of investors may lose validity over time and with the imposing or lowering of MREL guidance. Prediction of default probabilities and pricing is complicated, as discretion must be anticipated of not only one authority but of at least two different authorities.

722 Tröger, 'Why MREL won't help much', p. 12.

723 That again can pose further problems in respect of inter-authority cooperation, see Stiefmüller, *Ten Years After - The 2017 Banking Package: One Step Forward, Two Steps Back*, p. 13.

724 Tröger, 'Why MREL won't help much', p. 12.

725 Art. 45e TLAC implementation proposal states that the resolution authority can exceed the amount of the combined buffer requirements if a higher level is necessary to ensure that. Following the event of a resolution, the entity continues to meet the conditions for its authorization for an appropriate period of time that is not longer than one year.

Calculation Process

The integrated approach, although partly aligned in certain points, still distinguishes significantly between GSIBs and non-GSIBs when it comes to the calculation process. While GSIBs are subject to the integrated and harmonized TLAC minimum level, now called the Pillar 1 MREL requirement, that will be incorporated into the CRR and will constitute the fixed minimum requirement of MREL equivalent to the one required by the FSB's TLAC standard, all other non-GSIBs do not fall under such an obligation, and are subject only to a highly individualistic case-by-case[726] Pillar 2 MREL requirement arising out of the BRRD and the SRMR according to the MREL methodology[727] determined by the Commission Delegated Act on RTS for MREL. Despite the unequal calculation mechanisms, the integrated approach aligned the measurement metrics of MREL with those of the TLAC for GSIBs, resulting in a uniform underlying metric for both MREL requirements. Accordingly, the institution-specific MREL for non-GSIBs should now be expressed as a percentage of the total risk exposure amount (RWA) and of the leverage ratio exposure (LRE) measure of the specific institution, and institutions should simultaneously meet the levels resulting from both measurements.[728]

The MREL requirement for non-GSIBs is composed of two components, the loss-absorption amount[729] (LAA) and the recapitalization amount[730]

---

726 The case-by-case basis is slowly implemented. The SRB started to use MREL targets in 2016 but only within a preliminary approach and with informative targets, gearing such targets towards the default formula set in the MREL RTS. Since 2017, the SRB slowly moved away from informative targeting and started to set bank-specific, tailored MREL targets with bank-specific adjustments for the majority of large and complex banks, including all GSIBs. However, even today, a number of non-GSIB banks are still only subject to the default MREL without adjustments, see Single Resolution Board, *Minimum Requirements for Own Funds and Eligible Liabilities (MREL) - SRB Policy for 2017 and Next Steps*, recital 5, 16 *et seq.*

727 LAA max (P1+P2R+CBR; Basel 1 floor) + RCA max (P1+P2R; Basel 1 floor) + MCC (CRB – 125 basis points).

728 See explanatory memorandum, p. 9 of TLAC Implementation Proposal.

729 SRB Default Loss Absorption Amount (LAA) = Max (P1+P2R+CBR; Basel 1 floor). The default LAA is considered to be the higher of either the sum of a bank's minimum capital requirements (Pillar 1), its Pillar 2 requirements (P2R), and its fully-loaded combined buffer requirements (CBR) or the amount required to meet the Basel 1 floor.

730 SRB Default Recapitalization Amount = Max (P1+P2R; Basel 1 floor) plus SRB Default Market Confidence Charge = CRB – 125 basis points.

(RCA), occasionally complemented by the Market Confidence Charge (MCC) or market confidence buffer, new Article 45e (1)(b) BRRD. While the LAA must be met by each bank, the RCA can be set at zero for banks that are subject to liquidation under national insolvency proceedings (gone concern) or at any level that is deemed necessary for the application of the predefined resolution tools (going concern). In addition, the integrated approach proposal introduced Article 45e (1)(a) BRRD, which allows authorities to require institutions to meet higher levels of MREL to cover losses in resolution that are higher than those expected under a standard resolution scenario (that is, above the level of the current own funds requirement), namely the so-called loss-absorption guidance (that is attached to the capital guidance in Articles 104b and 128 CRD). While the denomination base of MREL was adjusted according to the FSB's standard, the denomination and calculation of the TLAC remains mostly the same under the integrated approach. With the originally envisaged minimum TLAC amount incorporated in the CRR and now labeled as a minimum Pillar 1 MREL requirement, it is still calculated as a fixed amount of 16/18 % of RWA or 6/6.75 % of LRE respectively. The new Article 45d (1)(b) BRRD allows for institution-specific (Pillar 2) add-ons to said minimum level, if the Pillar 1 MREL minimum is insufficient to absorb losses and recapitalize the given GSIB under the envisaged resolution strategy.[731] In addition, under the new minimum Pillar 1 MREL, GSIBs may also be subject to loss-absorption guidance, new Article 45e (1)(a) BRRD, and a market confidence buffer, new Article 45e (1)(b) BRRD.

Table 1: Calculation of GSIB MREL and non-GSIB MREL

GSIB MREL =	18 % RWA/ 6.75 % LRE, new Art. 92a(1)(a), (b) CRR	Individual add-on, new Art. 45d (1)(b) BRRD	Loss-absorption guidance, new Art. 45e (1)(a) BRRD	Market confidence buffer, new Art. 45e (1)(b) BRRD
			Pillar 2 Guidance, new Art. 104b CRD	Combined buffer requirement, Art. 128(6) CRD
non-GSIB MREL = max. 2x	8 %, new Art. 45c(3) BRRD	Pillar II requirement, new Art. 45c (3)(a) BRRD	Loss-absorption guidance, new Art. 45e (1)(a) BRRD	Market confidence buffer, new Art. 45e (1)(b) BRRD

731 TLAC Implementation Proposal, explanatory memorandum, p. 10.

However, even if some of the initial misalignments[732] between MREL and the TLAC are smoothed-out by the proposed integrated approach (*i.e.* through the introduction of the denominators of RWA and LRE[733]), some reservations remain. The clear-cut 'equation' for calculating the needed MREL for GSIBs and non-GSIBs looks good on paper but veils deeper problems when elaborating more closely on the components and trying to retrace their underlying functioning, especially with respect to the very discretional non-GSIB MREL. Although a certain amount of discretion is certainly justifiable in order to meet banks' particularities, discretion always produces some uncertainty among investors who are dependent on forecasts regarding the risk, and therefore price, of MREL instruments to make economically reasonable investments. Impeding investors' forecasts on the default probabilities of MREL instruments by incorrectly or discretionally setting, reducing, or increasing the requirements, even after the initial investment decision has already been taken, can lead to undesirable under- or over-pricing of MREL debt.

In this regard, concerns have been raised about the 'new' denomination base RWE and LRE in general. Secondly, the distorting influence of recovery and resolution planning on MREL is critically assessed. Thirdly, in light of the second point, the wide discretion of authorities in setting the recapitalization amount for MREL is questioned. Lastly, different MREL adjustment mechanisms are evaluated.

Denomination – Underlying Uncertainty

The denominator that causes the most controversy here is the RWA[734] measurement. It is suspected that, although it seems an attractive and

---

732 See, for example, Ayadi and Ferri, *"Total Assets" versus "Risk Weighted Assets": does it matter for MREL requirements?*; Hellwig, *"Total Assets" versus "Risk Weighted Assets": does it matter for MREL requirements?*; Berger, Hüttl and Merler, *"Total Assets" versus "Risk Weighted Assets": does it matter for MREL requirements*; Groen, *"Total Assets" versus "Risk Weighted Assets": does it matter for MREL requirements?*

733 The TLAC would, under the new integrated approach, be calculated both on a risk-based denominator, RWA, and on a non-risk-based denominator, LRE, new Art. 92a CCR. According to the new proposed changes, the MREL would also be calculated according to the denominators of total risk exposure amount (RWA) and leverage ratio exposure (LRE).

734 A number of proposals aiming to improve the methodology issued by the Basel Committee on Banking Supervision suggested that the BCBS itself has reservations about the adequacy of risk modeling, see Basel Committee on Banking

sophisticated approach, RWA as an assessment of risk is more a matter of judgment than a matter of measurement,[735] indicating that it can – intentionally or unintentionally – be manipulated. Meanwhile, underlying data enabling the assessment of the risk may not be reliable, as they are notoriously changeable and correlations between risks are always moving,[736] especially in a systemic crisis or a local, regional, or national recession.[737] Furthermore, banks may not be best incentivized to model risk properly, as they are always anxious to make their activities appear less risky.[738] It might therefore be assumed that RWA leaves some leeway[739] because of its attachment to risk positions. For example, IFRS 9, in its current design, penalizes smaller banks that are subject to the use of the standardized approach (SA) to calculate their RWA in contrast with the bigger competitors that use the internal-model-based approach, as only the latter can count general provisions as Tier 2 capital,[740] which creates a double standard.[741] Internal models of different banks can lead to widely diverging results, and the same asset portfolio can lead to widely diverging RWA calculations.[742] This indicates that some banks might exploit their privilege of having an internal model for their own benefit.

Supervision, *Report on risk-weighted assets for counterparty credit risk (CCR)*, Regulatory Consistency Assessment Programme (RECAP) (2015); Hellwig, *"Total Assets" versus "Risk Weighted Assets": does it matter for MREL requirements?*, p. 16.

735 Hellwig, *"Total Assets" versus "Risk Weighted Assets": does it matter for MREL requirements?*, p. 15; Bank for International Settlements, *Annual Economic Report 2018* (2018), pp. 45 *et seq.*

736 Hellwig gives the example of the correlation between counterparty credit risk in a hedge contract and the underlying risk, against which the hedge contract should insure, and how it changes in the case of AIG, see Hellwig, *"Total Assets" versus "Risk Weighted Assets": does it matter for MREL requirements?*, p. 15.

737 Groen, *"Total Assets" versus "Risk Weighted Assets": does it matter for MREL requirements?*, p. 18.

738 See, for further critique on RWA, Hellwig, *"Total Assets" versus "Risk Weighted Assets": does it matter for MREL requirements?*, pp. 16 *et seq.*

739 Bank for International Settlements, *Annual Economic Report 2018*, p. 45.

740 Stiefmüller, *Ten Years After - The 2017 Banking Package: One Step Forward, Two Steps Back*, p. 10.

741 Bank for International Settlements, *Annual Economic Report 2018*, p. 46.

742 A study by the Basel Committee on Banking Supervision (BCBS) found that two banks with identical banking book assets might report capital ratios differing by up to 4 percentage points, see Basel Committee on Banking Supervision, *Regulatory Consistency Assessment Programm (RCAP) - Analysis of risk-weighted assets for credit risk in the banking book* (2013); Basel Committee on Banking Supervision, *Analysis of risk weighted assets for credit risk in the banking book*, Regulatory Consistency Assessment Programme (RECAP) (2016).

However, even if risk-weighting is at the center of attention in the ongoing criticism, and LRE is said to be a counterweight and backstop to the potentially inadequate and cyclical RWA, reservations can also be found in relation to the definition of the leverage ratio. Since 2010, it has been revised substantially and is now in its third iteration[743] and is much altered from its initial design. Its intended simplicity and transparency has been diluted with every revision, and this dilution has now created a complicated measurement that still leaves some problems untreated.[744]

The Impact of Recovery and Resolution Planning – First Level of Uncertainty

One of the topics to have gained relatively little attention in the academic discussion takes place in the run-up to the determination of the MREL. The distinction of the new integrated approach between minimum Pillar 1 MREL for GSIBs and Pillar 2 MREL for non-GSIBs shifts the focus of the problem onto MREL for non-GSIBs, as the resolution authority determines the amount of necessary MREL for the institutions on a case-by-case basis.

Resolution authorities are allowed and obliged – already under the BRRD and still under the new integrated approach – to take into consideration the specific features of a given institution, such as its resolution strategy, its regulatory capital needs after a potential resolution, excluded liabilities, size, business model, funding model, risk profile, DGS contributions, or adverse effects of its failure on financial stability, new Article 45c(1) BRRD. The described determination process is supplemented by the RTS on MREL, which will most likely need to be revised once the

743 The original standard, published by the Basel Committee in December 2010 (Basel Committee on Banking Supervision, *Basel III: A global regulatory framework for more resilient banks and banking systems* (2010)), was replaced by a January 2014 definition (Basel Committee on Banking Supervision, *Basel III leverage ratio framework and disclosure requirement* (2014)). A final definition may be found, for the time being, in Basel Committee on Banking Supervision, *Basel III: Finalising post-crisis reforms* (2017), see also https://www.bis.org/fsi/fsisummaries/b3_lrf.htm accessed 1 October 2022, for a summary on leverage ratio.

744 For example, the different treatment of derivatives under IFRS and the US GAAP accounting rules, see Stiefmüller, *Ten Years After - The 2017 Banking Package: One Step Forward, Two Steps Back*, p. 9.

proposed changes to the BRRD take effect.[745] However, even if an overhaul of the RTS will be necessary (*e.g.* in light of the aligned denomination base),[746] the fundamental principles for the calculation of non-GSIB MREL remain. What also remains is the basic collection process of the data and information on which the resolution authorities ground their decisions about the MREL.[747] This applies both to the underlying data that is collected, as well as to the information on the different above-mentioned features and criteria that need to be taken into consideration when setting and subsequently adjusting the MREL. This debilitates the MREL determination process for non-GSIBs.

To recapitalize, problems were detected, *inter alia*, in bank employees' ability to generate, assess, and process the needed information and data, the costliness and unpredictability of future events and – most importantly – in the deficient data-collection process especially with regard to the use of templates[748]. These problems were discussed in full range and depth above under Part 3, A.II.1. and 2. – *Impediments Concerning Both Recovery and Resolution Planning* and *Impediments Concerning Resolution Plans.* Problems emerge if one transfers the above-identified shortcomings in recovery and resolution planning in the present context of resolution authorities setting the MREL according to recovery and resolution plan

745 So far, new Art. 45c(8) BRRD envisages the delivery of new regulatory technical standards by the EBA to the Commission within 1 month of the entry into force of the proposed amendments, meaning the beginning of 2019 at the earliest.

746 Both MREL requirements for GSIBs and non-GSIBs are denominated either in the total risk exposure amount (RWA) or in the leverage ratio exposure (LRE). While GSIB MREL is calculated on a fixed percentage (16/18 % of RWA and 6/6.75 % LRE), non-GSIB MREL is calculated by determining the loss-absorption amount, the recapitalization amount and the combined buffer requirements, expressed as a percentage of RWA/LRE, see new Arts. 45 and 45c BRRD.

747 Even though MREL targets are also partly set up using supervisory data of SREP decisions, information deriving from recovery and resolution planning plays an important role in the MREL determination process. However, even if not part of the current discussion, it may be that the SREP process suffers from similar problems and shortcomings like the recovery and resolution planning process, as both are to a certain extent intertwined.

748 In the context of MREL determination, the Liability Data Template gains massive importance. However, as resolution authorities take into consideration a wide range of criteria, all collected data, whether through recovery planning by the institution or through resolution planning templates, make an impact. See Single Resolution Board, *Guidance to the Completion of the SRB's Liability Data Template for 2016*; Single Resolution Board, *Guidance on the 2018 Liability Data Report*; Single Resolution Board, *Guidance on the 2019 Liability Data Report*.

information – both with respect to underlying general information and information regarding the adjustment criteria (such as excluded liabilities, size, business model, funding model, risk profile, etc.). Just as the accuracy and reliability of recovery and resolution plans suffer under the set-up of the current recovery and resolution planning process, the setting of specific MREL quotas for non-GSIBs suffers equally from the inaccuracy and unreliability of the provided information.

Besides the outlined problems regarding the inaccuracy of underlying data and data pertaining to information regarding specific adjustment criteria, a third information source for the determination of MREL is worth examining more closely. For the purpose of setting the MREL, given that resolution authorities require detailed insight into the liability structure in order to assess the eligibility of liabilities for MREL, a ten-sheet template for reporting was introduced in 2017. The Liability Data Report (LDR)[749] is an additional reporting requirement that authorities are obliged to request from the institutions.

Throughout the financial industry, there is a widespread consensus that the correct population of the LDR is an enormous and very complex task. Auditing companies, consultant firms, as well as lawyers have recognized the struggle experienced by institutions in dealing with the LDR and already offer services to institutions to help with data management and LDR assistance.[750] To give some insight into the dimensions of the LDR, institutions are required to report their entire liability structure including a detailed breakdown of liabilities, such as those excluded from bail-in, product types, and counterparties as a starting point for the assessment of their potential MREL fulfillment. This requires detailed single contract data, which is often unavailable in institutions. In its official guidance document,[751] seven pages are dedicated to trying to explain the correct use of the template entailing cross-references, abbreviations, references to

749 See the Liability Data Reporting template 2018 v1.5 available at https://srb.europa.eu/en/content/liability-data-report, accessed 1 October 2022, as well as Single Resolution Board, *Guidance on the 2018 Liability Data Report.*

750 Many auditing companies offer explicit assistance for managements of institutions in order to fulfil this task, see PricewaterhouseCoopers, *MREL, TLAC and Banking Resolution* , slide 45 *et seq.*, retrievable at https://digital.pwc-tools.de/basel-iv/wp-content/uploads/sites/23/2017/03/4174_RZ_Booklet_Toolbox_MREL_A6_SCREEN.pdf, accessed 1 October 2022.

751 Single Resolution Board, *Guidance to the Completion of the SRB's Liability Data Template for 2016*; Single Resolution Board, *Guidance on the 2018 Liability Data Report*; Single Resolution Board, *Guidance on the 2019 Liability Data Report.*

(old) BRRD provisions, and encrypted explanation formulas.[752] It is highly doubtful, in light of the findings on general recovery and resolution planning, that institutions are going to be able to fill-out the LDR correctly and that the senior management, as demanded[753] by the SRB, is going to be capable of discussing the data with the SRB. The data collection will most likely be done by revision, compliance, or internal audit employees, who themselves only collect the information without attempting to verify the deliverables, especially not in an international multi-entity institution with complicated liability structures.

Parallel to the problem in basic recovery and resolution planning, outdated or incompatible IT further impede the process of collecting the needed data. The process is exhausting and requires strenuous efforts to be completed manually, while the progress of automated solutions is insufficient[754] and therefore not an option at the current stage. Missing or unavailable information might tempt institutions to guess or estimate instead, thereby inevitably mixing false or incorrect information with conjectured data. The quality of data from the LDR has remained a critical issue until now and is acknowledged by the SRB itself as a current and future critical point on the agenda of the SRB.[755] Aggravating the situation further, the SRB intends to increase the information requested in the LDR by 2020 to support the implementation of the planned internal MREL requirements and to better understand the bail-inability of a bank's liabilities.[756] This will complicate the situation around the LDR even more.

This aspect, paired with the wide range of criteria that resolution authorities are supposed to take into consideration when determining the MREL for each institution, destabilizes the entire process of setting up non-GSIB MREL. Admittedly, the more aspects and features of the institution under question that flow into the decision, the more proportional and tailored the decision will be. On the other hand, the more aspects and criteria that can be discretionally considered, the more error-prone and complex the

752 Single Resolution Board, *Guidance on the 2018 Liability Data Report*, pp. 8–14.

753 The SRB intends to communicate with the senior management based on the LDR data and expects the senior management "to be aware and familiar with this data and ensure an appropriate level of confidence with respect to its accurateness," see ibid.

754 PricewaterhouseCoopers, *MREL, TLAC and Banking Resolution*, slide 47.

755 D. Laboureix, *SRB MREL Policy*, SRM-EBF Boardroom Dialogue (Brussels, 2018), slide 10 retrievable at https://srb.europa.eu/sites/srbsite/files/srm_boardroom_dialogue_mrel_d_laboureix.pdf accessed 1 October 2022.

756 Ibid., slide 10.

decision will be. Considering that, in the paragraphs immediately above, one of the fundamental problems of loss-absorbing capacities outlined is in their complexity and the resulting difficulty potential investors face in evaluating, pricing, and handling investment in such instruments, it is evident that the concerns raised in the *current* paragraph further exacerbate this problem.

Discretion in Setting the Recapitalization Amount – Second Level of Uncertainty

As explained in the above paragraph, the resolution authority is allowed to make bank-specific adjustments to the MREL quotes for non-GSIBs. Mostly, such adjustments relate to the components of the recapitalization amount (RCA), including the market confidence charge (MCC), as these amounts are highly discretional and dependent on the institution in question. In contrast, the loss-absorption amount (LAA) is less discretionary[757] and mainly consists of the capital instruments already issued by the institution in order to comply with supervisory capital requirements. In other words, if a bank gets into financial trouble, loss-absorption will always be necessary while the need for recapitalization depends on the resolution strategy and can be set at zero if the institution can be liquidated under normal insolvency proceedings, Article 2(2) RTS on MREL. Furthermore, depending on which resolution tools are foreseen in the resolution plan, the resolution authority can set the recapitalization amount accordingly.

Therefore, the resolvability assessment and resolution planning of the respective institution, laid down in the resolution plan, is of crucial importance for the purpose of setting the MREL through determination of the re-

757 Although the resolution authority mainly sets a default loss-absorption amount, it can set a loss-absorption amount higher or lower than the default loss-absorption amount if the institution's business model, funding model, risk profile, impediments to resolvability, additional own funds requirements according to the outcome of stress tests, or combined buffer requirements assessment requires, see Art. 1 RTS on MREL. However, the SRB decided preliminarily not to make any adjustments to the LAA, see Single Resolution Board, *Minimum Requirements for Own Funds and Eligible Liabilities (MREL) - SRB Policy for 2017 and Next Steps*, recital 24.

capitalization amount.[758] Although there are various ways to influence the recapitalization amount, as will be demonstrated in the next paragraph, the initial determination according to the chosen resolution strategy sets the grounds for each further adjustment. If the resolution plan foresees a specific resolution tool, such as a bail-in tool (resulting in a high RCA) or the sale-of-business-tool (resulting in a low RCA), resolution authorities will set the MREL TCA accordingly. If, in an actual resolution scenario, the (non-binding) resolution plan is abandoned and the resolution scheme provides for a different resolution tool, the RCA might be either over- or under-planned. This scenario worsens in cases where the institution is designated to undergo normal insolvency proceedings, hence the recapitalization amount is set at zero. But once it fails, authorities or governments decide to resolve the institution under the resolution framework. Market conditions might have changed, the liability structure of the institution might have altered, or other factors might have arisen which shed more light on the past decision with regard to normal insolvency proceedings. As a consequence, the institution might absorb its losses with the loss-absorption amount even though it is undercapitalized for further business and continues to carry out its potentially critical functions. Due to the fear of disruptions to the market or political and social pressure, governments and authorities might be forced to help an institution to fulfil necessary capital requirements again to continue operating. Such help would most likely entail public money. Reservations about the occurrence of such adverse scenarios and inadequate planning therefore can be brushed aside: they have already happened, whether it be in the case of Banco Popular Español[759] or the two Venetian banks in Italy.[760] Therefore, the setting of Pillar 2 MREL for non-GSIBs might be flawed from the outset.

---

758 Maragopoulos, *Minimum Requirements for own Funds and Eligible Liabilities (MREL): A Comprehensive Analysis of the New Prudential Requirement for Credit Institutions*, p. 23.

759 See *supra* under Part 3, A.II.1.f. – *Predictability of the Actual Crisis Scenario at Some Future Date*.

760 Federico, 'Crisi delle banche venete ad "aiuti di Stato"', pp. 214 *et seq.*; Banca D'Italia, *Informazioni sulla soluzione della crisi di Veneto Banca S.p.A. e Banca Popolare di Vicenza S.p.A.*; Mesnard, Margerit and Magnus, *The orderly liquidation of Veneto Banca and Banca Popolare di Vicenza*.

Unclear Adjustment Mechanisms – Third Level of Uncertainty

The last level of uncertainty in the calculation process can be found in the many ways authorities can adjust each bank's MREL requirement. At the end of 2017, the SRB issued its policy for the next steps to be taken with regard to its MREL approach. The SRB gave a glimpse on how it intends to deal with and use possible adjustment mechanisms.[761] The discussion above expressed some underlying concerns about the adequacy of the denomination base, the influential role of imprecise recovery and resolution planning, and also voiced doubts about the discretion of authorities in setting the recapitalization amount. The following discussion on potential adjustment mechanisms reveals another contributor to uncertainty when it comes to MREL calculation.

While the SRB only started setting default MREL targets at the beginning of 2016, it has slowly moved away from default targeting and started to set bank-specific, tailored amounts for all banks under its remit.[762] Such MREL targets are – so far – mostly just subject to adjustments to the recapitalization amount (RCA), including the option of using a different basis for the risk-weighted assets from that of the most-recently reported balance sheet figure, see Article 2(3) RTS on MREL. According to the SRB, the RWA basis for the calculation of the RCA and the MCC can be adjusted by including: (a) the effect of balance sheet depletion directly following resolution up to 10 % of total assets, as the balance sheet might shrink; (b) the use of certain recovery options that can reduce the RWA; and (c) the impact of restructuring plan divestments and sales on the RWA. Furthermore, the SRB might consider implementing other adjustments in relation to the RWA basis. These could include RWA adjustments to take into consideration the potential liquidation of entities in a banking group or adjustments to the Pillar 2 requirement to reflect potential post-resolution requirements.[763]

Even if deviation from the RWA must be identified, explained, and quantified in the resolution plan and such changes must be feasible and credible without adversely affecting the bank's critical functions during resolution, the option of deviation and discretion reflects the concerns raised above regarding the adequacy of MREL setting. Furthermore, resolution

761 Single Resolution Board, *Minimum Requirements for Own Funds and Eligible Liabilities (MREL) - SRB Policy for 2017 and Next Steps.*

762 Ibid., recital 5, 11 *et seq.*

763 Ibid.

authorities will be allowed to make adjustments to the Pillar 2 own-funds requirements used for the default RCA, see Article 2(5) RTS on MREL, and the level of the combined buffer requirements that are used for setting the default market confidence buffer, Article 2(7–8) RTS on MREL. Both factors can be tailored accordingly.

In addition, it is expressly provided that adjustments to the LAA and the RCA can be made based on the institution's business model, funding model, and risk profile. Decisions pertaining to said influential factors are based on information received from the supervisory authority and the Supervisory Review and Evaluation Process (SREP) assessment. Although resolution authorities are required to provide a reasoned explanation to the supervisory authority, it is an exclusively internal process with little to no possibility of challenging or retracing the decision. Further adjustments can be made, assuming the potential involvement of the DGS,[764] thereby lowering the MREL requirement. However, the potential involvement of the DGS hinges on the fraction of covered deposits with respect to the total liabilities of the institution. As the amount of covered deposits can shift, so too can MREL prescriptions, causing problems for long-term investors when trying to price relevant risks at the time of purchase of the MREL instrument.[765]

Howsoever such adjustment of MREL quotas would look, it is clear that the sheer possibility of institution-specific choices being made by supervisory and resolution authorities can prove problematic for potential investors that are dependent on pricing risk *ex ante* as accurately as possible, especially when adjustment mechanisms are as opaque as they seem to be here. As a result, the market for bail-inable debt might be unsettled, which weakens the concept of MREL.

The TLAC as an International Standard Being Transposed into National Law

In contrast to MREL, an exclusively European project, the TLAC derives from a global initiative, namely the FSB's Standard on Total Loss-absorbing Capacity (TLAC) incorporated in the TLAC Term Sheet. However,

---

764 This point is included despite the claim of the SRB that, taking into account DGS contributions, is not consistent with the preferred resolution strategy for most of the banking groups under its direct responsibility, see ibid., p. 13.

765 Tröger, 'Why MREL won't help much', p. 10.

since the standard was globally agreed upon, each relevant home and host jurisdiction of an affected GSIB has translated, or is in the course of translating, the defined TLAC Term Sheet provisions into the relevant national law. Such transposition can vary significantly across jurisdictions and become fragmented, especially when the TLAC is integrated into local legislation by units smaller than the European Union.

Indeed, the FSB called for public feedback[766] on the technical implementation of the FSB's TLAC standard in June 2018 and received responses indicating that certain trends in implementation adopted by different national regulators in key provisions could have significant consequences[767] for the functioning of the TLAC concept. Such consequences will almost inevitably affect GSIBs as they operate across implementation borders, even though their headquarters are incorporated in only one jurisdiction. Without going into specific detail, as doing so would go beyond the scope of this thesis, it may be noted concerns were raised, *inter alia*, about the calibration of internal TLAC for a material sub-group in a host jurisdiction. Here, the Term Sheet determines a fixed range of 75 % up to 90 % of the respective external TLAC requirements applicable if the material group is a resolution group.[768] While regulators in some jurisdictions have calibrated, or are about to calibrate, the internal TLAC requirement at the low end of the bounded range (i.e. near 75 %),[769] other jurisdictions have or might calibrate their internal TLAC near the higher end (i.e. near 90 %).[770] It is obvious that in cases of crisis, a risk arises that such distribution of internal TLAC does not match the actual distribution

766 Financial Stability Board, *Monitoring the Technical Implementation of the FSB Total Loss-absorbing Capacity (TLAC) Standard – Call for public feedback*.

767 J. Court, A. Parent and A. Portilla, *Letter to the FSB regarding call for public feedback on Monitoring the Technical Implementation of the FSB Total Loss-Absorbing Capacity (TLAC) Standard* (2018).

768 Financial Stability Board, *Principles on Loss-absorbing and Recapitalisation Capacity of G-SIBs in Resolution*, p 18.

769 Such as intended by the Bank of England, see Bank of England, *The Bank of England's approach to setting a minimum requirement for own funds and eligible liabilities (MREL) - Statement of Policy* (2018), retrievable at https://www.bankofengland.co.uk/-/media/boe/files/paper/2018/statement-of-policy-boes-approach-to-setting-mrel-2018.pdf?la=en&hash=BC4499AF9CF063A3D8024BE5C050CB1F39E2EBC1 accessed at 22 November 2018; or by the Hong Kong Monetary Authority, see https://www.hkma.gov.hk/eng/key-information/press-releases/2018/20180725-3.shtml accessed 1 October 2022.

770 For example, the Federal Reserve set the internal TLAC requirement at around 89 %; Court, Parent and Portilla, *Letter to the FSB regarding call for public feedback on Monitoring the Technical Implementation of the FSB Total Loss-Absor-*

of losses, complicating or even impeding the resolution process.[771] While this serves only as an example for many[772] international implementation and coordination issues, it is a significant example illustrating that the hovering global TLAC standard poses problems when different jurisdictions transpose the international standard differently, and that different transpositions can thereupon cause fragmentation and deterioration of the TLAC's quality and credibility for GSIBs, even while already (solidly) transposed into European law.

Current Shortfall and Transposition

The integrated approach is intended to be adopted by the end of 2018/beginning of 2019. However, because of the demanding design of applicable LACRs, it is estimated that the European financial sector will need to make up a considerable shortfall of eligible liabilities. Available calculations provide for a shortfall that could exceed 120 billion euros and the SRB indicated corresponding data for the banks under the remit of the SRB as of 31 December 2016.[773] Others, such as the EBA, estimate the shortfall to be even higher, up to 285 billion euros.[774] Some research has even estimated a shortfall of up to 526 billion euros, depending on the ultimate design

bing Capacity (TLAC) Standard, see Annex 1–1 to 1–3 of the latter for calculation examples of different scenarios.

771 Ibid., p. 3.

772 For an exhaustive discussion of potential queries arising out of different national implementations of the TLAC standard see ibid.; Japanese Bankers Association, *Comments on the document: Monitoring the Technical Implementation of the FSB Total Loss-absorbing Capacity (TLAC) Standard - Call for public feedback, issued by the Financial Stability Board* (2018); Credit Suisse AG, *Monitoring the Technical Implementation of the FSB Total Loss-absorbing Capacity Standard Call for public feedback dated June 6, 2018* (2018) all retrievable at http://www.fsb.org/2018/08/public-responses-to-the-call-for-public-feedback-on-monitoring-the-technical-implementation-of-the-fsb-total-loss-absorbing-capacity-tlac-standard/ accessed 1 October 2022.

773 Restoy, *Bail-in in the new bank resolution framework: is there an issue with the middle class?*

774 EBA, *Quantitative Update of the EBA MREL Report: December 2016 Data* (2017), summary, p. 2 retrievable at https://www.eba.europa.eu/documents/10180/1720738/Quantitative+update+of+the+EBA+MREL+Report.pdf accessed 1 October 2022.

of the MREL framework.[775] The currently envisaged deviation from the initial BRRD eligibility criteria in the proposed Article 72b(2) CRR would exclude a significant amount of already-issued liabilities from the scope of MREL eligibility, resulting in the worsening of the current shortfall and in the necessity of issuing new eligible liabilities.[776] Because of the different funding and business structures amongst European countries, the shortfall would be even worse in 'peripheral countries' such as Greece, Italy, Ireland, Portugal, and Spain (*i.e.* countries whose banking sectors are stricken anyway) and would cause issuance costs above the European average. Therefore, complying with MREL requirements will prove more challenging for banks from such countries.[777] In addition, the potential consequences of Brexit are not considered in the above estimation of shortfalls. After Brexit, all issuances under UK law will be treated like other third-country issuances, which are generally excluded. As a vast majority of MREL-eligible liabilities are issued in and sold to the UK, this will most likely have a further impact on the shortfall.[778] The SRB allows banks to build up their MREL targets within a transition period of four years[779] and has implied that it would also consider lengthening the transition period in the future.[780]

Such an excessively long transition period – although more of an inevitable element than a shortcoming of the new integrated approach to MREL- may have negative consequences. The shortfall until transition, even though partially covered by smooth transitional arrangements, in combination with the already-in-force 8 % bail-in requirement, could undermine the credibility of entire bail-ins or make them a tedious and

775 García and Rocamora stated that the estimated shortfall could vary from 195 billion euros under the light scenario (subordination recommended by the EBA), to 301 billion euros under the medium scenario (Council's compromise text subordination), and up to 526 billion euros under the hard scenario (full subordination), see García and Rocamora, *How prepared are European banks to comply with MREL?*, p. 1.

776 Bundesverband der Deutschen Volksbanken und Raiffeisenbanken e.V. and Die Deutsche Kreditwirtschaft, *Stellungnahme zum Vorschlag der Kommission für Änderungen der BRRD/CRR im Zusammenhang mit MREL/TLAC Vorgaben*, p. 2.

777 García and Rocamora, *How prepared are European banks to comply with MREL?*

778 Single Resolution Board, *Minimum Requirements for Own Funds and Eligible Liabilities (MREL) - SRB Policy for 2017 and Next Steps*, recital 52; König, *SRB Conference 2018 - 10 years after the crisis: are banks now resolvable?*

779 Single Resolution Board, *Minimum Requirements for Own Funds and Eligible Liabilities (MREL) - SRB Policy for 2017 and Next Steps*, recital 7.

780 Ibid., recital 47.

complicated task. This can be illustrated by the example of an institution that does not meet MREL requirements upon transition but is in need of SRF financing. Such SRF financing would then only be possible if the 8 % bail-in quota is fulfilled, if necessary with unsecured deposits – an undesirable scenario for institutions, investors, clients, and politicians.[781]

Result of Part 4

This part has examined the instrument of LACRs as a remedy to the identified *ex post* problems of credibility of resolution. After confirming the general potential for serving as an antidote, it elaborated on the instrument's inherent impediments. The analysis showed that the current framework for recovery and resolution planning suffers from an array of problems that might have a negative impact on its remedial character. Initial shortcomings of MREL and the TLAC were partially reinforced by the Commission's integrated approach, even though the latter was intended to eradicate discrepancies and flaws in the two initial concepts. The current framework is characterized by enhanced complexity, induced by the alleged need for proportionality,[782] flexibility, and fine-tuning[783] and by uncertainty faced by investors in loss-absorbing debt instruments. Many provisions (such as the eligibility of instruments, the discretional subordination requirements, and the unstable calculation process) of the integrated approach distort the prerequisite of effective loss-absorbing capital: correct pricing and risk valuation by investors. But even if investors are somehow capable of evaluating the price and risk of their investment correctly, relaxations and discretion can alter the initial calculations significantly. Combined with the absence of provisions regulating the holdings of bail-in instruments, together with numerous minor defects (high costs, flooding the market with non-preferred senior debt, the level of applicati-

781 Restoy, *Bail-in in the new bank resolution framework: is there an issue with the middle class?*

782 Outlining the problematic aspects of proportionality in the resolution framework J.-H. Binder, 'Proportionality at the Resolution Stage: Calibration of Resolution Measures and the Public Interest Test: he Principle of Proportionality and Its Applicability in EU Banking Regulation', *SSRN Electronic Journal* (2017), p. 22 retrievable at SSRN https://ssrn.com/abstract=2990379 accessed 1 October 2022.

783 Tröger, 'Why MREL won't help much', p. 21.

on, and the underlying deficient determination process through RRP), the *status quo* is unsatisfactory.

Despite the identified problems, loss-absorbing capacities are a meaningful remedy for the detected lack of sufficient non-public funding in resolution. Since the integrated approach has not yet been adopted, improvements to the proposed framework can still help to achieve the intended aim of enhancing the credibility of bail-in through boosting loss-absorbing capacities. Therefore, this part has attempted to find solutions to the identified problems. The detailed outline of impediments herein will serve as a robust starting point for proposals to improve LACRs.

PART 5 – ATTEMPTS TO FIND SOLUTIONS TO THE IDENTIFIED IMPEDIMENTS

The purpose of the following section is to devise and present solutions to the identified impediments with respect to RRP and LACRs where possible, as well as to give some indications as to what direction should be taken in order to improve relevant instruments specifically. The section does not purport to find exhaustive solutions to each raised problem, since this would hardly be possible in the rapidly changing and highly complex environment of banking resolution. It instead aims to contribute to making an improvement to the resolution framework as a whole, especially through pointing out current deficiencies and their causes in light of the ongoing legislative process and the fluid developments in the field. Eventually, legislators or policy makers can take such considerations into account. Preferably, if RRP as well as loss-absorbing capacities can really be improved, this can enhance the credibility of bail-in and resolution in general, making the banking union more resilient and sounder.

Possible Solutions to the Identified Impediments of Recovery and Resolution Planning

The legislative framework for RRP eventually suffered from several shortcomings and difficulties, some of which are outlined above under Part 3, A.II. – *Identification of Possible Impediments to the Potential of Recovery and Resolution Planning.* Below, the identified problematic points are taken up again, with each of them allocated a potential solution.

Is Improvement of Recovery and Resolution Planning Necessary at All?

Before going into detail, it is important to clarify whether, despite the unequivocal impediments, improving the concept of RRP is necessary at all. The line of argument against the need for improvement rests on two assumptions. First, RRP is extremely costly. Therefore, the current framework may already provide a sufficient cost-benefit tradeoff in the sense that it is Pareto-efficient.[784] Indeed, enhancing the current framework might trigger costs no longer compensated by the generated benefits. The second assumption meshes with the first, and revolves around the implication that estimates are satisfactory and are 'doing the job,' meaning that *perfect* planning is not needed. Even if RRP information may not be completely accurate, a rough orientation given in the plans could be enough.[785] The rationale here can be illustrated by taking the example of sending out invitations to a party in which invitees are asked to RSVP. Even though some people may not respond to the invitation but attend anyway (or vice versa), or some guests indicate the wrong number of attendees, an approximate number of attendees can more or less be derived from the received answers. Subsequently, in light of the estimated attendance, preparations can be made accordingly (*e.g.* the amount of food or the number of seats) and minor adjustments can be made on the day of the event to accommodate the true number of attendees. This logivc might be transferred to RRP, where imperfect plans can still give enough guidance to deal with recovery and resolution, with only minor adjustments required (if any). Considering the cost and effort that go into the enhancement of RRP, it might not be worth improving the process as it already produces sufficient and satisfactory results from a cost-benefit perspective.

However, such an assumption cannot be proved in reality. Even if RRP is undeniably costly[786] for institutions as well as for the EU, especially during and shortly after implementation, it has not yet reached maximum synergy. As is the case with any newly-introduced task, RRP also carries initial costs that will eventually be recouped in the following years once the synergies between supervisory reporting, internal compliance, revision, or other related bodies attain their full potential. Costs will most likely diminish in the course of developing better information-gathering and

---

784 Pareto-efficient is a state in which it is impossible to readjust factors so as to make one individual or preference criterion better-off without making another individual or preference criterion worse-off. See, among many, I. Berthonnet and T. Delclite, 'Pareto-Optimality or Pareto-Efficiency: Same Concept, Different Names? An Analysis Over a Century of Economic Literature', *Research in the history of economic thought and methodology* 32.2014 (2014), 129–45.

785 Thole, 'Bank Crisis Management and Resolution', p. 8.

786 See the estimated budgetary implications in *Proposal for a Directive of the European Parliament and of the Council establishing a framework for the recovery and resolution of credit institutions and investment firms and amending Council Directives 77/91/EEC and 82/891/EC, Directives 2001/24/EC, 2002/47/EC, 2004/25/EC, 2005/56/EC, 2007/36/EC and 2011/35/EC and Regulation (EU) No 1093/2010: BRRD Proposal* (2012), explanatory memorandum, p. 18.

reporting frameworks and will be priced-in by institutions over the long term. Undeniably, costs will still arise but it can be assumed that such costs will then be counterbalanced by the overall benefits of the task that go beyond the fulfillment of the planning requirement. Moreover, there is no evidence to prove whether the cost-benefit calculation here has reached its optimum level yet. On the contrary, the qualitative level of RRP seem to offer questionable benefits, especially when looking at cases such as Banco Popular Español[787] where the plans were ultimately not put into practice due to discrepancies between the plan and the actual situation faced. There is no indication that initially-drafted but subsequently-unused plans currently provide estimates that prove helpful in resolution actions. As a consequence, the resolution framework should strive to become as accurate and precise as it can be in its planning processes, and accurate information should determine RRP to make it as effective as possible.

Proposals in Detail: Measures to Improve Recovery and Resolution Planning

After having ascertained the need to enhance the recovery and resolution framework, the following section introduces a set of potential solutions and approaches to improve the current planning framework. With this purpose in mind, suggestions to solve the identified problems listed under Part 3, A.II. – *Identification of Possible Impediments to the Potential of Recovery and Resolution Planning* have been grouped under wider measures. Four main measures were identified, covering most of the detected lacks in RRP. First, there is a strong case for strengthening the framework for cross-border cooperation of competent and resolution authorities as well as among the authorities themselves. Second, and this measure covers the majority of open issues pertaining to problems of RRP, the data collection and management process for recovery and resolution information is in urgent need of improvement in a variety of aspects. Third, recovery and resolution plans need to be made enforceable to a certain extent, penalizing discretionary non-compliance with the predefined plans and preventing political influence *ex post*. Lastly, a structural reform of the banking sector would provide for a multitude of improvements to the planning process. However, while these four potential measures have been identified, some

787 See *supra* under Part 3, A.II.1.f. – *Predictability of the Actual Crisis Scenario at Some Future Date* for a description of the Banco Popular case.

issues remain open and these are considered in the last paragraph of this section.

Strengthening and Clarifying the Framework for Cross-Border Cooperation of Supervisory and Resolution Authorities

The first proposed measure to be taken in order to improve RRP can be grouped under the wider topic of "strengthening and clarifying vertical as well as horizontal cross-border cooperation of authorities involved in RRP."[788] As was outlined above, under Part 3, A.II.1.a. – *Potential Divergences between Authorities – Cross-Border Coordination* as well as under Part 3, A.II.1.b. – *Protection of Own Markets, Market Players and Depositors*, some of the problems pertaining to the current recovery and resolution framework stem from deficits arising from cooperation within the EU and in the non-EU cross-border context. The focus of the criticism here has been primarily on coordination for a, such as Internal Resolution Teams (IRT), (European) Resolution Colleges, or Crisis Management Groups (CMGs). It has also been noted that shirking, as well as the conflicting opinions and interests of different authorities and parties involved can negatively influence the highly-intertwined RRP process, where mutual information, recommendation, and consultation are integral parts of the process, ultimately leading to distorted planning for groups, semi-optimal compromises, and unsatisfactory trade-offs for weaker host countries that could affect the efficiency of the regime. In a cross-border context with third countries, where different national authorities are not only obliged to reach joint decisions but are also required to liaise with a number of foreign authorities which maintain different standards and attitudes towards RRP, the problem worsens. The complicated legal framework and the number of bodies and pieces of legislation involved serve to complicate the process further. Home bias and the protection of own markets, market players,

788 This is a rather common and mainstream proposal, repeatedly emphasized by scholars, legislators, and politicians. See, among many and only recently, Financial Stability Board, *Thematic peer review on bank resolution planning* (2018), pp. 5 *et seq.* retrievable at http://www.fsb.org/wp-content/uploads/P040618.pdf accessed 1 October 2022 and A. Carstens, *Post-crisis bank resolution: what are the main challenges now?: Concluding remarks by Mr Agustín Carstens, General Manager of the BIS, at the 8th FSI-IADI conference on "Bank resolution, crisis management and deposit insurance", Basel, 2 February 2018*, FSI-IADI conference on "Bank resolution, crisis management and deposit insurance" (2018).

and depositors exacerbate this problem as well. Often, and especially within Resolution Colleges, where the cross-border activities of an institution are of systemic importance in a specific host country but immaterial to the institution as a whole, interests are diametrically opposed in the resolution planning process (frequently between 'stronger' and 'weaker' countries). In order to address the cross-border problem, certain approaches should be contemplated.

First, a palatable way must be found of both eliminating extraneous considerations from the cross-border RRP process *and* aligning the incentives of countries and players involved. Second, there is a strong need for simplification and clarification of cross-border RRP. Operational frameworks must be reviewed and internal processes for coordination must be clearly communicated to all parties involved.[789] This may prove difficult under the current set-up, as each affected authority of a cross-border institution can potentially be included in the process: supervisory authorities of cross-border institution subsidiaries review the Union parent undertaking's recovery plan together with the consolidated supervisor, and a similar process applies to resolution planning with respect to the review and approval of the resolution plan within IRTs, Resolution Colleges, or CMGs. However, within such cross-border for a, frequently only the authorities of significant subsidiaries are involved. Whether the significance criteria pertain to the significance of the group or only within the respective state is left at the discretion of the group resolution authority. And, despite the progress that Resolution Colleges have achieved since the introduction of the BRRD, there is clearly still room for improvement.[790] College meetings are not held regularly, resolution-planning information is not circulated properly,[791] and dissenting authorities can still decide to take their own decisions contrary to a joint decision, despite existing (albeit not really

789 A similar line of reasoning can be found in J. Cunliffe, 'Ending Too-Big-to-Fail: How Best to Deal with Failed Large Banks' in G. B. Navetti, G. Calzolari and A. F. Pozzolo (eds.), *European Economy: Banks, Regulation, and the Real Sector* (Rome: Europeye, 2016), pp. 59–74, pp. 73 *et seq.*

790 Also highlighted in EBA, *EBA Report on the Functioning of Resolution Colleges in 2017*, executive summary.

791 Ibid., p. 3.

binding[792]) EBA mediation.[793] Understandably, the current set-up's complexity and outline owes to the nature of the European Union and does serve a reasonable purpose. However, it carries the danger of misaligned incentives, poor information management, so-called national go-it-alone, and the excessive influence of national interests.

Therefore, as a third proposal, a body could be established that sits above the consolidated supervisor or responsible resolution authority, to be consulted if needed when reservations about the objectiveness and uninfluencedness of plans are raised. Additionally, the internal organization within a Resolution College must be reviewed and complemented in order to prevent power imbalances and inconsistent or unduly-influenced behavior of home and host authorities. There must be confidence that *all* available information is passed along and that all objections are heard and considered. Even though the latter might only be achieved by letting the concept of cooperation fora such as IRTs, Resolution Colleges, or CMGs ripen, since most of them are only in their second iteration,[794] active restructuring and modification of the current cross-border cooperation design is necessary.

Finally, as a last proposal with respect to cross-border problems, it is suggested that common communication interfaces be introduced. Such interfaces could take the form of an online tool that authorities and other participants can use to participate in international resolution fora. Participation would be easily accessible, and convenient coordination could also be achieved. This would facilitate information-sharing between all parties involved and would enhance the participation of all members in such international coordination fora. Information could be uploaded and voting tools could even be introduced to ensure the participation of all members in important decisions.

In addition to specific techniques to enhance cross-border cooperation in specific fora, another suggestion is made. Specifically, easing cross-border cooperation and the improvement of resolution planning could be

---

792 Although mediation is binding when a resolution authority refers the decision of the consolidating or subsidiary resolution authorities' resolution plan to the EBA, resolution authorities may argue that the subject matter under disagreement impinges on its financial responsibilities, thereby excluding the issue from EBA mediation, see World Bank Group, *Understanding Bank Recovery and Resolution in the EU: A Guidebook to the BRRD*, p. 77.

793 Ibid., p. 77.

794 EBA, *EBA Report on the Functioning of Resolution Colleges in 2017*, executive summary.

realized in the mandatory introduction or incentivized[795] reinforcement of the SPE approach in the European Union.[796] If EU financial firms were to move to a holding company structure, the focus of resolution could be at the holding company level, thereby minimizing disruption of ordinary businesses of other subsidiaries[797] and lifting the burden of heavy resolution planning from the shoulders of host authorities, which would be especially welcomed in less-advanced Member States. Additionally, organizing large bank or cross-border resolutions using an SPE approach would further facilitate resolutions that go beyond European borders, since, for example, the US and the UK favor the SPE resolution approach.[798] This would also be favorable in light of the forthcoming internal MREL and the existing internal TLAC requirements, which would then facilitate resolution financing.

As indicated by a survey on the European banking landscape, most institutions are decentralized and have no single holding company, and this is why the MPE approach might be the best fit for the eurozone at first glance. When looking at the existing literature, however, there are some indications that the SPE procedure has many advantages including the clarity, credibility, and transparency of the process. It is cross-border friendly and allows the operating subsidiaries to continue with their business as normal.[799] The cross-border argument is an especially strong one in this respect: MPE recovery or resolution would mean that, where a banking group is separable in each jurisdiction, multiple authorities act independently at a national level, causing, at the very least, coordination

795 The hope that banking groups in the EU would voluntarily move away from an operating holding company to an SPE holding company was expressed by König, *SRB Conference 2018 - 10 years after the crisis: are banks now resolvable?*

796 Bolton and Oehmke argue in favor of SPE approaches, however they also recognize implementation constraints. See P. Bolton and M. Oehmke, 'Bank Resolution and the Structure of Global Banks', *Columbia Business School Research Paper* (2018), pp. 1, 4.

797 J. N. Gordon and W.-G. Ringe, *Bank Resolution in Europe: the Unfinished Agenda of Structural Reform*, ECGI Law Working Paper (2015), p. 2, retrievable at https://ecgi.global/working-paper/bank-resolution-europe-unfinished-agenda-structural-reform accessed 1 October 2022.

798 Schoenmaker states that the appropriate procedure depends on the intensity of cooperation between the countries and with outside countries. When a corporation in uncooperative, an MPE approach might be better suited for dealing with resolution. However, a combination of SPE and MPE would also be possible. See Schoenmaker, *The different legal and operational structures of banking groups in the euro area, and their impact on banks' resolvability*, p. 16.

799 Ibid., p. 16.

problems.[800] This, of course, would mean an extensive remodeling of the European baking landscape and would also mean that several financial groups are required to put up a holding company for their business operations in the Banking Union area since many of them operate as decentralized groups for now. However, such remodeling could either be achieved through the RRP process under the BRRD, since supervisors or resolution authorities can decide that a holding company is essential for resolution and may insist on implementing them[801] during the recovery planning phase. Otherwise, it could be achieved through a structural reform of the banking sector,[802] although recent European reform endeavors in this respect were ultimately rejected.[803]

Enhancing Data Management

The core weakness of the RRP regime can be found at the root of the process, namely the production, assessment, processing, and provisioning of information and data necessary to generate recovery and resolution plans. Above, under Part 3, A.II. – *Identification of Possible Impediments to the Potential of Recovery and Resolution Planning*, a number of problems have been detected in that respect, all revolving around defective data management before or during planning by institutions and authorities.[804]

---

800 Karamichailidou and Mayes, 'Plausible recovery and resolution plans for cross-border financial institutions', p. 44.

801 Binder, 'Resolution Planning and Structural Bank Reform within the Banking Union', pp. 140 *et seq.*; Gordon and Ringe, *Bank Resolution in Europe: the Unfinished Agenda of Structural Reform*, p. 18.

802 For some discussion as to whether structural banking reform can provide solutions to impediments to recovery and resolution planning, see *infra* Part 5, A.II.4. – *Structural Reform of the Banking Sector.*

803 Gordon and Ringe state that the implication of an SPE structure can further be achieved through capital requirements under the Capital Requirements Regulation and Directive (CRR/CRD IV), through the assessment of extra capital charges for a bank without a holding company structure in the stress tests administered by the ECB, or through a structurally-sensitive systemic risk assessment of a GSIB as contemplated by Basel III, see Gordon and Ringe, *Bank Resolution in Europe: the Unfinished Agenda of Structural Reform*, p. 3.

804 The importance of functioning and up-to-date data management for carrying out nearly all resolution-related tasks effectively was recently stressed by D. Laboureix, *SRB Conference 2018 – 10 years after the crisis: are banks now resolvable?*, SRB Annual Conference (Brussels, 2018).

Amongst these detected problems are some of the key problems to have arisen in recent resolution cases.

The greatest improvement of RRP can therefore be obtained by enhancing the underlying data management process for institutions and authorities, making available a better information base for planning, and thereby enhancing the quality of the latter.

Special Training to Enhance Internal Data Provision

A number of problems pertaining to RRP lie in the inability of institutions to provide the necessary data correctly, both for their own recovery planning and for resolution planning as part of their obligation to provide information to the resolution authority. Employees of institutions entrusted with RRP might not be sure where to get the relevant information, at which level this information is to be obtained (entity, jurisdiction, or group), which data need to be included, what the denominator or ratio is, and how the figures are to be presented, among other aspects.

A possible action response would be to educate and train the institution's employees who are responsible for data and information procurement. This could be done through mandatory workshops with mock planning scenarios hosted by supervisory or resolution authorities of the Member States or through briefings, online seminars, or on-site courses. Such training would explain the key points of recovery and resolution planning, including the used templates and especially the abbreviations, ratios, indicators, and measurements contained in those templates. Despite having various documents to explain how recovery plans should look[805] and how templates should be filled-out,[806] face-to-face training would undoubtedly achieve a better result. Furthermore, during on-site trainings, responsible employees could pose questions as to where to obtain specific information in the specific institution or whether the IT systems are sufficient to do the job. To intensify the effect, participation in such training

805 EBA, *Guidelines on the range of scenarios to be used in recovery plans EBA/GL/2014/06; EBA final draft Regulatory Technical Standards on the content of recovery plans under Article 5(10) of Directive 2014/59/EU establishing a framework for the recovery and resolution of credit institutions and investment firms*; Commission Delegated Regulation (EU) 2016/1075 on RTS of Recovery and Resolution Plans.

806 EBA Draft ITS on Resolution Plans; Commission Implementing Regulation (EU) 2016/1066 on ITS on resolution plans; Single Resolution Board, *The Single Resolution Mechanism – Introduction to Resolution Planning*.

could be made a prerequisite for being allowed to work on an institution's recovery plan or for being allowed to fill-in the templates and work with the resolution authority, at least for the supervising or executive employees in this area. Such an approach would entail having at least one specialist in each institution that is available to resolution authorities to respond to questions and queries pertaining to RRP assistance, without the need for various decentralized employees to delve into details. Such intra-institution experts would also assume supervision of the internal planning and data provision process and would be the responsible contact person for the authorities and within cross-border coordination resolution planning in the resolution fora.

Full-Time RRP Employees

This leads us to a second proposal that pursues a similar direction but goes one step further. While training internal employees as experts would most likely ameliorate the problem of gathering and providing wrong data due to a lack of knowledge and/or ability, this may not eliminate the problem of institution-specific biases, shirking, and conflicts of interest. Such a tendency was detected above, under Part 3, A.II.1.c. – *Planning as an Inconvenient Standard Exercise – Adding More Complexity*, Part 3, A.II.1.d. – *Drawing Up of Plans Takes Place in Times of Stability – Optimism Bias* and Part 3, A.II.2.b.iii. – *Intentionally Incorrect Information.* Intentional or unintentional attempts to influence RRP for the benefit of the institution and in order to avoid unpleasant actions being taken by authorities (changes in the course of recovery planning or removal of impediments to resolvability in the context of resolution planning[807]) can put pressure on internal employees to adjust information accordingly or may make them vulnerable to managerial influence. Therefore, it would be best to hire external people for the monitoring of internal RRP assistance. Potential candidates for this position would work full-time on recovery and resolution matters within the institution and would be obliged to attend regular training given, for example, by the competent or supervisory authority. Alternatively, taking the concept one step further, such experts could be domiciled with the

807 See *supra* Part 3, A.II.2.b.iii. – *Intentionally Incorrect Information* for examples how and why institutions may want to influence recovery and resolution planning.

SRB and will only be borrowed or assigned to the institutions.[808] As a side-effect, this would create a market for full-time RRP employees, which, in turn, incentivizes the latter to work well and efficiently. Similar proposals, such as setting up specific resolution teams that consist of analysts and seconded experts from consultancy firms or banks, known as "ex-experts brigades,"[809] all incorporate the same elements: specialization, expertise, no conflicts of interest, and full-time employment only for RRP purposes.

Development of a Standardized Template for a Single Distributor that Shares Relevant Data with Recipient – Information Intermediary

The attempt to remedy problems surrounding data collection for RRP by introducing specifically-trained employees, or even a new profession of full-time RRP employees, remedies only one side of the problem. In addition to the problem of not having appropriate staff, a second issue massively impedes functional recovery and especially resolution planning. That problem is described above, under Part 3, A.II.1.h. – *Opaque Data Production and Collection Process – Templates*, which covers concerns with regard to the collection vehicle, such as the templates used for planning and their handling. Like so many other issues here, this mainly concerns resolution planning because this is realized through the query of templates while recovery planning is done at institutional level only, under the general guidance of what the recovery plan should entail.[810] These templates, as set out above, often cause confusion, are redundant, and are subject to constant change. Moreover, the indicators and ratios used in the templates do not always correlate to those used in the course of supervisory reporting. Right from these templates' introduction, smaller institutions

---

808 Although in a slightly different context (namely the determination of critical functions of an institution), Schoenmaker states that, if the SRB suspects that there is relevant information being withheld from them, either by the banks themselves or by national resolution authorities, the SRB should be given more staff with direct access to the institutions, as can be seen in the US Federal Deposit Insurance Corporations FDIC. See Schoenmaker, *The different legal and operational structures of banking groups in the euro area, and their impact on banks' resolvability*, p. 17.

809 Franke, Krahnen and Lüpke, *Effective Resolution of Banks: Problems and Solutions*, p. 15.

810 Arts. 3–21 of Commission Delegated Regulation (EU) 2016/1075 on RTS of Recovery and Resolution Plans.

in particular complained about the complexity, incomprehensibility, and volatility of the used templates. Indeed, the resulting uncertainty has certainly contributed to the delivery of incorrect information. However, bigger banks have also struggled massively with the requested task and expressed concerns and indignation accordingly.[811]

It can be argued that this situation presents a clear case for letting things develop and mature on the assumption that a best-practice approach will ultimately be found over time. This is true to a certain extent, as all novelties and legal innovations need time to be implemented and tested. However, as the approach that needs to be pursued is fairly clear, suggestions in this respect can be made to accelerate the process. For such acceleration to materialize, there are two requirements. First, the templates need to be enhanced; and, second, a solution must be found to remedy the criticized double-reporting in supervision and resolution matters to avoid confusion and the imposition of an unnecessary burden on institutions.

Therefore, efforts should be made pursuant to the development of a standardized, pan-European reporting format, comprising all prudential, regulatory, and statistical information. This reporting format, whether it remains in the form of Excel sheet templates or ultimately has a totally different design (such as, for example, an online portal or a log-in area on a homepage) should be the only vehicle for conveying information to all authorities in need of institution-specific data. To eliminate double-reporting and confusion with respect to different reporting standards for different purposes, this reporting format should be submitted electronically, at given intervals, to one single point of contact, which is then responsible for managing the sharing of data between the relevant national and European authorities. Authorities would, in turn, be both authorized and obliged to share relevant data amongst themselves, if appropriate (for example, for authorities'internal reporting of competent and resolution authorities to the EBA).[812] This would guarantee the conveyance of consistent infor-

811 EBA, *Consultation Paper for Draft Implementing Standards on the provision of information for the purpose of resolution plans under Article 11(3) of Directive 2014/59/EU EBA/CP/2017/15*; Deutsche Bank, *Deutsche Bank response to the European Banking Authority's consultation paper of the Draft ITS on the provision of information for the purpose of resolution plans under Article 11(3) of Directive 2014/59/EU*; European Banking Federation, *EBF response to EBA Consultation on Draft ITS on the provision of information for the purpose of resolution plans under Article 11(3) of Directive 2014/59/EU*.

812 *Commission Implementing Regulation (EU) 2016/962 of 16 June 2016 laying down implementing technical standards with regard to the uniform formats, templates and*

mation between all information recipients. Therefore, a body such as the EBA should be mandated to design appropriate reporting formats and, eventually, new online tools to execute such reporting. However, it should be noted that the efficiency of reporting processes also depends largely on the quality of the bank's internal processes and controls, and the deployment of up-to-date IT infrastructure. The efficiency of a bank's reporting system, as well as its effectiveness, should be reviewed regularly as part of the SREP.[813]

The first endeavors in the direction of a pan-European information intermediary have been observable at the European level, such as for example AnaCredit (analytical credit datasets). The latter is a project designed to set up a dataset containing detailed information on individual bank loans in the euro zone,[814] harmonized across all Member States. The project was initiated in 2011 and data collection was scheduled to start in September 2018.[815] However, a central data collection system in Europe for the purpose of recovery planning, and especially resolution planning, is still missing. Objectives for the future will include the setting up of a European reporting framework, probably under the initiative of the European central banks or with parties outher than the authorities that use the data.[816]

Updating of Institutions' IT Infrastructure

This leads to the next crucial point with regard to enhancing data management for recovery and resolution purposes. The underlying problem here is less of an inherent, RRP-related problem but rather a broader issue of the banking sector that interferes with the prerequisites for the optimal

---

definitions for the identification and transmission of information by competent authorities and resolution authorities to the European Banking Authority according to Directive 2014/59/EU of the European Parliament and of the Council OJ L 160, 17.6.2016, p. 35–49.

813 Stiefmüller, *Ten Years After - The 2017 Banking Package: One Step Forward, Two Steps Back*, p. 8.

814 Deutsche Bundesbank, *Richtlinien zur Kreditdatenstatistik (AnaCredit)*, 3rd edn. (2018).

815 *Regulation (EU) 2016/867 of the European Central Bank of 18 May 2016 on the collection of granular credit and credit risk data (ECB/2016/13), OJ L 144, 1.6.2016, p. 44–98.*

816 Sachverständigenrat zur Begutachtung der Gesamtwirtschaftlichen Entwicklung, *Für eine zukunftsorientierte Wirtschaftspolitik*, 54.2017/18, ch. 5, para. 466.

functioning of RRP. However, RRP fails to combat this well-known[817] problem in its current set-up; indeed, it almost ignores it. The problem here is that institutions, for various reasons,[818] use outdated and fragmented IT infrastructure, often from 30 or more years ago. Sometimes, systems are antiquated and no longer state-of-the-art. The result is that younger employees cannot work with the old systems anymore, as universities no longer include them in their courses, thus forcing banks to engage specialists or retired bankers to operate these outdated structures.[819] More frequently, IT structures of banks are incompatible across branches, subsidiaries, or jurisdictions due to mergers or acquisitions or simply because the initially-implemented systems were never replaced but only extended and supplemented with various add-ons. The consequences of this problem were outlined above under Part 3, A.II.1.h. – *Opaque Data Production Collection Process – Templates.*

As RRP stands or falls on the availability and accuracy of the underlying data, it is clear that improvements in this respect must be achieved, not only to enhance RRP but for the benefit of the banking sector's technical evolvement.[820] Here, national authorities can spring into action, and require institutions to update their systems and introduce IT actuality checks within the SREP or as a stand-alone test.

Automated Data Submission

With the introduction of updated IT systems, another data management problem could be solved. As was described above under Part 3, A.II.1.g. – *Impermanence of Banks Structures and the Topicality of Recovery and Resolution Plans*, banks and their balance sheets change constantly. Even though

817 The problem with legacy IT systems in banking is well-known across the sector and already acknowledged by authorities. See BaFin, *Rundschreiben 10/2017 (BA) in der Fassung vom 14.09.2018 – Bankaufsichtliche Anforderungen an die IT (BAIT)*, BaFin Rundschreiben (2018).

818 See a description of reasons why institutions have fragmented and outdated IT infrastructure *supra* under Part 2, A.II.1.b. – *Complexity in Banks Structures.*

819 A. Irrera, 'Banks scramble to fix old systems as IT 'cowboys' ride into sunset', Reuters, 10 April 2017 retrievable at https://www.reuters.com/article/us-usa-banks-cobol/banks-scramble-to-fix-old-systems-as-it-cowboys-ride-into-sunset-idUSKBN17C0D8 accessed 1 October 2022.

820 BaFin, *Rundschreiben 10/2017 (BA) in der Fassung vom 14.09.2018 - Bankaufsichtliche Anforderungen an die IT (BAIT)*, p. 3.

recovery and resolution plans need to be updated at least annually, and major changes need to be communicated to the competent or resolution authority, it is questionable whether RRP can keep pace with the volatile developments of an institution in the course of one year. With the implementation of new IT systems – which is perhaps a standardized or at least a compatible solution – data submission could be automated.[821] This would involve the automated transfer of available data to the respective authority or authorities, placing such updates under their responsibility and discretion. The submitted data would then be automatically retrieved by the system. Moreover, discrepancies between plans and reality would be reduced, as submission errors or failures would be eliminated. Obviously, such an approach would also touch on data protection issues that would need to be solved before implementation.

RegTech as an Antidote to Major Data Management Problems

All proposed measures above can be further examined in light of a new phenomenon: regulatory technology (RegTech).[822] Although steered in a slightly different direction, namely supporting effective regulatory management and compliance through IT solutions in light of the demanding new regulatory framework, RegTech could be serve RRP purposes too. The first initiatives[823] in this area already point in this direction, but these are a long way from fulfilling the vast potential here. Even though there is no clear definition of what RegTech includes exactly, the underlying idea indicates that RegTech involves, *inter alia*, effective and updated IT

821 First approaches in this direction can recently be observed. The EBA states that the "[…] extension of the EBA's data point model (DPM) to resolution reporting templates will improve data quality and allow for automated collection, quality control and exchange." See EBA, *Draft final report - Draft Implementing Standards on the provision of information for the purpose of resolution plans under Article 11(3) of Directive 2014/59/EU EBA/ITS/2018/02*, p. 3.

822 Institute of International Finance, *RegTech in Financial Services: Technology Solutions for Compliance and Reporting* (2016) retrievable at https://www.iif.com/system/files/regtech_in_financial_services_-_solutions_for_compliance_and_reporting.pdf accessed 1 October 2022; D. Arner, J. N. Barberis and R. Buckley, 'FinTech, RegTech and the Reconceptualization of Financial Regulation', *Northwestern Journal of International Law & Business* 37 (2017), 371–413, pp. 412 *et seq.*

823 See, for example, the monitoring tool "zeb.regulatory.information" or "zeb.control"; https://control.zeb.eu/sites/default/files/broschure_zeb_control_deu.pdf.

solutions, a common understanding of pan-European data availability, streamlining and automation of processes, and the implementation of useful data governance. Such features, if fully exploited, could certainly help RRP to overcome its data management sufficiency problem. However, since RegTech is a new concept that is not sufficiently developed yet, it remains to be seen whether (and to what extent) it can really contribute to RRP.

Make Plans Enforceable – Penalize Non-Compliance – Prevent Political Influence

The next proposal designed to improve RRP concerns the enforceability of agreed plans. So far, as demonstrated under Part 3, A.II.1.j. – *Gateway to Political Influence – Enforceability of Plans*, plans do not have legal force nor is non-compliance with, or deviation from, a predetermined plan penalized. This has been identified as a gateway for political influence *ex post* planning: while the resolution plan aims for bail-in, governments can decide to deviate from the foreseen resolution strategy, as they realize the impact on the bank's customers and the influence on the state's economy.[824] Notwithstanding the heavy consequences of non-enforceable plans, a mandatory application is still not a good solution. Indeed, in some cases, sticking to the plan can make the situation even worse. This may be due to changes in the underlying conditions of the institution or the occurrence of scenarios not foreseen at the time of a resolution plan. In these cases, forced execution of plans into a respective resolution scheme might damage the institution even further. Therefore, exceptions are necessary, but such exceptions must not be excessively loose in order not to lead politicians and governments into temptation. Most importantly, intended deviation from a predetermined plan must be reasonably explained, preferably publicly, so that political considerations become transparent. The more precise and exhaustive plans are from the beginning, the less likely it is that deviation will be necessary. Pre-made proposals, the strengthening and clarifying of cross-border coordination, and the enhancement of data management can all make a contribution in this respect.

---

824 Even though the plan itself is not disclosed to the public and only known to the resolution authority, governments can influence the transposition of the plan into the resolution scheme, even though no official mechanism exists where governments can exert their influence.

Structural Reform of the Banking Sector

The last potential redress for problems pertaining to RRP is the implementation of a structural reform[825] of the European banking sector. For the United States[826] or the United Kingdom[827] (as examples outside the eurozone), and for Belgium,[828] France,[829] and Germany[830] (as examples *inside* the eurozone), a structural reform of the entire European banking landscape might ease some of the detected problems in the current resolution design. Even though the objective of reform endeavors is the prevention of contagious effects in times of crisis by separating certain macro-economically important business functions, rather than the enhancement of RRP through the reduction of organizational complexity. Indeed, it may be expected that it would be easier to recover and resolve a structurally-reformed institution. This is due to the underlying concept of structural reform proposals that create separated, and therefore simplified, business units and legally, organizational, and technically segregated structures. This could make things easier not only in cases of crisis management in recovery or resolution, but also beforehand, during the setting-up of recovery and resolution plans, by reducing organizational complexity and simplifying corporate structures in the interest of enhanced resolvability.[831] Less intervention by authorities in the course of removing impediments to

825 For an overview of existing structural reform efforts, see J.-H. Binder, 'To ring-fence or not, and how?: Strategic questions for post-crisis banking reform in Europe', *SSRN Electronic Journal* (2014) retrievable at SSRN https://ssrn.com/abstract=2543860 accessed 1 October 2022.

826 See § 619 of the Dodd-Frank Wall Street Reform and Consumer Protection Act of 2010, Pub. L. No. 111–203, 124 Stat. 1376(2010).

827 See Financial Services (Banking Reform) Act 2013 (ch. 33).

828 See Loi relative au statut et au contrôle des établissements de crédit, 25 April 2014, Moniteur Belge Ed. 2, 7 June 2014, p. 36794, articles 117–33.

829 See Loi no. 2013–672 du 26 juillet 2013 de separation et de regulation des activités bancaires, Journal Officiel de la République Francaise no. 0173 du 27 juillet 2013, p. 12530.

830 See Gesetz zur Abschirmung von Risiken und zur Planung der Sanierung und Abwicklung von Kreditinstituten und Finanzgruppen, 7 August 2013, Bundesgesetzblatt Part I, p. 2090.

831 The same approach may be found in Schoenmaker, *The different legal and operational structures of banking groups in the euro area, and their impact on banks' resolvability*, not calling his recommendations a structural banking reform but indicating that he would propose to separate the legal structures to simplify the structures and procedures. Similar arguments can further be found in Weber, 'Structural regulation as antidote to complexity capture', p. 691.

resolution would be necessary and cross-border resolution planning would be simplified. Therefore, the aim of structural reforms in this regard can be considered the removal of impediments to effective crisis resolution and enhancing RRP.[832] Effective resolution as a response to individual or systemic crises in the long term may only be possible with greater convergence in terms of funding models and group structures. The FSB already acknowledged this tendency when stating that "structural reforms promote greater alignment of business lines with legal structures within a group [...] by simplifying internal management and supervision."[833]

Although using structural reforms as a simplifier of complexity, and therefore as an enhancer with regard to information-gathering, does seem to provide a good solution, certain problems exist. The legislation concerning RRP was already adopted ahead of the potential implementation of respective structural reform proposals and ahead of a possible Europe-wide structural reform. This has implications for potential future endeavors: recovery and resolution plans were drawn up in times of organizational confusion, as shown, in which data production is a hard task and where plans are susceptible to potential misinformation. Therefore, it might be the case that all existent recovery and resolution plans need to be at least reviewed or possibly even redrawn in the event that a proposal for structural reform is adopted. Processes need to be changed and templates need to be redesigned, possibly setting back the recovery and resolution implementation process by years.

Despite potential inconveniences for RRP arising out of a structural reform, it has been argued that only both approaches together – resolution planning and concepts for a structural bank reform – can represent a possible solution[834] to the too-big-to-fail problem and to foster market dis-

---

832 E. Liikanen, *High-level Expert Group on reforming the structure of the EU banking sector - Final Report* (2012), pp. 95–97; Gordon and Ringe, *Bank Resolution in Europe: the Unfinished Agenda of Structural Reform*, p. 1.

833 Financial Stability Board, *Structural Banking Reforms: Cross-border consistencies and global financial stability implications: Report to G20 Leaders for the November 2014 Summit* (2014), p. 13 retrievable at http://www.fsb.org/wp-content/uploads/r_141027.pdf accessed 1 October 2022.

834 Some scholars disagree with this view and state that the concept of resolution planning (along with the concept of extended capital requirements) is only a behavioral regulatory tool that delegate the primary responsibilities to the banking industry itself. It is argued that these reforms are the sort of regulation that is susceptible to complexity capture and regulatory dysfunction. It is argued that only a focus on promoting structural regulatory reforms is the key to building a

cipline among bank owners, bank managers, and investors in bank debt.[835] Interference with existing corporate and group structures of institutions, both at the level of structural reforms and consecutively within RRP, would be inevitable in the process of heightening the credibility of resolution. Furthermore, it is also argued that a resilient resolution-planning framework and a structural reform of the banking sector would need to be reconciled and aligned[836] in order to effectively promote the credibility of resolution.[837]

However, recent developments[838] in Europe make structural reform unlikely in the near term. Therefore, a European structural reform, as initially envisaged, is no longer available for the enhancement of RRP. Although RRP alone might not accomplish the identified objectives, action in this regard is required nevertheless. A structural reform – or at least something similar in order to enforce consistency of business models, funding arrangements, and legal structures of institutions and groups – must be achieved in some way. Therefore, a feature of RRP might redress this situation, and may have an effect similar to that of structural reform of the banking sector.[839] As described in the above sections, resolution[840]

more resilient financial system, see Weber, 'Structural regulation as antidote to complexity capture', p. 647.

835 Stiefmüller, *Ten Years After: Back to Business as Usual*, p. 26.

836 Binder, 'Resolution Planning and Structural Bank Reform within the Banking Union', p. 129.

837 Binder states that a real European structural banking reform is no longer probable, therefore the success of the resolution framework hinges on how the relevant authorities will use their powers to alter recovery plans in order to force institutions and groups to reorganize themselves in a way that removes potential impediments to the resolution action. Binder therefore understands the re-planning powers of the supervisory authority as substitute to the structural banking reform, see ibid., pp. 140 *et seq.*

838 European Commission, *Annex IV to the Communication from the Commission to the European Parliament, the Council, the European Economic and Social Committee and the Committee of the Regions - Commission Work Programm 2018 - An agenda for a more united, stronger and more democratic Europe, COM(2017) 650 final*, p. 2, no. 2.

839 Gordon and Ringe argue that the structural reform in the EU could be achieved by supervisory implementation of the recovery and resolution planning requirement for effective resolution or irresistible incentives through capital charges, but that it would be best obtained through addition to the EU's proposed structural measures regulation, which for now is rejected, see Gordon and Ringe, *Bank Resolution in Europe: the Unfinished Agenda of Structural Reform*.

840 Also supervisory authorities can influence banks' structures and business models to a certain extent and under certain conditions in the course of assessing

authorities have the power[841] to demand structural, financial, or planned information-related changes to institutions which could lead to the simplification of structures and procedures to enhance the resolution process, allowing for the consistent application of the resolution plans and its tools across – at least – the Banking Union. Subject to the proportionality tests that banks can rely upon in defending their existing business models and organizational structures, authorities can use their powers given by the BRRD to alter recovery and resolution plans as well as the respective institutions' structure and business model. In doing so, they can accomplish substantial changes to the banking landscape under their control. A certain streamlining of business models and group structures can be the consequence of this, for example through eliminating superfluous entities in the group's structure or by requiring the institution to take precautions in order to legally and economically separate critical functions from other functions in resolution.[842]

This approach is not new and has already been applied. Rabobank, a large Dutch cooperative, was instructed to streamline its rather complicated cooperative banking decision-making procedures. It moved from a complex cooperative bank to a single, more centralized, legal structure comprising a parent bank and local cooperative entities in 2015.[843] Another example, although outside Europe, was when the Federal Reserve System of the US and the FDIC rejected the living wills that were submitted by the 11 largest and most complex GSIBs as first-round filers. The Federal Reserve and the FDIC stated that the submitting GSIBs failed "to make, or even identify, the kinds of changes in form structure and practices that would be necessary to enhance the prospects for an orderly resolution."[844] Both authorities subsequently demanded that the next submission of living wills establish "a rational and less complex legal structure that

---

the recovery plan. However, the influence of supervisory authorities in this respect seems to be smaller than the one exerted by resolution authorities.

841 EBA, *Guidelines on the specification of measures to reduce or remove impediments to resolvability and the circumstances in which each measure may be applied under Directive 2014/59/EU.*

842 Possible measures are outlined in Art. 17(5) BRRD and subdivided into structural, financial, and information-related. See also ibid., pp. 4 *et seq.*

843 Schoenmaker, Véron, Gehrig, Messori, Leite, Sapir, Steffen, Tibi, Vegara Figueras, Vries and Xafa (eds.), *European banking supervision*; Schoenmaker, *The different legal and operational structures of banking groups in the euro area, and their impact on banks' resolvability.*

844 Board of Governors of the Federal Reserve System, *Agencies provide feedback on second round resolution plans of "First-Wave" filers* (2014) retrievable at https://ww

would take into account the best alignment of legal entities and business lines to improve the firm's resolvability."[845]

Despite some positive examples (presented above), where structural-reform-like effects were achieved, such developments have not been successfully replicated in the eurozone. Indeed,, the enforcement of changes to institutions during RRP is rare.[846] Therefore, some argue that the current promise of RRP is that, by drafting plans, banks will confront their operational complexity and will decide for themselves to streamline their operations, thereby achieving structural-reform-like effects.[847] However, as banks can currently externalize their costs of complexity onto taxpayers and as policy establishment is only committed to behavioral regulation (*i.e.* RRP and loss-absorbing capacities) rather than meaningful structural reform,[848] it is yet to be seen if such voluntary streamlining and reduction in complexity is a widespread phenomenon, or simply an exception.

Nevertheless, as structural reform is not in sight, the potential of 'camouflaged' structural reforms through RRP should instead be reinforced, and supervisory and resolution authorities should exercise their powers in this respect. By doing so, they might also find a potent option to address the structural-reform-deprived eurozone.

Open Issues

Despite the various suggestions for improvements, some identified issues remain unresolved, without a tangible solution in sight. Three such issues are related to the inherent unforeseeability of crises, while one issue pertains to an inevitable factual problem. The former are composed of: the problem of planning for a systemic crisis (Part 3, II.1.i. – *Planning Capacity for Systemic Crisis*); the problem of planning for an exact future crisis scenario (Part 3, A.II.1.f. – *Predictability of the Actual Crisis Scenario*

---

w.federalreserve.gov/newsevents/pressreleases/bcreg20140805a.htm accessed 1 October 2022.

845 Ibid.

846 EBA, *EBA Report on the Functioning of Resolution Colleges in 2017*, recital 34, p. 12.

847 Recovery (and resolution) planning is also argued to be a valuable corporate governance instrument for institutions. See L. Amorello and S. Huber, 'Recovery Planning: A New Valuable Corporate Governance Framework for Credit Institutions', *Law and Economics Yearly Review* 3 (2014), 296–317, pp. 286, 315.

848 Weber, 'Structural regulation as antidote to complexity capture', p. 713.

at some Future Date); and the problem of planners being optimistically biased (Part 3, A.II.1.d. – *Drawing Up of Plans Takes Place in Times of Stability – Optimism Bias*). The first two of these issues can presumably never be solved entirely, even though they might be improved with enhanced planning and through implementing the suggestions presented above. Nevertheless, at the point at which plans are made up, no-one will ever be capable of predicting exactly how a systemic crisis will take shape or how a future crisis scenario will look in detail. Furthermore, the optimism bias contributes to these predictability problems.

The last open issue is linked to the costs that RRP triggers for both the institutions and the planners (Remedy to Part 3, A.II.1.e. – *Costliness of the Recovery and Resolution Plans*). As outlined above, such costs are not only of a monetary nature. RRP is also costly in terms of time, resources, and labor. As long as these costs are high (even higher than the experienced benefits), institutions in particular will try to cut costs by lowering the quality or quantity of work put into planning. In the next few years, it cannot be expected that costs will decline significantly. On the contrary, costs could rise further in the course of implementing new technologies (*e.g.* the increase of information requested by the LDR), higher requirements, and more sophisticated information requests for future RRP. Ultimately, a low-cost approach for RRP is not in sight.

Possible Solutions to the Identified Impediments of Loss-Absorbing Capital Requirements

Much like the recovery and resolution framework, the proposal to design an integrated loss-absorbing capital framework within the European Union turned out to suffer from several shortcomings and difficulties (some of which are assessed above under Part 4, A.III. – *Identification of Possible Impediments to the Potential of Loss-Absorbing Capital Requirements*). Below, the identified problematic points are taken up again, with a possible solution assigned to each problem.

Proposals in Detail: Measures to Improve Loss-Absorbing Capital Requirements

Contrary to the suggestions put forward in order to find possible solutions to the identified impediments of RRP above, the suggestions for problem-solving in relation to LACRs cannot be grouped into overarching broader categories. This may be due to the fact RRP in its legal framework and design has already been in use for some time and is more impaired by external factors as well as the setting in which it is embedded. Therefore, broad and general proposals that change more than just legal subtleties are needed. Specifically, even if it cannot be precluded that a more holistic underlying problem also exists, the functioning of LACRS suffers more evidently from internal problems, such as its design and setup, as the framework has barely been used in practice yet. More specific and punctual measures that improve the legal framework and design of the instrument are required, as these can be considered when further developing the legal and policy framework for loss-absorbing capacities in Europe. Besides numerous smaller proposals aimed at tweaking LACRs in a specific yet smaller respect, the only comprehensive approach to improving the new integrated MREL pertains to the enhanced clarity and predictability of eligible instruments for investors and the market. This can be considered a general remedy to most of the detected impediments inherent in the current set-up of LACRs. However, this approach entails taking multiple smaller measures and the resulting overall enhancement of the entire framework, since there is no single curative solution in this respect.

Adoption and Maturation of the Reforms

A first step to improving the application of LACRs at this stage would certainly be to wait for the final adoption of the reforms and to allow them to mature. In contrast with RRP, where initial experience has already been gained, LACRs in their current and presumably final design, after the decision to incorporate TLAC into MREL, are not even agreed upon. Certain points, such as the definite design of the subordination rules, are still under discussion. Such discussions and further consultations will generate valuable inputs for the application of the new LACRs regime. Some of the cited points with regard to possible impediments of MREL – namely, the chaotic implementation phase, confusion and unsureness in the market, and the ultimate shortfall – have a good chance of remedying themselves once the legal framework is fully developed. Nevertheless, it has already become apparent that the majority of problems will not vanish in the course of deciding on a final legal framework of the integrated MREL framework, as the problems are either already inherent in the initial setting of the MREL or TLAC or because the problems have not been dealt with in the proposals. With this in mind, the following paragraphs will touch upon these issues.

Defining Dependable Eligibility Criteria

As was set out above under Part 4, A.III.3. – *Eligibility of Instruments – Qualitative Requirements*, the core problem with respect to the eligibility criteria of the new integrated approach is less that it might not perfectly align with MREL and TLAC, or even the reservations against the integrated approach not adequately mirroring the internationally agreed standards, but rather that the new integrated eligibility criteria produce uncertainty in the market. Through its discretional features (*e.g.* allowance of derivative features in eligible instruments, and discretional fulfillment of quotas with non-subordinated debt), the new integrated eligibility criteria do not help investors to correctly gauge risk and set pricing for instruments. The conditions for and characteristics of investment in the debt of a GSIB, for example, can vary significantly if one GSIB is allowed to fulfil certain LACRs with non-subordinated debt while another GSIB would not be granted this exception. Even if an investor can produce such information upon investment, it is costly in terms of money and time, which excludes some investors from participating in engaging with MREL debt. Furthermore, the structure of loss-absorbing debt can change discretionally after the time of investment, thereby altering the risk structure and price of already-issued debt instruments.

Therefore, moving toward making investments in loss-absorbing instruments more transparent and marketable requires that discretions that cannot be assessed at the time of investment must be limited to the greatest extent possible. Investment in loss-absorbing debt should be comparable among similar institutions, influenced only by the performance and default probability of the institution, not by the exertion of legislative discretion. This might contribute to transparency with regard to notification of holders of instruments of changes in the loss-absorbing structure of the institution because of the exertion of discretion in order to give them the chance to readjust their strategy and structure accordingly. The same effect would be achieved if holders of instruments were granted the right to redeem or return their investment in the event of significant changes compared to the situation at the time of the initial investment. Regardless of how exactly measures would look, they should primarily be aimed at simplifying investors' pricing and their subsequent handling of instruments. This is a key element in building-up a resilient and strong market for bail-inable debt and, therefore, setting the preconditions of a functioning MREL regime.

Enhancing the Pricing of MREL Instruments

The last point pertaining to the definition of non-discretional eligibility criteria leads directly to one of the acutest problems of the regime: investors are, and most likely will continue to, be unable to price issued instruments correctly. As explained above under Part 4, A.III.4. – *Pricing of LAC Instruments*, the problem has its roots in the instrument's current complicatedness, complexity, and discretional character. However, the correct pricing of loss-absorbing instruments is key to the functioning of the loss-absorbing requirements concept. Without a sound and fit market for said instruments, MREL debt will be over- or under-priced, leading to suboptimal outcomes (moral hazard or high refinancing costs).

The main desideratum in this respect would therefore be to enhance the investor's positions by introducing more transparency in this field.[849] This could be achieved by the interplay of multiple measures, such as making the LACRs framework less discretional. This, in turn, would make the instruments more transparent and would make the process of investing in those instruments more feasible. The above-described exceptions to bailing-in certain debt instruments must be eliminated to the maximum extent, and should go hand-in-hand with the prevention of political influence on the process that has the potential of interfering with the prescribed bail-in plan. Lastly, subsequent adjustments of authorities within their wide administrative discretion regarding the MREL arrangement must be limited insofar as they do not change the loss-participation of MREL instrument holders significantly, as this renders initial risk and price calculations void.

849 Interestingly, enhancing transparency in respect of investors' pricing was one of the main proposals at this year's SRB annual conference. However, no explicit proposals or measures where identified that could achieve transparency, see Enria, *SRB Conference 2018 - 10 years after the crisis: are banks now resolvable?*

Solution to the Subordination Problem

Even though a major leap forward was achieved by introducing harmonized insolvency hierarchies, problems remain. The still not-agreed-upon approach as to the extent to which subordination will be required unsettles investors, markets, and the industry, as the exact amount of necessary Pillar 1 and Pillar 2 subordinated MREL instruments for GSIBs and even non-GSIBs cannot be estimated. Moreover, even if an approach is finally agreed upon, the looming discretional power of authorities within the applied approach to defining the amount of subordination and exceptions for institutions' loss-absorbing instruments further complicates the situation for investors. Therefore, it is essential that the legislator takes further action as it is their responsibility to create a reliable legal framework at the European level.[850]

To provide clarity, both for investors in pricing MREL instruments as well as for the industry and the market regarding the expectable shortfall, a consistent approach must be found in the short term, and authorities must come to an agreement. Some claim that, in order to avoid any doubts, all liabilities eligible for the fulfillment of MREL requirements – GSIB or non-GSIB – need to be subordinated to senior unsecured (*pari passu*) creditors, indicating that the "hard"[851] subordination scenario shall be pursued.[852] This would be beneficial in providing clarity, both for investors (i.e. easing their investment decisions) and about the quality of bail-in. Consequently, going down this path, the proposed definition of eligible instruments, new Article 72b(2)(d) CRR, must be rephrased and all senior unsecured *pari passu* claims must be excluded from eligibility for MREL but not however, for the avoidance of doubt, from the eligibility to be bailed-in altogether, which is defined in Article 44(2) BRRD, but for the fulfillment of loss-absorbing requirements.[853]

---

850 Stiefmüller, *Ten Years After - The 2017 Banking Package: One Step Forward, Two Steps Back*, p. 13.

851 For a display of the possible subordination scenarios, see either *supra* under Part 4, A.III.5. – *Debt Subordination – New Art. 108 BRRD* or García and Rocamora, *How prepared are European banks to comply with MREL?*, p. 5.

852 Currently demanded by Balz, *SRB Conference 2018 - 10 years after the crisis: are banks now resolvable?*

853 This, however, would make massive issuances of subordinated non-preferred senior debt necessary, with a considerable initial shortfall. Nevertheless, this solution would provide the most clarity.

Furthermore, the exemptions from the subordination requirement in the new Article 72b(3–6) CRR, which is based on Section 11 of the TLAC Principles and Term Sheet, should be reconsidered as well. First, it is difficult to see how including claims that may give rise to material risk of successful legal challenge or valid compensation claims if bailed-in would not also have "a material adverse impact on the resolvability of the institution", new Article 72b(3)(c) CRR.[854] Second, exceptions of any kind will trigger the pricing and risk-guessing problem addressed multiple times above, under Part 4, A.III. – *Identification of Possible Impediments to the Potential of Loss-Absorbing Capital Requirements.* Therefore, if the investor problem is to be taken seriously, it would be best to opt for the "hard" subordination scenario,[855] in terms of both subordination requirements and exemptions, even if this would imply a considerable initial shortfall.

Solving the Investor Problem – Adequacy of Holders of Loss-Absorbing Debt

Another rather prominent issue revolves around the adequacy and suitability of holders of MREL/TLAC eligible instruments. As extensively described above under Part 4, A.III.6. – *Potential Investors and Holders of MREL Eligible Instruments*, and given the fact that the current BRRD provides for no differentiation in the treatment[856] of liabilities based on the nature of the holder, not all investors can be considered appropriate when investing in core bail-inable debt, and the requirements for being allowed to invest must be high in order to set-up a strong and reliable base for loss-absorption. Taking all of this into account, a balance must be found with regard to restricting the group of potential investors.

854 Stiefmüller, *Ten Years After - The 2017 Banking Package: One Step Forward, Two Steps Back*, p. 13.

855 See *supra* under Part 4, A.III.5. – *Debt Subordination – New Art. 108 BRRD* and García and Rocamora, *How prepared are European banks to comply with MREL?*, p. 5.

856 Even if a special treatment (namely exemption from bail-in) of existing and future retail holders in resolution could be achieved under the current rules by declaring them an impediment to resolvability according to the BRRD, such an approach cannot be supported in light of moral hazard considerations.

To tackle the current[857] problem of potentially unlimited participation of all possible kinds of investors, and to prevent the distortion of LACRs through inadequate holdings, different measures could possibly be applied. These range from small-impact measures such as mandatory information and education of possible investors, to moderate measures such as monitoring and supervision of holders, to deep-impact measures such as the legal exclusion of certain investors.

Disclosure Requirements and Provision of Mandatory Information to Potential Investors

In order to prevent scenarios such as those witnessed in Italy,[858] this dissertation proposes making mandatory information and disclosure of risk available to all current and potential investors of debt.[859] Such attempts, which would be in accordance with the investor protection provisions of the MiFID II,[860] could include institution-provided information over the unsecuredness of their instruments, making it clear to such investors that their claims are subject to resolution or insolvency and that the outstanding amount may be reduced to zero in the event of resolution. This could be realized through the mandatory signing of information forms by each

857 The EBA and the ESMA conducted data analysis in which it was discovered that retail investors, especially in some EU countries, hold important parts of EU debt securities issued by institutions. See the EBA and ESMA, *Statement of the EBA and ESMA on the treatment of retail holdings of debt financial instruments subject to the Bank Recovery and Resolution Directive*, recital 4.

858 For a detailed description of the alleged mis-selling in the Italian MPS case, the resulting complications, and the final refrainment from bailing-in the affected investors, see *supra* under Part 2, A.II.2.a.ii. – *Application of Precautionary Recapitalization in Italy – Unveiling the Problems.*

859 EBA and ESMA, *Statement of the EBA and ESMA on the treatment of retail holdings of debt financial instruments subject to the Bank Recovery and Resolution Directive*, pp. 9 *et seq.*

860 The MiFID II, that entered into force on 3 January 2018, establishes requirements on product governance, sale of complex debt instruments, and assessment of suitability that can be relevant to the cases related to retail investors purchasing instruments eligible for bail-in. See *Directive 2014/65/EU of the European Parliament and of the Council of 15 May 2014 on markets in financial instruments and amending Directive 2002/92/EC and Directive 2011/61/EU Text with EEA relevance OJ L 173, 12.6.2014, p. 349–496* ; EBA and ESMA, *Statement of the EBA and ESMA on the treatment of retail holdings of debt financial instruments subject to the Bank Recovery and Resolution Directive*, pp. 2, 11 *et seq.*

potential investor prior to investing. Information forms would outline the risk(s) associated with the investment and how such risk(s) can be calculated. The client would have to specifically consent to the provision of information in that specific form and must be notified accordingly, either electronically or via mail, with information being continuously accessible to them.[861]

First attempts in this regard have already been taken at the national level, for example in Germany, where the BaFin introduced a three-step voluntary[862] approach to informing clients about BRRD implications. Similar attempts have been seen in Portugal, where the Portuguese Securities Market Commission (CMVM) intends to introduce measures to inform investors about bail-in risks.[863] Moreover, Italy, known for having the most retail-held debt security investments in Europe, has also taken action. The Consob has put in place various supervisory and enforcement measures, published several guidelines and clarifications, and even introduced pecuniary sanctions on banks where necessary with regard to the self-placement of debt instruments.[864]

Such an approach would probably eliminate information deficiencies among unsophisticated investors, thereby scaring unfit holders away outright by making them aware of probable losses. However, this method has several problems and is short-sighted. First, it would not address the problem of negligent or intentional mis-selling to investors with no or less loss-absorption capacity. Moreover, it would not prevent selling to potentially capable but undesirable holders, by banks for instance, that can lead to the accumulation of massive amounts of debt holdings in other institutions, producing contagion and systemic effects. Lastly, it does not provide a solution to the massive amounts of already-issued debt to retail investors and other unfit holders. With regard to harnessing the MiFID into the investor selection process for MREL debt, strong indicators suggest that even if the legislative framework is strong and represents an important positive factor in the ability of resolution authorities to bail-in retail debt liabilities,[865] weak enforcement of the rules will continuously

861 EBA and ESMA, *Statement of the EBA and ESMA on the treatment of retail holdings of debt financial instruments subject to the Bank Recovery and Resolution Directive*, p. 11.

862 With the exception of cooperative banks, it has been followed by the majority of German institutions, see ibid., p. 21.

863 Ibid., p. 22.

864 See for an extensive description of measures taken in Italy ibid., pp. 22 *et seq.*

865 Ibid., p. 16.

be a cause of mis-selling.[866] Therefore, the present suggestion can only be seen as a starting point for further problem-solving.

Find Resilient and Adequate Holders for Loss-Absorbing Instruments – Buy-Side Monitoring

Another suggestion that points in a similar direction is the establishment of comprehensive buy-side monitoring.[867] Going one step further than providing only mandatory information and leaving the decision up to the interested investor, buy-side monitoring would establish a list of criteria that must be fulfilled in order to be able to invest in MREL/TLAC instruments. Proposals of this ilk suggest that potential investors must comply with a certain standard and must meet criteria such as storm resilience, sufficiently high levels of reserves (for example, from coupon payments on debt instruments), and being the ultimate risk bearer (*e.g.* there must be no risk transfer).[868] Such criteria must be communicated via national central banks or supervisory authorities and optimally monitored.

In the case of Italy,[869] the legislator proposed a solution that generates a similar effect, even though no direct monitoring is carried out: non-preferred senior unsecured debt – the instrument primarily used to comply with loss-absorbing requirements within MREL – is issued only with a minimum denomination of 250 000 euros in order to stress that institutional investors are targeted holders of such instruments. Introducing a threshold would effectively prevent retail investors from engaging in MREL debt without employing time-consuming information or monitoring structures. The introduction of minimum MREL issuance denominations in all Member States, maybe even with a smaller denomination of 50 000 or 100 000

866 For the reasons behind mis-selling and why the MiFID will most likely not work as a remedy against it, see Conac, *Subordinated debt and self-placement*, pp. 27 *et seq.*

867 Tröger, 'Optimal Bail-In Tools - Observations From A European Perspective', pp. 14 *et seq.*

868 Ibid., p. 15.

869 Spain introduced similar legislation in 2013 to avoid the mis-selling of subordinated debt to non-qualified retail clients by introducing mandatory institutional investor participation and a minimum threshold of 25 000, respectively 100 000 euros.

euros[870] according to their ranking in the insolvency creditor hierarchy and their complexity, could make a substantial contribution to problem-solving in this respect. However, this approach does not prevent the investment by sophisticated but run-prone investors, such as banks. Therefore, the implementation of an investment threshold together with buy-side monitoring would be the optimal solution.

Setting-up Specific Bail-in Bonds

Another initiative pursuing the same objective would entail setting up specific bail-in bonds, as will be established over the next months and years in any case, but to market and sell them only to suitable investors[871] within a specific framework, such as a special trading platform or through a designated sales agent (essentially through self-placement[872]). Access to bail-in bonds marketing platforms or trading venues is only granted if the potential buyer demonstrates their ability to hold bail-in instruments adequately and to absorb losses without further risk. A similar attempt made in Spain, where legislation[873] requires that, in cases of self-placement of subordinated liabilities or other junior debts, 50 % of the issue should be sold to at least 50 different institutional investors.

What to do with Legacy Holdings – Resolution Planning?

Even if the future investment of inadequate holders in bail-inable debt can be forestalled by the suggestions made in the last paragraphs, the question

870 EBA and ESMA, *Statement of the EBA and ESMA on the treatment of retail holdings of debt financial instruments subject to the Bank Recovery and Resolution Directive*, p. 20.

871 A similar approach was already proposed in 2014 in A. Baglioni and M. Esposito, *Modigliani-Miller Doesn't Hold in a "Bailinable" World: A New Capital Structure to Reduce the Banks' Funding Cost*, Dipartimento di Economia e Finanza, Working Paper n. 52 (2016), p. 13 retrievable at SSRN https://ssrn.com/abstract=2875880 accessed 1 October 2022.

872 Conac, *Subordinated debt and self-placement*, pp. 11 *et seq.*

873 Ley del Mercado de Valores, Article 214 Evaluación de la conveniencia. Disposición adicional cuarta. Comercialización a minoristas de participaciones preferentes, instrumentos de deuda convertibles y financiaciones subordinadas computables como recursos propios.

of what to do with the notable amount of current[874] retail and other problematic holdings remains and this concerns banks and governments across all Member States.[875] This is a crucial issue to solve: if investors, and especially retail investors, retain their holdings and a crisis occurs, it is highly likely that Member States will try to protect their retail investors from the full consequences of a bail-in by using various tricky strategies, as was seen in the Italian case, which will pose obstacles to regular BRRD resolution proceedings. Furthermore, since those holdings are mostly long-term holdings, this problem will not solve itself in the near future. Arguably, some retail investors have already taken action with respect to mis-selling and have challenged their holdings in court or through arbitration.[876] Nevertheless, the majority of retail investors subject to potential mis-selling still hold their investments, and bailing them in may affect overall confidence in the financial markets and may adversely impact the economic situation of the retail client and their household. To avoid bank runs, Member States are tempted to intervene, thus making the new resolution legislation obsolete. Moreover, when debt is placed with its own clients, institutions would damage their own customer base by bailing them in, making it even harder for them to restore their viability after resolution.[877] Therefore, as long as retail debt holdings are present in the market, a solution must be found for occasions where a bank gets into financial trouble.

A clear solution would be that resolution authorities consider the amount of retail debt liabilities in their resolution planning and that – where no other solution is apparent and under specific and exceptional circumstances – such liabilities can be exempted from bail-in, Articles 27(5) or 44(3) BRRD.[878] This approach may redress the problem of negative soci-

---

874 Conac, *Subordinated debt and self-placement*, p. 16; A. Resti, *Should the marketing of subordinated debt be restricted in one way or the other? What to do in the case of mis-selling?*, In-Depth Analysis for the Economics and Monetary Affairs Committee of the European Parliament (Brussels, 2016) retrievable at http://www.europarl.europa.eu/RegData/etudes/IDAN/2016/497754/IPOL_IDA(2016)497754_EN.pdf accessed 1 October 2022.

875 For samples of mis-selling to retail investors *e.g.* in Spain, Slovenia, Portugal and Italy see Conac, *Subordinated debt and self-placement*, pp. 18–27.

876 Ibid., pp. 33 *et seq.*

877 EBA and ESMA, *Statement of the EBA and ESMA on the treatment of retail holdings of debt financial instruments subject to the Bank Recovery and Resolution Directive*, p. 16, recital 47.

878 However, such exemptions must be duly justified and have to be regarded as very exceptional. Nevertheless, the Commission Delegated Regulation 2016/860

al effects on retail holders and households, however it might not eliminate the problem of potential runs on the institution by retail investors, who are not aware of the content of the resolution plan. Furthermore, because the exemption of subordinated liabilities from bail-in is highly exceptional, retail investors in Europe cannot fully count on the exemption of their holdings from bail-in for their respective institution. Indeed, additional problems with this approach arise, since it is unclear whether the resolution authority is capable of obtaining comprehensive information about retail debt holders from the institutions. Such information should be hard to obtain, especially where retail holdings did not occur in the context of self-placement,.[879] Lastly, the exclusion of technically eligible debt from the scope of bail-in, and therefore from the scope of MREL requirements, would require the fulfillment of the MREL quote with additional issuance of MREL-eligible liabilities or other already-available liabilities, as authorities otherwise face the risk that the available MREL and other liabilities would not be sufficient for the implementation of the envisaged resolution strategy.[880] This could give rise to NCWO claims.

Another approach to addressing the situation of retail debt holdings in resolution can be seen in the incentivizing and influencing of institutional behavior towards retail-held debt instruments. Since they run the danger of providing 'additional' MREL liabilities due to the exclusion of retail-held debt in the resolution plan, institutions might be encouraged to proactively reduce their retail-held liabilities through voluntary programs

---

sets out that a potential exemption can be justified considering 'the number of natural persons directly and indirectly affected by the bail-in, visibility and press coverage of the resolution action, insofar as that has a significant risk of undermining overall confidence in the banking or broader financial system', see Art. 8(2)(b) of *Commission Delegated Regulation (EU) 2016/860 of 4 February 2016 specifying further the circumstances where exclusion from the application of write-down or conversion powers is necessary under Article 44(3) of Directive 2014/59/EU of the European Parliament and of the Council establishing a framework for the recovery and resolution of credit institutions and investment firms, OJ L 144, 1.6.2016, p. 11-20.*

879 For a detailed analysis of institutions' problems with regard to information procurement and the subsequent sharing of data with the resolution authorities, see *supra* under Part 3, A.II.1.h. – *Opaque Data Production and Collection Process – Templates.*

880 EBA and ESMA, *Statement of the EBA and ESMA on the treatment of retail holdings of debt financial instruments subject to the Bank Recovery and Resolution Directive*, p. 16, recital 50.

of conversion into saving deposits, thereby slowly shifting their structure into liabilities that are suitable for funding and MREL purposes.[881]

As a last step, information should be provided to all European retail debt holders. This would enable them to prove that they are entitled to compensation under the MiFID due to violations of information requirements or similar. The compensation would be paid by the responsible financial institution and the respective holding would be redeemed. If, however, the institution is already subject to resolution procedures before investors have had the chance to take action and their instrument is bailed-in, it may be worth considering the resolution fund or the deposit guarantee scheme stepping in or even the creation of a special national or European compensation fund.[882]

Whichever solution is pursued in order to deal with existing retail holdings, resolution procedures will be influenced by retail holdings until the amount of retail investments becomes so small that interference with the resolution process is no longer politically or economically appealing.

Flexibility Needs of Different Business Models

Another problem that needs to be solved is the issue of diverging business models under the remit of integrated MREL application in the EU. As stated above under Part 4, A.III.7. – *Problem of Certain Banks in Complying with Loss-Absorbing Requirements*, the business models and structures of banks across the European Union differ significantly and, as a result, some banks might have a hard time fulfilling the necessary MREL quotes imposed on them. Even though the affected institutions are the smaller ones, subject only to a discretionary Pillar 2 MREL, it has been demonstrated that even small requirements can pose a problem. In particular, institutions that have little or no market access and are mostly active in deposits and lending, serving mainly retail customers, might find themselves in trouble when confronted with MREL requirements.[883] The industry therefore demands flexibility and proportionality, not only with respect to the

881 Ibid., p. 19, recital 61.

882 Conac, *Subordinated debt and self-placement*, p. 50.

883 Especially when retail holdings are excluded from the scope of MREL-eligible instruments in the course of resolution planning, as envisaged by some resolution authorities, see *supra* Part 5, B.I.5.d. – *What to do with Legacy Holdings – Resolution Planning?* Institutions must then top-up their MREL requirements with non-retail-held instruments, making it even more difficult for them.

well-known issues of supervisory reporting, disclosure requirements, and RRP. Moreover, even though such claims might be justified, they always need to be confronted with the consequences of flexibility and proportionality, namely uncertainty and the exercising of discretion. Therefore, a compromise would be to define clear-cut exceptions that apply uniformly in all participating Member States and that can reliably be considered at the time of investment in respective MREL instruments. Such 'simplified' or proportionate MREL requirements, however they are designed, can be attached to the criteria of risk or materiality, or simply the size of the institution.[884]

Such proportionality endeavors can, for example, be pursued in the context of initiatives such as the German approach of setting up a "Small Banking Box."[885] So far, the latter has only been aimed at easing the operational burden for smaller institutions. However, including proportionality with respect to LACRs might be a possible next step, with the second step being the introduction of such an approach on a European level. With further elaboration of this concept, either in its detail-oriented approach or the envisaged two-fold approach,[886] a reliable framework for proportionality for small banks can be realized that is both predictable and calculable. Nevertheless, the question regarding the scope of application of a "Small Banking Box" remains. The German Federal Bank proposed to include institutions that fulfil the combination of a small balance sheet total and further qualitative criteria such as resolution under national insolvency proceedings, no significant capital markets or cross-border activities, small trading book, and no internal models.[887] Even though this provides a rather clear approach, a 'perfect catalogue' that considers all eventualities[888]

884 C. Hadjiemmanuil, *Reflections on the Concept of Proportionality & Its Implications for Banking Regulation*, Conference on 'Fostering a Diversified Banking Market through Proportionality: An Academic Review' (Brussels, 2018).

885 C. Schiele, J. Ankert and J. Kleinow, *Small Banking Box - mehr Proportionalität in der Bankenaufsicht für mittelständische Institute: Aktuelle Diskussion über Erleichterungen in der Regulierung mittelständischer Institute* (2017), retrievable at https://bankinghub.de/banking/steuerung/small-banking-box-proportionalitaet-banken aufsicht-fuer-mittelstaendische-institute accessed 1 October 2022.

886 Ibid.

887 A. Dombret, *Auf dem Weg zu mehr Verhältnismäßigkeit in der Regulierung? Vorschlag für eine Small Banking Box*, Vortrag bei der Strategietagung des Rheinischen Sparkassen- und Giroverbands (RSGV) (Bonn, 2017).

888 For example, institutions that themselves are considered admissible for the "Small Banking Box" but present a systemic risk by being connected and are therefore "too many to fail."

will most likely never exist. Therefore, even if MREL requirement easements were to be included in a concept such as the "Small Banking Box," insecurities would remain.

O/DSIBs – Scope and Level of Application

As set out above under Part 4, A.III.8. – *Scope and Level of Application*, sometimes GSIBs and non-GSIBs are very similar in terms of size, risk, or business model. As a matter of fact, they can even be 'bigger' than some GSIBs with respect to certain activities. This observation leads to a general criticism of the sharp distinction between GSIBs and the big and otherwise systemically important non-GSIBs. An obvious solution in this respect would be the application of the minimum Pillar 1 requirement to O/DSIBs or to adapt the Pillar 2 requirement for such institutions to the level prescribed in the minimum Pillar 1 for GSIBs where institutions are similarly situated (*e.g.* where the resolution authority prescribes institution-specific add-ons according to Article 45d of the BRRD's TLAC implementation proposal). They could further require the O/DSIBs to fulfil all, or parts, of the quota with instruments eligible for GSIB MREL.[889] As helpful as this approach may be, it still poses another familiar issue: without clear-cut rules regarding the application and scope of institutions concerned, discretion is the only criterion. Discretion always produces insecurity and problems for investors when it comes to pricing respective capital instruments. Under the here-proposed approach, an investor in O/DSIB debt will never be able to predict if the resolution authority will change its mind and impose stricter Pillar 1 minimum or, vice versa, less strict Pillar 2 requirements on the institution in the future. Non-subordinated debt instruments held by a certain investor might suddenly be subject to MREL, even though the investor acquired the instrument at a time when the institution was only subject to Pillar 1 minimum requirements with a strict subordination requirement. Consequently, parallel to the "Small Banking Box" approach, reliable criteria must be defined if and when stricter Pillar 1 minimum requirements are imposed on non-GSIBs. This could be done, for example, by expanding the Pillar 1 minimum requirements

889 Tröger, 'Why MREL won't help much', p. 11.

to the OSIBs that are listed annually by the EBA.[890] However, this list also changes annually and OSIBs can be added or drop out. If such criteria cannot be defined robustly, it might be better to adhere to the sharp – and sometimes random – distinction between GSIBs and non-GSIBs.

MREL Guidance

Aiming to facilitate the pricing process of potential investors in MREL instruments, this proposal with respect to concerns raised in the context of MREL guidance points in the same direction. If a resolution authority deems additional MREL instruments necessary, it might be best to impose them on the institution in the course of the regular process of setting the MREL as additional Pillar 2 either for GSIBs or non-GSIBs, rather than within a second concept that is essentially the same but much more discretional. The alleged advantage, namely that no direct consequences follow from a breach of MREL guidance requirements, is only valid to a certain extent. The new Article 45c of the TLAC Implementation proposal specifies that, where "an entity consistently fails to have additional own funds and eligible liabilities as expected under the guidance", the "resolution authority may require that the amount of the requirement referred to in Article 45c(2) be increased to cover the amount of the guidance [...]." Regardless of what "consistently" means in this respect, be it two or even 20 times, authorities can top-up the regular MREL with the amounts required under the guidance. Where institutions consistently fail to produce additional guidance requirements, it might be best to threaten them with consequences attributed to a regular MREL breach. Such institutions can, and need to, be required to fulfil additional MREL guidance within the regular MREL requirements from the outset in order to avoid voluntary postponement and reluctance to fulfil the guidance. Institutions that comply with the guidance right from its imposition would not benefit from the relaxed punishments for breaches, as they comply both under the regular MREL as well as under the guidance. For the sake of the clarity and calculability of potential investors in MREL debt, the concept of guidance should be reconsidered and eventually revised or even repealed. This would eliminate at least two additional stages of predicting authorities'

890 EBA, *List of OSIIs notified to the EBA* (2017), retrievable at https://www.eba.europa.eu/risk-analysis-and-data/other-systemically-important-institutions-o-siis-/2017 accessed 1 October 2022.

discretional decisions and would enhance investors' comprehension of MREL quotes of respective banks.

Solutions to Calculation Problems

In terms of feasible solutions to the calculation problem outlined above under Part 4, A.III.10. – *Calculation Process*, the first line of reasoning pertains to making the calculation process for MREL requirements understandable and less discretional, to enable investors to gauge the requirements imposed on the institution in which they want to invest, especially during future rounds of MREL determination and the changed situation in envisaged resolution procedures. The second solution argues in favor of a more precise calculation process in order to avoid miscalculations, leading to inadequate MREL quotes that potentially impede envisaged resolution procedures.

Making the Calculation Process More Predictable

In order to make the MREL calculation process more predictable, the discretion of authorities in setting the recapitalization amount for MREL must be reviewed critically, both with regard to setting the general direction of the RCA according to the envisaged resolution strategy in the resolution plan as well as their discretion to make specific adjustments to the MREL due to institutional particularities. Again, banks' need of a proportionate treatment before and during a resolution[891] clash with the needs of investors and markets to gauge default probability and pricing for MREL instruments. In order to achieve the latter, investors must understand *ex ante* the likelihood and extent of their loss-bearing.[892] Admittedly, this problem derives largely from post-resolution discretional decisions, however it can also become apparent during the pre-resolution calculation of MREL. Therefore, it is important to limit the use of discretionary elements of the MREL calculation process as far as possible, especially where investors have already invested in MREL debt and are confronted with the annually-revised MREL calculation. The same applies to the various

891 Zhou, Rutledge, Bossu, Dobler and Jassaud, *From bail-out to bail-in*, 2012/3, pp. 10 *et seq.*

892 Tröger, 'Too complex to work', p. 11.

adjustment mechanisms that resolution authorities can apply to the final MREL quote (see above under Part 4, A.III.10.d. – *Unclear Adjustment Mechanisms – Third Step of Uncertainty*). It is not particularly worthwhile to only ban possibilities to adjust the MREL requirements according to institutional particularities. Instead, a way must be found to ensure the consistency of MREL requirements over the medium term and to prevent substantial differences in the annual MREL settings.

Making the Calculation Process More Accurate

In order to make the calculation process more accurate, an overhaul of the design of the underlying denominators (RWE and LRE) might be needed. Instead of complicating their approach further by constantly issuing new guidance or versions of the denomination bases, a radical approach should be taken to streamline the denominators, as they tend to become excessively sophisticated and convoluted. In addition, problems arising from the use of different models for different sizes of institutions under the IFRS9 should be addressed as, under the current approach, systemically relevant, larger, more market-oriented and publicly-owned banks are subject to relatively low average requirements compared to smaller banks that, due to their different internal models, can lead to different RWA calculations despite having the same portfolio of assets.[893]

Furthermore, the demanded enhancement of data management (see above under Part 5, A.II.2. – *Enhancing Data Management*) within RRP would play a crucial role in making the calculation process for setting the MREL requirements more accurate. Through this measure, the underlying database that resolution authorities need in order to set and specify the required level for MREL would be more precise and would mirror the capital needs of the institution in a potential resolution more accurately. As long as the foundation on which the resolution authorities ground their decision cannot be considered reliable, such errors will seep into MREL planning and eventually into the MREL requirements. As institutions are right at the beginning of the information supply chain, information that seeps through will always tend to be in favor of the institutions. Therefore, Pillar 2 MREL requirements might perpetuate this tendency. Hence, a

893 For an analysis of how MREL requirements and allocation differs with the application of different denominators, see Groen, *"Total Assets" versus "Risk Weighted Assets": does it matter for MREL requirements?*

review of the underlying process, but especially of the much-criticized Liability Data Report templates, would also enhance the calculation process for MREL requirements.

International Transposition of TLAC

As for the point raised about nationally diverging transposition of the globally-agreed TLAC standard and the resulting potential difficulties arising from different transposition across jurisdictions,the FSB must be called upon. In this respect, the FSB is well on track having called for public feedback[894] globally and trying to engage and orchestrate a consistent approach within a global forum that has no common jurisdiction. A yearly review of the implementation of the global standard into national law would also contribute to a consistent transposition of the TLAC standards.

Shortfall and Transposition

Lastly, in order to tackle the inevitable problems arising during and shortly after transposition of the integrated approach on MREL described above under Part 4, A.III.12. – *Current Shortfall and Transposition*, adequate grandfathering rules are necessary to deal with the expectable shortfall of eligible MREL instruments. In the absence of favorable transitional agreements regarding existing debt, the MREL shortfall would in any case be significantly increased, in addition to the shortfall expected because of the new eligibility criteria (especially in peripheral countries). Therefore, the ultimate design of the grandfathering rules will have a strong impact on the market of subordinated debt instruments.

In order to not swamp the market with enormous amounts of non-preferred unsecured senior debt, grandfathering rules should be rather extensive when it comes to already-issued debt instruments, and such debt instruments should be admitted to fulfil the MREL requirements until their expiry. Unambiguous grandfathering rules prior to complete transposition of the proposal are necessary to preclude uncertainty about the ultimate eligibility criteria of existing senior unsecured bonds that are not subject to retroactive subordination clauses. Uncertainty over the eligibility of

894 Financial Stability Board, *Monitoring the Technical Implementation of the FSB Total Loss-absorbing Capacity (TLAC) Standard – Call for public feedback*.

existing senior unsecured debt could hamper the market when it comes to issuance over subsequent years as well as banks' ability to meet the minimum requirements, starting from January 2019.[895] In light of a confined transitional period, and in order to speed up banks' compliance with the envisaged MREL levels, liberal grandfathering rules must be found.

Result to Part 5

The section above presented possible solutions to the identified impediments to RRP on the one hand and those to LACRs on the other, and tried to give advice and put forward approaches on how to tackle the examined shortcomings of both instruments. Despite various smaller-scale suggestions, two underlying notions can be extracted that contain most of the proposed approaches either directly or indirectly. Firstly, resolution procedures – which include the recovery and resolution framework to the same extent as the loss-absorption capital framework – need to be reduced in terms of their degree of complexity. Secondly, bearing in mind the necessary balance between discretion and predictability, discretion in resolution must be reduced to the greatest extent possible. Both notions here provide feasibility of resolution procedures, and of course feasibility creates credibility. Endeavors in this direction that can be pursued by legislators and policy makers in the ongoing legislative process might help to enhance the remedial effect of the instruments that were introduced to revive the trust of markets, their participants, and of society in a credible resolution framework. A credible and unquestionable resolution framework will finally tackle the last legacies of long-standing bailout practice and the financial crisis of 2007.

895 As for example in the US, where the final TLAC rule incorporated a grandfathering clause for debt issued before its finalization in December 2016, see Association for Financial Markets in Europe, *Resolution aspects of the EU Risk Reduction Measures Package*, p. 2.

PART 6 – SUMMARY OF THESES

The results of the above discourse can be summarized in the following theses.

1. To tackle the negative aftermath of the financial crisis, both with respect to lingering mindsets and old habits of financial actors as well as with respect to trust issues of tormented taxpayers, a credible resolution regime with credible private loss-participation is needed. The credibility of the already-implemented rules is of the utmost importance, as the success of the entire European bank resolution framework hinges on the credible application of the rules in future bank failure cases (Part 2, A.I.).
2. The current resolution framework lacks credibility in two respects. *Ex ante* a specific resolution decision, it lacks predictability, the structure of the banking industry is too complex and no measures are available to modify existing complex structures. *Ex post* a specific resolution decision, sufficient and adequate private funding for resolution is lacking, which – together with the absence of a credible backstop financing mechanisms from within the industry itself – leads to frequent deviation from the envisaged burden-sharing cascade and exploitation of easy-to-use public-funding loopholes. Those two aspects render the application of resolution procedures according to the BRRD in general, and the bail-in tool in particular, uncredible. That the lack of credibility in the resolution framework already pervades financial markets, as was demonstrated by the recent use and provision of ELA (Part 2, A.II.).
3. Through analysis, it was found that two instruments proposed at the European level hold the potential to remedy the detected lacks. While RRP entails features that remedy the current *ex ante* lacks, LACRs entail provisions that are able to tackle the current *ex post* lack. As both instruments were examined more closely, it became apparent that both instruments suffer from inherent shortcomings, which have an impeding effect on their remedial power (Part 2, A.III.).
4. Prominent shortcomings of RRP arise out of deficient cross-border planning structures, poor data management in numerous respects, an absence of coping mechanisms for the complexity of institutions, and the unpredictability of planning for the future. Together with more fundamental issues, which were already detected as current *ex ante*

resolution credibility lacks and which RRP has failed to tackle, such as institutions' outdated IT infrastructures, human imperfection, and biases, RRP has been found to fall short of its promised potential (Part 3).

5. The most significant shortcomings of LACRs include a lack of transparency with regard to the MREL debt investment, ample discretion of authorities in numerous aspects (resulting in pricing problems), and a suboptimal debt-holder structure. LACRs are characterized by ambiguities and uncertainty, as definitive consensus on its final design is not yet agreed upon. Just like RRP, the LACRs in their current state are bereft of opportunities (Part 4).
6. Through scrutiny of the inherent shortcomings of RRP and LACRs, it was found that the identified impediments can be tackled. Possible solutions include more holistic approaches as well as several more specific proposals. An overarching desideratum to make both instruments less discretionary, more precise, and more transparent was at the forefront of such proposals. It was found that the identified solutions would enhance the remedial potential of RRP and LACRs in a way that would facilitate the reinstatement of credibility in the current resolution framework (Part 5, A. and B.).
7. Despite various proposals being made to better the instruments, not all shortcomings of RRP and LACRs can be solved. Some issues remain open, as these solutions are either not yet feasible or not realistic. It seems that such open issues coincide to a significant extent with the *ex ante* and *ex post* lacks of credibility of resolution identified at the outset. Examples for this are the rejection of beneficial structural reform proposals or the inability to totally eliminate the necessary discretion, political influence, and human imperfection. It remains to be seen whether unsolved issues will outweigh the benefits gleaned from enhanced RRP and LACRs.
8. Against this backdrop, it must be noted that both instruments have failed to tackle the current lacks of credibility in each identified aspect. Early indications, however, suggest that at least a positive impact of the instruments can be ascertained, for example the intrinsic efforts of institutions to reorganize themselves in light of the new regulatory regime, raised awareness about the respective institution's characteristics, and the recognized rise in resorbable debt instruments. Therefore, in an overall assessment and after the implementation of the suggested solutions, RRP and LACRs are no panacea against distorted credibility but can still certainly be involved in enhancing the credibility of resolution,

resolution financing, and especially the credible application of bail-in in the future.

9. Despite its potential contribution to enhancing credibility, RRP and LACRs will only achieve their full potential with the help of additional measures outside their own scope. Indeed, general measures, such as de-politicizing and removing the precautionary recapitalization loophole from the BRRD, would be necessary. Moreover, the public-interest test should be harmonized (or even reconsidered) and eventually removed, thereby mandatorily placing all institutions that are failing or likely to fail, with no reasonable alternatives for preventing failure, under resolution procedures.[896] Moreover, the problem of lingering amounts of NPLs in peripheral eurozone Member States must be tackled.[897] Lastly, an overhaul of the various insolvency regimes in the Member States by aligning, and eventually integrating burden-sharing in the spirit of the BRRD into, the various national insolvency legislations, or an amendment to the 2013 Banking Communication,[898] would drive integration of RRP and LACRs further.

896 Schillig, 'The (Il-)Legitimacy of the EU Post-Crisis Bailout System', p. 76, retrievable at SSRN https://ssrn.com/abstract=3202118, accessed 1 October 2022.

897 Avgouleas and Goodhart are proposing to introduce a euro asset management company to buy NPLs, see Avgouleas and Goodhart, 'An Anatomy of Bank Bail-ins: Why the Eurozone Needs a Fiscal Backstop for the Banking Sector', pp. 84 *et seq.*

898 Balz, *SRB Conference 2018 - 10 years after the crisis: are banks now resolvable?*.

References

ABLV Bank, *Voluntary Liquidation of ABLV Bank, AS to Protect the Interests of Clients and Creditors*. https://www.ablv.com/en/legal-latest-news/voluntary-liquidation-of-ablv-bank-as-to-protect-the-interests-of-clients-and-creditors.

Acharya, V. V. and Yorulmazer, T., 'Too many to fail – An analysis of time-inconsistency in bank closure policies', *Journal of Financial Intermediation* 16 (2017), 1–31.

Amorello, L. and Huber, S., 'Recovery Planning: A New Valuable Corporate Governance Framework for Credit Institutions', *Law and Economics Yearly Review* 3 (2014), 296–317.

Angeloni, I., *SRB Conference 2018 – 10 years after the crisis: are banks now resolvable?*, SRB Annual Conference (Brussels, 2018).

Armour, J., 'Making Bank Resolution Credible' in N. Moloney, E. Ferran and J. Payne (eds), *Oxford Handbook of Financial Regulation* (Oxford: Oxford University Press, 2015), pp. 453–86.

Arner, D., Barberis, J. N. and Buckley, R., 'FinTech, RegTech and the Reconceptualization of Financial Regulation', *Northwestern Journal of International Law & Business* 37 (2017), 371–413.

Association for Financial Markets in Europe, *Resolution aspects of the EU Risk Reduction Measures Package: Recommendation for effective implementation of TLAC, MREL and related reforms* (2017).

Avgouleas, E. and Goodhart, C., *A Critical Evaluation of Bail-ins as Bank Recapitalisation Mechanisms*, Centre for Economic Policy Research Discussion Paper (2014).

Avgouleas, E. and Goodhart, C., 'Critical Reflections on Bank Bail-ins', *Journal of Financial Regulation* 1 (2015), 3–29.

Avgouleas, E. and Goodhart, C., 'An Anatomy of Bank Bail-ins: Why the Eurozone Needs a Fiscal Backstop for the Banking Sector' in G. B. Navetti, G. Calzolari and A. F. Pozzolo (eds), *European Economy: Banks, Regulation, and the Real Sector* (Rome: Europeye, 2016), pp. 75–91.

Avgouleas, E., Goodhart, C. and Schoenmaker, D., 'Bank Resolution Plans as a catalyst for global financial reform', *Journal of Financial Stability* 9 (2013), 210–8.

Ayadi, R. and Ferri, G., *"Total Assets" versus "Risk Weighted Assets": does it matter for MREL requirements?*, In-Depth Analysis for the Economics and Monetary Affairs Committee of the European Parliament (2016).

Ayadi, R. and Groen, W. P. de, 'Banks' Business Models in Europe' in T. Beck and B. Casu (eds), *The Palgrave Handbook of European Banking* (London: Palgrave Macmillan UK, 2016), pp. 81–102.

Ayadi, R., Groen, W. P. de, Sassi, I., Mathlouthi, W., Rey, H. and Aubry, O., *Banking Business Models Monitor 2015 Europe* (Montréal: International Research Centre on Cooperative Finance, 2016).

Ba, H., 'The systemic causes of financial crises in the long nineteenth century', *Business and Politics* 20 (2018), 208–38.

BaFin, *Übersicht über die Haftungskaskade im Rahmen der Bankenabwicklung*. https://www.bafin.de/SharedDocs/Veroeffentlichungen/DE/Merkblatt/BA/mb_haftungskaskade_bankenabwicklung.html.

BaFin, *Rundschreiben 10/2017 (BA) in der Fassung vom 14.09.2018 – Bankaufsichtliche Anforderungen an die IT (BAIT)*, BaFin Rundschreiben (2018).

Bagehot, W., *Lombard Street: A description of the money market*, Wiley investment classics (New York: Wiley, 1999).

Baglioni, A. and Esposito, M., *Modigliani-Miller Doesn't Hold in a "Bailinable" World: A New Capital Structure to Reduce the Banks' Funding Cost*, Dipartimento di Economia e Finanza, Working Paper n. 52 (2016).

Balz, B., *SRB Conference 2018 – 10 years after the crisis: are banks now resolvable?*, SRB Annual Conference (Brussels, 2018).

Banca D'Italia, *Informazioni sulla soluzione della crisi di Veneto Banca S.p.A. e Banca Popolare di Vicenza S.p.A.* (2017).

Banca D'Italia, *La ricapitalizzazione precauzionale di MPS: domande e risposte* (2017).

Bank for International Settlements, *Annual Economic Report 2018* (2018).

Bank of England, *The Bank of England's approach to setting a minimum requirement for own funds and eligible liabilities (MREL) – Statement of Policy* (2018).

Barbagallo, C., *Interventi – Banca Monte dei Paschi di Siena: Senato della Repubblica – Camera dei Deputati, Commissione Parlamentare di inchiesta sul sistema bancario e finanziario* (2017).

Barker, A. and Sanderson, R., 'Brussels and Rome seal rescue deal for Monte dei Paschi: Investor bail-in and deep restructuring agreed for Italy's oldest bank', Financial Times, 01 June 2017.

Basel Committee on Banking Supervision, *Basel III: A global regulatory framework for more resilient banks and banking systems* (2010).

Basel Committee on Banking Supervision, *Global systemically important banks: Updated assessment methodology and the higher loss absorbency requirement: Updated assessment methodology and the higher loss absorbency requirement*, July 2013 (Basel: Bank for International Settlements, 2013).

Basel Committee on Banking Supervision, *Regulatory Consistency Assessment Programm (RCAP) – Analysis of risk-weighted assets for credit risk in the banking book* (2013).

Basel Committee on Banking Supervision, *Basel III leverage ratio framework and disclosure requirement* (2014).

Basel Committee on Banking Supervision, *The G-SIB assessment methodology: Score calculation* (Basel: Bank for International Settlements, 2014).

Basel Committee on Banking Supervision, *Report on risk-weighted assets for counterparty credit risk (CCR)*, Regulatory Consistency Assessment Programme (RECAP) (2015).

Basel Committee on Banking Supervision, *Analysis of risk weighted assets for credit risk in the banking book*, Regulatory Consistency Assessment Programme (RECAP) (2016).

Basel Committee on Banking Supervision, *Basel III: Finalising post-crisis reforms* (2017).

Bauer, E., Mrusek, F., Metka, K. and Schöll, M., *Complexity kills – How European banking models have to change in a complex world*, Results from zeb's European Banking Study 2015 (2015).

Benczur, P., Cannas, G., Cariboni, J., Di Girolamo, F., Maccaferri, S. and Petracco Giudici, M., 'Evaluating the effectiveness of the new EU bank regulatory framework: A farewell to bail-out?', *Journal of Financial Stability* 33 (2017), 207–23.

Berger, B., Hüttl, P. and Merler, S., *"Total Assets" versus "Risk Weighted Assets": does it matter for MREL requirements*, In-Depth Analysis for the Economics and Monetary Affairs Committee of the European Parliament (2016).

Berthonnet, I. and Delclite, T., 'Pareto-Optimality or Pareto-Efficiency: Same Concept, Different Names? An Analysis Over a Century of Economic Literature', *Research in the history of economic thought and methodology* 32.2014 (2014), 129–45.

Binder, J.-H., 'Institutionalisierte Krisenbewältigung bei Kreditinstituten: Ausländische Gestaltungsvorbilder und mögliche Konsequenzen für die Weiterentwicklung des deutschen Aufsichtsrechts', *Zeitschrift für Bankrecht und Bankwirtschaft* (2009), 19–32.

Binder, J.-H., 'To ring-fence or not, and how?: Strategic questions for post-crisis banking reform in Europe', *SSRN Electronic Journal* (2014).

Binder, J.-H., 'Gleichung mit (zu?) vielen Unbekannten: Nachhaltige Bankenstrukturen durch Sanierungs- und Abwicklungsplanung?', *Zeitschrift für Bankrecht und Bankwirtschaft* 27 (2015), 153–65.

Binder, J.-H., 'Cross-border coordination of bank resolution in the EU: All problems resolved?', *European Company and Financial Review* 13 (2016), 575–98.

Binder, J.-H., 'Resolution Planning and Structural Bank Reform within the Banking Union' in J. E. Castañeda, D. G. Mayes and G. E. Wood (eds), *European Banking Union: Prospects and challenges* (Routledge, 2016), pp. 129–56.

Binder, J.-H., 'Resolution: Concepts, Requirements, and Tools' in J.-H. Binder and D. Singh (eds), *Bank Resolution: The European Regime* (Oxford: Oxford University Press, 2016), pp. 25–59.

Binder, J.-H., 'Proportionality at the Resolution Stage: Calibration of Resolution Measures and the Public Interest Test: he Principle of Proportionality and Its Applicability in EU Banking Regulation', *SSRN Electronic Journal* (2017).

Binder, J.-H., 'Systemkrisenbewältigung durch Bankenabwicklung? Aktuelle Bemerkungen zu unrealistischen Erwartungen', *Zeitschrift für Bankrecht und Bankwirtschaft* 29 (2017), 57–71.

Binder J.-H., *Wunderkind is Walking? The Resolution of Banco Popular as a First Test for the Single Resolution Mechanism*. https://www.law.ox.ac.uk/business-law-blog/blog/2017/06/wunderkind-walking-resolution-banco-popular-first-test-single.

Binder, J.-H., 'The Relevance of the Resolution Tools Within the SRM', *European Banking Institute Working Paper Series* (2018).

Binder, J.-H. and Gortsos, C. V. (eds), *The European Banking Union: A compendium* (München, Oxford, Baden-Baden: C.H. Beck; Hart; Nomos, 2016).

Binder, J.-H., Krimminger, M., Nieto, M. J. and Singh, D., 'The Choice between Judicial and Administrative Sanctioned Procedures to Manage Liquidation of Banks: A Transatlantic Perspective', *SSRN Electronic Journal* (2018).

Binder, J.-H. and Singh, D. (eds), *Bank Resolution: The European Regime* (Oxford: Oxford University Press, 2016).

Black, L., Correa, R., Huang, X. and Zhou, H., 'The systemic risk of European banks during the financial and sovereign debt crises', *Journal of Banking & Finance* 63 (2016), 107–25.

Board of Governors of the Federal Reserve System, *Agencies provide feedback on second round resolution plans of "First-Wave" filers* (2014).

Bolton, P. and Oehmke, M., 'Bank Resolution and the Structure of Global Banks', *Columbia Business School Research Paper* (2018).

Bonfatti, S., 'Crisi bancarie in Italia 2015–2017', *Rivista di Diritto Bancario* (2018).

Bookstaber, R., *A Demon of Our Own Design: Markets, Hedge Funds, and the Perils of Financial Innovation* (New York, NY: John Wiley & Sons, 2007).

Brown, C. and Dinc, S., 'Too Many to Fail? Evidence of Regulatory Forebearance when the Banking Sector is Weak', *Review of Financial Studies* 24 (2011), 1378–405.

Brunnermeier, M. K., 'Deciphering the liquidity and credit crunch 2007 – 2008', *The Journal of Economic Perspectives: a Journal of the American Economic Association* 23 (2009), 77–100.

Bruyckere, V. de, Gerhardt, M., Schepens, G. and Vander Vennet, R., 'Bank/sovereign risk spillovers in the European debt crisis', *Journal of Banking & Finance* 37 (2013), 4793–809.

Buckley, R. P., Avgouleas, E. and Arner, D. W., 'Three Major Financial Crises: What Have We Learned' in D. Arner, D. Busch, E. Avgouleas and S. Schwarcz (eds), *Systemic Risk in the Financial Sector: Ten Years After the Great Crash* (Centre for International Governance Innovation, 2019).

Bundesverband der Deutschen Volksbanken und Raiffeisenbanken e.V. and Die Deutsche Kreditwirtschaft, *Stellungnahme zum Vorschlag der Kommission für Änderungen der BRRD/CRR im Zusammenhang mit MREL/TLAC Vorgaben* (2017).

Bundesverband Öffentlicher Banken Deutschlands, VÖB, e.V., *Aktuelle Positionen zur Banken- und Finanzmarktregulierung, 2. Quartal 2018*.

Busch, D., 'Governance of the Single Resolution Mechanism' in D. Busch and G. Ferrarini (eds), *European Banking Union* (Oxford: Oxford Univ Press, 2015), part III, ch. 9.

Busch, D., van Rijn, M. and Louisse, M., 'How Single is the Single Resolution Mechanism?', *European Business Law Review* (2019).

Cai, J., Eidam, F., Saunders, A. and Steffen, S., 'Syndication, interconnectedness, and systemic risk', *Journal of Financial Stability* 34 (2018), 105–20.

Camera dei deputati ed il Senato della Repubblica, *Conversione in legge, con modificazioni, del decreto-legge 25 giugno 2017, n. 99, recante disposizioni urgenti per la liquidazione coatta amministrativa di Banca Popolare di Vicenza S.p.A. e di Veneto Banca S.p.A. (17G00133) (GU Serie Generale n.184 del 08–08–2017).*

Carlson, M. A. and Rose, J. D., 'Can a Bank Run Be Stopped? Government Guarantees and the Run on Continental Illinois', *Finance and Economics Discussion Series* (2016), 1–44.

Carmassi, J., Gros, D. and Micossi, S., 'The Global Financial Crisis: Causes and Cures', *Journal of Common Market Studies* 47 (2009), 977–96.

Carmassi, J. and Herring, R., 'Corporate Structures, Transparency and Resolvability of Global Systemically Important Banks', *Wharton School Working Papers* (2014).

Carmassi, J. and Herring, R., 'The Cross-Border Challenge in Resolving Global Systemically Important Banks' in K. E. Scott, T. H. Jackson and J. B. Taylor (eds), *Making failure feasible: How bankruptcy reform can end "too big to fail"*, Hoover Institution Press publication (Stanford, California: Hoover Institution Press, Stanford University, 2015), pp. 249–75.

Carmassi, J. and Herring, R., 'The Corporate Complexity of Global Systemically Important Banks', *Journal of Financial Services Research* 49 (2016), 175–201.

Carstens, A., *Post-crisis bank resolution: what are the main challenges now?: Concluding remarks by Mr Agustín Carstens, General Manager of the BIS, at the 8th FSI-IADI conference on "Bank resolution, crisis management and deposit insurance", Basel, 2 February 2018*, FSI-IADI conference on "Bank resolution, crisis management and deposit insurance" (2018).

Cavelaars, P., Haan, J. de, Hilbers, P. and Stellinga, B., *Key Challenges for Financial Supervision after the Crisis* (2013).

Cetorelli, N. and Goldberg, L., 'Measures of Global Bank Complexity', *FRBNY Economic Policy Review* (2014), 107–26.

Champsaur, A., 'Stressed tests', *International Financial Law Review* 35 (2016), 43–4.

Chen Chen, H., 'The Recovery Framework in the BRRD and its Effectiveness', *International Company and Commercial Law Review* 10 (2015), 26.

Cichy, P., Buchmüller and Igl, '§ 15 Sanierungs- und Abwicklungsplanung' in J.-H. Binder, A. Glos and J. Riepe (eds), *Handbuch Bankenaufsicht* (Köln: RWS, 2017).

Commission Delegated Regulation (EU) 2016/1075 of 23 March 2016 supplementing Directive 2014/59/EU of the European Parliament and of the Council with regard to regulatory technical standards specifying the content of recovery plans, resolution plans and group resolution plans, the minimum criteria that the competent authority is to assess as regards recovery plans and group recovery plans, the conditions for group financial support, the requirements for independent valuers, the contractual recognition of write-down and conversion powers, the procedures and contents of notification requirements and of notice of suspension and the operational functioning of the resolution colleges OJ L 184, 8.7.2016, p. 1–71 (2016).

Commission Delegated Regulation (EU) 2016/1450 of 23.05.2016 supplementing Directive 2014/59/EU of the European Parliament and of the Council with regard to regulatory technical standards specifying the criteria relating to the methodology for setting the minimum requirements for own funds and eligible liabilities OJ L 237, 3.9.2016, p. 1–9.

Commission Delegated Regulation (EU) 2016/860 of 4 February 2016 specifying further the circumstances where exclusion from the application of write-down or conversion powers is necessary under Article 44(3) of Directive 2014/59/EU of the European Parliament and of the Council establishing a framework for the recovery and resolution of credit institutions and investment firms, OJ L 144, 1.6.2016, p. 11–20.

Commission Implementing Regulation (EU) 2016/1066 of 17 June 2016 laying down implementing technical standards with regard to procedures, standard forms and templates for the provision of information for the purpose of resolution plans for credit institutions and investment firms pursuant to Directive 2014/59/EU of the European Parliament and of the Council OJ L 181, 6.7.2016, p. 1–38.

Commission Implementing Regulation (EU) 2016/962 of 16 June 2016 laying down implementing technical standards with regard to the uniform formats, templates and definitions for the identification and transmission of information by competent authorities and resolution authorities to the European Banking Authority according to Directive 2014/59/EU of the European Parliament and of the Council OJ L 160, 17.6.2016, p. 35–49.

Communication from the Commission on the application, from 1 August 2013, of State aid rules to support measures in favour of banks in the context of the financial crisis ('Banking Communication'), 2013/C 216/01 (2013).

Conac, P.-H., *Subordinated debt and self-placement: Mis-selling of financial products*, Study requested by the ECON Committee (Brussels: European Parliament).

Coppola, F., 'Italy's Latest Bank Bailout Has Created A Two-Speed Eurozone', Forbes, 26 June 2017.

Coppola, F., 'Why The U.S. Treasury Killed A Latvian Bank', Forbes, 28 February 2018.

Council of the EU, *Treaty establishing the European Stability Mechanism between the Kingdom of Belgium, the Federal Republic of Germany, the Republic of Estonia, Ireland, the Hellenic Republic, the Kingdom of Spain, the French Republic, the Italian Republic, the Republic of Cyprus, the Republic of Latvia, the Republic of Lithuania, the Grand Duchy of Luxembourg, Malta, the Kingdom of the Netherlands, the Republic of Austria, the Portuguese Republic, the Republic of Slovenia, the Slovak Republic and the Republic of Finland.*

Council of the EU, *ESM Direct Bank Recapitalisation Instrument – Main Features of the Operational Framework and Way Forward* (2013).

Council of the European Union, *Presidency Progress Report on Work in the AHWP on strengthening the Banking Union 9819/1/18 REV 1* (2018).

Court, J., Parent, A. and Portilla, A., *Letter to the FSB regarding call for public feedback on Monitoring the Technical Implementation of the FSB Total Loss-Absorbing Capacity (TLAC) Standard* (2018).

Credit Suisse AG, *Monitoring the Technical Implementation of the FSB Total Loss-absorbing Capacity Standard Call for public feedback dated June 6, 2018* (2018).

Crotty, J., 'Structural causes of the global financial crisis: a critical assessment of the 'new financial architecture'', *Cambridge Journal of Economics* 33 (2009), 563–80.

Cunliffe, J., 'Ending Too-Big-to-Fail: How Best to Deal with Failed Large Banks' in G. B. Navetti, G. Calzolari and A. F. Pozzolo (eds), *European Economy: Banks, Regulation, and the Real Sector* (Rome: Europeye, 2016), pp. 59–74.

Dam, L. and Koetter, M., 'Bank Bailouts and Moral Hazard: Evidence from Germany', *Review of Financial Studies* 25 (2012), 2343–80.

Deslandes, J. and Magnus, M., *Banking Union: Towards new arrangements to finance banks under resolution?*, Briefing of the European Parliament (2018).

Deutsche Bank, *Deutsche Bank response to the European Banking Authority's consultation paper of the Draft ITS on the provision of information for the purpose of resolution plans under Article 11(3) of Directive 2014/59/EU* (2017).

Deutsche Bundesbank, *Richtlinien zur Kreditdatenstatistik (AnaCredit)*, 3rd edn. (2018).

Deutscher Bundestag, *Antrag zu dem Vorschlag für eine Verordnung des Europäischen Parlaments und des Rates zur Änderung der Verordnung (EU) Nr. 806/2014 im Hinblick auf die Schaffung eines europäischen Einlagenversicherungssystems KOM(2015) 586 endg; Ratsdok. 14649/15 – Drucksache 19/2525* (2018).

Dewatripont, M., 'European banking: Bailout, bail-in and state aid control', *International Journal of Industrial Organization* 34 (2014), 37–43.

Dimova, S., *Resolution Planning: Too Complex to Work or Cornerstone of a Stable Financial Architecture?: The Perspective of Regulators*, SAFE/BaFin Conference (House of Finance, 2018).

Directive (EU) 2017/2399 of the European Parliament and of the Council of 12 December 2017 amending Directive 2014/59/EU as regards the ranking of unsecured debt instruments in insolvency hierarchy, OJ L 345, 27.12.2017, p. 96–101: Insolvency Hierarchy Directive (2017).

Directive 2014/49/EU of the European Parliament and of the Council of 16 April 2014 on deposit guarantee schemes, OJ L 173, 12.6.2014, p. 149–178.

Directive 2014/59/EU of the European Parliament and the Council of 15 May 2014 establishing a framework for the recovery and resolution of credit institutions and investment firms and amending Council Directive 82/891/EEC, and Directive 2011/24/EC, 2004/25/EC, 2005/56/EC, 2007/36/EC, 2011/35/EU, 2012/30/EU and 2013/36/EU, and Regulations (EU) No 1093/2010 and (EU) No 648/2012, of the European Parliament and of the Council OJ L 173, 12.6.2014, p. 190–348.

Directive 2014/65/EU of the European Parliament and of the Council of 15 May 2014 on markets in financial instruments and amending Directive 2002/92/EC and Directive 2011/61/EU Text with EEA relevance OJ L 173, 12.6.2014, p. 349–496.

Dohmen, C., *Finanzwirtschaft: Wie alles zusammenhängt*, Zeitbilder, 1. Aufl. (Bonn: Bundeszentrale für Politische Bildung, 2014).

Dombret, A., *Auf dem Weg zu mehr Verhältnismäßigkeit in der Regulierung? Vorschlag für eine Small Banking Box*, Vortrag bei der Strategietagung des Rheinischen Sparkassen- und Giroverbands (RSGV) (Bonn, 2017).

Donato, L., Rotondi, Z. and Scognamiglio, A., 'From the Rescue of Banks to the Single Resolution Mechanism: Institutional and Empirical Analysis', *SSRN Electronic Journal* (2017).

Draghi, M. to J. Almunia, 30 July 2013, 'Banking Communication – treatment of subordinated debt in precautionary recapitalisation', Letter.

Dübel, H.-J., *The capital structure of banks and practice of bank restructuring: Eight case studies on current bank restructurings in Europe; final report*, CFS working paper series (2013), No. 2013,04.

Dübel, H.-J., *Creditor Participation in Banking Crisis in the Eurozone – A Corner Turned?: Empirical analysis of current bank liability management and restructuring policies with conclusions for the European bank restructuring and resolution framework*, Study commissioned by Bundestagsfranktion Bündnis90/ Die Grünen (Berlin, 2013).

EBA, *Consultation Paper for Draft Implementing Standards on the provision of information for the purpose of resolution plans under Article 11(3) of Directive 2014/59/EU EBA/CP/2017/15.*

EBA, *Guidelines on the range of scenarios to be used in recovery plans EBA/GL/2014/06* (2014).

EBA, *Guidelines on the types of tests, review or exercises that may lead to support measures under Article 32(d)(iii) of the Bank Recovery and Resolution Directive: EBA/GL/2014/09* (2014).

EBA, *EBA Final Draft Regulatory Technical Standards on the content of resolution plans and the assessment of resolvability EBA/RTS/2014/15* (2014).

EBA, *Guidelines on the specification of measures to reduce or remove impediments to resolvability and the circumstances in which each measure may be applied under Directive 2014/59/EU* (2014).

EBA, *Final Report – Draft implementing technical standards on procedures, forms and templates for the provision of information for resolution plans under Article 11(3) of Directive 2014/59/EU of the European Parliament and the Council EBA/ITS/2015/06* (2015).

EBA, *Guidelines specifying the conditions for group financial support under Article 23 of Directive 2014/59/EU* (2015).

EBA, *2016 EU-Wide Stress Test Results* (2016).

EBA, *List of OSIIs notified to the EBA* (2017).

EBA, *Quantitative Update of the EBA MREL Report: December 2016 Data* (2017).

EBA, *Draft final report – Draft Implementing Standards on the provision of information for the purpose of resolution plans under Article 11(3) of Directive 2014/59/EU EBA/ITS/2018/02* (2018).

EBA, *EBA Report on the Functioning of Resolution Colleges in 2017*, Resolution Colleges Annual Report (2018).

EBA and ESMA, *Statement of the EBA and ESMA on the treatment of retail holdings of debt financial instruments subject to the Bank Recovery and Resolution Directive* (2018).

EBA final draft Regulatory Technical Standards on the content of recovery plans under Article 5(10) of Directive 2014/59/EU establishing a framework for the recovery and resolution of credit institutions and investment firms: EBA/RTS/2014/11 (2014).

Ebner, A., 'The Financial Stability Aspects of the EU-wide Stress Test', *Journal of Financial Regulation* 4 (2018).

Engelbach, S. and Friedrich, T., 'Die Umsetzung der BRRD in Deutschland: WM 2015 Heft 14, 662', *Zeitschrift für Wirtschafts- und Bankrecht* (2015), 662–71.

Enria, A., *SRB Conference 2018 – 10 years after the crisis: are banks now resolvable?*, SRB Annual Conference (Brussels, 2018).

Ervin, W., *SRB Conference 2018 – 10 years after the crisis: are banks now resolvable?*, SRB Annual Conference (Brussels, 2018).

ESM Board of Governors, *Resolution of the Meeting of 8 December 2014: Establishment of the instrument for the direct recapitalisation of institutions* (2014).

European, *Directive 2013/36/EU of the European Parliament and of the Council of 26 June 2013 on access to the activity of credit institutions and the prudential supervision of credit institutions and investment firms, amending Directive 2002/87/EC and repealing Directives 2006/48/EC and 2006/49/EC, OJ L 176, 27.6.2013, p. 338–436.*

European Banking Federation, *EBF response to EBA Consultation on Draft ITS on the provision of information for the purpose of resolution plans under Article 11(3) of Directive 2014/59/EU* (2017).

European Banking Federation, *Facts and Figures – Banking in Europe 2018* (2018).

European Central Bank, *ECB determined ABLV Bank was failing or likely to fail*, Press Release.

European Central Bank, *Economic Bulletin Issue 6/2015.*

European Central Bank, *'Failing or Likely to Fail' Assessment of Banco Popular Espanol.*

European Central Bank, *Consolidated financial statement of the Eurosystem as at 20 April 2012* (2012).

European Central Bank, *Annual Report 2012* (2013).

European Central Bank, *Communication on Emergency Liquidity Assistance*, Press Release (2015).

European Central Bank, *List of supervised entities – cut-off date for significance decisions: 1 April 2017* (2017).

European Central Bank, *Agreement on emergency liquidity assistance* (2017).

European Central Bank, *Report on financial structures* (2017).

European Central Bank, *List of supervised entities – cut-off date for significance decisions: 1 July 2018* (2018).

European Commission, *Annex IV to the Communication from the Commission to the European Parliament, the Council, the European Economic and Social Committee and the Committee of the Regions – Commission Work Programm 2018 – An agenda for a more united, stronger and more democratic Europe, COM(2017) 650 final.*

European Commission, *Communication from the Commission to the European Parliament and the Council – A Roadmap towards a Banking Union COM(2012) 510 final.*

European Commission, *Communication to the European Parliament, the Council, the European Central Bank, the European Economic and Social Committee and the committee of the Regions on completing the Banking Union COM(2017) 592 final.*

European Commission, *Completing the Banking Union by 2018*, Fact Sheet.

European Commission, *Impact Assessment accompanying the document Proposal amending Regulation (EU) No 575/2013 on prudential requirements for credit institutions and investment firms; – Directive 2013/36/EU on access to the activity of credit institutions and the prudential supervision of credit institutions and investment firms; – Directive 2014/59/EU establishing a framework for the recovery and resolution of credit institutions and investment firms; – Regulation (EU) No 806/2014 of the European Parliament and of the Council of 15 July 2014 establishing uniform rules and a uniform procedure for the resolution of credit institutions and certain investment firms in the framework of a Single Resolution Mechanism and a Single Resolution Fund SWD(2016) 377 final*, Commission Staff Working Document.

European Commission, *State Aid Scoreboard 2017: Aid in the context of the financial and economic crisis.*

European Commission, *The effects of temporary State aid rules adopted in the context of the financial and economic crisis, SEC(2011) 1126 final*, Commission Staff Working Paper (2011).

European Commission, *Banking Union – restoring financial stability in the Eurozone*, Press Release/Memo (2014).

European Commission, *State Aid SA.43364 (2015/N) – Greece – Amendment of the restructuring plan approved in 2014 and granting of new aid to Piraeus Bank* (2015).

European Commission, *State Aid SA.43365 (2015/N) – Greece – Amendment of the restructuring plan approved in 2014 and granting of new aid to National Bank of Greece C(2015) 8930 final* (2015).

European Commission, *Capital requirements (CRR/CRD IV) and resolution framework (BRRD/SRM) amendments*, Fact Sheet – Frequently Asked Questions (2016).

European Commission, *EU Banking Reform: Strong banks to support growth and restore confidence*, Press Release (2016).

European Commission, *Reflection Paper on the Deepening of the Economic and Monetary Union COM(2017) 291 of 31 May 2017* (2017).

European Commission, *State aid: How the EU rules apply to banks with a capital shortfall – Factsheet* (2017).

European Commission, *Commission sets out Roadmap for deepening Europe's Economic and Monetary Union*, Press Release (2017).

European Parliament, *Emergency Liquidity Assistance – moving away from "constructive ambiguity"?*, Briefing of the European Parliament (2017).

European Parliament, *Ranking of unsecured debt instruments in insolvency hierarchy*, Briefing of the European Parliament (2017).

European Parliament, *Global Systemically Important Banks in Europe*, Briefing of the European Parliament (2017).

European Parliament, *Amending the bank resolution framework – BRRD and SRMR*, Briefing of the European Parliament (2017).

European Parliament, *Banking Reform Package – Impact Assessment (SWD(2016)377) of five European Commission proposals amending EU banking legislation*, Briefing of the European Parliament (2017).

European Stability Mechanism, *Guideline on Financial Assistance for the Direct Recapitalisation of Institutions* (2014).

Faia, E., Hackethal, A., Haliassos, M. and Langenbucher, K. (eds), *Financial Regulation: A Transatlantic Perspective* (Cambridge, United Kingdom, New York: Cambridge University Press, 2015).

Farhi, E. and Tirole, J., 'Deadly Embrace: Sovereign and Financial Balance Sheets Doom Loops', *The Review of Economic Studies* 85 (2018), 1781–823.

Farnè, M. and Vouldis, A., *Business models of the banks in the euro area*, ECB Working Paper (2017).

Federico, G., 'Crisi delle banche venete ad "aiuti di Stato"', *Questione Giustizia* (2017), 212–20.

Financial Stability Board, *Structural Banking Reforms: Cross-border consistencies and global financial stability implications: Report to G20 Leaders for the November 2014 Summit* (2014).

Financial Stability Board, *Principles on Loss-absorbing and Recapitalisation Capacity of G-SIBs in Resolution: Total Loss-absorbing Capacity (TLAC) Term Sheet* (2015).

Financial Stability Board, *Guiding Principles on the Internal Total Loss-absorbing Capacity of G-SIBs ('Internal TLAC')* (2017).

Financial Stability Board, *Thematic peer review on bank resolution planning* (2018).

Financial Stability Board, *Monitoring the Technical Implementation of the FSB Total Loss-absorbing Capacity (TLAC) Standard – Call for public feedback* (2018).

Fisher, P., 'Practical issues for the lender of last resort' in European Central Bank (ed), *ECB Legal Conference 2015: From monetary union to banking union, on the way to capital markets union: new opportunities for European integration, 1–2 September 2015* (Frankfurt am Main: European Central Bank, 2015), pp. 86–9.

Flinders, K., 'Big banks' legacy IT systems could kill them', computerweekly.com.

Franke, G., Krahnen, J. P. and Lüpke, T. von, *Effective Resolution of Banks: Problems and Solutions*, White Paper Series (2014).

Frignani, R., 'Choc a Civitavecchia – Salvabanche, il pensionato morto', Corriere Della Sera, 10 December 2015.

Gandrud, C. and Hallerberg, M., *How not to create zombie banks: lessons for Italy from Japan*, Bruegel Policy Contributions.

García, J. and Rocamora, M., *How prepared are European banks to comply with MREL?: The importance of the subordination requirement*, BBVA Research.

Gardella, A., 'Bail-in and the Financing of the SRM' in D. Busch and G. Ferrarini (eds), *European Banking Union* (Oxford: Oxford Univ Press, 2015), part III, ch. 11.

Geithner, T., *Stress test: Reflections on financial crises*, First paperback edition (New York: Broadway Books, 2014).

Geithner, T., *Are We Safer? The Case for Strengthening the Bagehot Arsenal*, Per Jacobsson Lectures (2016).

German Council of Economic Experts, *Annual Economic Report 2014/2015: The Long Road to More Financial Stability in Germany and Europa* (2015).

Gesetzesentwurf der Bundesregierung – Entwurf eines Gesetzes zur Abschirmung von Risiken und zur Planung der Sanierung und Abwicklung von Kreditinstituten und Finanzgruppen, Drucksache 17/12601 vom 04. 03. 2013.

Gleeson, S. and Guynn, R., *Bank Resolution and Crisis Management: Law and Practice*, First edition (Oxford: Oxford University Press, 2016).

Göhner, M. M., *Bail-in oder Bail-out?: Bankeninsolvenzen aus wirtschaftspolitischer Perspektive*, Wirtschaftspolitische Forschungsarbeiten der Universität zu Köln (Baden-Baden: Tectum Verlag, 2018), Band 63.

Gordon, J. N. and Ringe, W.-G., *Bank Resolution in Europe: the Unfinished Agenda of Structural Reform*, ECGI Law Working Paper (2015).

Gortsos, C. V., *The Impact of the Current Fiscal Crisis in the Euro Area on the Greek Banking System and the Measures Adopted to Safeguard its Stability: An Institutional, Supervisory and Regulatory Perspective* (2016).

Gortsos, C. V., *A Poisonous (?) Mix: Bail-Out of Credit Institutions Combined with Bail-In of Their Liabilities Under the BRRD – The Use of 'Government Financial Stabilisation Tools'* (2016).

Götz, M. G., Krahnen, J. P. and Tröger, T. H., 'Taking Bail-in Seriously – The Looming Risks for Banking Policy in the Rescue of Monte Paschi di Siena', *SAFE Policy Letter* No. 54 (2017).

Götz, M. R., Haselmann, R., Krahnen, J. P. and Steffen, S., *Did emergency liquidity assistance (ELA) of the ECB delay the bankruptcy of Greek banks?*, SAFE Policy Letter (2015).

Götz, M. R., Krahnen, J. P. and Tröger, T. H., 'Testfall Monte dei Paschi, Frankfurter Allgemeine v. 3.2.2017', *Frankfurter Allgemeine Zeitung* (2017), 19.

Götz, M. R. and Tröger, T. H., *Should the marketing of subordinated debt be restricted/different in one way or the other?: What to do in the case of mis-selling?*, In-Depth Analysis for the Economics and Monetary Affairs Committee of the European Parliament (2016).

Groen, W. P. de, *"Total Assets" versus "Risk Weighted Assets": does it matter for MREL requirements?*, In-Depth Analysis for the Economics and Monetary Affairs Committee of the European Parliament (2016).

Groen, W. P. de, *The different legal and operational structures of banking groups in the euro area, and their impact on banks' resolvability*, In-Depth Analysis for the Economics and Monetary Affairs Committee of the European Parliament (2016).

Groen, W. P. de, *Cash outflows in crisis scenarios: Do liquidity requirements and reporting obligations give the Single Resolution Fund sufficient time to react?*, In-Depth Analysis for the Economics and Monetary Affairs Committee of the European Parliament (2018).

Groen, W. P. de and Gros, D., *Estimating the bridge financing needs of the Single Resolution Fund: How expensive is it to resolve a bank?*, In-Depth Analysis for the Economics and Monetary Affairs Committee of the European Parliament (Brussels, 2015).

Grünewald, S., 'Legal challenges of bail-in' in European Central Bank (ed), *ECB Legal Conference 2017: shaping a new legal order for Europe: A tale of crises and opportunities: 4–5 September 2017* (Frankfurt am Main: Europäische Zentralbank, 2017), pp. 287–310.

Haas, R., 'Recent Trends in Cross-Border Banking' in T. Beck and B. Casu (eds), *The Palgrave Handbook of European Banking* (London: Palgrave Macmillan UK, 2016), pp. 475–97.

Hadjiemmanuil, C., 'Bank stakeholders' mandatory contribution to resolution financing: principles and ambiguities of bail-in' in European Central Bank (ed), *ECB Legal Conference 2015: From monetary union to banking union, on the way to capital markets union: new opportunities for European integration, 1–2 September 2015* (Frankfurt am Main: European Central Bank, 2015), pp. 225–49.

Hadjiemmanuil, C., 'Bank Resolution Financing in the Banking Union' in J.-H. Binder and D. Singh (eds), *Bank Resolution: The European Regime* (Oxford: Oxford University Press, 2016), pp. 177–210.

Hadjiemmanuil, C., 'Limits on State-Funded Bailouts in the EU Bank Resolution Regime' in G. B. Navetti, G. Calzolari and A. F. Pozzolo (eds), *European Economy: Banks, Regulation, and the Real Sector* (Rome: Europeye, 2016), pp. 91–117.

Hadjiemmanuil, C., *Reflections on the Concept of Proportionality & Its Implications for Banking Regulation*, Conference on 'Fostering a Diversified Banking Market through Proportionality: An Academic Review' (Brussels, 2018).

Haldane, A. G., *Rethinking the Financial Network* (Financial Student Association, Amsterdam, 2009).

Handelsblatt, 'Bankenrettung kostet Steuerzahler bis zu 17 Milliarden Euro', Handelsblatt, 25 June 2017.

Helleiner, E., 'Understanding the 2007–2008 Global Financial Crisis: Lessons for Scholars of International Political Economy', *Annual Review of Political Science* 14 (2011), 67–87.

Hellwig, M., *Yes Virginia, There is a European Banking Union! But It May Not Make Your Wishes Come True* (2014).

Hellwig, M., *"Total Assets" versus "Risk Weighted Assets": does it matter for MREL requirements?*, In-Depth Analysis for the Economics and Monetary Affairs Committee of the European Parliament (2016).

Herring, R. and Carmassi, J., 'Complexity and Systemic Risk: What's Changed Since the Crisis?' in A. N. Berger (ed), *The Oxford handbook of banking*, 2. ed. (Oxford: Oxford Univ. Press, 2015).

Herring, R. and Carmassi, J., 'The Corporate Structure of International Financial Conglomerates: Complexity and Its Implications for Safety and Soundness' in A. N. Berger (ed), *The Oxford handbook of banking*, 2. ed. (Oxford: Oxford Univ. Press, 2015), p. 195.

Herring, R. and Santomero, A., 'The Corporate Structure of Financial Conglomerates' in M. H. Kosters and A. H. Meltzer (eds), *International Competitiveness in Financial Services: A Special Issue of the Journal of Financial Services Research* (Dordrecht, s.l.: Springer Netherlands, 1991).

Herrmann, S. and Heinke, U., 'Kernbanksysteme müssen moderner werden', SpringerProfessional, 05 April 2017.

Hett, F. and Schmidt, A., *Bank Rescues and Bailout Expectations: The Erosion of Market Discipline During the Financial Crisis*, Safe Working Paper Series (2016).

Hoenig, T. M., *Credibility of the 2013 Living Wills Submitted by First Wave Filers* (2014).

Honohan, P., *Management and Resolution of Banking Crises: Lessons from Recent European Experience*, Peterson Institute for International Economics Policy Brief (2017).

Huertas, T. F., 'A Resolvable Bank' in K. E. Scott, T. H. Jackson and J. B. Taylor (eds), *Making failure feasible: How bankruptcy reform can end "too big to fail"*, Hoover Institution Press publication (Stanford, California: Hoover Institution Press, Stanford University, 2015), pp. 129–74.

Hüpkes, E., 'Lines of defense against systemic crises: Resolution.' in G. Caprio and P. Bacchetta (eds), *Handbook of safeguarding global financial stability: Political, social, cultural, and economic theories and models* (London, Waltham, MA: Academic Press, 2013).

Hüpkes, E., *Resolution: overcoming credibility gaps*, EFDI International Conference 2016 (Vilnius, 2016).

Hüser, A.-C., Hałaj, G., Kok, C., Perales, C. and van der Kraaij, A., 'The systemic implications of bail-in: A multi-layered network approach', *Journal of Financial Stability* 38 (2018), 81–97.

Institute of International Finance, *RegTech in Financial Services: Technology Solutions for Compliance and Reporting* (2016).

International Monetary Fund, *2014 Article IV Consultation – Staff Report; Press Release; and Statement by the Executive Director*, IMF Country Report No. 14/198 (2014).

International Monetary Fund, *2016 Article IV Consultation – Press Release; Staff Report; and Statement by the Executive Director for the Euro Area*, IMF Country Report No. 16/219 (2016).

Irrera, A., 'Banks scramble to fix old systems as IT 'cowboys' ride into sunset', Reuters, 10 April 2017.

Jahn, U., Schmitt, C. and Geier, B. M. (eds), *Bankensanierung und -abwicklung: Handbuch*, 1. Auflage (München: C.H. Beck, 2016).

James, H., *Keynote speech – Lehman in a Broader Perspective*, Lehman – 10 Years After (Goethe-Universität Frankfurt am Main, 2018).

Japanese Bankers Association, *Comments on the document: Monitoring the Technical Implementation of the FSB Total Loss-absorbing Capacity (TLAC) Standard – Call for public feedback, issued by the Financial Stability Board* (2018).

Jensen, M. C. and Meckling, W. H., 'Theory of the Firm: Managerial Behavior, Agency Costs and Ownership Structure', *Journal of Financial Economics* 3 (1976), 305–60.

Kapur, E., 'The Next Lehman Bankruptcy' in K. E. Scott, T. H. Jackson and J. B. Taylor (eds), *Making failure feasible: How bankruptcy reform can end "too big to fail"*, Hoover Institution Press publication (Stanford, California: Hoover Institution Press, Stanford University, 2015), pp. 175–241.

Karamichailidou, G. and Mayes, D. G., 'Plausible recovery and resolution plans for cross-border financial institutions' in J. E. Castañeda, D. G. Mayes and G. E. Wood (eds), *European Banking Union: Prospects and challenges* (Routledge, 2016), pp. 38–66.

Key Attributes of Effective Resolution Regimes for Financial Institutions (2014).

King, M. A., *The And of Alchemy: Money, banking and the future of the global economy*, First edition (London: Little Brown, 2016).

Kleftouri, N., 'European Union Bank Resolution Framework: can the objective of financial stability ensure consistency in resolution authorities' decisions?', *Journal of the Academy of European Law – ERA Forum* 18 (2017), 263–79.

Knips, S. E., *Bankenanleihen in Deutschland: Neue Preferred Senior Anleihen vor dem Start*, Helaba Volkswirtschaft/Research Credit Special (2018).

König, E., *SRB Conference 2018 – 10 years after the crisis: are banks now resolvable?*, SRB Annual Conference (Brussels, 2018).

Krahnen, J. P., *Banking Failures: Consolidation is Better than Rescue: Bailing out ailing banks distorts competition*, SAFE Policy Blog (2017).

Krahnen, J. P. and Moretti, L., 'Bail-In Clauses' in E. Faia, A. Hackethal, M. Haliassos and K. Langenbucher (eds), *Financial Regulation: A Transatlantic Perspective* (Cambridge, United Kingdom, New York: Cambridge University Press, 2015).

Laboureix, D., *SRB MREL Policy*, SRM-EBF Boardroom Dialogue (Brussels, 2018).

Laboureix, D., *SRB Conference 2018 – 10 years after the crisis: are banks now resolvable?*, SRB Annual Conference (Brussels, 2018).

Laboureix, D. and Decroocq, V., 'Enhancing the Capacity to Apply a Bail-in Through the MREL Setting' in G. B. Navetti, G. Calzolari and A. F. Pozzolo (eds), *European Economy: Banks, Regulation, and the Real Sector* (Rome: Europeye, 2016), pp. 117–30.

Laeven, L., Ratnovski, L. and Tong, H., *Bank Size and Systemic Risk* (2014).

Laeven, L. and Valencia, F., *IMF Working Paper – Systemic Banking Crises Revisited*, IMF Working Paper (2018).

Langenbucher, K., Tröger, T. H., Milione, L., Roth, A., Kolassa, D., Honnefelder, S., Krischel, A. K., Lemos Peixoto, S. d., Lindemann, C., Maier, R., van Es, I. and Silvestri, R., *EU Mapping 2017: systematic overview on economic and financial legislation: Study for the ECON Committee* (Luxembourg: Publications Office of the European Union, 2017).

Lannoo, K., *Pursuing Multiple Objectives with the Banking Reform Package: Who can still follow?*, CEPS Commentary (Brussels, 2017).

Lannoo, K., *Uneven progress in implementing cross-border bank resolution in the EU* (2017).

Lastra, R., Ayadi, R., Olivares-Caminal, R. and Russo, C., *The different legal and operational structures of banking groups in the euro area, and their impact on banks' resolvability*, In-Depth Analysis for the Economics and Monetary Affairs Committee of the European Parliament (2016).

Lehmann, M., 'Bail-in and Private International Law: How to Make Bank Resolution Measures Effective Across Borders', *International & Comparative Law Quarterly* 66 (2017), 107–42.

Levitin, A. J., 'In Defense of Bailouts', *Georgetown Law Journal* 99 (2011), 435–514.

Liikanen, E., *High-level Expert Group on reforming the structure of the EU banking sector – Final Report* (2012).

Lippe, P., Putnis, J., Katz, D. M. and Hurst, I., *How smart resolution planning can help banks improve transparency, increase profitability and reduce risk* (2015).

Littmann, S., Welp, A. and Welp, C., 'Computersysteme der Banken veraltet – Opa sitzt im Serverraum', Wirtschaftswoche, 19 April 2017.

Liu, X., 'Some Comments on Central Banks' Lender of Last Resort Function in the Post-Crisis World' in European Central Bank (ed), *ECB Legal Conference 2015: From monetary union to banking union, on the way to capital markets union: new opportunities for European integration, 1–2 September 2015* (Frankfurt am Main: European Central Bank, 2015), pp. 90–7.

Manns, J., 'Building Better Bailouts: The Case for a Long-Term Investment Approach', *Florida Law Review* 63 (2013), 1350–405.

Maragopoulos, N. G., *Minimum Requirements for own Funds and Eligible Liabilities (MREL): A Comprehensive Analysis of the New Prudential Requirement for Credit Institutions*, ECEFIL Working Paper Series (2016).

Mayes, D. G., 'Top-down restructuring of markets and institutions: The Nordic banking crises', *Journal of Banking Regulation* 18 (2017), 213–32.

Memorandum of Understanding on Cooperation between the Financial Supervisory Authorities, Central Banks and Finance Ministries of the European Union on Cross-Border Financial Stability.

Mendicino, C., Nikolov, K. and Suarez, J., *Equity Versus Bail-In Debt in Banking: An Agency Perspective*, CEPR Discussion Paper (2017).

Merler, S., *Comfortably numb: ESM direct recapitalization*, bruegel Blog Post (2014).

Merler, S., 'Bank liquidation in the European Union: clarification needed', *Bruegel Policy Contributions* Issue no. 1 (2017).

Merler, S., *Critical functions and public interest in banking services: Need for clarification?*, In-Depth Analysis for the Economics and Monetary Affairs Committee of the European Parliament (2017).

Merrouche, O. and Nier, E., *What Caused the Global Financial Crisis? – Evidence on the Drivers of Financial Imbalances 1999–2007*, IMF Working Paper (2010).

Mersch, Y., *The limits of central bank financing in resolution*, IMFS Distinguished Lecture Series (Goethe-Universität Frankfurt am Main, 2018).

Mesnard, B., *Loss absorbing capacity in the Banking Union: TLAC implementation and MREL review*, Briefing of the European Parliament (2016).

Mesnard, B., *"Bail-ins" in recent banking resolution and State aid cases*, In-Depth Analysis for the Economics and Monetary Affairs Committee of the European Parliament (2016).

Mesnard, B. and Katopodi, C., *Hearing with Mrs Elke König, Chair of the Single Resolution Board*, Briefing of the European Parliament (2017).

Mesnard, B., Magnus, M. and Margerit, A., *The precautionary recapitalisation of Monte dei Paschi di Siena*, Briefing of the European Parliament (2017).

Mesnard, B., Margerit, A. and Magnus, M., *Precautionary recapitalisations under the Bank Recovery and Resolution Directive: conditionality and case practice*, Briefing of the European Parliament (2017).

Mesnard, B., Margerit, A. and Magnus, M., *The orderly liquidation of Veneto Banca and Banca Popolare di Vicenza*, Briefing of the European Parliament (2017).

Micossi, S., Bruzzone, G. and Cassella, M., 'Fine-tuning the use of bail-in to promote a stronger EU financial system', *CEPS Special Report* No. 136 (2016).

Munoz, D. R., 'Bank resolution and insolvency ranking and priorities' in European Central Bank (ed), *ECB Legal Conference 2017: shaping a new legal order for Europe: A tale of crises and opportunities: 4–5 September 2017* (Frankfurt am Main: Europäische Zentralbank, 2017), pp. 256–86.

Navetti, G. B., Calzolari, G. and Pozzolo, A. F., 'Bail-in, up to a point' in G. B. Navetti, G. Calzolari and A. F. Pozzolo (eds), *European Economy: Banks, Regulation, and the Real Sector* (Rome: Europeye, 2016), pp. 9–33.

Niskanen, W. A., *Bureaucracy and representative government* (Chicago: Aldine Atherton, 1971).

Oldfather J., Gissler S. and Ruffino D., *Bank Complexity: Is Size Everything?* https://www.federalreserve.gov/econresdata/notes/feds-notes/2016/bank-complexity-is-size-everything-20160715.html.

Onaran, Y., 'Zombie Banks', Bloomberg, 11 July 2017.

Pagano, M., 'Lessons from the European financial crisis' in E. Faia, A. Hackethal, M. Haliassos and K. Langenbucher (eds), *Financial Regulation: A Transatlantic Perspective* (Cambridge, United Kingdom, New York: Cambridge University Press, 2015), pp. 23–48.

Papanikolaou, N. I., 'To be bailed out or to be left to fail? A dynamic competing risks hazard analysis', *Journal of Financial Stability* 34 (2018), 61–85.

Perrow, C., *The Next Catastrophe: Reducing Our Vulnerabilities to Natural, Industrial, and Terrorist Disasters* (Princeton: Princeton University Press, 2011).

Petrella, G., 'The Interplay Between Banks and Markets: Supervisory Stress Test Results and Investor Reactions' in T. Beck and B. Casu (eds), *The Palgrave Handbook of European Banking* (London: Palgrave Macmillan UK, 2016), pp. 409–47.

Philipp, W., 'Systemänderung: Amputiertes Aktienrecht für Banken – Das Sanierungs- und Abwicklungsgesetz (SAG)', *Die Aktiengesellschaft* (2015), 77–82.

Philippon, T. and Salord, A., *Bail-ins and bank resolution in Europe: A progress report*, Geneva reports on the world economy Special report (Geneva, London: ICMB International Center for Monetary and Banking Studies; CEPR, 2017), vol. 4.

Plenderleith, I., *Review of the Bank of England's Provision of Emergency Liquidity Assistance in 2008–09: Presented to the Court of the Bank of England* (2012).

Posner, E. A. and Casey, A., 'A Framework for Bailout Regulation', *Notre Dame Law Review* 91 (2015), 479–536.

Presidency of the Council of the European Union, *Note to the Council; Subject: Banking package – General approach* (2018).

PricewaterhouseCoopers, *MREL, TLAC and Banking Resolution*.

Proposal for a Directive of the European Parliament and of the Council amending Directive 2014/59/EU on loss-absorbing and recapitalisation capacity of credit institutions and investment firms and amending Directive 98/26/EC, Directive 2002/47/EC, Directive 2012/30/EU, Directive 2011/35/EU, Directive 2005/56/EC, Directive 2004/25/EC and Directive 2007/36/EC – Presidency compromise (2018).

Proposal for a Directive of the European Parliament and of the Council amending Directive 2014/59/EU on loss-absorbing and recapitalisation capacity of credit institutions and investment firms and amending Directive 98/26/EC, Directive 2002/47/EC, Directive 2012/30/EU, Directive 2011/35/EU, Directive 2005/56/EC, Directive 2004/25/EC and Directive 2007/36/EC, COM(2016) 852 final (2016).

Proposal for a Directive of the European Parliament and of the Council establishing a framework for the recovery and resolution of credit institutions and investment firms and amending Council Directives 77/91/EEC and 82/891/EC, Directives 2001/24/EC, 2002/47/EC, 2004/25/EC, 2005/56/EC, 2007/36/EC and 2011/35/EC and Regulation (EU) No 1093/2010: BRRD Proposal (2012).

Proposal for a Directive of the European Parliament and of the Council on amending Directive 2014/59/EU of the European Parliament and of the Council as regards the ranking of unsecured debt instruments in insolvency hierarchy, COM(2016) 853 final.

Proposal for a Regulation of the European Parliament and of the Council amending Regulation (EU) 806/2014 in order to establish a European Deposit Insurance Scheme COM/2015/0586 final – 2015/0270 (COD).

Proposal for a Regulation of the European Parliament and of the Council amending Regulation (EU) No 575/2013 as regards the leverage ratio, the net stable funding ratio, requirements for own funds and eligible liabilities, counterparty credit risk, market risk, exposures to central counterparties, exposures to collective investment undertakings, large exposures, reporting and disclosure requirements and amending Regulation (EU) No 648/2012 – Presidency compromise (2018).

Rasmussen, R. K. and Skeel, D. A., 'Governmental Intervention in an Economic Crisis', *University of Pennsylvania Journal of Business Law* 19 (2016), 7–48.

Regulation (EU) 2016/867 of the European Central Bank of 18 May 2016 on the collection of granular credit and credit risk data (ECB/2016/13), OJ L 144, 1.6.2016, p. 44–98.

Regulation (EU) No 1022/2013 of the European Parliament and of the Council of 22 October 2013 amending Regulation (EU) No 1093/2010 establishing a European Supervisory Authority (European Banking Authority) as regards the conferral of specific tasks on the European Central Bank pursuant to Council Regulation (EU) No 1024/2013 OJ L 287, 29.10.2013, p. 5–14 (2013).

Regulation (EU) No 1093/2010 of the European Parliament and of the Council of 24 November 2010 establishing a European Supervisory Authority (European Banking Authority), amending Decision No 716/2009/EC and repealing Commission Decision 2009/78/EC OJ L 331, 15.12.2010, p. 12–47: EBA Regulation (2010).

Regulation (EU) No 575/2013 of the European Parliament and of the Council of 26 June 2013 on prudential requirements for credit institutions and investment firms and amending Regulation (EU) No 648/2012 OJ L 176, 27.6.2013, p. 1–337.

Regulation (EU) No 806/2014 of the European Parliament and of the Council of 15 July 2014 establishing uniform rules and a uniform procedure for the resolution of credit institutions and certain investment firms in the framework of a Single Resolution Mechanism and a Single Resolution Fund OJ L 225, 30.7.2014, p. 1–90.

Resti, A., *Should the marketing of subordinated debt be restricted in one way or the other? What to do in the case of mis-selling?*, In-Depth Analysis for the Economics and Monetary Affairs Committee of the European Parliament (Brussels, 2016).

Restoy, F., *Bail-in in the new bank resolution framework: is there an issue with the middle class?*, IADI-ERC International Conference: "Resolution and deposit guarantee schemes in Europe: incomplete processes and uncertain outcomes" (Naples, 2018).

Richard van Tilborgh, *Managing Information and Data Requests for Recovery & Resolution*, European Recovery and Resolution Plan Summit (Frankfurt am Main, 2016).

Sachverständigenrat zur Begutachtung der Gesamtwirtschaftlichen Entwicklung, *Für eine zukunftsorientierte Wirtschaftspolitik*, Jahresgutachten (Wiesbaden, 2017), 54.2017/18.

Schäfer, A., Schnabel, I. and Di Weder Mauro, B., 'Bail-in expectations for European banks: Actions speak louder than words', *CEPR Discussion Paper* DP11061 (2016).

Schelo, S., *Bank recovery and resolution*, International banking and finance law series (Alphen aan den Rijn: Kluwer Law Internat, 2015), vol. 26.

Schelo, S. and Steck, A., 'Das Trennbankengesetz: Prävention durch Bankentestamente und Risikoabschirmung', *Zeitschrift für Bankrecht und Bankwirtschaft* (2013), 227–43.

Schiele, C., Ankert, J. and Kleinow, J., *Small Banking Box – mehr Proportionalität in der Bankenaufsicht für mittelständische Institute: Aktuelle Diskussion über Erleichterungen in der Regulierung mittelständischer Institute* (2017).

Schillig, M. A., 'The (Il-)Legitimacy of the EU Post-Crisis Bailout System', *King's College London Law School Research Paper* 2018 (2018).

Schoenmaker, D., 'A fiscal backstop to the banking system' in M. Haentjens and B. Wessels (eds), *Research Handbook on Crisis Management in the Banking Sector* (Edward Elgar Publishing, 2015), pp. 42–54.

Schoenmaker, D., 'The Banking Union: An Overview and Open Issues' in T. Beck and B. Casu (eds), *The Palgrave Handbook of European Banking* (London: Palgrave Macmillan UK, 2016), pp. 451–74.

Schoenmaker, D., *The different legal and operational structures of banking groups in the euro area, and their impact on banks' resolvability*, In-Depth Analysis for the Economics and Monetary Affairs Committee of the European Parliament (2016).

Schoenmaker, D., Véron, N., Gehrig, T. P., Messori, M., Leite, A. P., Sapir, A., Steffen, S., Tibi, P., Vegara Figueras, D., Vries, C. G. d. and Xafa, M. (eds), *European banking supervision: The first eighteen months*, Blueprint series (Brussels, Belgium: Bruegel, 2016).

Sciorilli Borrelli S., *Q and A with Andrea Enria of European Banking Authority*. https://www.politico.eu/pro/q-and-a-with-andrea-enria-of-european-banking-authority/.

Scott, K. E., Jackson, T. H. and Taylor, J. B. (eds), *Making failure feasible: How bankruptcy reform can end "too big to fail"*, Hoover Institution Press publication (Stanford, California: Hoover Institution Press, Stanford University, 2015), no. 662.

Serière, V. de, 'Recovery and Resolution Plans of Banks in the Context of the BRRD and the SRM: Some Fundamental Issues' in D. Busch and G. Ferrarini (eds), *European Banking Union* (Oxford: Oxford Univ Press, 2015), part III, ch. 10.

Serière, V. de and Milione, L., 'De-Politicizing Bail-in', *Journal of International Banking Law and Regulation*, 34, Issue 2 (2019), pp. 71 *et seq*.

Singh, D., 'Recovery and Resolution Planning: Reconfiguring Financial Regulation and Supervision' in J.-H. Binder and D. Singh (eds), *Bank Resolution: The European Regime* (Oxford: Oxford University Press, 2016), pp. 1–24.

Single Resolution Board, *Guidance to the Completion of the SRB's Liability Data Template for 2016*.

Single Resolution Board, *Banco Popular Group Resolution Plan* (2016).

Single Resolution Board, *Data collection for resolution planning and the determination of the Minimum Requirement for own funds and Eligible Liabilities (MREL)* (2016).

Single Resolution Board, *The Single Resolution Mechanism – Introduction to Resolution Planning* (2016).

Single Resolution Board, *Decision of the Single Resolution Board concerning the adoption of a resolution scheme in respect of Banco Popular Espanol, S.A.: Executive Session* (2017).

Single Resolution Board, *Decision of the Single Resolution Board concerning the assessment of the conditions for resolution in respect of Banca Popolare di Vicenza S.p.A.* (2017).

Single Resolution Board, *Decision of the Single Resolution Board concerning the assessment of the conditions for resolution in respect of Veneto Banca S.p.A.* (2017).

Single Resolution Board, *Guidance on the 2018 Liability Data Report* (2017).

Single Resolution Board, *Minimum Requirements for Own Funds and Eligible Liabilities (MREL) – SRB Policy for 2017 and Next Steps* (2017).

Single Resolution Board, *Ex-ante publicity notice – negotiated procurement procedure: Call for Tender for the Provision of Access to Financial Data through a Data Vendor* (2018).

Single Resolution Board, *Guidance on the 2019 Liability Data Report* (2018).

Single Rulebook Q&A, *Question ID: 2015_1779*.

Single Rulebook Q&A, *Question ID: 2016_2951*.

Sirletti S. and Weber A., *Italy Commits $19 Billion for Veneto Banks in Biggest Rescue*. https://www.bloomberg.com/news/articles/2017-06-25/italy-mobilizes-up-to-19-billion-to-keep-veneto-banks-afloat.

Sjöberg, G., 'Banking Special Resolution Regimes as a Governance Tool' in W.-G. Ringe and P. M. Huber (eds), *Legal challenges in the global financial crisis: Bail-outs, the euro and regulation*, Studies of the Oxford Institute of European and Comparative Law (Oxford: Hart, 2014), pp. 187–96.

Sommer, J. H., 'Why Bail-In? And How!', *Economic Policy Review* 20 (2014), 207–228.

Stern, G. H. and Feldman, R. J., *Too Big to Fail: The Hazards of Bank Bailouts* (Washington, DC: Brookings Institution Press, 2009).

Stiefmüller, C. M., *European Parliament ECON Public Hearing on the new banking legislation package*, European Parliament's ECON Committee Public Hearing (Brussels, 2017).

Stiefmüller, C. M., *Ten Years After – The 2017 Banking Package: One Step Forward, Two Steps Back*, Finance Watch Policy Brief (2017).

Stiefmüller, C. M., *Ten Years After: Back to Business as Usual: The Pit and the Pendulum – Post-Crisis Financial Regulation in Europe*, Finance Watch Report (2018).

The Economist, 'What would Bagehot do?: Should central banks act as buyers of last resort?', The Economist, 16 August 2007.

Thole, C., 'Bank Crisis Management and Resolution: Core features of the Bank Recovery and Resolution Directive', *SSRN Electronic Journal* 2014.

Tim Skeet to Thomas Jorgensen (ECB), 20 December 2016, 'Bail-in Working Group of the AMIC -International Capital Markets Association (ICMA)', Letter.

Triantafyllakis, I., 'Italienische Banken: Wenn nicht alle Wege zum Bail-in führen', *Zeitschrift für Wirtschafts- und Bankrecht* (2016), 2248–55.

Tröger, T. H., 'Effective Supervision of Transnational Financial Institutions', *Texas International Law Journal* 48 (2012), 177–221.

Tröger, T. H., 'Regulatory Influence on Market Conditions in the Banking Union: the Cases of Macro-Prudential Instruments and the Bail-in Tool', *European Business Organization Law Review* 16 (2015), 575–93.

Tröger, T. H., 'Too complex to work: A critical assessment of the bail-in tool under the European bank recovery and resolution regime', *SAFE Working Paper* No. 179 (2017).

Tröger, T. H., 'Why MREL won't help much: Minimum requirements for bail-in capital as insufficient remedy for defunct private sector involvement under the European bank resolution framework', *SAFE Working Paper* no. 180 (2018).

Tröger, T. H., 'Optimal Bail-In Tools – Observations From A European Perspective' in D. Arner, D. Busch, E. Avgouleas and S. Schwarcz (eds), *Systemic Risk in the Financial Sector: Ten Years After the Great Crash* (Centre for International Governance Innovation, 2019).

van Roosebeke, B., *The ESM's Direct Recapitalisation of Banks: Looking Forward in Backstop-Questions* (2014).

Véron, N., *Precautionary recapitalisation: time for a review?*, In-Depth Analysis for the Economics and Monetary Affairs Committee of the European Parliament (Brussels, 2017).

Vollmer, U. and Wiese, H., 'Minimum capital requirements, bank supervision and special resolution schemes. Consequences for bank risk-taking', *Journal of Financial Stability* 9 (2013), 487–97.

Vovolinis, D., 'The European Stability Mechanism Direct Recapitalisation Instrument: An Element for a Complete European Banking Union', *ECEFIL Working Paper Series* (2015).

Walter, J. R., 'The 3–6–3 rule: An urban myth?', *Economic quarterly* 92 (2006), 51–78.

Weber, A., 'Monte Paschi Bailout Plan Has Some ECB Supervisors Grumbling', Bloomberg.

Weber, A. and Speciale, A., 'ECB Weighs Emergency Cash Injections to Smooth Bank Rescues', Bloomberg, 09 April 2018.

Weber, R. F., 'Structural regulation as antidote to complexity capture', *American business law journal: the official publication of the American Business Law Association* 49 (2012), 643–738.

Weiß, G. N.F., Bostandzic, D. and Neumann, S., 'What factors drive systemic risk during international financial crises?', *Journal of Banking & Finance* 41 (2014), 78–96.

Wiggins, R., Tente, N. and Metrick, A., *European Banking Union D: Cross-Border Resolution – Dexia Group*, Yale Program on Financial Stability Case Study 2014-5D-V1 (2015).

Wiggins, R., Tente, N. and Metrick, A., *European Banking Union C: Cross-Border Resolution – Fortis Group*, Yale Program on Financial Stability Case Study 2014-5D-V1 (2015).

Wihlborg, G., *Bail-ins – Issues of Credibility and Contagion*, SUERF Policy Note (2017).

Wojcik, K.-P., 'Bail-in in the Banking Union', *Common Market Law Review* 53 (2016), 91–138.

World Bank Group, *Understanding Bank Recovery and Resolution in the EU: A Guidebook to the BRRD* (Vienna, 2017).

World Bank Group, Financial Sector Advisory Center (FinSAC), *Bank Resolution and "Bail-In" in the EU: Selected Case Studies Pre and Post BRRD* (2016).

Xiouros, C., *Handling of the Emergency Liquidity Assistance of Laiki Bank in the Bailout Package of Cyprus* (2013).

Yiatrou, M., *Bank Resolution Credibility and Economic Implications*, ADEMU Working Paper Series (2016).

Zhou, J., Rutledge, V., Bossu, W., Dobler, M. and Jassaud, N., *From bail-out to bail-in: Mandatory debt restructuring of systemic financial institutions*, IMF staff discussion note (Washington, DC: Internat. Monetary Fund, 2012), 2012/3.